Heroes in Our Midst

From The Pages of
The Valley Patriot

FORWARD

In March of 2004, the first edition of The Valley Patriot rolled off the presses at Graphic Development in Hanover, Massachusetts. As a local, monthly newspaper, one of our primary missions was to honor the lives and sacrifices of local veterans who not only fought for our country, but then came back and made significant contributions to our nation here at home.

Each month since then, the Valley Patriot has published stories of these local heroes in a feature called "Valley Patriot of the Month, Hero in Our Midst". In the early months of our publication we honored local veterans with a few paragraphs and a photo. But, as time went on it became clear these veterans deserved to have their stories told in much more detail. This book is dedicated to every man and woman who put on a uniform and served our country.

***

"We owe so many of our freedoms and liberties to the sacrifices of our veterans. Combat and military service is an experience that few Americans endure. Of those who have served in the armed forces, few open up and share their memories after returning home. I am personally grateful to every veteran who has taken the time to share their experiences with The Valley Patriot for their monthly feature, "Valley Patriot of the Month, Heroes in Our Midst" over the last 13 years. Through this collection of their individual stories, let every American read about the heroism and valiant service these men and women gave to our country. They are Truly Heroes in Our Midst and as you will see, they are true 'Valley Patriots'. The least we can all do in return for the brave service of our veterans is to remember their stories, their sacrifices, and experiences."

~ Francisco Urena, Massachusetts Secretary of Veterans Services

"The Valley Patriot has provided a great service to the Merrimack Valley in honoring veterans each month for the last 13 years. They have made great and successful efforts to reach out to so many veterans and their families. This compilation of all of the men and women who were honored with "Valley Patriot of the Month" in one book, will be a memorable and a treasured keepsake for the veterans and their families, and a reminder to all of us the many Heroes in our Midst."

~ State Rep. Linda Dean Campbell, (D) Methuen, Massachusetts

HEROES
IN OUR
MIDST

PHOTO: TOM DUGGAN, Jr. - Thomas Hudner in North Andover, Massachusetts at the Memorial Day ceremony.

Remembering the
Fallen Heroes of Memorial Day

Captain Thomas J. Hudner, Jr., U.S.
Navy, Korean War, Medal of Honor

Terrorists Must Be
Confronted & Destroyed

May, 2014 - The following speech was given by Captain Thomas J. Hudner, Jr., U.S. Navy, Korean War, Medal of Honor recipient at the North Andover Memorial Day Ceremony on May 28, 2007.

"It was 232 years ago, within a day's march of where we are now gathered, that the first shots were fired in Concord that marked the start of a war that changed history. It signaled the start of "A new nation, conceived in liberty and dedicated to the proposition that all men are created equal."

In that battle and the ensuing war, a tiny nation stood up to the world's greatest power in its quest for freedom. Because of brilliant leadership, a dedication to the belief that all men are created equal and a relentless determination to attain liberty in the face of almost insurmountable hardships, that small group of colonies conquered its former oppressor and has since evolved into the greatest nation in the history of mankind.

Close by are memorials to all those patriots of generations past who gave their lives to preserve those liberties, not only for us Americans, but also for the people of those nations around the globe who looked to us to attain or maintain theirs

Today we are observing Memorial Day which commemorates all those who gave their lives in the defense of that "New nation's freedoms and equality of all men which are articulated in our Declaration of Independence and our Constitution." It is an occasion for the American people to reflect on the sacrifices of human lives which led to the independence and the growth and the maturation of our country and of the freedoms we now enjoy.

My generation has experienced three major wars; World War II, The Korean War and the Vietnam War. World War II was fought by the great generation of Americans who saved the world from fascist aggression and secured the blessings of liberty for hundreds of millions of people around the world. Four hundred thousand Americans sided in that war and of over 16 million who fought in it, less than 4 million are still alive today. And, 100,000 more American lives were lost in Korea and Vietnam in the cause of freedom.

Today, their descendants are fighting a global war against terrorism. They are serving and sacrificing in Afghanistan and Iraq and at other outposts on the front lines of freedom. The lives of every one of them are precious to their loved ones and to our nation. And each life given in the name of liberty is a life that has not been lost in vain."

This war in which we are now engaged, truly another world war, is a vicious guerrilla war, one in which religious zealots are determined to destroy us. It is a war between two cultures, one which values life and the dignity of man and the other which considers that any lives sacrificed for violation of Islamic Law, regardless of sex or age, are a tribute to Allah.

Although most fighting is in Iraq and Afghanistan, the enemy is striking in locations all throughout the world, intent on destroying the civilized world we live in. And it WILL be a long war.

© Copyright 2007, The Valley Patriot

We have taken the position that the terrorists must be confronted and destroyed where possible. We offer prayers every day for the safety of our troops and for their success in subjugating the evil that has been infiltrating through our and other societies for many years.

Our precious freedoms and our way of life envied throughout the world have been attained only through great sacrifice and the wisdom of those who came before us.

Today, also, we share the sorrow of the mothers and fathers and families and friends of those who never returned from the field of battle. They have suffered the greatest human tragedy – the loss of sons and daughters, spouses, and brothers and sisters.

America has always been a beacon of hope for freedom for oppressed and threatened people of the world over. We have used our military might to enable other people, as well as our own, to enjoy life, liberty and the pursuit of happiness. And it has been our veterans throughout history who have been the key players in making the world a safer and better place to live.

We must give special thanks to those veterans who bear the scars of combat, many of whom are disabled and in need of constant medical care. Our hospitals are full of veterans suffering from illnesses and injuries incurred during combat or from the rigors of military service, afflictions that prevent them from living pain free lives enjoyed by most Americans.

So, today we express our honor to those men and women who have followed in the footsteps of our forefathers starting with the colonists and the minutemen. They were, and are today, those who were willing to fight as necessary to perpetuate the way of life passed down to them by warriors of earlier generations. They know there is no glory in war; it can be utter hell. But, thanks to them, we are living here in peace.

In closing, let us be reminded of President Abraham Lincoln's words in 1863 at the cemetery by the battlefield of Gettysburg, and I quote;

"The world will little note nor long remember what we say here, but it can never forget what they did here. It is for us the living rather to be dedicated here to the unfinished work which, they who fought here have thus far so nobly advanced. It is rather for us – that from these honored dead we take increased devotion to that cause for which they have the last full measure of devotion – that we here highly resolve that these dead shot have died in vain...."

With Americans fighting in the cause of freedom in a land almost half a world away, think of how applicable Lincoln's words are today. Although he spoke of the dead, his words apply equally to those men and women in uniform who are devoted to the cause of freedom and peace.

We are blessed to be Americans. Let us not, in the selfishness of forgetfulness betray those we honor this morning. Our legacy from them, obtained at the cost of the blood of millions, is priceless.

God Bless them, – And god bless us all."

Capt. Thomas J. Hudner, Jr.
U.S. Navy - Korean War
Medal of Honor

Ted Tripp - May, 2007

CONCORD/ANDOVER – Tom Hudner was sitting in the commons area after lunch at Phillips Academy in Andover when word spread that the Japanese had just bombed Pearl Harbor. As with most young people of the era, he had no idea where Pearl Harbor was but he knew it meant the U.S. was at war. And like many of the students in the Class of '43, Tom expected to become part of the war effort after graduation. But fate would take him to the U.S. Naval Academy at Annapolis where he would  not graduate until 1946, well after the conclusion of World War II.

Four years after Annapolis, however, Tom would find himself in another war, the Korean War. Here he would lead a heroic effort to save a downed pilot when his flight was on patrol over the Chosin Reservoir. For this extraordinary rescue attempt, President Harry Truman would present the first Congressional Medal of Honor of the Korean War to Tom Hudner.

Born in 1924, Tom grew up in Fall River, Mass. where the family had a chain of meat and grocery stores called Hudner's Markets. His father and uncle had attended Phillips Academy and later he and his brothers would do so as well. While at Phillips, Tom was co-captain of the track team, a member of the football and lacrosse teams, a senior class officer and student council member. These endeavors would later help prepare him well for the responsibilities of a military career.

Tom's father had attended Harvard after Phillips, but Tom had always thought about going to Annapolis and subsequently into the Navy. In 1943,

Congressman Joe Martin, then Speaker of the House of Representatives, appointed Tom as his second alternate to the U.S. Naval Academy. As luck would have it, a position opened up and Tom was told to report to Annapolis on July 7, 1943.

During the next few years Tom would train to be a naval officer. His ultimate goal was to be stationed aboard a destroyer or battleship. In 1946 Tom graduated from the Academy and now Ensign Thomas Hudner was assigned to the cruiser USS Helena. That September, Tom became a communications watch officer on the Helena stationed off of Tsing-Tao, China, about 150 miles north of Shanghai. Although the Nationalists were still in control of China, the communists and Red Army were making it increasingly difficult for Americans. It was Tom's duty to read incoming and outgoing messages, decode/encode them, and pass them along to interested officials.

After six or seven months on the ship, the Helena sailed back to Long Beach, California. There, Tom received new orders to report to Pearl Harbor as a communications officer. Unhappy at his new post because he was not at sea, several classmates serving with him eventually convinced him to put in a request for flight training. Tom was accepted and in April 1948 reported to Pensacola Naval Air Station in Florida for flight school. He learned to fly in the North American SNJ, the naval equivalent of the Air Force T-6 trainer. He had to complete six successful, arrestor-hook carrier landings to graduate.

Then it was on to Corpus Christi, Texas for advanced training with the Corsair F4U and finally back to Pensacola where he received his aviator wings in August of 1949. His first duty was at the Naval Air Station at Quonset Point, Rhode Island where he was assigned to VA-75, an attack squadron of Douglas AD-1 Skyraiders, as part of Air Group 7. About a month later, VA-75 was decommissioned and he was reassigned to VF-32, a Corsair squadron aboard the USS Leyte aircraft carrier. On May 1, 1950 the Leyte sailed to the Mediterranean for a six-month deployment.

Tom was now Lt. J.G. Tom Hudner.

It was at Quonset Point where Tom would first meet Ensign Jesse Brown, another aviator assigned to the same squadron. Ensign Brown was the Navy's first black aviator. Although the Tuskegee Airmen had paved the way for black aviators in World War II, it still took years for the other services to accept this cultural change.

Brown had grown up in Mississippi, was valedictorian at his high school, and attended Ohio State University. While at Ohio State, a naval officer encouraged him to apply to the Navy's flight school. Jesse had always wanted to fly, so this became his goal. He eventually went through the same training as Tom Hudner, first at Pensacola and then Corpus Christi. Tom believes Jesse was eventually assigned to Quonset Point to get him away from the bigotry that was still widespread in the South.

The USS Leyte was off the coast of Cannes, France, about a month and a half into its deployment, when North Korea attacked South Korea. Like Pearl Harbor, the first question on most people's minds was "Where is Korea?" On August 8th, five to six weeks after the initial attack, and after being relieved by another carrier stationed off Lebanon, the Leyte was ordered to Korea. The first port of call was back to Norfolk for war preparation and to take on six Marine Sikorsky helicopters and ten Marine pilots. The USS Leyte left Norfolk and after traversing the Panama Canal headed west into the Pacific. She dropped off the Marines and their helicopters in Japan and then arrived off the east coast of Korea on 8 October 1950. The Leyte joined with three other carriers to provide close ground support to U.S. troops ordered in that summer by President Truman.

The Leyte at this point had one squadron of Grumman F9F-2 Panther jets, two squadrons of Chance Vought Corsair F4U-4 fighters, and one squadron of Douglas AD-1 Skyraiders. The jets were the superior fighters, but they could only stay in the air half as long as the other aircraft. Thus, close ground support missions were generally left to the Corsairs and Skyraiders.

Flight operations started immediately and consisted of 12-hour days where Tom, Jesse and the other pilots would fly one, sometimes two, missions a day, standing down every fourth day for replenishment and refueling. Every one-and-a-half hours the carrier was launching or recovering aircraft. Early on, one of the Leyte pilots brought back word that the Chinese appeared to be entering the war.

When hordes of Chinese troops suddenly appeared everywhere on November 28th, all hell broke loose. Air operations then shifted to protecting the retreating American troops, now well north of the 38th Parallel.

On December 4, 1950, Tom Hudner, Jesse Brown and four other Corsair pilots left the USS Leyte at about 1330 hours to fly an armed reconnaissance mission over the northwestern part of the Chosin Reservoir, a mountainous, snow-covered, inhospitable area about 70 miles from the Chinese border. They were flying low, only 500-700 feet above the terrain, looking for enemy targets of opportunity.

Suddenly, Jesse radioed that he was losing oil pressure and power. He would have to land. Another pilot noticed a small clearing only about a quarter mile in size on the side of one of the slopes and radioed the location to Jesse. Tom also radioed to him, "Jesse, make sure your shoulder harness is locked and the canopy is open!" Then Jesse, wheels up with no power, brought his Corsair in for a hard, crash landing. The impact buckled the fuselage at the cockpit.

Other flight members who were circling the area at the time first thought he had been killed because of the force of the impact. The flight leader had even started climbing to a higher altitude so he could radio for a helicopter to come in and retrieve the body. But then some of the pilots could see Jesse waving from the damaged craft. He was still alive although he didn't appear able to get out of the aircraft. There was also smoke coming from the cowling, an ominous sign.

It was obvious that Jesse was trapped and, with the imminent threat of a fuel fire, he needed immediate help to survive. The helicopter wouldn't arrive in time to do any good. Then Tom Hudner radioed the rest of his formation, "I'm going in to get him out!" He says there was silence on the radio after that. No one tried to talk him out of it.

Then he turned towards a nearby hillside and fired off all his rockets and ammunition to both lighten the plane and reduce the hazards of a crash landing. Looking for how best to land, he slowed to about 85 knots and maneuvered the Corsair into an area near Jesse on a slope of about 20 degrees. Wheels up, he landed hard about 100 yards from Jesse's Corsair. The snow didn't help the impact at all, as the ground below was frozen solid. The crash landing broke his windscreen and injured his back. Tom later said, "That was the hardest landing I ever made."

With adrenaline pumping, Tom ran through the snow to Jesse's plane. It was cold, perhaps no more than 5 or 10 degrees. He didn't see any enemy soldiers, but was confident that his air cover, now increased to 10-12 planes, would keep them away. When he reached Jesse, he saw that he had his helmet off and his gloves were missing. Tom surmised that Jesse had taken the gloves off to unbuckle his chute and dropped them. Tom then put a woolen watch hat on Jesse and wrapped his hands in a scarf that he had brought with him. Jesse was obviously badly injured.

A quick glance showed that Jesse's knee was pinned between the bent fuselage and the central instrument column. The snow made it slippery and Tom struggled to maintain his footing as he leveraged himself to free Jesse. It didn't take him long to realize that he would need some kind of tool to help. Tom returned to his plane and radioed his flight leader to have the helicopter bring an ax and fire extinguisher. Then he returned to Jesse's plane to consider what else he could do. He started packing snow into the cowling openings to suppress the smoldering fire. At this point, Jesse was fading in and out of consciousness from the injuries and the cold.

Meanwhile, the helicopter which had been launched from a nearby Marine camp was already in the air when it got word that that there were two pilots on the ground and they needed an ax and fire extinguisher. The news meant that the chopper had to return to base and drop off the crewman that the pilot had taken with him and pick up the requested items. Finally, in what seemed like forever, the helicopter arrived over the crash scene.

As it circled the area, Tom fired a flare/smoke emitter to show the pilot how the wind was blowing. But the helicopter took its time landing because, as Tom later learned, the brakes on the chopper were poor and the pilot was afraid that if he landed on a slope the helicopter might slide off the hill. Also, the engine on this chopper had a history of trouble starting so the pilot would have to leave it running.

The Sikorsky finally landed and out stepped 1st Lt. Charlie Ward. Instantly, Tom recognized him as one of the Marine pilots the Leyte had ferried to Japan several months earlier. The two then hurried over to Jesse to try to free him. But the ax was ineffective on the metal fuselage no matter what they did. Try as they might, they could not get Jesse out of the aircraft. At one point when Jesse was conscious, he told Tom, "If anything happens to me, tell my wife Daisy I love her."

It was now getting late in the day and Ward turned to Tom and said, "We have to leave. I can't fly out of these mountains in the dark." Tom reluctantly agreed. He then turned to Jesse and told him they had to leave to get some equipment. He knew, however, that there was no chance they could get back before morning and Jesse wouldn't survive the night.

Charlie and Tom then boarded the chopper and flew south to the Marine base camp at Hagaru-ri. It was cold and Tom would have to spend the night in a tent. A young Marine appeared and gave Tom his bedroll. He said, "Sir, tonight I think you will need this more than me." Tom says he didn't sleep at all because of the cold and his thoughts of Jesse.

The next morning, December 5th, Tom was flown to another Marine base at Yonpo where he would spend the next two days because of bad weather. Finally, on December 7th a Skyraider from the Leyte came in to take him back to his ship. On the way to the carrier, Tom learned that the captain wanted to see him as soon as he came on board. Radio communication had been poor over the past several days and Captain Thomas Sisson had little information on what actually happened.

After listening to Tom's story, Capt. Sisson said he would send in a helicopter with a flight surgeon to retrieve Jesse's body. Tom advised him that would be too dangerous and needlessly risk the lives of two more men. The captain then said he had a backup plan. He would send in planes with napalm to incinerate the crash area – a makeshift warrior's funeral. Within the hour, seven aircraft from Squadron 32, all flown by Jesse's friends, left the carrier for the crash site. Six carried napalm and while they were diving to drop their ordinance, the lone seventh plane climbed above them in the traditional tribute to a fallen comrade.

After the mission had been completed, Capt. Sisson started the process recommending Tom for the Medal of Honor. Meanwhile, Tom's injured back now started to really bother him and he was grounded for the next month while recovering. Shortly after he returned to flight operations, the USS Leyte got orders to head back to San Francisco. In mid-February, VF-32 returned to Quonset Point.

On April 1st Tom got word that the Joint Chiefs of Staff and Congress had approved him for the Medal of Honor. On Friday, April 13, 1951,

President Truman presented the medal to Tom in a White House ceremony before family and friends.

Tom would also find out later that Charlie Ward, the Marine helicopter pilot, received the Silver Star for his heroic efforts on that day. Jesse Brown was posthumously awarded the Distinguished Flying Cross for his Korean War combat service.

Tom now settled in as a career Navy aviator. He spent time as an instrument instructor, admiral's aide, assistant air officer, executive officer of an aircraft carrier, exchange pilot flying Air Force interceptors, and finally a tour with the Joint Chiefs of Staff at the Pentagon before retiring in April 1973 with the rank of captain.

Tom returned to Massachusetts and over the years worked for several Boston area companies in various consulting, management and administrative capacities. In 1988 Governor Dukakis appointed him to Deputy Commissioner of Veterans Services. He eventually became Acting Commissioner and in 1991 Governor Weld appointed him to Commissioner, where he remained until retirement in 1999. Tom is currently vice president of Battleship Cove, the USS Massachusetts war memorial and museum complex in Fall River.

In 1963, while undergoing jet training in San Diego, Tom met the recently widowed Georgea Smith at a Christmas party. They started dating and were married in August of 1968. The Hudners have a son, Tom, who lives in Concord. Georgea has three children from her prior marriage: Kelly, Stan and Shannon. Between them, the Hudners have 11 grandchildren.

Captain Thomas J. Hudner, Jr., we thank you for your extraordinary service to our country.

PHOTO: TOM DUGGAN, JR.

The very first veteran to be honored by The Valley Patriot was in our very first edition in March of 2004 when we paid tribute to our good friend Jim Cassidy, or as his friends called him, "the commander" as he was Commander of The American Legion, Post 219 in North Andover, Massachusetts. While we had no idea back then that our Valley Patriot of the Month feature would grow to what it is now, we knew for sure that someone needed to honor our servicemen and women here at home. Prior to his passing, The Valley Patriot was fortunate enough to publish several Hero in Our Midst stories on the commander as well as covering him at local events in the community. Jim Cassidy also published a monthly column in the pages of our paper before falling ill. We have included just some of his tributes and submissions in this section.

In Memory of
Corporal Jim Cassidy
WWII - U.S. Army

By: Ted Tripp - February, 2007

NORTH ANDOVER, MA – On the morning of June 6, 1944, the Allies finally began the liberation of Europe from the Nazi nightmare. Tens of thousands of American, British, and Canadian troops poured onto the shores of Normandy to engage the Germans and drive them out of France. The Allies had trouble at first fighting through the treacherous French hedgerows, but by late fall General Eisenhower's armies were nearing the German border.

As the Americans advanced, Pfc. Jim Cassidy and his machine gun squad were attempting to enter a Rhineland town when almost immediately they were pinned down by a German sniper perched in the church steeple. There was little they could do as they hunkered down in their foxholes to avoid the bullets whizzing by. Finally, late in the day, supporting artillery moved up and demolished the church. Once again, the squad, as they had so many times before, picked up their gear and pushed forward with the rest of their unit during that miserable winter of 1944-45.

Eighteen-year-old Jim Cassidy was just one of the many young men who had stepped forward to risk their lives in the worldwide struggle for freedom against the Axis powers. He and his men were typical of what Tom Brokaw calls "The Greatest Generation."

Jim was born in 1926 and grew up in Worcester. He vividly remembers the day World War II began. On the evening of December 7, 1941, he and his brother Bill were on their way home from the movies. Jim noticed that there was a lot of talk on the trolley car about the Japanese bombing of Pearl Harbor and some women were crying.

The brothers didn't know what or where Pearl Harbor was, but they knew that the news was bad. The next day the Cassidy family heard over the parlor's Philco radio that the country was at war.

When Jim turned 17, he tried to enlist in the Navy but was turned away because of a minor vision problem. So he returned to Worcester South High School for his senior year.

He graduated early, in February of 1944, and

Jim Cassidy is given the Bronze Star by WWII Hero Commander George Henderson in 2007. PHOTO: TOM DUGGAN

shortly after his 18th birthday was drafted into the Army. He remembers that his mother, Grace, went to pick up his diploma later that spring in the high school gym and she remarked on how many empty seats there were for those who had already gone into the service. On May 15, 1944 Jim reported to Ft. Devens in Ayer for induction. The Army then shipped him to Ft. McClellan, Ala. for 17 weeks of infantry training in the tropical heat of summer.

Then Jim was sent to Ft. Leonard Wood in Missouri for additional training and, after a short leave at home, was ordered to Camp Myles Standish where he arrived in a blinding snowstorm. This was his final stop before "shipping out" to Europe. At this point, Jim was assigned to the 70th Infantry Division, famously known as the Trailblazers. For all this, Jim was paid $30/month.

In November 1944 Jim Cassidy boarded the SS Mariposa troop ship in Boston and headed to Marseilles, France. The trip over was uneventful, but Jim remembers well his arrival on December 10th. There was mud everywhere and it was cold. He pitched his tent in the ever-present mud and awaited orders to the front. That didn't take long.

Ten days later he and the other troops were loaded onto cattle cars and started towards Brumath, France. Five hundred miles later they arrived at their destination on Christmas Eve. Jim remembers the next day, Christmas 1944, very well. He went to open his C rations for dinner and found them full of ice.

At this point, Jim had been assigned to Company H, 274th Regiment of the 70th Division, 7th Army. Company H carried heavy weapons to support the infantry, primarily machine guns and mortars. Jim was part of a "machine gun squad," an eight-man unit operating the water-cooled Browning .30-caliber machine gun. The unit consisted of a #1 Gunner, who carried the heavy support tripod, the #2 Gunner who carried the machine gun itself, and six ammo carriers who each hauled two boxes of the 250-round cartridge belts.

Jim began as an ammo carrier but quickly moved up to Gunner as other squad members became casualties. Promotion during the war was as likely to be based on survival as it was on battlefield prowess.

The 274th Division fought just south of Patton's 3rd Army during Hitler's last-gasp Panzer attack in the Battle of the Bulge. As Jim and his Division moved forward from France into Germany, they endured constant shelling and sniper fire. They lived in foxholes in what was one of the coldest winters that Europe had seen in many years. Jim remembers carrying extra socks and innersoles in his parka to keep his feet dry. Dry feet were important because it meant warm feet and no frostbite.

Perhaps Jim's closest brush with death came when a "screaming meemie," the nickname for a German 88 mm rocket or artillery shell, landed no more than ten feet from his position. Fortunately, it was a dud and did nothing more than to spray him with lots of dirt and debris. Did I mention that it also scared the hell out of him?

As the 274th fought its way into Germany, Jim recalls that his unit was pulled back every so often and allowed a one-minute hot shower, given clean underwear and served some hot meals. One time Jim was even given a 3-day pass to Paris. It was the first time he had seen electricity since leaving Marseilles.

Jim also remembers sending V-mail back home. "V" stands for victory and the mail itself might be called the predecessor of today's e-mail. The soldier would write his letter on a special form and the Army would then shrink it onto microfilm for transport back to the states. There the letters would be restored to actual size and sent on to the intended recipients.

Despite the primitive conditions, the troops were kept up to date on the news by the Armed Forces Radio and Stars and Stripes. Jim remembers the sad day when their Commander in Chief, President Roosevelt, died.

As the war wound down in the spring of 1945 and Germany's surrender was near, Jim recalls the 274th taking many prisoners. A substantial number were no more than 12-13 years old as the German Army had exhausted its supply of regular troops.

After the Germans had surrendered to the Allies, Jim and the 274th started planning to go to the Pacific for one more battle. This was for the invasion of Japan where Jim knew the casualties would be very high. He was still in Europe when the atomic bombs were dropped on Hiroshima and Nagasaki and he remembers the jubilation and relief of the troops when Japan surrendered. Instead of one more battle to fight, thankfully, they would be going home.

In early January of 1946, Jim boarded the Liberty Ship SS John Holland for New York. He had been in Europe for 13 months and was eager to get back to the states. He will always remember that wonderful site of the Statue of Liberty as his ship made its way into New York harbor. On May 1, 1946 Jim was discharged from the Army.

For his service, Jim was awarded the Victory Medal, the Distinguished Presidential Unit Badge, the European African Middle Eastern Theater Campaign Ribbon with Two Battle Stars, and the Combat Infantry Badge. At the 2004 North Andover Memorial Day Service, Jim was also finally awarded the Bronze Star, the third highest award the U.S. Army bestows upon a soldier for "distinguishing oneself by heroic or meritorious achievement or service ... in connection with military operations against an armed enemy... ."

After the war, Jim used the GI Bill to attend UMass at the Ft. Devens campus. He studied agriculture and, after graduation, went on to a distinguished career with the Massachusetts Department of Agriculture. For 37 years he was the state's Director of the Bureau of Farm Products and enforced the regulations on all fruits and vegetables. He even had a long running and popular gardening program with a Boston radio station.

On July 4th, 1947 Jim met his future wife, Lorraine, while on an outing at Hampton Beach. They were married in 1950 and in 1954 moved from the Tower Hill section of Lawrence to a home on Perry Street in North Andover. They lived there until 2005 when they decided to move into a townhouse just across the line in Bradford. Sadly, Lorraine passed away this last year after a sudden illness.

Jim Cassidy is perhaps best known for his efforts to help veterans and seniors, and promote the American spirit. He is past commander and current vice commander of American Legion Post 219 in North Andover and a member of VFW Post 2104. After the 9/11 terrorist attack, Jim also helped champion the effort to get the American flag painted on the Bradford Street water tower in North Andover.

As many of you know, until recently Jim was a regular contributor to The Valley Patriot with his column on "Senior Moments." He always had great stories to share with us and wanted to pass along his famous "lessons on life." We are all appreciative for having the opportunity to read them.

Jim Cassidy, we thank you for your service to our country.

Editor's Note: Jim Cassidy was featured as this paper's first Valley Patriot of the Month in March 2004. However, at that time stories were not included with the veteran's picture. This month's column finally shows why he so richly deserved our prior acknowledgement.

LST-345 Commander George Henderson

WWII

By: Dr. Charles Ormsby - December, 2004

NORTH ANDOVER, MA - Meeting North Andover resident George Henderson for the first time, you wouldn't guess what he did during his first three years after college. Born in 1921, he graduated from St. Michaels College in 1942, approximately six months after Pearl Harbor.

George immediately signed up for duty in the Navy and, after being transformed into a "90-day wonder", he was assigned to the Naval amphibious forces; more precisely, he was assigned to serve on Landing Ship Tank 345 (LST 345). Given

Retired Commander George Henderson holds a model of the LST 345.

the option of choosing a specialty in Supply, Communications, or Gunnery, George picked Gunnery ... "because it seemed more glamorous!"

LST 345 departed US shores for northern Africa on May 1, 1943. George downplays the crossing, but consider the circumstances. LST convoys averaged 5-6 knots (under 7 mph) and the North Atlantic was still plagued by numerous German U-boats. If hit by a German torpedo, an LST would rapidly sink and other ships in the convoy were under orders to "just keep steaming" … any ship that stayed behind to pick up survivors would also be sunk. There would be no rescue.

LST 345's service in WWII was divided into three phases: Support of Allied Operations in Northern Africa (immediately after the fall of Axis forces in May 1943), support for the invasions of Sicily (July 1943) and Salerno (September 1943), and support of the D-Day invasion of Normandy (June 1944) and subsequent Allied Operations in Northern Europe. For LSTs, supporting an invasion meant going right up to the beach under fire to unload supplies and then take Allied wounded (or enemy prisoners) back to the staging area.

While operating out of Bizerte, Tunisia, LST 345 was exposed to German air raids every night for three months. George recalled one such air raid during a Bob Hope concert. Hope and his staff quickly retired to a dark hiding place until the raid was over. When the lights went on, Hope's troupe discovered they were hunkered down in an ammo dump!

LST 345Prior to the invasion of Sicily, military planners estimated casualties would reach 75-80%. But sometimes, good fortune intervenes. A barrage balloon tethered to LST 345 during the invasion at Sicily (that George had been unable to cut away when ordered to do so during the crossing of the Med) probably saved LST 345, George, and its crew. At the last second, a German FW190 fighter swerved to miss the balloon (which was tethered approximately 300 feet above the ship). That swerve sent a 500lb bomb, which would have landed in George's lap (he was standing on the bridge), into the water next to the ship. The explosion was still close enough to wound four crewmen.

henderson4The number of exciting events during these momentous months is too numerous to tell. Here is just a small sampling: * George and LST 345 were mistakenly ordered to sail into Salerno harbor while it was still firmly occupied by the Germans. Being the last ship to receive the order to "get out!"; they were exposed to 88 mm shells raining in from all directions. Only a smoke-screen lay down by HMS Tartar probably saved their lives.

* Sailing to Britain from the Mediterranean, LST 345 encountered a Nazi Wolfpack in the Atlantic. The ship was fortunate to survive as their escorts sunk 5 German subs. LST 345 then hit a storm in the Bay of Biscay where 40-foot waves nearly tore the ship apart.

* George and LST 345 were at Gold beach on the morning of June 6, 1944 unloading men, tanks, and supplies (see photo). LST 345 was the first ship to return to Britain with wounded Allied soldiers.

* LST 345 made 56 trips between Britain and France in support of the Allied offensive in Europe. Some of these trips extended well in-land (up the Seine River) and provided critically needed supplies for our troops engaged in the month-long Battle of the Bulge.

* On one trip, LST 345 carried rail cars in its hold. When they broke loose during a storm, the rail cars threatened to punch holes in the ship and sink it. George and his men crawled under the run-away cars and, with split second timing, forced wedges behind their wheels to prevent a disaster.

LST 345 2One chapter in George's history, thankfully, is missing. Upon returning to New York in July 1945, after Germany had surrendered, George Henderson was assigned to be the commanding officer of an LSM-R [Landing Ship Medium – Rockets] to be used in the invasion of Japan, scheduled for November 1, 1945. His role would be to sail in close to a selected invasion beach (before the actual invasion) and bombard the shore. Research conducted after the war (see Book Keepers Corner) indicated that the planned mission was likely to be suicidal. Hiroshima and Nagasaki intervened (thank you, Einstein and Truman) and, fortunately, George is still with us today.

George was awarded, among others, The American Defense Medal, The Victory Medal, and The European, Middle East, and African Campaign Medal with four stars (signifying the invasions of North Africa, Sicily, Italy, and Normandy). The Captain of LST 345 was awarded the Bronze Star on behalf of all of the Officers and crew of the ship for their heroism.

George, thank you for your service. P.S. If you are ever fortunate enough to meet George, ask him about the Top Secret Invasion Plans for Sicily that were mistakenly dropped overboard and, to this day, are resting somewhere on the bottom of the Mediterranean!

Francisco Urena
U.S. Marines

By Tom Duggan. Jr., - September, 2007

LAWRENCE MA - Most Lawrence residents know Francisco Urena as the city's Veterans' Services Director, but long before Urena came to work for the city of Lawrence he was serving the United States Marines in the 1st Tank Battalion in Iraq.

Urena was born in the Dominican Republic and grew up in Lawrence, attending the Lawlor, Tarbox and Arlington Schools before his family moved to Florida. In June of 1998 Urena joined the Marines, training at Parris Island in South Carolina and then attending 2 ½ months of training as a tank commander where he learned how to operate the M1A1 tank, graduating as a tank crewman.

From there Urena was selected to go to Twenty-Nine Palms, California, where he trained with tanks in the California desert. "There were hundreds of miles of desert," Urena explained. "We were trained to be as efficient as possible in combat situations." Little did he know that the training lie was receiving would be critical to the United States effort in Iraq to secure the country against international terrorists.

Urena served as a security officer at the United States Embassy after completing a rigorous course at Quantico, Virginia, "They wanted to make sure that the people they selected for security for the U.S. embassies were of sound mind and capable of handling diplomatic and security situations overseas," he explained.

"My first post after completing training was in Damascus, Syria where I spent a year and a half." There, Urena learned how to speak Arabic fluently, "which was very handy later on" he admits.

Urena also learned how to speak fluent Russian when he was assigned to his second post at the United States Embassy in Bishkek, Kyrgyzstan, a country which was formerly part of the Soviet Republic. Kyrgyzstan is located on the western border with China.

After returning home for a brief period of time in 2004, Urena found himself on his way to Iraq as a tank commander in the Spring of 2005. Urena was sent to the el Anbar province of Iraq on the eastern border of Syria "It was pretty much a no-mans-land out there," Urena says.

"Even Saddam Hussein had no power in that region when he was in power. There was no law enforcement at all, no rule of law it was total lawlessness, total chaos" he described.

During his time in Iraq, Urena was part of three major operations; Operation Matador, Operation Spear and Operation Quick Strike. During operation Matador Urena was issued a navy achievement medal for heroic actions and quick decisiveness during combat operations where he and his company were ambushed by Islamic terrorists. Urena was credited for saving numerous lives and evacuated civilians from the area safely while under heavy fire.

During "Operation Spear" Urena showed his heroism once again when he was hit with shrapnel in the face, "We were engaged in operations and the vehicle next to me was engaging a suspected enemy target with 40MM rounds. That's when the van next to the house we were near exploded, blowing fragments into my tank," he explained.

"I could see the shrapnel coming towards me when the van exploded but I couldn't duck fast enough. I didn't realize I was hit at first."

Urena refused to leave the area until several civilians and military personnel could be evacuated and have their medical needs tended to. "I had no idea I was bleeding profusely at the time all I could think about was evacuating the civilians and protecting my men."

Urena laughed nervously as he

Francisco Urena being interviewed by Ret. Lt. Colonel Oliver North in Iraq for Fox News.

described how he found out that a piece of shrapnel was still lodged in his cheek weeks later when he went for x-rays. "There it was, embedded in my cheek and I never knew it was there," he said. "I never reported the injury because I didn't want to leave my men behind, so a crewman gave me first aide and I just continued on with the mission. I was on my way out of the Corps. By the time I was nominated and when the investigation of the incident was completed I wasn't in the Marines anymore." Urena was out of the Corps. for more than a month when he was awarded the purple heart.

Francisco Urena was honorably discharged on June 15, 2006, but his service to his country did not end there. Like most real heroes who serve in the United States Military, Urena came back to the states looking for ways to continue serving, only this time serving his local community.

"When I left the military I decided to return to Lawrence, Massachusetts" Urena continued.

"It was May of 2006 and the flood was just hitting Lawrence, so I decided to become involved and help out in any way I could."

Urena immediately dropped off his bags at home, didn't bother to unpack, and went directly to the tent that Lawrence city officials had set up at the Hayden Schofield Playstead to help the area flood victims. At first, Urena served as a translator, helping Spanish speaking flood victims receive critical information from government officials, but when a local cable access television crew said they needed someone to volunteer as a cameraman Urena didn't hesitate to help.

At one point they asked Urena to take the microphone and speak on camera about the emergency services that were available and as soon as he began talking they recognized his communication skills in front of the camera, asking if he would help report on emergency procedures and news of the flood. Soon Urena was translating for local, state and federal officials, disseminating critical information to the community as part of the city's emergency response."

"Really, that's how I became involved in cable access," he said.

"Two months later, while the turmoil was going on in the Veteran's Services Office [in Lawrence City Hall] I started helping out Jorge DeJeus, (Lawrence's Acting Veteran's Services Director) doing paperwork and helping him catch up on a backlog of cases."

Urena volunteered in Lawrence city hall during the day while attending college at Northern Essex, taking a full semester of classes in the evening and logging more than 200 hours as a volunteer for the city.

"When the position of Veteran's Services Director became available I applied for the job, but in the mean time I signed up for a five day session of training that's put upon by The Department of Veteran's services."

Lawrence Mayor Michael J. Sullivan, recognizing Urena's heroic record in the military and having seen his zealous efforts to help the community as a volunteer, nominated him to be the city's Veteran's Services Director. Urena was hired on February 13, 2007.

But Urena's service to the community doesn't end there. Urena also volunteers his time reading to children in the Lawrence public schools, an activity he began while he was in the service. He's also a member of the VFW, American Legion, is a member of the board of directors for cable access, and works with Boy Scout Troop #2 training adult leaders as a unit commissioner.

Urena is still attending college classes at Northern Essex where he is studying political science.

Francisco Ureana, the Valley Patriot would like to thank you for your heroic service to your country and your community. We are honored to be able to tell a small part of your story as our Valley Patriot of the Month. The people of the Merrimack Valley and the United States owe you a great debt of gratitude that can never be repaid.

EDITOR'S NOTE: Francisco Urena is now the Secretary of Veterans Services for Massachusetts Governor Charlie Baker.

PHOTO: RICH RUSSELL

The Valley Patriot newspaper holds an annual BASH to honor veterans, police officers, and Firefighters. Left to right: 2016 Hero Veteran Award Winner J.T. Torres of New England Veterans Liberty House was presented his Valley Patriot, "Hero Veteran" award by Francisco Urena, Massachusetts Secretary of Veteran's Services (2016). Urena himself is a Valley Patriot "Hero Veteran" award winner in 2014. The amount of help these two men, have given to local veterans is immeasurable.

Staff Sgt. John Katsaros, USAAF (ret.), Haverhill, received the French Legion of Honor–Chevalier award from the Consul General of France Christophe Guilhou, who holds the 3rd edition of Katsaros' book "Code Burgundy: The Long Escape." Katsaros will speak Nov. 16, 7 p.m., VFW, No. Andover.

POW - Ssgt. John Katsaros Author of "Code Burgundy" Part I

By: Helen Mooradkanian - September, 2011

HAVERHILL, MA - Out of the darkness, engines roaring, hundreds of American B-17 Flying Fortresses took off on March 20, 1944, in World War II, from Deenethorpe, England. Destination: Frankfurt. Mission: destroy production of dreaded Luftwaffe FW-190 fighter planes.

At 30,000 feet, under heavily overcast skies and turbulent winds, two B-17s collided over the base.

Formation flying over Germany was impossible. Miraculously avoiding a B-17 that plunged out of control, the pilot dived thousands of feet. On regaining altitude, he lost formation. Then the bombers were recalled to another target but due to radio silence all turned back except one.

He kept going to Frankfurt. Alone.

Staff Sergeant John Katsaros, 20 years old, Haverhill, Mass., was on that doomed aircraft, as aerial engineer, gunner and photographer with the 612th Bomb Squadron, 401st Heavy Bomb Group, 8th Air Force. This was his 11th mission on the B-17 "Man O' War" Flying Fortress.

While successfully bombing their target, the B-17 was hit by 88mm anti-aircraft fire, losing two of four engines. Five ME-109s strafed the bomber, chasing it to France—but the crew shot down three of them. Outside Reims, their plane exploded in flames—seconds after the crew bailed out!

In the darkness–a beacon of hope

Yet, what appeared to be "a mission to hell" turned into a drama of divine intervention and miraculous escapes.

Although France had surrendered to Germany in 1940, the darkness could not quench the spirit of freedom.

Out of the darkness of despair, the French Resistance arose like a beacon of hope—one of the greatest mass movements of freedom-fighting patriots. For downed American and Allied airmen, it meant the difference between life—and death.

Because of their sacrifices, John Katsaros is alive today.

Beyond man's control

Two days after Pearl Harbor, with "patriotism jumping in my veins," 17-year old Katsaros joined the Navy Air Cadets, later enlisted in the U.S. Army Air Corps and sworn in December 7, 1942.

He flew 11 combat missions against Germany, February 11 to March 20, 1944: Frankfurt (3 missions), Leipzig (producing ME-109 fighter planes), Lippstadt, Wilhelmshaven, Cologne, Berlin, Berlin/Erkner, Augsburg, and Landsburg am Lech.

He took part in the massive operations that blitzed Germany—the "Big Week," February 20-25, 1944—"the largest and most successful missions ever run." For their role, the 401st received two Presidential Distinguished Unit Citations, for raids against Leipzig and Frankfurt.

The day his plane was shot down, four crew members were KIA, Katsaros' body was riddled with shrapnel, his mangled right arm hung paralyzed. Yet before bailing out, he wrapped his scarf around the neck of a fellow gunner, hemorrhaging from a severed artery, and helped him bail out.

With seconds to spare, Katsaros bailed out at 27,000 ft. in a 25,000 foot free-fall, losing consciousness. But first he said a fast prayer.

Valley of the shadow of death

His prayer was answered.

Katsaros landed on the "Bonne Maison Farm." Alive, but shattered with six broken ribs, a fractured left ankle, a badly twisted and sprained right ankle and severe contusions to his head, back and leg.

A farm worker saw him and carried him to the farmhouse.

Then the Gestapo arrived . . .

Thus began "the long escape"— a three-month, 3,000-mile journey from the north of France to the south, climbing the Pyrenees Mountains before reaching Spain, then Gibraltar and freedom.

Thanks to the French underground, Katsaros survived. They whisked him from one safe-house to another, often right under the nose of the Gestapo.

The Germans offered a $10,000 reward for Katsaros.

Twice the Gestapo captured him. After his bail-out, and later when an undercover German collaborator betrayed him.

Each time the French Resistance stormed the scene, guns blazing and rescued him!

Repeatedly, he narrowly escaped death.

John Katsaros literally walked "through the valley of the shadow of death"—and beyond it to life.

Code Burgundy–the long escape

The French Resistance, working with British Intelligence, code-named Katsaros "Burgundy" and mapped out his entire escape route. Slipping through enemy lines, he gathered strategic information.

Katsaros took on many disguises. He was a cell leader's deaf-and-dumb nephew injured in a Paris raid, a French "gendarme," complete with uniform and cap that walked the beat with his rescuer and a French citizen, with papers and photo expertly forged.

Messengers of mercy

Through it all, the brave men and women of the French Resistance sacrificed their lives and endured torture to save his life. Among his many angels of mercy:

• The underground doctor, a French Jew, who performed three surgeries in three days on his right arm, with little or no anesthesia available. When he advised amputation because gangrene had set in, the Resistance leader pointed a pistol at his head and shouted, "NO!" Katsaros' arm was saved.

• The elderly woman who came daily to feed him, though fearing for her life. Her son was a German POW.

• The family who loved and cared for him like their own son, when he was weak and emaciated. His extended stay put their lives at peril.

• The men who hid him in a winery's storage cellar, deep underground.

• The farmer who hid him in a covered dry well, 20 to 30 feet underground.

Above him, Katsaros heard the Gestapo interrogating the farmer!

Enemy's eyes are blinded

Often the Gestapo looked right at Katsaros without "seeing" him.

Katsaros says that once he lay crumpled in the street, while German soldiers strolled by.

On Easter Sunday, he says he received Holy Communion in a church filled with German soldiers. Not one of them recognized him. Later he celebrated Easter dinner with three resistance leaders and their families. Before eating, "we had special prayers, rejoicing in the resurrection of our Lord Jesus Christ," Katsaros recounted

"One more mountain"

The unexpectedly long, four-day, four-night trek, with a Basque guide, across the Pyrenees into Spain was grueling and torturous. The trail circuitous, rated "severely difficult."

No food. Virtually no water.

No winter climbing clothes.

German patrols with dogs. Spotter planes circling overhead.

Since Katsaros' right arm was useless, others often pulled him up, using a branch.

Worse yet, he had only dress shoes, two sizes too small! His feet became cramped and frozen. The soles wore thin. Over snow covered rocks and steep, icy slopes they hiked, fording rivers with stony beds.

Yet he kept walking. One step at a time. In faith.

"One more mountain, one more mountain," their Basque guide kept urging.

Weak, exhausted, weighing 87 lb, Katsaros says he told the others to go on without him, but they refused. "You're one of us. We will not leave you. See, we're getting closer to freedom. We're all going to make it."

Someone slipped him two sugar cubes. Their kindness kept him going.

Finally, they reached Spain. Another lockup. Another rescue. Freedom at last!

The Light shines in darkness

What sustained a 20-year old in such fiery trials? John Katsaros says, "Faith in God, knowing He was always with me. That gave me courage to act in the face of death. I firmly believed He always heard me when I prayed. He sent His people to save my life. When you experience the miracles of God, you know!"

Ultimately, good always triumphs over evil.

As the Apostle John wrote, "The Light shines on in the darkness, for the darkness has never overpowered it."

(To order the book "Code Burgundy: The Long Escape," contact author: jkatsaros3@comcast.net).

PART II

By: Helen Mooradkanian - October, 2011

Last month we described the miraculous escape of downed airman, John Katsaros, USAAF, of Haverhill, Massachusetts, whose life was saved during WWII by the French Resistance. Smuggled out of Nazi-occupied France in a 3-month, 3,000-mile escape, he gathered strategic intelligence used to liberate France. For this, he received France's highest honor.

Legion of Honor: Chevalier

On September 6, 2011, in Haverhill, Massachusetts, in a ceremony attended by military and political dignitaries, Staff Sergeant John Katsaros, USAAF (ret.), received the Chevalier in the French Legion of Honor for his "outstanding contribution to the liberation of France from Nazi occupation in World War II."

Consul General of France, Christophe Guilhou, granted this prestigious medal to Katsaros, on behalf of French President, Nicolas Sarkozy, who signed the decree. The medal was created in 1802 by Emperor Napoléon.

"This honor," the Consul General said, "is a token of France's eternal gratitude. France has never forgotten the tremendous sacrifice and contribution that went into helping liberate our country. Mr. Katsaros, thank you for your courage, perseverance, and dedication. You are a true hero."

On his three-month, 3,000-mile escape through enemy lines, he gathered extensive, strategic military information for the USAAF Intelligence and Britain's Special Operations Executive (SOE), founded by Winston Churchill.

The escape route Katsaros followed was mapped out by the British SOE working with the French Resistance. They code-named him "Burgundy," and smuggled him in various disguises from the north of France near Reims, where his B-17 was shot down, to the south, across the Pyrenees into Spain, then Gibraltar and England. He flew home on President Roosevelt's personal plane.

As Consul General Guilhou pointed out, "It is imperative we honor men such as Mr. Katsaros for their courage and sacrifices. Moreover, younger generations must never forget that it is due to their sacrifices that we are able to live in a free and democratic world today."

French Ambassador to the United States, Pierre Vimont, wrote to Katsaros: "The French people will never forget your courage and devotion to the great cause of freedom . . . and your personal, precious contribution to the United States' decisive role in the liberation of our country."

BEHIND ENEMY LINES

John Katsaros became the vital link exposing enemy secrets as he moved within the vast network of cells within the Resistance.

Newly declassified government documents reveal his espionage in the 3rd edition of "Code Burgundy: The Long Escape."

Among them: Hitler's top-secret weapons, the Jet Bomber and the ME-262 Jet Fighter; the V-2 bomb that flew undetected then dropped, silently; the Ho 2-29 stealth bomber (600 mph at 60,000 ft.) that could fly undetected by radar from Berlin to NYC and back without refueling—carrying the Atomic Bomb before we had it!

He uncovered the European-wide holocaust of Jews, Catholics, and Gypsies; sites of German stalags (POW camps), names of German commanders, transport of POWs and their number; anti-aircraft machine-guns stationed along key railway routes.

Journey without a roadmap

Little did the Resistance know, when they stormed "La Bonne Maison" farmhouse near Reims and rescued Katsaros in a blaze of gunfire, that their daring rescue would have such far-reaching impact—linking men, nations, and generations.

"I owe my life to the French Resistance," said Katsaros, who formed a deep bond with all his helpers, especially the three Resistance leaders who executed his first rescue: Pierre Demarchez, leader of the Chaumuzy cell, Jean Joly, leader of the Reims cell, and René Felix, Reims cell.

"These men were focused, shrewd, and calculating in their strategy. They were fearless, driven only by their love for France and their love of freedom."

His second rescue was orchestrated by the Reims police chief, another resistance leader. Katsaros, captured at the bakery run by Pierre and Julienne Demarchez, was being transported when the resistance led a clever ambush of the German convoy. A surprise blockade. "official" vehicles. A stunned Gestapo. And Katsaros sped away in a cloud of dust! Not a shot was fired!

Often, instructions came one at a time. "Follow me." "Go to . . ."

"Look for a man who…"

"Wait there until . . ."

People slipped in and out of his life, whispering instructions, giving messages.

General Dwight D. Eisenhower, Supreme Allied Commander, wrote in his book, "Crusade in Europe," that "without the great assistance (of the French Resistance), the liberation of France and the defeat of the enemy in Western Europe would have consumed a much longer time and meant greater losses to ourselves."

Lessons in survival

Katsaros assumed many disguises: deaf-and-dumb nephew injured in a British air raid, police deputy, "gendarme" (military police) who walked the beat with his rescuer, "French citizen" with photo ID and documents expertly forged.

"These men and women showed me what courage is. Their boldness gave me strength and hope. "I never felt lonely because I became part of their family. From them, I learned how to survive: devise plans, avoid capture, escape when seized, endure hardships and never lose hope."

"This was not just my war. It was our war, and we fought it together, side by side. They felt it was their duty to protect me, save my life, and send me home safely."

John Katsaros became the beloved son of Pierre and Julienne Demarchez, who nursed him to health in their home for several weeks, at great risk to themselves. When discovered, Julienne was tortured by the Gestapo, but steadfastly refused to reveal anything. Later imprisoned at Ravensbruk, she said she would do it all over again for the cause of freedom.

CLARION CALL: PROTECT FREEDOM

John Katsaros' mission did not end with WWII. He is part of a greater purpose linking freedom-loving patriots, and nations.

Today his mission continues to unfold, honoring the heroes of the past and inspiring future generations to fight for freedom.

The French Resistance was like a swift-flowing river underground, invisible, bringing life, freedom, and hope to those bound in darkness. Nothing could stop it.

When walking the line between life and death, a bond develops with those who saved you. It can never be broken. It spans generations. Katsaros' visits to his rescuers, and their visits here, attest to this.

It also crosses continents. The international Air Forces Escape and Evasion Society (AFEES), which Katsaros heads as president includes 300 living WWII airmen and the more than 600 helpers who saved them, who meet annually.

As a gift to the people of France, a French translation of Katsaros' book "Code Burgundy" is now being prepared, which he will donate to schools and libraries as a memorial to the heroism of these patriots and an inspiration to future generations.

To Americans, Katsaros urges, "Cherish your freedom!" During his escape, he said, "every close call made freedom taste even sweeter." He has given more than 100 talks across the United States before the Air Force Academy, aviation groups, grammar and high schools, colleges and universities, veterans groups and churches, to keep alive our precious heritage—and to remind us how fragile freedom is.

As President Ronald Reagan observed:

"Freedom is never more than one generation away from extinction. We didn't pass it to our children in the bloodstream. It must be fought for, protected, and handed on for them to do the same."

(To order book, contact author: jkatsaros3@comcast.net, 978-869-3035)

Photo provided by John Katsaros 1

To see the video of Valley Patriot publisher Tom Duggan, Jr.'s interview with John Katsaros on 980WCAP in Lowell visit: valleypatriot.com

Colonel Kris Mineau
USAF (Ret.)

By: Helen Mooradkanian - March, 2012

NORTH READING, MA - Colonel Kris Mineau, USAF (Ret.), of North Reading, flew 100 combat missions into North Vietnam in 1966 as fighter pilot in the supersonic F-4C Phantom II. Capable of speed Mach 2.23, more than twice the speed of sound, the Phantom was key to downing the Soviet MiG-21s used by the North Vietnamese to intercept U.S. bombing missions.

Flying out of Ubon, Thailand, with the 8th Tactical Fighter Wing (TFW), Mineau flew deep into North Vietnam as part of "Operation Rolling Thunder," the first sustained—and the longest—aerial bombing assault in the history of American air power. It cut off the flow of supplies moving south down the Ho Chi Minh Trail to the Viet Cong invading South Vietnam.

Supersonic fighter jets. Lightning-speed maneuvers. Aggressive warfare. Suicide missions. "I was a cocky fighter pilot who thought I was invincible," Mineau says.

The Wolf Pack"—Record breakers

As a young lieutenant, Mineau was a member of the famed "Wolf Pack," renowned for their aggressiveness and teamwork in destroying enemy aircraft. Their wing commander was the legendary WWII ace Colonel Robin Olds who, in 1944-1945, had 12 kills against the German Luftwaffe. Then, at age 44, he led the 8th TFW, as commander and pilot, to 24 aerial victories and 38.5 kills in Vietnam—both records unsurpassed by any other wing in the war. Olds also masterminded "Operation Bolo," a clever ambush of MiG-21s. The 12-minute engagement destroyed seven MiG-21s—the highest number in any combat operation of the war—without a single American loss. Col. Olds got his first MiG kill in "Bolo" and went on to shoot down a total of 4 MiG-21s. Mineau also flew with another Air Force legend, Colonel Daniel "Chappie" James, Jr., the first black American promoted to four-star general.

Supersonic ejection— toward hell

Following his combat tour, Mineau was assigned to fly F-4Cs in Europe where in 1969, his life as an intrepid aviator suddenly crashed. Not in an air battle, but during a routine combat training mission. "I was stationed in England," he says, "leading the life of a rascal with wine, women, and song."

On Tuesday, March 25, 1969, his F-4 Phantom II fighter jet developed a mechanical flight-control malfunction. From an altitude of 15,000 ft., it nosedived at the speed of sound. His electronic weapons officer in the rear seat ejected. But Mineau's seat would not fire due to a design problem — no matter how many times he tried.

As the jet plummeted, reaching an altitude too low for ejection, Mineau says, "My life passed before me. Although never a religious person, I cried out, 'Please, God, help!' Instantly the ejection seat fired."

"Now at an altitude of 1000 feet, I'm diving at 1,280 ft. per second. My parachute takes 3 to 4 seconds to open. Only a miracle can save me."

It was later determined his parachute opened in half a second! "Absolutely impossible, mechanically speaking!" he said.

"I looked down and saw this enormous fireball as my plane hit the ground and exploded. I tried to steer away from the fireball but couldn't. The 750-mph supersonic wind-blast had broken all four limbs. I hit the ground like a 200-lb rag doll, unable to move or cry for help."

Mineau is one of the very few pilots in the world to have survived a supersonic ejection.

From brokenness—a new creation

For the next four months, he was totally immobilized in traction, all four limbs, followed by a total body cast. When doctors in the States removed the cast, they found he had not healed properly. They had to re-break his bones and start all over again. At one point, they even prepared to amputate a leg. For six years, Mineau was in and out of military hospitals undergoing major surgeries.

Worse yet, doctors gave him no hope of ever flying again. His dream of flying, his all-consuming passion, lay shattered. Just like his body. Driven to despair, he hit rock bottom

At that point, an Air Force chaplain and former pilot on two-week active reserve duty, walked into his hospital room unexpectedly. He talked to Kris of Jesus' love for him. Slowly Kris opened up.

"In that hospital bed," he says, "I asked Jesus Christ to be my Savior. A vision of Jesus on the cross flooded my mind. For the first time, I understood with my heart everything I knew about Jesus in my head. A deep warmth and wondrous love enveloped me. Then this rough, tough barroom-brawling fighter pilot began crying like a baby because I knew Jesus loved me. All my sins were forgiven, erased!"

From that point on, Kris Mineau began a rapid recovery. His doctors were amazed. Within a month, he was walking again, although with multiple casts and crutches. A year later, he relinquished his will and dreams completely to the Lord. Then he heard the words, "Welcome, home, my prodigal son." Like the parable of the father and his prodigal son, Jesus embraced him: "For this my son was dead and is alive again; he was lost and is found" (Luke 15:24).

The healing of his shattered life began and he was ultimately made whole in spirit, soul, and body.

On August 28, 1974, the Air Force declared Mineau medically fit for flight status.

On January 1, 1975, Kris Mineau returned to active duty as a pilot.

Six years to the day after his crash, he climbed into a T-38 supersonic trainer. Like "déjà vu," it was again Tuesday, March 25, with 4:30 p.m. take-off. The T-38's tail number was 898, the same as the F-4C that crashed.

At the start of the seventh year after his crash, his new life began.

"Wild Weasels"—suicide missions

For five years, Mineau flew the F-15 Eagle, one of the world's most formidable interceptor fighters, capable of speed Mach 2.5 (1,875 mph).

A second close call with death came in 1981, while serving as F-15 Eagle instructor pilot and squadron commander. Shortly after take-off, a violent engine explosion tore the Eagle apart. Again he called out to the Lord for help. Instantly, the molten mass of engine debris fell out. With flames extinguished, he maneuvered the jet to the runway and awaiting fire trucks.

Later promoted to Colonel and deputy commander for the maintenance group of three squadrons, Mineau spent two years flying the highly sophisticated supersonic jet, the F-4G Weasel, reminiscent of the "Wild Weasels" that flew in suicide missions in Vietnam. Armed with anti-radar missiles for "hunter-killer" operations, the Weasel "trolled" for enemy surface-to-air missile (SAM) sites, waited for the SAM to launch, attacked, then guided bombers to finish the job—before veering off sharply. They called this "dancing with the SAMs."

The eagle soars to new heights

After retiring from the military in 1992, Mineau served three years in Saudi Arabia under a USAF contract to build F-15 air bases. Then his career took a sharp turn. The U.S. Air Force Academy graduate, with a master's in aeronautical engineering was called to the ministry. He graduated from Gordon-Conwell Theological Seminary and became a pastor. Today he is president of the Massachusetts Family Institute, a public policy organization where he serves on the frontlines in the battle to strengthen and protect the traditional family.

The Eagle has landed.

Mike Beshara
U.S. Navy - WWII

By: Tom Duggan, Jr. - September, 2007

METHUEN, MA - When Methuen resident Mike Beshara tried to join the Navy in January of 1942, he was initially told that he could not join the service because of his age.

"I was only 17 years old at the time," Beshara recalled. "After December 7, 1941 I really wanted to enlist in the Navy, but my parents had passed away and my uncle couldn't sign the papers for me to join because he was not considered my legal guardian."

So, Beshara made an appeal to the Navy and, because his uncle didn't drive, the Navy arranged to have a judge come up to Superior Court in Lawrence to have his uncle designated as his legal guardian.

By the time the red tape was cleared away it was April of 1942 and the young senior in high school dropped out to serve his country. It would be 57 years later before Beshara would graduate from high school. "My Diploma was issued to me at the Methuen High School in 1999, they gave diplomas to a whole bunch of us who had gone into the service and never finished high school.

Once accepted by the Navy, Beshara says he went to boot camp training at Great Lakes Naval Training Station in Illinois. After boot camp training, he was assigned to the Navy Pier in Chicago where he was trained as an aircraft mechanic and graduated aviation machinist mate 3rd class. From there he was shipped to Hollywood, Florida for Air Crewman training and then to Fort Lauderdale for flight training.

"We did extensive training with machine guns and learned trap and skeet shooting to get use to hitting a moving target," Beshara said. "Then I went to Clinton Oklahoma. There, I joined what was called STAG ONE, which stood for Special Task Air Group One.

Secret Drone Spy Program is Born

From there, Beshara was sent to Travis City, Michigan where he trained with the first-ever secret spy drone airplanes. "This was a secret outfit with radio controlled drones," Beshara says. "By this time it was 1943 and we didn't know it at the time, of course, but we were working on the forerunner of the guided missile system."

"It was really remarkable. We were working with a mostly plywood, twin engine, unmanned airplane with a television camera built into the nose of the plane. These drones carried 2000lb bombs. The canopy on the cockpit was for training only, but when the training was over and these drones were ready for use in battle, they removed the cockpit completely to make it less wind resistant. The landing was also dropped after takeoff to reduce wind resistance."

Beshara recalls how the drone planes were just like the Japanese kamikaze planes except there were no pilots to give up their lives.

"Tokyo Rose called us 'the American Kamikazes' because they didn't know this was an unmanned plane. The mother ship, which was a torpedo bomber, could sit four or five miles off the target and direct the drones in. They had a television screen in there so they could see what the drone was seeing, and direct the plane to the target without risking American lives."

"While the pilot flew the plane, there was a man behind him flying the drone by radio control, a radio man and a machine gun man in the turret." That's where Beshara flew with a 50 caliber machine gun in case their plane was attacked.

Some of the drones were stationed on aircraft carriers, but Beshara recalls being sent to the island of Benika in the Russell Islands, northwest of Guadalcanal. "We had set up a small airfield on the island. Some of the targets were anti-aircraft placements and storage caves in Bougainville, but we couldn't bomb the caves successfully because, when the planes would drop a bomb, they would be too close to the ground and pull up a little too late so the drones would blow up."

Beshara says the program was not all that successful during World War II and, though the drones were designed to prevent the loss of American and allied soldiers, one very famous American soldier died working on the drones.

"Joe Kennedy, JFK's older brother, was killed in Europe working on the drones. They were flying a B24 or B17. They had them all loaded with about 25,000 lbs. of explosives, but the munitions experts were all marines and General George Marshall said that, as long as he had anything to say about it, there would never be any marines in Europe. Marshall didn't like the marines, so the marine munitions expert couldn't go over there to make sure the explosives were set up properly. That's when they asked for two volunteers. Joe Kennedy and a guy named Whiley agreed to go." Beshara conjectured that, "While they were arming the explosives there was short circuit somewhere and it exploded and killed them both."

"While we were overseas in Benika, our outfit was suddenly decommissioned. Our commanding officer, Commodore Oscar Smith was not a pilot and Admiral Tower, sitting back in Washington D.C., was making the decision that you can't have an aircraft unit without a pilot as a commanding officer. So that was the end of the drone program," Beshara said, "at least until after the war. But this was the forerunner of the guided missile system and the drones being used today in Iraq are just a smaller version of the drone program we started in the South Pacific."

A Chance Encounter

After Beshara's STAG ONE group was permanently decommissioned in 1944, he wound up in the Philippines on Clark Field. "We were servicing bombers going to Okinawa. At that point in time we couldn't say where we were when we were on the island. We could put in our letters home that we were in the Philippines, but we couldn't tell them exactly where we were, we couldn't designate an island."

"My older brother Herbie was in the Army Signal Corps and surprised me one day when he just showed up on the Island of Sumar. He had been stationed in the South Pacific and, when he found out I was in the Philippines, he spoke to his commanding officer to try and find out where I was. They had to courier the mail to the troops and he let my brother come to find me. The day after I met him, I received orders to come back to the states. All air crewmen were being reassigned to the states to train for the invasion of Japan in June 1945."

Mike says he was shipped back to the U.S. and was given a 30 day leave of absence. "I was home for 4th of July, in 1945." Beshara remembered how he visited the center at Salisbury Beach wearing his flight jacket, "because it was just so cold for me after spending all that time in the South Pacific. People thought I was crazy because, to them, it was a hot summer day, but, compared to the South Pacific, it was like winter to me."

After his leave of absence, Mike Beshara was sent to the University of Oklahoma for further training "Of course," Beshara added, "in August they dropped the atomic bomb on Japan." Beshara was discharged honorably in January of 1946.

"That's when," Beshara said laughing, "I was a member of the 52/20 club. It was our funny name for unemployment. It was $20 a week for fifty-two weeks or until we found a job." Beshara did find work in the Wood Heel factory on Osgood Street in Methuen, which is now home to luxury apartments.

Continuing His Service to America Here at Home

Mike Beshara's dedication to service and country did not end when he was discharged from the Navy in 1946. He joined the American Legion and the VFW, and was active in local politics and community service in the city of Methuen.

Beshara served 4 years on the Methuen School Committee and served as chairman of the committee when proposition 2 ½ took effect. "After four years of beating my head against the wall and getting nothing done, I decided not to run for another term." Mike volunteered as a member of the Methuen Cable Advisory Committee and served on the board for 18 years. He spent several years as chairman of the board. Beshara was also chairman of the Methuen Soil Removal Board for a number of years as well as chairman of the School Renovation Committee where he was responsible for the renovation of three schools: the Marsh, Tenny and Timony schools.

"Before that, we did some extensive work on the Oakland school; we put in new windows, new floors and brand new boilers. We renovated the Ashford School and put in windows in the Central School. After we renovated the three schools they closed Oakland and Ashford. The Ashford was sold and turned into apartments and the Oakland school is a mosque now.

Beshara also volunteers his time on a cable television program run by Methuen City Councilor Kathleen Corey Rahme titled "Call to Serve". The television program highlights the heroic service of military men and women from Methuen. "I remember when Kathleen was getting ready to tape her first show and she asked me to sit down and do an interview for practice, and I said yes. We sat down and did the interview and immediately afterwards the other volunteers in the studio said that it was great, so Kathleen said, 'Let's just use this interview as our first "Call to Serve" show,' so my story was the first in the series that was aired."

Beshara said all the veterans who have been honored on "Call to Serve" were asked to sign a waiver release for the library of congress in Washington D.C. so that the public could view the tapes for years to come.

Mike Beshara is so typical of the men and women who are willing go off to war, putting their lives on the line for our freedoms here at home. He doesn't consider himself a hero despite the fact that he sat in the machine gun turret of a fighter plane and was the most at risk of losing his life when they encountered enemy plane gunfire.

Like so many of those who answer the call to serve, Mike Beshara didn't stop serving his country when his military service was over. He continued to fight for a better community and a better America through his community activism and the way he has lived his life right here in the city of Methuen.

We thank you Mike Beshara for your military service, for your undying loyalty to your country and your community, and we are honored to call you our Valley Patriot of the Month. You are truly a hero in our midst and the people of Methuen should recognize forever the sacrifices you have made to make life better for the rest of us who have reaped the benefits of your service and sacrifice.

Capt. Terrance Hart
U.S. Coast Guard

By: Ted Tripp - October, 2006

GEORGETOWN, MA – Late on the night of December 26, 1970, in stormy seas 600 miles off Cape May, New Jersey, the aging 540-foot Finnish tanker Ragny broke in half without warning. An SOS went out and was relayed to the Coast Guard station in New York which immediately initiated rescue operations. Thirty-one crewmembers were stranded on the stern section and six, including the captain, were believed to be on the bow.

The Coast Guard cutter Escanada, on its way to Atlantic station Echo and 170 miles away, was immediately diverted to assist in the rescue. After 20 hours traveling at full speed, the Escanada reached the stricken tanker in the middle of the following night. Another vessel, the SS Platte, had reached the Ragny earlier but had already lost a crewman when a rescue lifeboat capsized in the rough seas. The Escanada established

47

communications with the stern's survivors by sending them a portable radio by shot line. The cutter's commanding officer then made the decision to wait until first light to attempt any further rescue efforts for obvious safety reasons.

But several hours later the Ragny crew reported that the stern was sinking and the commanding officer of the Escanada ordered a dangerous nighttime rescue. Two lifeboats were lowered from the cutter into 10-15 foot seas and, with great risk, successfully rescued all 31 crew from the stern. The bow of the Ragny, unfortunately, disappeared from the radar screen just after the stern rescue was completed. Throughout the following day, the Escanada continued to search for the captain and five missing crewmembers from the bow, but they were never found.

Ensign Terry Hart, fresh out of the Coast Guard Academy, was the boat officer of one of the lifeboats involved in the daring rescue. He and nine other members of the rescue team would later be awarded the Finnish Lifesaving Medal by President Urho Kekkonen of Finland. The Commandant of the U.S. Coast Guard, Admiral C.R. Bender, also awarded a Unit Commendation Medal to the crew of the Escanada for "exceptionally meritorious service ... while engaged in the dramatic rescue of 31 survivors ... ."

Terrance P. Hart was born in 1948 in Chicago, the son of a career Coast Guardsman. As part of a military family, Terry traveled throughout the country while growing up but eventually would spend the last two years of his secondary education at Mt. Diablo High School in Concord, Calif. During his senior year he was student body president and participated on the cross-country and track teams.

Always knowing he was destined for a military career, he applied to and was accepted at both the Coast Guard Academy and Annapolis. He chose the Coast Guard, mostly because of his father, but also because he was excited about sailing on the Coast Guard's tall ship, the Eagle. He would subsequently spend three summers hauling lines, climbing masts and furling sails on the Eagle. Hart says that the first thing a cadet is required to do is climb a mast – to overcome any fear of heights.

Terry graduated from the Coast Guard Academy in 1970 – only a third of the entering class made it to graduation that year - and was assigned to the Cutter Escanada as an Assistant Gunnery Officer and Deck Watch Officer.

The 255-foot Escanada was an ocean station vessel which would travel out to a specific point in the Atlantic and stay on watch for 30 days, collecting weather information, providing navigation assistance to aircraft, and monitoring radio traffic.

Terry spent two years on the Escanada where he would participate in a number of rescues, recoveries and the towing of disabled fishing boats. However, he was also fortunate to participate in the exciting America's Cup races off Newport, R.I. in 1970 where the Intrepid defeated the Australian challenger, Gretel II.

In 1972, after being promoted to lieutenant junior grade, Terry Hart became the commanding officer of the 95-foot Cutter Cape Horn out of Woods Hole, Mass. He will never forget his first tow job. It was the carcass of a huge 65-foot humpback whale which had washed up on the beach at Provincetown. Most of the time, however, the cutter performed search and rescue operations around Cape Cod and out to George's Bank.

Two years later Terry was transferred to the Coast Guard District in New Orleans as a controller in the rescue center. This station was responsible for all air and sea, search and rescue operations in the entire Gulf of Mexico. The controller coordinates all operations much like an air traffic controller at an airport. The shifts were 24 hours on and 48 hours off, but that was only if you were lucky. It was here that Terry became an expert on hurricanes and was preparing for the worst when one headed directly towards New Orleans – but then took a left turn at the last moment.

In 1974 Terry volunteered to become Commanding Officer of the Cutter Flagstaff, an experimental hydrofoil formerly belonging to the Navy. This was an era when Washington was beginning to emphasize drug enforcement and the 50+ knot Flagstaff was thought to be ideal for interdiction of drug smugglers.

Although stationed out of Woods Hole, Hart says the cutter spent much of its time up in Boston for repairs. Because of the continuing maintenance problems, the Flagstaff was decommissioned after two years of trials. Hart still remembers the thrill – and awe from the bystanders on shore – going through the Cape Cod Canal at 50 knots without creating a wake.

In late 1978 Terry Hart was transferred to Coast Guard Headquarters in Washington, D.C. in the military readiness division. He would subsequently become the Current Operations Officer for all international law enforcement activities involving the Coast Guard. During his tenure he would be involved in 480 drug-bust cases, all involving foreign boat seizures.

In 1980, Cuba's Fidel Castro emptied his prisons and told them and other "government-designated undesirables" that they could flee to the United States if they wished. This became known as the Mariel Boatlift and involved over a thousand boats and rafts headed for U.S. shores. President Jimmy Carter, alarmed at the huge influx of Cubans, ordered a stop to it. Coast Guard Headquarters sent Terry Hart to Miami to set up the law enforcement and engagement procedures. The program worked. Within two weeks, the number of Cubans fleeing to the U.S. had dwindled to just a trickle.

In the summer of 1983, drug problems were sweeping the country. President Ronald Reagan decided he needed a "Drug Czar" and appointed his vice president, George H.W. Bush, to that position.

Shortly afterwards, Terry Hart got a call from the White House to join the Bush team. He was assigned to the staff of the National Narcotics Border Interdiction System. He ended up spending three years with Bush fighting the war on drugs.

By now Terry Hart had been away from sea duty for seven and a half years. The Coast Guard had a stipulation that after seven years away from a sea command, you are no longer permitted to return to the sea.

So Terry was relegated to shore duty from here on. In 1986 he asked for and was appointed Chief Law Enforcement & Intelligence Officer for the First Coast Guard District in Boston. (The district encompassed all waters from Toms River, N.J. to the Maine/Canada Border.) Four years later he became Deputy Group Commander of Coast Guard units performing law enforcement, aids to navigation and search and rescue operations from the Cape Cod Canal to the New Hampshire border.

In 1992 Terry was the Coast Guard's "logistics coordinator" for Sail Boston '92, the international parade of tall ships through Boston Harbor. This was also the year that Terry was promoted to captain and became Director of the Coast Guard Auxiliary for all of New England.

After a short stint as Chief of Boating Safety, in 1994 Terry Hart was transferred to what was to become his last station – San Francisco. He was the Coast Guard's Group Commander of search and rescue, aids to navigation and law enforcement for most of the northern California coast as well as inland to Lake Tahoe.

In 1997, Terry retired after 27 years in the Coast Guard. His military awards include the Legion of Merit, the Meritorious Service Medal, six Coast Guard Commendation Medals, and the Life Saving Medal from Finland.

Terry is a life member of the Disabled American Veterans and the Military Officers Association, and a member of American Legion Post 104 in Hamilton.

While Terry was at the Coast Guard Academy, he met a young nursing student by the name of Barbara Haneberg.

He married her in 1970, in a ceremony just three hours after he graduated from the academy. Terry and Barbara have three children: Kari (Richards), John and Kevin; and five grandchildren. Only John acquired a taste for the sea; he is a merchant mariner currently aboard the USS Mercy hospital ship.

After he retired, Terry Hart eventually decided he wanted to help other veterans. In 1999 he became Director of Veterans' Services for the towns of Georgetown, Essex, Hamilton, Ipswich, Rowley, Wenham and West Newbury.

Terry says the job doesn't pay as much as some of his command posts, but the satisfaction of helping others more than makes up for the difference. Terry Hart, we thank you for your service to our country.

PHOTO: KATHLEEN COREY RAHME

Luther McIlwain
Tuskegee Airman
Part I

By: Ted Tripp- April, 2006

METHUEN, MA – Everyone meeting Luther McIlwain for the first time immediately realizes there is something special in the air.

Even a short conversation with the 85 year-old veteran of World War II causes you to think about the greater social and political issues of our time.

Every one of the many detailed stories he freely shares about his life is filled with lessons on determination, hard work, and the evils of racism, pride, humility, education, luck, and making a difference. Today, Lt. McIlwain still visits schools to teach these important messages to young people for them to use in their own lives. The subtle hint of optimism in all he says is pleasantly refreshing.

Luther McIlwain's story cannot be justifiably told without delving into his extraordinary family history.

Luther was born on September 23, 1921 in Lugoff, a small rural town in South Carolina. He was born to Simon and Katherine McIlwain in an era when racism and segregation were a way of life in the Deep South and the lynching of Negroes who got out of line was still practiced.

In spite of all this prejudice, Simon McIlwain worked hard and took advantage of nearby educational opportunities. In 1914 he graduated from the all-Negro Claflin College in Orangeburg and studied new and improved methods of farming.

About this time, the federal government instituted a program to bring more scientific methods of agriculture to rural farmers. Simon McIlwain was subsequently hired as a Farm Extension Agent to help teach local farmers the benefits of new technology. Unfortunately, the white farmers didn't take well to being told what to do by a Negro and a group of white "crackers" gave him "24 hours to get out of town." The McIlwains knew immediately what would happen if Simon stayed.

So Simon McIlwain traveled to Pittsburgh where he had heard the steel mills were looking for help. He found a job as a steel/iron worker, and in his spare time played second base for the Homestead Grays baseball club. The Grays were an independent Negro team formed in 1912 that played other regional ball clubs. Years later, the Homestead Grays would become part of the Negro National League and win a number of league championships and the Negro League World Series.

In 1923 the Grays traveled to Lawrence for a game and Simon saw a "Help Wanted" sign for one of the mills. He jumped the team and got a job at the Champion International Paper Mill – later to become Oxford Paper – and sent for his pregnant wife, Katherine, and two-year-old Luther to join him. Shortly afterwards, Luther's sister Glendora was born.

The family lived in a five-story walk-up on the site that is now Manzi Dodge. During this time in Lawrence, Simon McIlwain was accepted to Suffolk Law School and a young Luther began his education at the Saunders grammar school. In 1928, Simon was awarded a law degree from Suffolk and the family moved to a relative's farmhouse in the Pleasant Valley section of Methuen. Luther McIlwain still lives in that house today, where he once spent the early days of his youth.

Soon the Depression came and making a living was tough. Simon McIlwain used the farm to raise 400-600 hogs a year, which he sold to local mill workers for income. He was so good at hog farming that he later became a lobbyist and spokesman for the Hog Growers Association.

In the latter half of the 1930s, Luther attended the old Methuen High School – now City Hall – where he was captain of the track team and elected three years in a row to class vice president and a member of the Student Council.

Luther graduated in 1939 and the next year was off to the all-Negro Allen University in Columbia, S.C. to study pre-law. It was here on December 7, 1941 where he heard others yelling out a window that Pearl Harbor had just been bombed by the Japanese.

Like everyone else, he didn't know where Pearl Harbor was but he knew it meant war. He had already been designated as 1A by the draft board back in Methuen and was resigned to wait for the Army induction notice to show up in the mail. But he missed the first wave of the draft because of his age and in the spring returned to Methuen for the summer months where he worked in the mills and played baseball. This was also the summer he played ball with his old friend, Mike Buglione, a Valley Patriot of the Month highlighted in the April 2005 edition of this paper.

Another year of school passed and in the fall of 1943 he went back to Allen, knowing Uncle Sam would soon come looking for him. The services were still segregated then and he didn't relish being assigned a menial role in the war effort. In the early 1940s, the Marines didn't accept Negroes at all, the Navy accepted Negroes for minor positions like cooks and kitchen help, and although the Army allowed you to fight, assignment was to all-Negro units under white command.

Then, that September, fate intervened. On a Sunday afternoon, 2nd Lt. Willie Ashley came to the campus to visit his girlfriend. He looked sharp in his uniform with the Air Corps Eagle on his officer's cap, impressive bronze bars on the sleeve indicating his rank and pilot wings pinned to his chest. He was a Tuskegee Airman. He quickly drew a crowd and when Luther saw him, he immediately said to himself, "That's what I want to be."

Ashley told Luther that he had to apply to Washington to become part of the Tuskegee program, but that he could get the paperwork at the local recruiting office. The very next day Luther went down to the office to start the process. As he entered, there were five imposing white officers facing him, two from the Army, two from the Navy and a Marine. When he asked for the paperwork, they laughed at him. "Did you hear that?" one of them said, "the nigger wants to fly a plane!"

Luther McIlwain ran out of there as fast as he could, tears streaming down his cheeks, and that night went to his girlfriend's house looking for answers. It turned out that his girlfriend's mother was the head cook and good friend of C.C. Richardson, the state's Chief Game Warden, who was white and a powerful local politician. Luther's girlfriend, Lillian, – and later his wife - said she would see what she could do and told Luther to come back the next day. What happened could not have been better. Richardson offered to send his car and chauffeur J.J. White to pick up Luther and drive him the 14 miles to nearby Ft. Jackson where he could get the paperwork without a hassle. Luther will never forget that day when the guards at the fort recognized the warden's car as it approached and smartly stepped aside as J.J. drove right through the gate entrance.

Ten days after filling out the papers, Luther got a letter from Washington telling him to report to Ft. Jackson on October 10th, 1943, for tests and a physical. He passed with flying colors and was sworn in the next day. He was then put on a train to Ft. Bragg, N.C. where he was assigned to a Negro barracks. After a brief stint at KP, Luther's main job became teaching the other 32 soldiers in the barracks how to properly sign their names on the payroll cards so that the Army could pay them. He also assumed the task of reading letters from home to these mostly uneducated farm boys and writing out their own letters to their families.

This went on for four months until January of 1944 when Tuskegee finally called.

The orders were brought to Luther by a white major and a white captain and included a train ticket to Keasler Army Air Field in Biloxi, Miss. where he would undergo pre-aviation basic training. To his astonishment, the white officers picked up his two large duffel bags and threw them into the Jeep. This was the first time Luther had been shown any respect by the white Army establishment.

The officers drove him to the train station and put his bags on the train. But when Luther tried to board the Pullman car with his first-class ticket, a ruby-faced white conductor refused to let him on because he was a Negro. The Army major and captain took the conductor aside and after discussions with the depot agent, Luther was allowed onto the Pullman. From there on, a helpful Negro porter took good care of Luther for the two-day train trip.

477th Bombardment Group, February 1945 - Tuskegee AAF. Lt. Luther McIlwain is fourth from left, front row. All others in photo are deceased. Courtesy Smithsonian Institution.

PHOTO: COURTESY LUTHER McILWAIN

PART II

By: Ted Tripp - May, 2006

METHUEN, MA – As 85-year-old Luther McIlwain slowly walks around the kitchen table in his Pleasant Valley home, it is obvious that this Tuskegee Airman has a lot more story to tell about his military experience during World War II. Each little parcel of information he shares tells us about an era where Negroes were second class citizens that worked and fought hard to show that they were the equals of white soldiers and officers.

They had to prove to the military that they had the skills and knowledge to fly sophisticated aircraft in life-and-death combat situations.

Today we know they performed superbly with some of the best records of the war. In last month's The Valley Patriot, we followed Luther McIlwain's early life and the discrimination problems he endured simply trying to enlist in the Army's new Tuskegee program designed to train Negro pilots, bombardiers and navigators.

We pick up the story when, after a brief period at Ft Bragg, N.C., Luther was transferred in January of 1944 to Keesler Army Airfield at Biloxi, Miss. to become part of the 1120th training squadron. He was now a pre-aviation cadet undergoing three months of physical training, testing and evaluation in preparation for Tuskegee. Out of more than 400 original applicants, only 44 passed the rigorous program to go on to the next step. It was also here that Luther was assigned to be a bombardier/navigator rather than a fighter or bomber pilot, since that's where the Army needed men at the time. You had no choice in those days.

In April or May, Luther was sent to Tuskegee as a full-fledged Army Air Corps cadet. He had a propeller emblem on the front of his cadet cap and another one on the sleeve of his uniform. The first step was ground school, which consisted of 12-hour days studying aerodynamics, physics, radio transmission, Morse code, English and other related subjects. At this time there were 8000 to 9000 Negroes training at Tuskegee under white officers. By 1944 the Army had managed to replace the original white ground school instructors with qualified Negro instructors. As more Negroes were trained and promoted, they would eventually replace all of the white officers. Near the end of the war, only the base commander and his immediate staff were white.

Just 27 of Luther McIlwain's class of 44 graduated from ground school. They were then sent to Hondo Army Air Field near San Antonio, Texas for bomber navigation training. Here, Luther earned his navigator wings and was promoted to 2nd lieutenant. He also became a Rated Instructor. His graduation class was only the second of Negro cadets to be trained as bombardiers/navigators. Now his final class size was down to just 23 elite Air Corps soldiers.

From here it was on to San Angelo Army Air Field in Texas for bombardier training with the famous Norden bombsight. After a month of ground school, followed by simulator experience, Luther McIlwain honed his skills in twin-engine B-25 bomber trainers. At 22 years of age, he earned his second set of wings - the bombardier wings - and was making 50 percent more money than the equivalent non-flying officer.

By now it was mid-1944 and Luther's next stop was the University of Chicago's School of Meteorology for three months of weather instruction. He graduated as a Rated Weather Observer, the first and only Negro airman in a class of 200 other white officers. Then, after a brief return to Tuskegee, Luther was assigned to the Tyndall Army Air Base at Panama City, Fla. Here he practiced firing .30- and .50-caliber aerial guns from B-17s and B-24s at targets towed by nearby aircraft. After Tyndall, Luther's career took an unusual twist. He was sent to Midland Army Air Base, Texas for three months where he was one of only four Negro instructors assigned to help train the first group of Chinese flying officers from Chiang Kai-shek's army. At the time, the Chinese Nationalists were fighting both the Japanese army and the threat of an internal Communist takeover.

It was now early 1945 and Luther's next assignment was to Godman Army Air Field at Ft. Knox, Ky., where the all-Negro 477th (C) B-25 Bomber Group was being assembled. The Army was still wrestling with discrimination at this time, as the (C) designation was used to denote "colored." Luther McIlwain was given orders to become part of the group's 617th squadron.

From Godman, the 477th was sent to the much larger Lockbourne Army Air Base near Columbus, Ohio and became a composite group of bombers and fighters. Here, Luther McIlwain was given orders to return to Tuskegee for pilot training on twin-engine planes. He had accumulated 80 hours of flight instruction — just 10 hours short of what he needed for his pilot's wings — before the program was abruptly terminated. By now, Germany had already surrendered and the Japanese were only weeks away from surrender. The Army didn't need any more bomber pilots; they had a surplus. Although Luther had spent countless hours in the air as a navigator and bombardier, he never did qualify for his pilot's wings.

The 477th Bomber Group did not see combat during the war, primarily because its white commander, Colonel Robert Selway, as well as Major General Frank Hunter, were so bigoted that they did almost everything they could to sabotage the training of the unit. Their treatment of the Negro officers broke Army regulations and was so outrageous that 101 of the Negro officers mutinied and were arrested for refusing to stay out of a newly created "White Officers' Club." After the war ended, Luther stayed in the service until the end of 1946.

During the post war period, he was privileged to be the lead navigator in a group of 21 B-25 Bombers escorting General Jonathan Wainwright (captured by the Japanese at Corregidor in 1942) from Texas to Ohio for a special ceremony. Also, in 1946, Luther McIlwain and his crew took first place in precision bombing at an air show competition where 50 bomber squadrons were selected from various air bases around the country to compete in combat-style maneuvers. Upon completion of his military service, Luther McIlwain decided to become a police officer in New York City after the police force was finally integrated in 1946. He spent 20 years there, the last 13 as a plainclothes detective.

It was during this time, unfortunately, that all of Luther's pictures, patches, wings and other military memories as a Tuskegee Airman were stolen from his apartment. All he has left today is his old military ID and a fuzzy picture of him as a cadet that he had sent to his mother. Eventually, Luther made it back to Methuen where he worked for over 20 years as a special assistant to the mayor in the Office of Equal Opportunity. He officially retired in 1992. But Luther McIlwain wasn't through yet. In 1998, at the age of 77, he received a phone call from Harvard University to talk about his

Tuskegee experience in its Division of Continuing Education.

For two years this Tuskegee Airman taught to overflowing crowds of retired doctors, professors, and company presidents. Not surprisingly, Luther has also been the recipient of numerous awards. In 1996, the Massachusetts Black Legislative Caucus presented him with a pewter cup and its Public Service Award. In 1997, the Merrimack Valley Chapter of the NAACP also gave him its Public Service Award. In 1999, Hanscom Air Force Base presented him with a "Lifetime Honorary Membership" in the Hanscom Officer's Club. Also in 1999, the Merrimack Valley Planning Commission, on which Luther had served for 13 years, gave him its Regional Service Award. And this past February the Boston Celtics presented him with a "Heroes Among Us" award prior to a game with Cleveland at the Boston Garden.

As an aside, it should come as no surprise that Luther's younger sister, Glendora, also excelled in her career. She became a lawyer in 1951 like their father and would go on to serve as an Assistant Secretary of HUD in President Ford's administration. For many years she was also active on transition teams for newly elected Republican governors here in Massachusetts, including Governor Weld's 1990 move into the gubernatorial office.

At this point in the story about "Hero in Our Midst," it is traditional for this paper to thank the veteran for his service. Somehow, for Luther McIlwain this seems woefully inadequate. He not only served his country well, he helped lead the way by example for the subsequent integration of the Armed Forces after the war and the groundbreaking 1964 Civil Rights Act. This has all led to a much better America in which we live today. So, we will say simply and with great admiration, "Thank you, Luther McIlwain, for all that you and your family have done to make this a better country and us, a better people."

Methuen City Council Vice Chairman Kathleen Corey Rahme kisses Luther McIlwain as she presents a proclamation to the WW II Airman for his struggle with racism to serve his country (2006) Photo: Tom Duggan, Jr.

Brad MacDougall-Congressional Aide to Rep. Marty Meehan, Tuskegee Airman Luther McIlwain, Glendora McIlwain Putnam, and Kathleen Corey Rahme of The Valley Patriot.

Tuskegee Airman Luther McIlwain Honored in D.C.

By: Ted Tripp, April, 2006

WASHINGTON - On March 29, 2007 a grateful nation honored its black airmen of World War II with the presentation of the Congressional Gold Medal. The medal is the highest civilian award presented by Congress and was first given to George Washington in 1776. The presentation ceremony was held in front of approximately 130 remaining Tuskegee Airmen who came from all parts of the country. Many of the aged veterans walked with canes or were in wheelchairs, but they made the effort to attend on behalf of their fellow airmen who are no longer alive.

Methuen's Luther McIlwain (Valley Patriot of the Month in the April and May issues of 2006) attended the presentation with his sister Glendora

McIlwain Putnam of Boston. Kathleen Corey Rahme, city councilor in Methuen, also flew down to Washington to attend the reception following the ceremony.

Congressman Marty Meehan's office took care of all the travel and hotel arrangements for Luther and his sister. Brad MacDougal, an aide to the congressman, also went along to make sure that everything went smoothly without a problem.

The day started with a breakfast for the Airmen and their guests at the Renaissance Hotel and then they boarded a bus to the Capitol to prepare for the 1:00 p.m. presentation. The Airmen were first placed in a holding room where several congressmen came through to visit. Luther got a chance to speak with Congressman James Clyburn (D-S.C.), the majority whip and the highest-ranking African-American in Congress.

After the Airmen and their guests were seated in the Rotunda, Speaker of the House Nancy Pelosi called the gathering to order. This was followed by a presentation of the colors, singing of the national anthem and an invocation by the House chaplain. Senator Carl Levin and Representative Charles Rangel, sponsors of the original bill authorizing the award, then spoke on the merits of the medal and the exploits of the Tuskegee Airmen. Former Secretary of State and Chairman of the Joint Chiefs of Staff Colin Powell also spoke to the group. Luther McIlwain remembers one memorable moment of his speech. Powell looked directly at the Tuskegee Airmen and then expressed something along the lines of ... I never would have become what I did if you had failed.

There were other speakers and then President George Bush went to the podium. He thanked the Airmen for their service and at the end he raised his hand and offered a military salute as Commander in Chief to all the Tuskegee Airmen who had passed on as well as those still alive today. He said, "For all the unreturned salutes, and unforgivable indignities ... on behalf of the office I hold and a country that honors you, I salute you for your service to the United States of America." Almost immediately you could see the old veterans rise from their seats to return the salute. Even many of those in the wheelchairs struggled to stand, if even for a brief moment, to salute the president. Luther McIlwain was proud to return the salute. It was the emotional highlight of the ceremony.

Each Tuskegee Airman was given a bronze replica of the Congressional Gold Medal. On the front it says "Tuskegee Airmen 1941-1949" with a relief showing three Tuskegee Airmen and an eagle. On the back is inscribed "Act of Congress 2006 / Outstanding Combat Record / Inspired Revolutionary Reform in the Armed Forces."

Luther McIlwain was a second lieutenant in the all-black 477th B-25 Bomber Group and earned his wings as a bombardier and navigator. He was also a rated weather observer.

Walter Pomerleau

By: Tom Duggan, Jr. - August, 2004

LAWRENCE, MA - Lawrence Native Walter Pomerleau served in the Coast Guard during World War II from 1942 - 1945, earning two service medals before being honorably discharged. Mr. Pomerleau founded the Mount Vernon Neighborhood Association in 1988. Today, the Mount Vernon Neighborhood Association represents 1,200 families in Lawrence. He is fondly known as the Mayor of Mount Vernon.

Pomerleau is a neighborhood activist, a member of the Lawrence Veterans Memorial Stadium Restoration Committee, the Holy Family Men's Guild, the Police Station Building Committee, a former Grand Knight of the Knights of Columbus and a current member of the Elks Lodge in Lawrence.

For his service to the country and his continued service to the community, we are proud to name Walter Pomerleau of Lawrence as our Valley Patriot of the Month. We thank him for all of his efforts in making our country and community a better place.

.

Lawrence High Headmaster Edwin Reynoso, Walter Pomerleau and Francisco Urena. (Background Rick Parthum of the LHS Alumni Assoc.)

At 88 Walter Pomerleau Gets High School Diploma from Lawrence High

By: Tom Duggan, Jr.

At 88, Lawrence resident Walter Pomerleau is most known for being the "Mayor of Mount Vernon" for his years of organizing and running the Mount Vernon Neighborhood Association.

Now he will be known as the oldest graduate of Lawrence High School ever. Last month, Lawrence High School Principal Edward Reynoso presented Pomerleau with his high school diploma at the Lawrence High School Alumni Scholarship Dinner.

Reynoso explained that Pomerleau was supposed to graduate in the class of 1940. But working two jobs and trying to take care of his family meant he continued to slip in his grades before joining the US Coast Guard the country's last line of defense during WWII.

Veteran's Services Coordinator Francisco Urena had full military honors standing at the podium as he thanked Pomerleau for his service to his country and his community.

"Walter joined the US Coast Guard and headed for New Jersey where he served with a crash and rescue unit. He also served in Philadelphia. During his 3 years in the Coast Guard he achieved the rank of Seaman First Class," Urena said.

Walter attended Lawrence High School at a time when there was a war going on, He wasn't able to graduate and he also worked numerous hours every day and was unable to achieve his high school diploma," Rick Parthum of the Alumni Association said.

Lawrence High Principal Edward Reynoso explained to the crowd why Pomerleau was receiving his diploma so late saying the following;

"Mr. Pomerleau graduated from St. Anne's Grammar School in 1937 and because we were in the middle of the depression he had to go to work. He worked at St. Anne's Club until 11pm every night He was doing this while he was going to Lawrence High School.

At the same time he was also delivering milk, which went on from midnight to 7 am. So you can see his studies were not a priority at the time. But he kept his class schedule for three years. But in his senior year, a few months before his graduation, one of his teachers informed him he would not be able to graduate because he was failing his fourth quarter.

Obviously he was falling asleep but he kept his class schedule, going to work, school and work again to support his family."

"Walter should have received this diploma with the class of 1941, but because of his work and trying to support his family he was never given his diploma. So, 70 years later we stand here in front of you and we recognize him today. We thank the Lawrence School Committee for allowing us to do this as we present Walter Pomerleau his diploma from Lawrence High School."

This diploma certifies that Walter Pomerleau has satisfactorily completed the Course of study prescribed for graduation and is therefore entitled to this diploma. Given this 2nd day of June 2011."

Pomerleau choked up while Reynoso read his diploma out loud and was congratulated by friends and family while receiving a standing ovation from the young crowd of Lawrence High Graduates.

"Hey, Walter, now you can get a job," longtime friend Frank Incropera joked as Pomerleau left the podium.

Staff Sgt. Eldon Berthiaume, Infantryman WWII PART I

By: Ted Tripp - August, 2006

LAWRENCE, MA - When Eldon Berthiaume graduated from Lawrence High School in the spring of 1942, he had no idea that in less than three years he would end up with thousands of other Allied soldiers as a POW in Germany at Stalag 5A.

He would learn to subsist on a slice of bread, a chunk of lard and sometimes some green soup for much of the time, and endure the loss of 50 pounds during his four-month imprisonment.

Eldon was born on September 10, 1924 in Lawrence to Aldona and Clement Berthiaume. On December 7, 1941, a teenage Eldon was with his parents on the way to Gardner when a Boston Herald newsboy on a street corner yelled "Japs bomb Pearl Harbor. Read all about it!" They stopped to get a paper about the impending war.

After graduation, and like many young men of the era, Eldon went to work in the mills. He got a job in the weave room at the Shawsheen Mill in Andover.

When war was declared, Eldon knew the Army would eventually come after him and, in the summer of 1943, he was drafted. He was sent to Ft. Devens for basic training and subsequently assigned to an MP company.

After a short stint at an Army base in Michigan, he was ordered to Ft. Ethan Allen in Vermont where he continued his MP duties.

Late in 1943, Pvt. Eldon Berthiaume received orders to go overseas. He shipped out on the USS Mount Vernon troop transport as part of a convoy to England. After he arrived, he spent much of the year as an MP directing military traffic. This was during the massive build-up of equipment and troops in preparation for the Allied invasion on D-Day. Afterwards, as more tanks and equipment continued to arrive in support of the newly established front, Eldon's services as an MP were still needed. Then, suddenly, in late 1944 Eldon was reassigned as an infantryman to the 3rd Infantry Division, 7th Infantry Regiment, Company G … and sent to France.

In early 1945 Eldon's unit was ordered to take the small village of Utweiler in the Alsace-Lorraine area just across the border in Germany. This would be the first incursion of Allied forces onto German soil. Before the troops started out, Major General John "Iron Mike" O'Daniel gathered them together and told them that there was "no opposition" in front of them. Still, the troops were nervous because of the impending battle, and Eldon remembers that almost all skipped their meal that afternoon, including himself. At 6 p.m., the troops started out and marched all night long towards Utweiler to relieve the 26th Yankee Division. They reached the town around 5 a.m. and suddenly found the ridge above the town lined with German tanks and troops.

His radioman urgently requested tanks to counter the threat. Three scouts were sent out to meet the U.S. tanks to guide them in … but the GIs never made it. And the U.S. tanks never came.

There were minefields all around, so Eldon and five of his buddies took shelter in the open cellar of a nearby house, waiting for help. All of a sudden, a German soldier burst through a door – a kid no older than fifteen or sixteen – and in German ordered the Americans to put their hands up.

He marched them out of the cellar and headed them towards the German lines. They were passing a wounded German officer when one of the American GIs stopped to put a tourniquet on the German's leg to stop the bleeding. The officer then said something to the young German soldier which Eldon later interpreted to mean "Take care of these prisoners; don't let anything bad happen to them."

The six Americans walked all day long behind the German lines until they came to a house about 4 p.m. They were taken to the second floor where another German brought them each a slice of bread and a piece of lard. At this point Eldon wished he had taken advantage of the Army meal he had skipped the day before.

One by one the Americans were taken out of the room and disappeared, until Eldon was the last one left. He feared the worst as he could constantly hear rifle fire in the distance. A German soldier came and Eldon was taken to a sparse room with a German interrogation officer behind a desk. Then the officer spoke – in perfect English! He had been educated in the U.S. and had returned to Germany to settle some family matters when the war broke out. He couldn't get back to the U.S. and was drafted into the German Army as an interpreter.

Eldon gave the officer his name, rank and serial number. Then the officer told Eldon that he would be "alright" and shortly afterwards he was reunited with his five buddies. Suddenly, artillery began to rain down on the area as the Allies advanced.

The American prisoners were hastily put back on the road with long lines of German troops heading further back into Germany. It was here that Eldon noticed that the Germans were using horses to pull their artillery and supplies, and he thought, "the Germans don't have any gasoline left!"

Again, they marched all night long until they came to a POW camp where they stayed for three days. The prisoners were introduced to a green soup which they nicknamed "spinach soup." From here they were taken to a railroad depot to board a train. As they were assembling, Allied planes appeared and strafed and bombed the train, totally destroying it. Some Germans were killed in the attack, but, fortunately, the American prisoners were unharmed.

So it was back on the road where they were forced to march to Stalag VA [5A], a POW camp in Ludwigsburg. Here there were at least hundreds and maybe more than a thousand prisoners with large contingents of Russians, Americans, British, Poles, French, and Indians. Each ethnic group stuck together and always had something to trade to the other prisoners to make life more endurable.

Eldon remembers that the Russians always had tobacco for trade. The British had tea. The Americans sometimes had chocolate from Red Cross packages. The Indians, he said, were able to skip eating for several days and would trade food for other items. He noted that the French always seemed to have the latest intelligence on the Allied progress in the war. He was convinced that they had a daily source feeding information into the camp.

There was a day when Eldon was very hungry and he approached one of the Indian soldiers for food. Eldon was willing to trade his watch for a meal. The Indian carefully examined Eldon's watch.

Then the Indian took out a list from his pocket and on it were written the names Bulova, Hamilton and other well-known makers of fine watches. Eldon's watch, which was an inexpensive brand, was not on the Indian's list. The deal was off. Eldon stayed hungry that day.

PART II

LAWRENCE, MA - In early 1945, Pvt. Eldon Berthiaume of the Army's 3rd Infantry Division was captured by the Germans in the small village of Utweiler, Germany. He and other Americans taken prisoner were force-marched deeper into Germany and, after a temporary stay at a transitional POW camp, ended up at Stalag VA [5A] in Ludwigsburg.

Stalag VA consisted of wooden barracks surrounded by a perimeter of fences and barbed wire. There were large groups of POWs from Russia, France, Britain, Poland, India and the United States. The roofs of the buildings were marked with KG (for Kriegsgefangener, the German word for POW) and had a large, red cross painted on them so that Allied planes would not attack the prison complex.

There was never enough to eat and Eldon always looked forward to the K-rations delivered occasionally by the International Red Cross. Much of the rest of the time the food consisted of a green soup – nicknamed "spinach soup" – and chunks of lard. When Eldon was eventually liberated, he was about 50 pounds lighter than when he was captured.

Eldon remembers that every day like clockwork the Germans had a ritual where they would parade from the camp hospital - and purposely in front of the American POWs - a wooden box covered by an American flag. He never found out if there was an actual body inside the box or if the Germans were just using the "performance" for psychological reasons.

At the time of Eldon's imprisonment at Stalag VA, the Allies were quickly closing in on what was left of the German Army. Eldon and the other POWs could see dogfights overhead between the Messerschmitt and American fighters. If an American pilot was shot down and then brought to the camp, the prisoners would press him for the latest news on the war. They wanted to know how close the U.S. Army was to their location. Liberation was always on their minds.

After months at the POW camp, one night Eldon and the others noticed explosions on the distant horizon. The next morning the Germans suddenly moved all the prisoners out of Stalag VA and started marching them even further into Germany. The Russians led the column, as they always would in the days ahead. They marched from sunup to sundown and Eldon remembers how hard it was on some of the older GIs who were in their thirties or forties.

Younger soldiers like himself would help carry on their shoulders the ones who had trouble keeping up. For those who fell and couldn't rise, the butt of a German rifle was swiftly administered.

At night, the exhausted prisoners had to sleep in the open fields beside the road. It was still cold with snow on the ground from the harsh winter months. The cold made it especially hard to sleep. Eldon remembers one night when he was able to find a large wooden barrel which he shared with another GI to conserve body warmth.

Eldon also recalls a night where the prisoners could hear the drone of Allied bombers flying overhead – and, incredibly, it lasted all night long. The sound was particularly heartening to the prisoners, as it reinforced their hope that it was just a matter of time before the war would soon be over.

Food was always in short supply. Eldon noted that the POWs considered any fresh snails they found along the side of the road as "special treats." Another source of precious food was the half-rotten apples still hanging on nearby trees from the previous fall season.

During the daytime, the forced march turned out to be especially dangerous. American planes might suddenly appear overhead and strafe the column with machine gun fire. The pilots unfortunately didn't know that those on the road below were Allied POWs. The prisoners were then caught in a quandary. If they left the road to avoid the strafing – and went too far – the German guards would shoot them. If they stayed on the road, the American planes would kill them. It was always a gamble on what to do.

A section of the march took the prisoners through a small town which had just been bombed by Allied planes. The residents, many injured, were still searching for their relatives and neighbors when the prisoners went by. They yelled and screamed at the Americans as they passed and some spit in disgust towards those they blamed for the destruction.

During the long march, at one point Eldon had a sudden "nature call" and asked a nearby German guard for permission to briefly stop. The guard granted permission and then noticed that Eldon had a rosary draped around his neck. The German, an older man, then pointed to Eldon and asked, "Catholic?" Eldon nodded yes. The guard then pointed at himself and said, "Catholic." Incredibly, he then proceeded to take out his wallet and show pictures of his family to Eldon. This was one of those rare and short-lived moments when the instinctive "good" of human nature was able to transcend the horrors of wartime.

Late on one of the last days of the march, the Germans let some of the Indian prisoners take a quick bath in a nearby stream. When the Germans ordered them out of the water, three or four just started swimming away. So the German guards shot and killed them. The remaining Indian prisoners then sat down and refused to resume the march until the Indian bodies were recovered and accorded a proper burial on a ceremonial funeral pyre. Amazingly, the Germans relented and that evening the Indian POWs honored their dead comrades.

The delay worked to the advantage of all the prisoners. That same night, after the funeral ceremony, and with the march again underway, the Americans heard machine gun fire in the distance. There was no question that these were American machine guns because of the sharp, crisp, repetitive nature of the noise. The American Army was getting close. Very close.

Only hours later, the Germans unexpectedly separated the Americans from the rest of the prisoners and herded them into a large barn. There were hundreds of exhausted, sick and hungry American prisoners. The Germans left only three or four soldiers behind to guard them.

Somewhere around 6 or 7 a.m. that morning, Eldon and the other American prisoners suddenly heard the rumbling and clinking of tanks approaching. These were the sounds of American tanks. The German guards stood silent. The noise grew louder and then a tank from Patton's 2nd Armored Division crashed right through the wall of the barn. A GI popped out of the hatch and yelled: "Are there any Americans here!" Eldon remembers a huge roar went up from the prisoners. The few German guards surrendered. The GI in the tank then started throwing out cartons of cigarettes to the crowd and other GIs passed out rifles to the former prisoners.

Soon an Army colonel appeared and said, "My troops are now going after the rest of the prisoners." But Eldon never found out if the colonel and his men ever caught up and freed the remaining POWs.

The now-liberated Americans were eventually put onto trucks and taken to an airport where they were flown to Rheims, France, the site of Allied Supreme Headquarters. Here they were de-loused, cleaned up and given all the food they wanted. After weeks of rehabilitation, the former POWs were shipped back to the United States. Eldon arrived on U.S. soil in August of 1945 and was granted a 30-day leave to go home to Lawrence.

During Eldon's capture and imprisonment, the U.S. Army had no idea what had happened to him. All they knew was that he had been missing since sometime in early 1945. When the Army first realized he was missing, it sent a telegram to his parents explaining that Pvt. Eldon Berthiaume was listed as "missing in action," without further information. When Eldon's mother, Aldona, got the telegram, she started attending Mass every day praying for her son's safe return. She didn't find out that Eldon was actually alive until after he was liberated by Patton's forces some four months later.

When his leave at home was up, Eldon was sent by train to Lake Placid, New York where the Army had a special facility for treatment of returning POWs. Here Eldon recuperated from his ordeal along with many other former American prisoners.

After Lake Placid, Eldon was given orders to report to Ft. McClellan in Anniston, Ala. to become an Army instructor. He would subsequently be promoted to staff sergeant before being discharged from the service in 1946.

Upon returning home, Eldon went back to work at the Shawsheen Mill for several years before eventually taking a job at Western Electric in

Lawrence. In 1956 he was transferred to the company's huge new complex in North Andover on Rte. 125. He worked in various jobs making telephone equipment and ended up as a supervisor in microwave equipment engineering when he retired in 1983.

In the summer of 1943, before Eldon entered the service, he had attended a family outing in Canada on Prince Edward Island. Here he met Corinne Gallant and was immediately infatuated with her. While there was little contact between the two during Eldon's army service, he finally got back in touch with her after the war. In 1946, Corinne and Eldon were married in a Canadian ceremony. This past July 10th, the couple celebrated their 60th wedding anniversary.

The Berthiaumes have four daughters, Ruth Messina, Carole Bonin, Elaine Foley and Lisa Singleton; seven grandchildren; and seven great grandchildren.

Eldon is a member of American Legion Post 122 in Methuen and also a member of the Veterans of Foreign Wars.

Staff Sergeant Eldon Berthiaume, we thank you for your service to our country and the sacrifices you endured to protect our freedoms.

As a final note, Eldon would like to extend a special thanks to John Doherty, the Director of Veterans' Services in Andover, who was a tremendous help to him over the past two years in his application for POW benefits.

POW Paul Stillwell
U.S. Army, 12th Armored Division

By: Helen Mooradkanian - March, 2013

In the cold, foggy pre-dawn hours of January 17, 1945, PFC Paul Stillwell, U.S. Army, 17th Armored Infantry Battalion, 12th Armored Division, of North Andover, advanced into Herrlisheim, Alsace, France, to join in the Twelfth's bloodiest battle to date. Paul's battalion had just come from their first major combat engagement, on the Maginot Line—a line of concrete fortifications, tank obstacles, machine gun posts along France's borders with Germany and Italy.

Having arrived in France only in mid-November, they were somewhat inexperienced. Auffay, Luneville, Bining, and Rohrback did not really prepare them for the nightmare of Herrlisheim. Herrlisheim became their "baptism by fire." It was there that they lived up to their name, the "Hellcats" Division.

Snow 15 inches deep and heavy ground fog blanketed the region around the Rhine River. As Paul's battalion moved across the flat, open field, they advanced directly into the line of heavy machine gun fire. They had entered "a perfect kill zone." No place for concealment. The canals were swollen with ice and snow and all but one bridge had been destroyed. The Germans lay hidden behind the small clusters of woods and railroad embankments, along with major elements of the 10th SS Panzer Division—including a tank brigade with 88mm and 75mm guns, a mortar company, motorized infantry brigade and anti-tank guns. Not only did the

77

Germans far outnumber the Americans they also had more combat experience. Their Mountain Division had just returned from Norway

More than half the Americans in one company were killed in the first five minutes. The rest were pinned to the ground by the very intense fire, unable to move. Tracers "zinged" above them "like strings of angry bees." Some 35 men survived, including the wounded. The Germans were amazed any were still alive. They called the Twelfth the "Suicide Division." By 10 a.m., Paul's battalion had lost all radio contact with their division's 43rd Tank Battalion, which was to have come to their aid. Despite repeated calls for reinforcements, no help came. Only silence. Then from the top came the command, "No retreat."

Around 4 p.m., six Panther tanks that could maneuver over rough terrain, with their deadly long-range 75mm guns, attacked the flank of Paul's company. There was still no trace of the 43rd Tank Battalion. "Darkness fell. Throughout the night we continued fighting in hand-to-hand combat. At midnight, the Germans launched a large-scale infantry attack that never let up. Their heaviest assault came at 4 a.m. In the Germans' final push, about 140 Americans escaped across the Zorn River. The Germans infiltrated among our platoon positions, their white capes camouflaging them in the snow and fog.

"At dawn on January 18, there was still no word on the 43rd Tank Battalion. The one building we were using as a command post had exploded in flames. German tanks had blasted through our command post twice. Our platoon positions had all been overrun. We had nothing left to fight with. We were forced to surrender." Later it was reported that most of the 43rd's Sherman tanks had been destroyed or heavily damaged. "Bloody Herrlisheim" was indeed a nightmare.

A POW in Stalags 5A and 11B

Paul was in a group of 35 Americans captured together at Herrlisheim on January 18. He and his unit marched on foot from the Rhine through Baden-Baden and on to Stalag 5A at Ludwigsberg, near Stuttgart. There he was imprisoned for 10 days in a former cavalry stable, virtually unheated. "I remember being cold all the time. There were 350 of us in the American barracks, sleeping in tiered bunks with straw ticking—and no blankets. Toilet facilities were poor. We were covered with lice but received only two delousing's. Since we had only the clothes on our backs, we were not able to wash them in the frigid temperatures." After 10 days, they were transported in unheated boxcars for four days, with minimal food and water, to Stalag 11B at Fallingsbostel, 30 miles from Hanover. Temperatures at night fell between zero and 15 degrees. Everyone suffered badly from frostbite.

Paul remained at Stalag 11B for two and one-half months. It had about six barbed-wire compounds covering probably 10 acres of farmland. Guard towers could sweep the entire area in machine gun fire. "We were always cold—and hungry. Temperatures dropped to around zero at night. A single blanket covered the lice-ridden straw mattress. We had virtually no heat. Our feet were frostbitten.

"But worst of all was the constant hunger. It tormented us day and night. We thought of nothing but food. We talked of nothing but food, literally. Each day we were allowed a meager piece of ersatz black "bread"—a poor imitation of the real thing. Daily rations also included a cup of rutabaga soup which literally tore out your insides, 3 or 4 ounces of potatoes, a cup of barley water, occasionally a piece of so-called margarine, actually lard. Twice we had horsemeat. In three months, I lost 20 lb. My bunkmate, who was much heavier, lost 40 lb. We used cigarettes to barter for everything, from food and pens to clothing. Twenty cigarettes could buy a loaf of bread from a German guard.

"Occasionally we were given a Red Cross package to share four-ways. We Americans would share our meager rations with the Russian POWs whom the Germans hated and mistreated, denying them food and medical care until they all died of starvation and disease. "I had an acute case of jaundice but lay helpless for three days in my bunk since only severe cases, like pneumonia were transferred to the clinic. A British medical doctor, a POW for five years who had fought in North Africa, did a great job for us with the limited supplies he had (paper bandages and whatever he could get through the Red Cross). "We were never tortured or beaten but I did witness the German guards repeatedly beating the Russian POWs, for whom they had a long-standing hatred. They were quite open about it."

British "Desert Rats" liberate us

Finally the captives were set free! "On April 16, 1945, the British 7th Armored Division—the famed "Desert Rats" who had fought in North Africa and in most of the major campaigns in WWII—stormed in and liberated us! On April 26 we left Stalag 11B, were flown to Oxford, England, and the 318th Hospital. On June 3, 1945, I boarded the SS Tarleton Brown for the United States."

An emotional reunion took place when Paul Stillwell arrived home in Virginia, Minnesota on June 27, 1945. His father, a minister who had served in Congregational and Episcopalian churches in Illinois, Minnesota and South Dakota, had written to Paul several times a week, letters that could never be delivered. Although they had no chance for communication during his imprisonment, he says, "My dad told me he never stopped praying for my safe return.

He knew—he had a peaceful assurance deep in his heart—that the Lord would bring me home safely." Fervent prayers and the power of a father's love. It was the Father's love that sent Jesus to the cross to open wide the prison doors and set the captives free. Jesus said, "He has sent Me to heal the brokenhearted, to proclaim liberty to the captives...to set at liberty those who are oppressed [bruised, crushed in spirit]" (Luke 4:18).

John Lenotte

John Lenotte (center) with his Valley Patriot Hero Award (2013) flanked by
Valley Patriot publisher Tom Duggan, Jr. and Anabel Gutierrez.

The Valley Patriot's second Hero Award recipient is a man who honorably served his country. And while many veterans do their service and then continue on with civilian life when they return home, this man got involved with the local American Legion, raising money, helping veterans become more aware of the government services available to them, walking them through the process to receive those services and donated his time to help the men and women who sometimes get forgotten by the very government they put their lives on the line for.

On top of all that, he has been elected District Commander of the American Legion, and volunteers his time to write a column for our veterans every month in the pages of the Valley Patriot. American Legion District Commander John Lenotte is our veteran recipient this because of his volunteer work, activism, and selfless work in the community to caring for our veterans.

WWII B-17 Turret Gunner George "Gunner" Haynes

This is the first in the three-part series of "Heroes in Our Midst ~ The Mt. Vernon Neighborhood."

By: Lawrence "Lonnie" Brennan - August, 2009

NORTH ANDOVER, MA - A firm handshake revealed the surprisingly tremendous inner-strength of the 92 year old former WWII B-17 turret gunner, Valley Patriot of the Month George Haynes, as we parted company recently at Joe's Landing Café at Lawrence Municipal Airport.

Former staff sergeant Haynes and his wife Helen recently joined Mt. Vernon neighbors Jim Derby and Ed Hickey (each Valley Patriot Heroes, see note) to share some memories of a distant past, when the world was at war. The airport had recently hosted an open house and tour of a restored vintage B-17 bomber. The event drew large crowds from throughout the Merrimack Valley and beyond, and the event held particular personal interested to many Lawrencians, including those from the Mt. Vernon neighborhood.

As a turret gunner, Mr. Haynes and his American B-17G crew were stationed with the Eighth Air Force unit in England where they launched aggressive and dangerous daylight bombing runs across the English

Channel deep into German territory. Their mission: cripple the German war effort by inflicting critical damage to Nazi industrial targets. Mr. Haynes protected his crew and craft as they entered hostile airspace and attempted to fend off attacks by Luftwaffe fighters during daylight precision bomb runs.

The daylight 'precision' runs allowed better targeting of railroad yards, ball-bearing works, oil plants, foundries, and critical infrastructure, but lacked the limited 'cover' that nighttime missions provided. In a word, it was dangerous. When the effort began, the Americans suffered tremendous losses as German Luftwaffe intercept fighters swarmed the slower-flying bombers. Statistics from a 1943 October mission showed 59 B-17s shot down over Germany in one attack. The Eighth Air Force lost a total of 176 bombers in October 1943 alone, temporarily suspending future missions until P-51 Mustangs and other fighter planes were modified with extra external gas tanks to escort the B-17 bombers to and from targets. The result: a tremendous turning point against the Luftwaffe. The B-17 runs continued unabated, delivering punishing blows of heavy damage deep into Nazi territory.

"I tried to join the Navy, but when they took my blood pressure, it was so high they couldn't take me at the time," Mr. Haynes related. "Later, I found myself in the Air Corps (Force). I remember they couldn't find a pair of pants small enough to fit me. For the first six months, I wore a pair that hung down so low I had to pull them up in the middle to go up and down stairs" Mr. Haynes chuckled.

"Young people don't know what these people went through," Helen Haynes prompted her husband. "Yup. True," he nodded. "We would count the holes (in the plane) after we came back (from missions)" he said regarding the anti-aircraft flack. "I remember there was one mission I wasn't assigned to, and this other fellow he went instead. I never saw him again" he said.

Mr. Haynes was 21 years old when he entered the Air Force. He flew on 27 missions in the 306th Bombardment Group (Heavy), and often returned with his airplane shot up with holes. His B-17G heavy bomber held a crew of 10 and he served as flight engineer/turret gunner. "Anyone that flew combat over in Europe was at least a buck sergeant. The Germans were very rank conscious. They considered the sergeant as an enlisted officer," he explained. "Three over two. Three upper stripes, two lower stripes. They would be easier on you in a POW camp (if you were captured)", he said. "We had emergency kits too, with survival gear. Open in the case of an emergency. I never opened mine. Thank God," he added.

"One day, we had an extra mission. The German soldiers had a little town in France which they captured and we had to go and drop leaflets, not bombs, leaflets. Well, one of these packages got caught in the door, So now, we couldn't land with the door wide open, the bomb bay door. So the pilot who was a short guy, he was small, so he suggested that I hold his feet, and the other guys hold my feet, so we did that. It's scary. You can picture it. There was me holding him, they held me. He got it done. I'll tell you, he got it done," Mr. Haynes related with a chuckle.

Married to his bride Helen for 57 years, Mr. Haynes related how he returned from the war and began work at the Lawrence Fire Department. "I retired as a lieutenant, I think it was '82" he said. A native of Lawrence, and a member of the V.F.W. and the Knights of Columbus, Mr. Haynes was born of Ellen (Carr) and Thomas Richard Haynes both originally from England. He has two sisters, Helen and Dorothea. Mr. Haynes and his wife Helen have two sons, George and Tom. Mr. Haynes was also active with little league when his sons were younger. They have five grandchildren: Thomas Jr., Ellen, Alexandra, Elizabeth, and Mia. They spoke proudly of their families.

"Did you ever go to a school, with a bunch of kids, and tell them what you've done?" Mr. Haynes began. "I have a niece who volunteered me, second grade, so I had to go. It was the best day that I ever had. It was wonderful," he exclaimed, "the questions, how many did you kill, all kinds of things."

The Valley Patriot is proud to be able to share a bit of the service that Mr. Haynes gave to our nation, and will detail the profiles of his Mt. Vernon neighbors, including Jim Derby and Ed Hickney in upcoming issues. We ask that you please forward your Valley Patriot of the Month nomination to the editor so that we may honor more of our service men and women.

Gunners Mate 3rd Class Thomas Petrillo, U.S. Navy WW II Part I

By: Ted Tripp - April, 2007

METHUEN, MA – Sixteen million Americans served in World War II. Only a fraction of this number saw action in both the European and Pacific Theaters. And only a handful of those served on both a battleship and an aircraft carrier. This brings us to Seaman Tom Petrillo, who served on the Battleship Massachusetts during the 1942 landing in North Africa and later aboard the Escort Aircraft Carrier St. Lo in the Philippines.

On October 25, 1944, the St. Lo became the first U.S. ship sunk by a Japanese Kamikaze airplane. That day, five out of 13 ships in St. Lo's Taffi 3 Task Force would be sunk by a superior Japanese naval force which surprised the Americans in the Battle off Samara. Tom Petrillo, badly wounded, would spend most of that day in the water before being rescued by the Destroyer USS Raymond. One hundred and twenty eight of his shipmates were not so lucky and perished at sea.

Thomas J. Petrillo was born in 1917 and grew up in the Pleasant Valley section of Methuen. In 1934, in the midst of the Great Depression, he left the public schools to work at his brother's store, Al's Grocery, to help out the family. Some years later he would learn the carpentry trade from his father. By 1940-41 he was building apartments in Portsmouth, N.H.

On December 7, 1941 Tom was with his father at work when the radio announced that the Japanese had bombed Pearl Harbor. The following month Tom received a letter from Uncle Sam ordering him to report to Ft. Devens on March 1st for induction into the Army. One week before March 1st, Tom went down to the post office in Lawrence and joined the Navy instead. He just couldn't picture himself slogging through the mud and dirt and eating cold rations all the time.

On March 31st Tom reported to the Navy in downtown Boston for the mandatory haircut and physical. The next day he was sent to the Naval Air Station in Newport, R.I. for five weeks of basic training. Completing his basic, he was then ordered to South Boston to become part of the crew of the newly completed battleship USS Massachusetts (BB 59).

The Battleship Massachusetts, called "Big Mamie" by its crew, was built by the Bethlehem Steel Co. at the Fore River Shipyard in Quincy, Mass. She was delivered to the Boston Navy Yard in April of 1942 and commissioned the following month on May 12th. She was 680 feet long, displaced 35,000 tons and could travel at 27 knots. Her armament consisted of nine 16" guns, twenty 5" guns, twenty-four 40 mm guns and thirty-five 20 mm guns. The ship had a complement of 2200 enlisted men plus officers.

Seaman Tom Petrillo was assigned to be a shellman or shell loader on one of the 5" guns. It was his job to load the shells into the breech just ahead of the powder charge. Each shell weighed between 64 and 74 pounds, depending on type. There were three types of shells: anti-aircraft, armor piercing and explosive.

At this point in his service, Tom was being paid $21/month. Out of this he had to pay for insurance, haircuts and other miscellaneous items. He says there was only enough left over at the end of the month for about two beers.

For the first two or three months, Tom and the rest of the crew practiced their jobs while the ship stayed dockside. Then, finally, they went to sea. He remembers sailing up off the coast of Maine for gunnery practice. Some days ships would tow targets far behind them for the gunnery crews to shoot at. Other days it was airplanes towing drones for aerial target practice. All this would be put to good use in the coming months. Tom says that with perfect timing the gunnery crew could get off 60 rounds a minute with the 5" gun.

Then, on October 24, 1942, the Massachusetts left Casco Bay, Maine and headed south to rendezvous with the ships of the Western Naval Task Force. BB 59 was to become the flagship for Admiral H. Kent Hewitt as the task force headed east for the Allied invasion of North Africa. Known as Operation Torch, this was the first landing of American troops in the European Theater. General George Patton was in command of the American GI's as they opposed the Vichy French – then allies of the German Army.

Early in the morning on November 8th, 1942, the Battleship Massachusetts arrived off Casablanca, Morocco and took the defenders by surprise. The Massachusetts had orders not to fire first, but then the French Battleship Jean Bart, moored at the dock, fired her 13" guns at the American ship. The Massachusetts responded with her 16" guns and after five hits silenced the French ship. These were the first 16" guns fired in battle in World War II.

The Massachusetts then opened fire on other ships trying to flee the harbor. It sank two destroyers, two merchant ships, a floating dry dock, and destroyed shore batteries including an ammunition dump. During all this action, the Massachusetts was hit by four shells, but, fortunately, there were no injuries to the crew. At 2300 hours the night before the battle, Tom remembers that he and the crew were fed a steak dinner. He spent the night in the gun mount preparing for action. However, he did get a break to attend Mass early the next morning before the battle began.

By late on November 8th the shooting had ceased and that night the Massachusetts headed back across the Atlantic to Norfolk, Va. to take on a new supply of ammunition. While docked there, half the crew from the southern part of the country was given a one-week leave. Then the ship headed north to Boston to repair the damage it incurred off Casablanca. Here, also, the half of the crew from the northern part of the country – including Tom – got a one-week leave.

In December of 1942 the Massachusetts left Boston and headed north for two days of trials off the coast of Maine. Then it turned south towards the

Panama Canal for eventual action against the Japanese in the Pacific. It took two days to traverse the canal and Tom remembers it well. He says the Massachusetts was so wide that it brushed the sides of the locks and the crew had to hose down the contact points to promote slippage and thus prevent any damage.

Halfway through the canal, the ship anchored in one of the canal's lakes for the night. Tom remembers natives coming out in canoes selling bananas for $1 an entire bunch. You lowered a rope to the canoe and the natives would tie bananas to it. The money was transferred in the same way. Some sailors would throw coins into the water and watch the local natives dive for the money.

After leaving the canal, the Massachusetts headed out into the Pacific. On March 4th, 1943 the ship arrived at the French island of New Caledonia. The harbor at Noumea was horseshoe shaped with two ships on either side of the entrance. They would open and close the harbor with a submarine net as ships entered or left the naval base. The Massachusetts joined a fleet of carriers, cruisers and destroyers. It was the only battleship present.

Tom says the residents of Noumea were friendly. They spoke French and Japanese. You could go ashore and buy lemonade and fresh fruit. The town also had a local place called the Pink House where ladies would "entertain" the troops. Tom says the Army soldiers from a nearby camp were always lined up at the entrance to get in. The Navy, however, had commandeered a nearby island and set up baseball fields, picnic tables and other recreational pursuits. When the Massachusetts was in harbor, a third of the crew would be rotated to the island every third day for R & R. The sailors would come to call this island their Shangri-La.

During the period Tom was at New Caledonia, the Battleship Massachusetts' primary task was to shell Japanese installations on the islands before our troops made an amphibious landing. He says there were many such small islands and landings as the U.S. Navy and Marines started reclaiming the South Pacific from Japanese forces.

The Massachusetts would usually join with several cruisers and 4-5 destroyers on these missions and be gone for 2-3 days. The ship would then rendezvous at a designated meeting place and await the next invasion order.

By now it was the summer of 1943 and Tom had been on the Massachusetts for sixteen months. While docked in New Caledonia one day, an announcement suddenly came across the intercom. It listed 109 sailors and said they had one hour to get their things together and disembark from the ship. They were to return to the states for a new assignment. Tom Petrillo was on that list.

He and the others were put on a Merchant Marine ship headed back to San Francisco. When he arrived he had leave and so took a train across country to visit his folks. In September of 1943 he was back in Methuen for a brief stay. Then he was told he had 21 days to report to Naval Station Bremerton in Washington state for his next assignment. That would be aboard the USS Midway, an escort aircraft carrier just being completed in the nearby Kaiser Shipyard.

In next month's continuation of Tom Petrillo's story, we will see how the USS Midway became the USS St. Lo and how it was sunk off the Philippine coast in the Battle off Samara.

PART II

METHUEN, MA – It was late in the summer of 1943 and Tom Petrillo was a shell loader on one of the twenty 5" guns onboard the battleship USS Massachusetts. After serving 16 months on Big Mamie, and having participated in the invasion of North Africa and later in the support of numerous amphibious landings in the Pacific, Seaman Petrillo was suddenly given one hour to get his things together and ordered back to the states for a new assignment. He would become part of a new Navy program to mix battle-tested sailors with new recruits in an effort to accelerate the training on naval ships about to be launched.

A merchant ship brought Tom back to San Francisco and, after a short leave at home in Methuen, he was ordered to report to Naval Station Bremerton near Seattle for assignment to the USS Midway, an escort aircraft carrier almost finished in the nearby Kaiser Shipyard.

Escort carriers, sometimes called jeep carriers, were smaller, lighter and slower versions of the larger fleet carriers. The escorts were about half the length, one-third the displacement and had about one-third the crew of the larger ships. Each carried only 24-32 fighters and bombers. Amazingly, over 120 of these small carriers were built during the war.

The USS Midway (CVE-63), 512 feet long with a 65-foot beam, was launched on 17 August 1943. She had a top speed of 19 knots and a complement of over 1000 sailors and aviators. Her defensive armament consisted of sixteen 40 mm guns along the sides of the ship and a single 5" gun on the stern.

The Midway was commissioned on 23 October 1943 at Astoria, Oregon where Tom boarded the ship and set up station in the 5" gun turret. Unlike the Massachusetts' armored twin 5" gun turrets, this 5" gun was open to the elements and provided minimal protection from enemy fire.

Shortly after boarding, Tom was promoted from seaman to gunners mate 3rd class.

The Midway proceeded south to San Diego to load planes and spare parts for delivery to Pearl Harbor. Tom says every square inch of the flight and hangar decks was loaded with replacement aircraft. Upon return to the states, the Midway picked up another load of aircraft for delivery to Brisbane, Australia.

After one more trip ferrying aircraft, the carrier returned to San Diego where she picked up Air Composite Squadron VC-65 and headed west into the Pacific to fight the Japanese. She joined Admiral Bogan's Carrier Support Group 1 in June of 1944 for the conquest of the Marianas. During that summer and into the early fall, the Midway participated in strikes against Saipan, Tinian and the invasion of Morotai.

On 3 October the Midway returned to Seeadler Harbor at Manus Island for replenishment. There, the crew learned the name of the ship was going to be changed to the St. Lo to free up the name Midway for a super aircraft carrier then under construction. The new name St. Lo was to commemorate a hard-fought victory by American troops who had liberated the French town on 18 July 1944.

Tom remembers that the crew was quite upset over the name change. Apparently, it is bad luck to have the name of a ship changed while at sea and many on board tried to transfer to other ships. However, because of wartime conditions, that was virtually impossible.

The St. Lo departed Seeadler Harbor on 12 October to participate in the amphibious landings on Leyte in the Philippines. MacArthur landed on October 20th in his famous pledge to return and liberate the islands. The St. Lo provided air support for the invasion forces.

The St. Lo was now part of Rear Admiral C. Sprague's Task Unit 77.4.3, better known by its radio call sign of Taffy 3. The St. Lo was one of six escort carriers in the task force of 13 ships, which also included a protective screen of three destroyers and four destroyer escorts. From 18 to 24 October the planes of the escort carriers attacked enemy airfields and bases on Leyte, Samar, Cebu, Negros, and Pansy Islands.

On 25 October the task unit was off Samar Island when it launched its initial aircraft strike just before dawn. Shortly afterwards, an anti-submarine patrol plane spotted a large Japanese fleet approaching at high speed from the northwest. At first Admiral Sprague thought the pilot had mistaken U.S. ships for the Japanese, but then lookouts quickly confirmed that they were enemy ships. The surprise attack by Vice Admiral Takeo Kurita's Center Force had taken the Americans completely by surprise.

Composed of four battleships, eight cruisers and 12 destroyers, the overwhelming Japanese force was poised for a decisive victory. The largest ship, the 72,000 ton super-battleship Yamato, displaced more tonnage than all 13 American ships combined.

The faster Japanese force closed in and at 0658 opened fire on Taffy 3. What followed next was one of the most heroic naval battles of World War II.

Admiral Sprague immediately ordered the launching of all available aircraft to attack the Japanese fleet with instructions to rearm and refuel at Tacloban airstrip on Leyte to continue the attack. Meanwhile, as Japanese salvos fell around them, the ships of Taffy 3 took evasive action and the destroyers laid down a blanket of smoke to protect the carriers.

Several of the destroyers and destroyer escorts made torpedo runs at Kurita's fleet and continually harassed the Japanese forces. They would eventually pay a dreadful price. At 0855, the Destroyer USS Hoel, peppered by Japanese shells, was the first to be sunk, losing 267 men in the process. The Destroyers Roberts and Johnoton would also be sunk shortly afterwards with the combined loss of another 274 sailors.

The escort carrier Gambier Bay took a shot just below the waterline that knocked out one of her engines and reduced her speed. As she fell behind the others, the Japanese closed in to finish her off. She went down with the loss of another 131 men.

Meanwhile, the planes from Taffy 3 were inflicting considerable damage on the Japanese fleet. U.S. Task Units Taffy 2 and Taffy 3, to the south of the battle, sent additional torpedo planes and dive-bombers. The combined air assault sunk three Japanese heavy cruisers and relentlessly attacked the remaining ships. At about 0930, Admiral Kurita signaled his task force to withdraw, just as two of his heavy cruisers were within a few thousand yards of Taffy 3's escort carriers. One explanation given later was that Kurita, because of the unexpectedly fierce counterattack by U.S. forces, mistakenly thought he had stumbled upon Admiral Halsey's entire Third Fleet, and withdrew to fight another day.

During all this action, Gun Captain Tom Petrillo was directing fire from the St. Lo's 5" gun towards enemy ships. His crew hit one Japanese cruiser three times and left it burning. Another shell from the gun had deflected a torpedo away from the St. Lo's stern. As the Japanese ships fired their parting shots, Tom's 5" gunners scored a direct hit on a retreating destroyer.

Now the remaining ships of Taffy 3 began to pick up survivors from the water. But the battle wasn't over yet. At 1050 hours a flight of eight Japanese suicide planes attacked the escort carriers. Three were shot down before they could reach the ships but two of the remaining planes hit the Escort Carriers Kitkun Bay and Kalinin Bay; fortunately, the planes inflicted little damage. A third Kamikaze, with two 500-pound bombs under its wings, crashed onto the flight deck of the St. Lo. At least one of the bombs penetrated to the hangar deck below where crewmen were loading torpedoes and bombs onto returning aircraft. The ordinance exploded, creating a massive gasoline fire which led to additional explosions. The third explosion shook the entire ship and many knew at that point the St. Lo was mortally wounded. The word was passed to abandon ship.

Immediately after the plane hit, burned and injured men started fleeing the hangar deck. On the fantail, Tom Petrillo and two others started assisting the injured and putting life jackets on those that went into the sea. The three stayed behind to help as explosions rocked the structure and they were able to assist 25 to 30 injured sailors get off the ship safely.

The fifth explosion, however, was enormous and close. Tom suffered shrapnel wounds in his right shoulder and left leg and the blast shattered a portion of his hip. Dazed and wounded, he couldn't get up so he rolled off the deck into the sea below. Once in the water, Tom knew he had to get away from the ship before it went down, but he couldn't swim because of his injuries. Fortunately, a raft with five men on board came by and picked him up and paddled away from the ship. They also picked up a 17-year-old sailor with his left leg blown off.

Just thirty minutes after the Kamikaze attack, the St. Lo went down. Tom couldn't watch as it disappeared beneath the surface. The St. Lo became the first U.S. ship to be sunk by Kamikaze attack.

All of Taffy 3's remaining destroyers and destroyer escorts accelerated their rescue efforts for the many survivors still in the water. The recovery area was large and at one point the ships disappeared from the horizon where Tom and a handful of other survivors were waiting. They felt abandoned. There were sharks in the water that attacked some of the wounded sailors. Hours went by as Tom and the others waited for rescue. Suddenly, late in the day, they saw ships approaching on the horizon. At first they were jubilant, but then someone said they might be Japanese and fear spread throughout the survivors. Fortunately, however, the ships turned out to be Taffy 3's destroyers coming to the rescue.

Tom was eventually picked up by the Destroyer USS Raymond. As Tom lay in a stretcher on the deck, he will never forget watching the burial at sea of four fellow sailors who died after being brought on board. The captain said a prayer and made a few remarks, the bugler played taps, and the four bodies draped by the Stars and Stripes slipped into the sea. A total of 128 men were lost when the St. Lo went down.

Tom was finally brought below deck where a Navy corpsman administered morphine and marked his forehead. The destroyer headed for Leyte Harbor as Tom slept that night and the next morning he was transferred to a hospital ship. He was still in his wet and oil-soaked clothes when he remembers the doctors and nurses cutting off his uniform and administering anesthesia. When he woke up later, he was in a full body cast from his ankles to his chest. There was also a bar holding his leg casts apart so that his hip could heal in the proper position.

Another hospital ship, the USS Comfort, would eventually take Tom to a field hospital on New Guinea where he spent two months in a Quonset hut. Later on, the SS Lurline, a converted luxury liner, would bring Tom back to San Francisco after picking up additional wounded in Australia. Following a brief stay at the Oakland Naval Hospital, Tom was put on a train to Boston by way of Chicago. Because of the body cast, Tom could not enter the train through the narrow doorway. A window had to be removed and he was passed through it to a special area the train crew had prepared for him. The trip to Boston required three different trains and each time a window had to be removed to transfer him in and out.

On New Year's day 1945 Tom arrived at South Station in Boston and was taken by ambulance to the Chelsea Naval Hospital. On January 19th he had his third or fourth operation – Tom had lost count at this point. It wasn't until March that the doctors finally removed his body cast and allowed him to use crutches. On 19 July 1945, Tom Petrillo was discharged simultaneously from the hospital and the Navy. He was judged 60 percent disabled.

Tom returned to Methuen and, after a long recovery period, briefly worked at the Rockingham Race Track followed by the Arlington Shoe Factory. Then he got a job as a carpenter at Hanscom Field in Bedford and would spend the next 20 years helping to maintain the infrastructure of the base. When he retired, he started the Petrillo Construction Company which his son, Kevin, now runs.

In the late 1940s, Tom was filling out some insurance paperwork at the Clover Hill Hospital in Methuen when he met Margarite Fitzpatrick and asked her out to lunch. One thing led to another and the two were married in September of 1949. The Petrillos have four children: Kevin, Carrol, Susan, and Kathleen; 12 grandchildren; and 12 great grandchildren.

Tom Petrillo is a lifetime member of the Disabled American Veterans Post 2 in Lawrence (Methuen) and a member of VFW Post 8546 in Salem, N.H.

Gunners Mate 3/c Tom Petrillo, we thank you for your service to our country.

Final Note: Last summer Tom got a phone call from a former shipmate that he had never spoken with before. It was that of Shipfitter and Seaman 2/c Louis Casiami, the last injured sailor Tom had put a life jacket on and helped over the side on that fateful day in 1944. The sailor and his wife had finally tracked him down after 62 years to personally thank him for what he had done so heroically, so long ago.

Left to right: Gunners Mate 3/c John Welch GM 3.c John Rollo, Tom Petrillo, GM 2/c Gene Hughes and GM 3/c Robert Estele – San Diego, 1944. Estle would later perish when the St. Lo was sunk. PHOTO: Provided by Mr. Petrillo

.

Corporal Kenneth Killilea, U.S. Marines Corps (Ret.), 4th Division

By: Helen Mooradkanian - November, 2011

Corporal Kenneth Killilea, U.S. Marines Corps (ret.), 4th Division, is a survivor of Iwo Jima. He saw action in five major invasions in the Pacific during World War II. In all five, he took part in the first assault wave of Marines that secured the beachhead.

Killilea's Division was the first to go directly from the U.S. into combat without further training. It began with the Marshall Islands, on the perimeter of Japan's empire. It ended on Iwo Jima, closest to Japan's mainland.

During that "island hopping" expedition across the Pacific, the 22-year old Haverhill, Mass., native, who had once doted on his 8-cylinder Packard, was transformed into a member of the "Suicide Six," who repeatedly volunteered to scout out the enemy hiding in caves, bunkers and ravines. He willingly sacrificed his life for others.

The five invasions followed in quick succession. Each battle was more vicious than the one before.

• Roi and Namur in the Marshall Islands, January 31–February 3, 1944. The two tiny islands were secured pretty quickly.

• Saipan in the Marianas, June 15 July 9, 1944, was the bloodiest, a decisive battle that marked the beginning of the end for Japan. It also marked a pivotal moment for Killilea's faith.

• Tinian, also in the Marinas, July 24–August 1, 1944, was secured in 11 days. From its airstrip, the longest in the world, B-29 Super Flying Fortresses were able to drop the Atomic Bomb on Hiroshima and Nagasaki.

• Finally Iwo Jima, February 19–March 26, 1945, saw the most vicious fighting of all.

This "island hopping" was part of the U.S. Navy's strategy to bridge the vast expanse of the Pacific and reach the Japanese mainland.

For Killilea, it paralleled a spiritual journey, one that led him closer and closer to a crisis in faith.

Saipan: a scene out of hell

On June 15, 1944, by 9 a.m., the first wave of 8,000 Marines landed on Saipan, the largest of the Mariana Islands—the first U.S. troops on Japanese soil.

"Some 30,000 Japanese with massive tanks and artillery were waiting for us completely hidden from view.

"Our assault wave had to climb to the top of the hill, lugging bazookas, machine-guns, flamethrowers, and then position them for firing.

"By day, the Japanese hid in the numerous caves on that mountainous island, firing from ridges and ravines honeycombed with machine-gun emplacements and bunkers.

"In the dead of night, we'd suddenly hear the thundering roar of 44 massive tanks heading straight for us—but couldn't see them! Thankfully, our anti-tank grenades obliterated 24 of them.

"Those three weeks on Saipan were horrific. The Japanese were extremely cruel, unbelievably tenacious fighters. With dying breath, eyes bloodied and unseeing, they shot to kill. They never gave up. They preferred suicide to surrender."

On July 7, three weeks after the invasion, the Japanese staged the largest suicide charge ("banzai") of WWII. It was like a scene out of hell. "A tidal wave of nearly 4,000 out-of-control Japanese charged head-on—shrieking blood-curdling screams, hurling hand grenades, stabbing with bayonets, daggers, rifle butts and pitch forks. They were hell-bent on killing Americans.

"It was kill or be killed. We just fired in the dark, not knowing whether we were effective or not. The 4,000 enemy were killed.

A crisis in faith

There on Saipan, Killilea lost his fear of death, and his faith.

In his distress, he cried out, "God, please stop this slaughter! Please!"

"Nothing changed," Killilea told the Valley Patriot. "The slaughter continued. So I thought, 'I guess God is not there.' "

"At that point, I vowed: 'From now on, I will walk through the valley of the shadow of death without Jesus!' My machine-gun became my 'bible.' My hand grenades became the books of my 'bible.'

Unlike battlefield conversions, Ken Killilea experienced a dark night of the soul. In anguish, he turned his back on God. Yet God never abandoned him. He waited…

"It was a horrific 25-day battle," Killilea said. "But we focused on our objective. We advanced 1 foot at a time, 1 yard at a time. No distractions. We just moved forward. No retreat. No holding back. And we secured Saipan."

Battle of Iwo Jima

When Killilea hit the beach on Iwo Jima, just before 9 a.m. on February 19, 1945, the beach looked empty. "But the Japanese were watching, concealed within a vast network of bunkers and caves connected by 11 miles of tunnels. They waited till the beach filled with our troops, then opened heavy fire. We were sitting ducks.

"Confusion reigned. There were no front lines.

"The loose, jet black volcanic ash made it very difficult to gain a footing—or dig foxholes. We had virtually no cover. The stench of sulfur filled our nostrils.

"We won Iwo Jima only because of the tenacity of the foot soldier that advanced inch by inch."

On the morning of February 23, 1945, the Marines raised the American flag on Mount Suribachi. Killilea heard the victorious whooping and hollering, sirens and ship whistles blasting, but couldn't see anything. The battle raged another 32 days. Fighting to capture the airstrip, the six Marines with Killilea were killed when an artillery shell exploded. Only Killilea survived. Shrapnel broke his right leg and riddled his right side, and he was hospitalized States-side six months before discharge.

General Hagee, Commandant of the Marine Corps, told Killilea in 2005: "The Marines of Iwo Jima raised the bar of the Corps."

Divine appointment

Over the years, however, Killilea felt "lost, empty, without hope. I could not get rid of the despair. No pastor, no counselor, none of the psychiatrists I went to were able to help me," he said.

"For the sake of my children, I went to church, became a church member and even served as deacon for many years. But I was only going through the motions. Finally, I stopped going to church. I played golf instead."

Then about three years ago, in Naples, Florida, Ken Killilea had a Divine appointment.

His wife told him a Vietnam Veteran, a Marine, would be speaking in church. He decided to go.

When Killilea saw Lance Corporal Randy Kington, dressed in his Marine blues, paralyzed from the waist down since 1966 and wheelchair-bound for the rest of his life, then heard his conversion to Jesus Christ on the battlefield, something was released in him.

"Randy's face shone with a radiance that dispelled the darkest night," said Killilea, eyes glowing at the recollection. "You knew immediately that Randy holds the right hand of Jesus.

"I have to meet this man!" he told his wife. "For the first time, I revealed the vow I had made on Saipan. Randy and I talked as one combat Marine to another, although a generation apart. Randy understood.

"Finally Randy said to me, 'I forgive you, Ken. And if I forgive you, Jesus forgives you.'

"No lightning bolt hit me," said Killilea, "but I sensed an overwhelming Presence of love enveloping me. I no longer felt lost. I was found. I had peace and joy. My life became transformed. Now I tell everyone about my experience, Randy's testimony and his book "What A Life."

Amazing Grace.

Ken Killilea thought Jesus had abandoned him. But Jesus had been standing there all along, waiting for Ken to invite him in.

Corporal Ken Killilea, U.S. Marines, was a member of the "Suicide Six," volunteers who went on reconnaissance with their sergeant to search out the Japanese concealed on Saipan (the bloodiest battle) and Tinian in the Mariana Islands.

Randy Carter
USAF and U.S. Army

By: Beth D'Amato- December, 2016

HAVERHILL, MA - On any given day, you will find Randy Carter of the Veterans Northeast Outreach Center (VNOC) out buying groceries for local veterans, counseling a newly discharged vet about health care, or meeting with local politicians to try and get more resources dedicated to helping local veterans in need.

Carter and the other staff members at Veterans Northeast Outreach Center provide exceptional services for local veterans who have nowhere else to turn.

Located on 10 Reed Street in Haverhill, VNOC was established in 1985 as a private, non-profit organization. Their mission is to provide a variety of services to assist, support, and advocate for veterans and their families. The center is funded, in part, through contracts with the Department of

Veterans Affairs, MA Department of Veterans Service, US Dept. of Housing and Urban Development and private donations.

Administration fees to pay for staff come from grants allowing 100% of all private donations to go directly to the veterans.

Carter is the Projects / Programs Manager at VNOC and he is also a combat veteran. Carter joined the Army in 1983 and served until 1992. He joined the Air Force in 1992 and retired in 2007.

He was deployed to the Middle East three times in support of Desert Storm and Iraqi Freedom. Along the way, he was given numerous awards and medals for his service. Carter was honorably discharged as a Tech. Sergeant from the USAF and a Sergeant in the U.S. Army.

According to Carter, 90% of the staff at the Outreach Center are veterans, 80% are combat vets, and 60% are disabled veterans. He says that being a veteran lends a special understanding and expertise in dealing with those veterans who have unique issues like PTSD that others may have a hard time relating to.

The organization offers an array of counseling services to help assist all Veterans and their family members. Vets in these programs are not your stereotypical WWII aging Veteran but instead a group of young men and women who were recently discharged and facing combat and non-combat physical and psychological issues.

Carter also said that many of the newer veterans are homeless (some with children) living in the street or in their vehicles, not even knowing there is a place like VNOC they can reach out to. "When children are involved it makes the situation more urgent," he said. That's when the staff at the Outreach Center will act quickly by contacting local landlords to arrange three to six months' worth of rent to be paid up-front.

During this transition period the children are safely off the streets while the veteran-parent is undergoing treatment and/or job training through the Outreach Program. Carter also highlighted the difficulties in placing homeless female veterans (with or without children).

Carter says that Veteran facilities are populated only by men, and that adding women to the facility is not in the best interest of the vets or the staff, especially if veterans in the facility are suffering from PTSD or other illnesses. Other arrangements are made by the center to accommodate female veterans and their unique requirements. Carter says this is critical as all veterans need to feel safe and at ease in order for them to begin the healing process.

A FACILITY LIKE NO OTHER

Inside the remodeled church at 10 Reed St. is the activity center, which is a day program among the most unique of all VNOC programs. There, veterans are provided a structured environment where all vets, including disabled vets, can participate in recreational activities, work training, group support and other activities that are both satisfying and challenging.

There is also a food pantry available where food and clothing donations take place on Tuesdays and Thursdays between 10am-2pm. If there is a veteran and family in need, the staff at VNOC will make special arrangements to assist them immediately.

It's a friendly space for the vets to gather together and share a meal and play a game of billiards. This program is funded, in part, through the US Dept. of Housing and Urban Development.

The Outreach Center offers employment services which are provided by Career Resources Corporation and Valley Works Career Center. Services include job training, resume preparation, career assistance and job placement. The employment team works hard to assist Veterans within our local communities in every way possible. The ultimate goal is to help veterans get a job and have a safe place of their own to call home.

Veterans Northeast Outreach Center received a $2,000,000 Renewal Grant for the program called: Supportive Services for Veterans Families (SSVF). This grant helps veterans trying to get housing or in imminent risk of losing housing. VNOC is dedicated to helping end veterans homelessness. SSVF provides personal outreach and case management services and will assist participants to obtain VA benefits and other public benefits.

Also, through the SSVF Program, the VA aims to improve very low-income Veteran families' housing stability.

The following housing properties are owned and run by the Outreach Center. The first housing unit is the Veterans Mansion. The mansion serves twenty two homeless veterans and offers a supportive and working environment as they make their way back into society.

The second one is the Veterans Campus – this housing facility added 25 VA Grant Per Diem housing units in Haverhill, MA. Next is Bedford

Veterans – this facility is located on the campus of the Bedford VA Medical Center. It is a sixty unit facility that offers the services of both the VA Medical Center and VNOC.

The next facility is O'Neill Hall in Haverhill - this property was built in 2003 to add ten permanent affordable rental units to the Veterans Campus. Finally there is *Freedom House which is located in North Andover. This complex provides housing for three North Andover Veteran families.

Along with all the benefits and services offered to our veterans, the VNOC staff also hosts holiday parties, outings and other events all through the year for veterans and their families.

Thank you to Randy Carter and all the staff at VNOC for not only going off to serve our country abroad but for making the lives of returning veterans a little better here at home as well.

To contribute or learn more about this non-profit organization, please visit: northeastveterans.org

The Fitzgerald Family from Mann Orchards in Methuen held a fundraiser in the summer of 2016 at their ice cream stand to benefit local veterans. Pictured above are hero veteran John Ratka, Dennis Marcello from State Senator Katy Ives office and hero veteran Randy Carter from Veterans Northeast Outreach Center in Haverhill. PHOTO: Tom Duggan, Jr.

CPL. Harvey Gibeau

By: Dr. Charles Ormsby - November, 2005

METHUEN, MA - Harvey Gibeau was born in Lawrence in 1923 and after high school he joined the Civilian Conservation Corps in the late 1930s. He vividly remembers the ever-present sense of patriotism that prevailed. Patriotism was a common household word and was an expected personal trait in his family.

In July of 1942, Harvey enlisted in the Army with the fervent hope that he would be assigned to an anti-aircraft artillery (AAA) unit. He felt fortunate when his wish came true. He was sent to Ft. Eustis, Virginia for the standard 13 weeks of basic training and then shipped to Battery Park, New York for anti-aircraft defense of the city while awaiting an overseas assignment.

As part of the 414th AAA Battalion in New York, Harvey manned 40 mm anti-aircraft guns that were set up to defend the Squib and telephone company buildings. His unusually good stereoscopic vision was invaluable in using specially designed equipment to estimate the range of targets, and this became his specialty.

Although the accommodations in New York City consisted of army-issue tents, it was a relatively peaceful assignment since German warplanes never made it to the U.S. Harvey's stateside duty came to an end in June 1943 when he received orders for Iceland – a temporary duty station prior to shipping out to Europe to fight the Germans.

GIBEAU1eThe trip began with an 18-day voyage to Liverpool, England and ended up at Keflavik, Iceland. Harvey knew he wasn't in Lawrence any longer. The summer days at 65 degrees north latitude were nearly 24 hours long with the sun only dipping below the horizon for a few minutes each day. Winter was a different matter: twenty-four-hour nights with howling winds and bitter cold. Ropes had to be strung between Quonset huts to provide handholds for soldiers trying to walk from hut-to-hut.

Harvey remembers the people of Iceland being relatively pro-German. The Germans had only recently left Iceland and they had been instrumental in connecting many Icelandic homes to the hot springs for winter heating. In that cold, anyone who helps you stay warm is probably appreciated!

Unbeknownst to Pfc. Gibeau, the Allies were planning an early June invasion of France at Normandy. Part of that plan included moving Harvey – and thousands of others – to England in preparation for supporting operations in Europe after D-Day. Training and gunnery practice were over. It was time to put Hitler back on his heels.

Harvey left Iceland in early March of 1944 and made stops in Glasgow, Hereford, and Camp Foxley before arriving at the White Cliffs of Dover. While there, Harvey's unit tried to shoot down several German buzz bombs headed for London. Even though the soldiers hit them with several 90 mm anti-aircraft shells, the bombs kept flying. Eventually they were ordered to stop shooting to preserve ammunition. The buzz bombs kept flying overhead all night, but many were duds and didn't explode when they came down on London. Some were found and carefully dug up decades after the war.

GIBEAU1bHarvey didn't know when the invasion of France was scheduled to begin, but he had a hint in the early morning hours of June 6th when he looked up and saw the sky full of U.S. warplanes. Harvey noted, "I didn't know the U.S. had that many planes. The sky was dark with planes. It was an amazing sight."

Shortly thereafter, Harvey was on an LST bound for Normandy. He landed in France on D+8 days (June 14, 1944). Harvey remembers the backgrounds of the soldiers in his company. They were from Minnesota,

Chicago, Arkansas, and Baton Rouge, plus a Quaker from Pennsylvania Dutch Country, and a full-blooded American Indian. Mix in a Lawrence boy and this company had some real variety!

As Harvey's unit moved away from the Normandy beaches, he remembers seeing the pointed stakes the Germans put in the ground to impale U.S. paratroopers when they landed. French citizens buried many of the American paratroopers that died in the early part of the invasion, but kept the parachutes to make much needed clothing.

The 414th AAA Battalion moved with the Allied forces as they penetrated deeper and deeper into the French countryside. Harvey recalls that the lines between U.S. and German forces were disorganized and chaotic. It wasn't a clearly marked boundary and, on several occasions, his group found themselves behind enemy lines. Once, he woke up to a real racket, only to find himself on the edge of a raging battle on an adjacent hillside.

GIBEAUIfHarvey's tour of France included Marseilles, Nancy, and Rheims. His artillery unit, equipped with 90 mm anti-aircraft artillery, traveled in truck convoys and once was strafed by German fighters. It happened so fast that there was no time to jump in a ditch or take cover. Thankfully, the unit suffered no casualties.

As the last days of fall passed, U.S. troops became more and more confident that the war would soon be over. Some even spoke about being home by early 1945. The Germans had a different plan. On December 16, 1944 the Germans launched their Ardennes Offensive – what we call the Battle of the Bulge. Well over a million men fought in this battle consisting of three German Armies, three American Armies, and three British Divisions. The Germans suffered 100,000 casualties. We suffered approximately 81,000 casualties, including 23,554 captured and over 19,000 killed. Both sides lost approximately 800 tanks. The battle lasted for six weeks.

After the first few days of the battle, it was going very badly for Allied forces. We were losing men faster than we could replace them. Every soldier was needed at the front. Even though Harvey was trained in anti-aircraft artillery, his country needed him to take on the role of an infantry soldier. He remembers thinking at the time, "I have a lot of worrying to do!"

There was no time for training. Two weeks into the battle, Harvey joined the fight as an infantryman. His unit still had its 90 mm guns, but now they were not pointed up but, instead, were pointed at German tanks.

He remembers four tanks probably less than a half-mile away that had their sights on his unit. The British troops that Harvey's unit was supporting fired on the German tanks and they turned tail and ran.

On another occasion, Harvey was standing near a British military vehicle when, with no warning, a German armor-piercing shell hit the vehicle right between two seats. Fortunately for Harvey, the shell didn't explode, but it did leave a nasty-looking hole right through two inches of steel armor plating.

The weather during the first week of the battle was horrible. For over a week, U.S. aircrews couldn't launch a strike or provide air cover. The first U.S. air operation in the battle occurred on Christmas morning. That same morning, Harvey volunteered for a mission to clear German forces from a section of a nearby town. He and two other soldiers approached a farmhouse and, not knowing if there were German soldiers inside; one of the men threw a grenade towards a window. It missed the window but made a pretty impressive explosion nevertheless.

There were, in fact, approximately half a dozen German soldiers inside the farmhouse at the time. They decided it was best to vacate the premises while they still had a chance. Harvey and his two comrades subdued and captured the Germans as they ran from the house. As this was taking place, Harvey noticed a group of German soldiers in a nearby field. U.S. warplanes strafed the field and Harvey and his two companions captured another dozen German soldiers ... making 18 prisoners in all. He has several souvenirs taken from the Germans captured that day – three medals and a small package of Chesterfield cigarettes – but he regrets not getting one of the German P-38 pistols that one of his fellow soldiers confiscated. For this operation, Harvey was awarded the Bronze Star.

Several days later, Harvey recalls witnessing the gruesome sights of dead German snipers still hanging in the trees and, on another occasion, seeing the burnt remains of several German soldiers in a pillbox who had been killed by flamethrowers several hours earlier. It is apparently the smell that makes the most lasting impression. "I really got to me," he said.

With so many German prisoners taken in the Battle of the Bulge, the U.S. had to man numerous new prison camps. Harvey was assigned to supervise a section of a POW camp that housed captured German officers. They professed to not liking Hitler, but later Harvey found out that many of them had been members of the German Nazi Party since the mid-thirties – not exactly the makings of a pro-democracy group!

Harvey's POW camp assignment continued until the end of the war in Europe. Shortly after victory was declared, orders came to free the German prisoners and allow them to walk back home to Germany. Many were reluctant to leave the camp, fearing they would be shot as they walked away. Maybe that is a reflection of what they would have done if the tables were reversed.

After VE-Day, Harvey went to Brussels to await return to the U.S. The magic day finally came in September 1945 when he boarded the Queen Elizabeth. The Queen Elizabeth was a fast ship and the return voyage took only 5 days. Harvey was discharged from active duty in November of 1945, after more than three years and three months of active duty.

On the return voyage Harvey met another soldier from Lawrence and they became friends. Upon reaching New York, his new friend invited Harvey to his home to meet the family. Harvey took him up on the offer and, as he walked in the door, he saw his friend's sister, Flora, for the first time. They were married 8 months later and have been together now for nearly 60 years! At first, they took up residence in Lawrence, but have now lived in Methuen for the last 32 years. Although Harvey worked for several employers, he spent over 30 years with Borden Chemical in North Andover. He and Flora have two children, five grandchildren, and two great-grandchildren.

Harvey Gibeau, thank you for your service.

BRONZE STAR CITATION: Private First Class Harvey Gibeau, 11055053, Coast Artillery Corps, United States Army, for meritorious service in connection with military operations against the enemy on 25 December 1944. Private First Class Gibeau, together with a fellow soldier, volunteered to accompany a warrant officer of his battalion on patrol. Fully realizing the dangers they would encounter, he and his companions entered a town still partially held by the enemy and aided in clearing the area. After entering the town, Private First Class Gibeau and his companions assisted in capturing a number of enemy troops. By his courageous and voluntary actions, Private First Class Gibeau aided greatly in clearing the area of enemy forces. Private First Class Gibeau's courage and devotion to duty are a credit to himself and to the Army of the United States. "Cpl. Harvey Gibeau was awarded the Bronze Star, the Good Conduct Medal, and the European Theater of Operations medal."

Former Valley Patriots of the Month, Francisco Urena, Lawrence's Veterans Services Director (at the time) with Harvey Gibeau (now deceased) Commander of the Disabled American Veterans, Chapter 2 in Methuen, Massachusetts. Urena dropped in to meet the new commander and to drop off money recently collected from employees at the Buckley Transportation Parking Garage in Lawrence, Massachusetts. (2006). PHOTO: Tom Duggan, Jr. The Valley Patriot, 2006.

Col. Van T. Barfoot
Congressional Medal of Honor
WWII, Korea, Vietnam

By: Helen Mooradkanian - August, 2011

In May 1944 during World War II, near Carano, Italy, 24-year old Sergeant Van T. Barfoot risked his life in extraordinary heroism. Single-handedly, he killed seven German soldiers, destroyed three machinegun nests, faced down three armored tanks, and captured 17 German prisoners!

For his valor, he was commissioned a Second Lieutenant and awarded the Congressional Medal of Honor. Today at 92, Barfoot is one of our oldest living Medal of Honor recipients.

Combat service in three wars—World War II, the Korean War, and the Vietnam War—earned him twenty medals including the Silver Star, Bronze Star, and three Purple Hearts.

In December 2009, outside Richmond, Virginia, at the age of 90, Colonel (retired) Barfoot, engaged in warfare of another kind.

This time it required standing fast. He refused to remove the American flag from the 21-foot flagpole he put up in his front yard, on his property. The homeowners' association harassed him. Their lawyers threatened legal action.

Barfoot stood firm. He would fight them in court.

No surrender.

Where does such courage come from?

Who is the source of his strength?

When your back is against the wall

Born on June 15, 1919, on a farm in Edinburg, Mississippi, Colonel Barfoot says, "I'm just a country boy who grew up at Rye's Creek and was very fortunate that God has been very good to me," he told WLBT-Jacksonville.

In 1940, before the draft, Barfoot enlisted in the U.S. Army and was promoted to Sergeant in December 1941. In 1943 he was reassigned to the 157th Infantry, the 45th Division. He took part in the Allied invasions of Sicily (July 1943), Salerno, Italy (September 1943), and Anzio (late January 1944). At Anzio the 45th Division held off the Germans for four months.

By May 1944, near Carano, they found their backs against the wall.

Before them lay a wheat field, cemetery, and minefield—and the German army.

Behind them stretched the woods, and the Mediterranean.

There was only one way to go. Forward.

Barfoot knew the Germans were laying mines there. Each day, he closely observed them come out, work, and then go back in. By night, he led small patrols, 25 to 30 in all, mentally mapping out where the mines lay.

On the morning of May 23, 1944, Barfoot volunteered to lead a squad behind enemy lines, using his information. Early that morning, under cover of a light rain and artillery shelling, they advanced 300 yards beyond the cemetery. Then both the rain and the shelling stopped.

Now visible to the Germans, they were exposed to machinegun fire.

Worse yet, they were completely cut off!

No way to communicate with their commander.

No radio—it had been damaged by machinegun fire.

No runner—he had been wounded before setting off.

No artillery support.

No way to contact the unit on their flank.

Barfoot decided to go off alone. He crawled along the minefield until he came within 20 feet of the first German machinegun nest. He threw a hand grenade, killing two and wounding three Germans.

He kept on going down the trenches to the second German machinegun emplacement. With his Tommy gun, he killed two more Germans and captured three.

Since he had no way to communicate with his men, he said, he just kept going.

When the third German machinegun crew saw all this, they surrendered to Sergeant Barfoot.

Leaving the prisoners with his squad, Barfoot proceeded to seize more prisoners. In all, he single-handedly captured a total of 17 Germans! In three hours!

Slaying Goliath

Early that afternoon, the Germans launched a fierce counterattack.

Three German Mark VI tanks arrived, a "fortress on wheels" with their 88mm gun and four inches of armor. They aimed straight for Barfoot on patrol with another soldier (he had ordered the others to withdraw to a hill).

Grabbing the soldier's bazooka, Barfoot ran to an exposed position, directly in their path. From a distance of 75 yards, on his first shot he destroyed the tread of the lead tank, disabling it. As the crew jumped out, Barfoot killed three of them with his Tommy gun. The other two tanks turned away.

Knowing where the Germans would likely counterattack, Barfoot headed there. Finding an abandoned German fieldpiece on the way, he destroyed it with a demolition charge.

Then although "greatly fatigued by his Herculean efforts," while returning to his platoon Barfoot helped carry two of his seriously wounded men 1,700 yards (about a mile) to safety.

His Congressional Medal of Honor, presented before his troops near the frontlines in France on September 28, 1944, reads in part, for "extraordinary heroism, magnificent demonstration of valor, and aggressive determination in the face of pointblank fire."

Spiritual courage: the strength to endure

Asked if he were ever afraid, Barfoot replied, "Why should I fear when I have the Lord? The Lord will look out for me," daughter Margaret Nicholls told The Valley Patriot.

"My Dad was raised by a very devout Christian mother, and his faith in God has been at the very core of his being since childhood. That's what gave him courage in battle.

"Throughout the war, he carried the pocket Bible of his wife's mother, drawing strength from God's Word, and read the Bible to his men. At each military post, he taught Sunday School.

"To this day, he reads the Bible daily, often three times a day," she said.

On his shelves, books by Billy Graham, Oliver North, and Ronald Reagan sit next to histories of World War II.

In warfare, success leads to surprise attacks.

In October 2009, Mississippi designated a portion of Highway 16 as the "Van T. Barfoot Medal of Honor Highway," beginning from Carthage, Mississippi, where Barfoot had first enlisted in the Army, through Edinburg to the Leake/Neshoba County line.

Two months later, in December, his display of the American flag triggered a dispute.

The flagpole was too tall and "not aesthetically appropriate," the homeowners' association claimed. It must come down.

Barfoot refused. It was a matter of honor. "The flag should be flown from a height, not half-mast from a porch. It's not dignified that way."

The association's law firm threatened court action.

Barfoot stood firm. "I was raised to respect the flag." Since his Army days, he has raised the flag each sunrise and lowered it each sunset.

In the uproar that followed, the national media and even U.S. and state senators got involved. The association's lawyers dropped the charges.

"In the time I have left, I plan to continue to fly the American flag without interference," Barfoot told the Associated Press.

Barfoot remains humble about his WWII heroism. "People say I did something miraculous. I don't think so. I don't think I did any more than any good American would do," he told Ron Capps (Foreign Policy, 11/11/2010).

But for a grateful nation, the closing words of his Medal of Honor citation say it all, calling his heroism "a perpetual inspiration to his fellow soldiers."

And to his fellow Americans for generations to come.

Col. Barfoot has always honored God, country, and family.

May his legacy inspire us all to hold fast to this truth, "In God we trust."

Helen Mooradkanian is former senior editor of a national specialized business magazine and currently a freelance writer and book editor. A Wellesley College graduate, she has a master's from Fuller Seminary. Email her at: hsmoor@verizon.net

The American flag flies triumphantly from the 21-ft pole in Col. Barfoot's front yard. He won the hotly contested battle with a homeowners' association. Since then, Virginia (in 2010) and Texas (2011) enacted laws that ban these associations from interfering with the display of the American flag.

Ted Cole

By: Dr. Charles Ormsby - May, 2005

ANDOVER, MA – "I was furious at what they did," said Ted Cole, recalling his emotions after hearing about the bombing of Pearl Harbor. Less than 24 hours later he and his two brothers were in line at the recruiting station in Lawrence. "The line was out the door and down the sidewalk. It took all day to get signed up."

After seeing pictures of the attack in the paper, Ted wanted in on the action. He wanted to be in gunnery and in the Pacific to fight the Japs. Ted also hoped to use his skills in photography that he had acquired as a teenager. All his wishes came true, but the experiences almost certainly exceeded whatever he could have imagined in those early days of the conflict.

Ted was born in Andover in 1921 and was 21 years old when he enlisted on December 8, 1941. Because of a problem with the vision in his left eye, he was initially refused admission by the Navy. Instead, he was sent to Boston for further testing. Every two weeks he went back, but couldn't get past the eye test. Finally, the doctor told Ted to take the rest of the physical … if he had no other problems; he would be sent to Mass General Hospital to correct his vision.

After a successful eye operation, Ted was finally accepted by the Navy in June of 1942 and sent to Newport, Rhode Island for basic training in gunnery. At the end of basic, he was on the verge of being sent for additional training when the call came: crewmen were needed for a new light cruiser, the Columbia (CL-56, the "Gem"). Next stop: Camden, New Jersey.

The Columbia had been launched ten days after Pearl Harbor, but at that time it was still just a floating shell. When Ted arrived, the Columbia was fully outfitted and ready for sea trials. As a member of the ship's initial crew, Ted is officially a "plank owner" … a term derived from the time of wooden boats.

Ted remembers one very exciting test of the Columbia. Because of the immense complement of equipment, the weight of the big guns and the size of the superstructure, there was concern that under some extreme operating conditions the ship might capsize. So what can you do, but try to capsize it? The Columbia's guns were all pointed to one side, the ship put in a maximum rate turn, and, just as the ship was at its peak roll angle … all guns were fired simultaneously. The ship dramatically increased its roll angle.

Thank God all the crew had on life preservers and were kept away from the railings, because the ship heeled over to such an extreme angle that the ship's deck went under water. With all the crew praying the ship would right itself and not continue its roll … it hesitated … and then slowly rolled back to vertical. Such a test would never be performed today … computer simulations are much safer!

In November of 1942, the Columbia departed the U.S., passed through the Panama Canal and headed for Espiritu Santo in the New Hebrides. Ted recalls a fueling stop in Tongatabu with fond memories. The stop was for only a few days, but he remembers it as a South Sea paradise.

After the Columbia crew arrived in Espiritu Santo, they witnessed major units returning from the Battle of the Coral Sea. It was a rude awakening: there were ships with their bow shot off, superstructures badly damaged and numerous casualties.

Over the next three years the Columbia steamed 178,000 miles in war-torn seas. A mere listing of engagements cannot impart the magnitude of the effort, risks taken and sacrifices made, but to not list them would be a disservice. Ted Cole was one of less than 200 plank owners that served, start to finish, on all three cruises.

First Cruise: Guadalcanal (Dec '42), Rennell Island (Jan '43), Solomon Islands (Feb-Apr '43), New Georgia Operations (Jun-Sep '43), Bougainville Operations (Nov-Dec '43), Bismark Archipelago & Green Islands Landing (Feb '43), Truk Anti-shipping Sweep & Landing Emirau Island (Mar '44). Second Cruise: Caroline Islands (Sep '44), Leyte Landings (Oct '44), Battle for Leyte Gulf and Surigao Strait (Oct '44), Luzon Operation (Dec '44, Jan '45).

Third Cruise: Borneo Operation (Jun, Jul '45), Anti-shipping Sweeps of China Coast & Yellow Sea (Jul, Aug '45), and the Inspection/Occupation of Truk Atoll.

Ted's duty was both as a gunner's mate and as ship's photographer, 3rd class (a job he inherited when the ship's previous photographer was promoted). His primary duty was on the 40mm anti-aircraft guns (he manned the lower turret just below and to the left of the gap between the two largest towers ... see previous photo). Photo duty was clearly secondary to his fighting role, but Ted noted that he could control firing of the 40mm radar-directed gun with his feet and still take pictures of incoming Jap planes. And incoming they were ...

The Columbia's encounters with Jap Kamikaze attacks in early 1945 were incredible. During the Luzon Operation in January, concentrated Kamikaze attacks were made on numerous ships in the fleet. Several suicide planes were shot down by Columbia. For a while, Columbia turned attacking planes away; one diverting and hitting a nearby destroyer. Finally, a Kamikaze came in on a strafing run intending to end its attack in a suicide crash. The plane came in just above Ted and to his left, hit the antenna wires hanging between the main towers and crashed close aboard. The result was Ted and nearby crew members being showered with gasoline from the Jap's gas tanks.

That was the first of three Kamikaze pilots that succeeded in hitting the Columbia. Later that afternoon, the second Kamikaze to hit the Columbia struck. Luckily, it was hit by 40mm fire in its right wing before impacting or it would have hit the bridge directly. Instead, it swerved and crashed into the main deck near turret number four. The plane and bomb penetrated the deck and the 800 kg bomb (~1760 lb.) penetrated the second and third decks before exploding ... blowing six large holes in the bottom of the Columbia. Nine compartments flooded, but miraculously the ship's magazine didn't explode. If it had detonated, the Columbia would almost certainly have sunk. Seventy-seven casualties were sustained – 17 killed and 20 listed as missing in action.

On January 9th, a third Kamikaze succeeded in striking Columbia. Traveling at 400 mph, the plane was also hit by 40mm gun fire on its way in, but its momentum carried it into the Columbia's forward main battery director ... just above Ted's position. When the plane and its 250 kg bomb (~550 lb.) exploded, the main battery director was knocked off its tower and it, along with six crewmen, were thrown into the ocean. Seventeen men were killed or died of wounds sustained by this attack and ninety-seven others were wounded. The six crew in the battery director were never recovered.

When the third Kamikaze struck, an amazing event occurred. As the plane with its pilot exploded, a piece of the pilot's cloth flight jacket was thrown free and landed in Ted's gun turret. A fellow gunner was killed and fell on Ted, who was knocked unconscious by the explosion. Shipmates evacuated the wounded and took Ted's dog tags (and other personal effects) and those of his deceased crewmate. When Ted regained consciousness, he moved his dead crewmate so he could get up. That was when he discovered a torn piece of flight jacket which included an inside pocket containing the pilot's "Kamikaze flag". This is the only known Kamikaze flag ever recovered from a Kamikaze pilot who struck an American warship (see opening photo).

Amidst the horrors of war, occasionally a light moment is recalled. In the famous Battle of Leyte Gulf (the largest sea battle in the history of the world), a radioman on a nearby ship, concerned that Columbia (codenamed Greyhound) might draw Japanese fire, called the Columbia and said, "Greyhound, you have a light showing from you bow porthole." The Columbia responded, "We don't have a bow porthole." "You do now," said the radioman. And sure enough they did … a big hole from Japanese artillery fire. It is probably much funnier now than it was then.

After the Japanese surrender, Ted supported post-war activities in the Pacific (mostly on Truk Atoll) for several months and then left active duty in November of 1945. Ted continued to serve in the reserves for four more years. He was married in March of 1946 to Lucy, whom he had plans to marry before the war, but who faithfully awaited his return from active duty. After the war, Ted worked at Craig Systems for 14 years and then another 23 years for the Defense Contract Administration Services in Boston. Except for his years of service in the Pacific, Ted has been a lifelong resident of Andover.

Ted, thank you for your service to your country.

Edward "Ted" Cole was awarded Two Purple Hearts with Combat Action Ribbons, Two Navy Unit Commendation Ribbons, the Navy Good Conduct Medal, the China Service Medal, the American Campaign Medal, the Asiatic-Pacific Campaign Medal with Ten Battle Stars, the World War II Victory Medal, the Navy Occupation Service Medal, the Philippine Presidential Unit Citation, and the Philippine Liberation Ribbon with Two Battle Stars.

Charles Bruderer

By: Dr. Charles Ormsby - July, 2005

METHUEN, MA - Charles Bruderer of Methuen is just wrapping up his military career. He will be leaving the National Guard after 33 years of service to our country and a record that recently won him the Meritorious Service Medal.

Born in Ogden, Utah and raised in Brigham City, Charles found himself between jobs in 1969. With the draft actively "recruiting," Charles and two friends decided to enlist. Charles and one of his friends picked the Navy and together they signed up in May of that year. By September he was on active duty.

After basic training, Charles was sent to Radarman School in San Francisco where he was trained in radar operations, radar navigation, and radiotelephone procedures.

At the conclusion of his training in April of 1970, Bruderer was assigned to the Navy's River Forces, affectionately referred to as the "brown water Navy". One month later he was on a flight to Saigon and then on to Song Ong Doc, which translated means the river of Mr. Doc. The Song Ong Doc runs through the Ca Mau Peninsula, on the Southern tip of Viet Nam, and flows into the Gulf of Thailand near the South China Sea.

Charles lived in a "hooch" on a "base" floating in the mouth of the river. Moored at the base were River Assault Boats and PBRs, short for Patrol Boats – River. Charles served as a Radarman Seaman (RDSN) in the Advanced Tactical Support Base Operations Center. In this capacity he served as Army liaison and communicated both with Navy ships off the coast and with boats conducting operations on the river.

Enemy rocket and small arms fire were common near the Operations Center, but on the night of October 20, 1970 all hell broke loose when the base came under attack by a Vietcong company using heavy and medium weapons. Operations Specialist 3rd Class Bruderer (see photo at Song Ong Doc shortly before the attack) was just going to bed when he heard some unusual explosions.

Since the most valuable elements at the base were the boats and the men, the defensive plan when attacked called for immediate evacuation to the boats and then to fight the enemy from the river. As Bruderer was exiting his hooch, it was hit with an incoming B-40 Rocket Propelled Grenade, or RPG. Fragments from the explosion hit Bruderer and became embedded in his back. Two Americans were killed in the attack including one of Charles' hooch-mates. Several others were wounded by shrapnel.

With the base largely destroyed and Bruderer now wounded, he and most of the men from Song Ong Doc continued their operations on an LST offshore. After the Operations Center was rebuilt, approximately 10 km up-river at the Old District Capital of Song Ong Doc, Bruderer and his fellow resumed operations at their new base.

In December of 1970, Bruderer was reassigned to the Provincial Capital of Ca Mau where he stayed until his 21st birthday the following February. While at Ca Mau, an incoming enemy rocket hit a flagpole directly in front of Bruderer's quarters and exploded. Several Americans were killed in the attack and, had this round not hit the flagpole, Charles would have almost surely been among those killed.

Bruderer's final four months in Vietnam were served in Cat Lai (near Saigon), Ben Luc, and Tan An (the last two near the "parrot's peak" area of Cambodia). He finished his tour in Vietnam in May of 1971 as a Radarman 3rd Class.

Bruderer spent the remainder of his four-year enlistment on sea-going vessels. In 1971 he was assigned to the Destroyer USS Gurke (DD 783), which was briefly deployed to Japan and then stationed off the coast of Vietnam to provide Naval gunfire support to operations ongoing within South Vietnam.

By 1973, while the US was engaged in withdrawing troops from Vietnam, the North Vietnamese were streaming troops southward. To discourage this, the Gurke was assigned to the waters off North Vietnam to provide some well-deserved shelling. DD 783 was the target of intense hostile fire during many of her naval gunfire missions while operating close to the North Vietnam coast. While no incoming shells directly hit the Gurke, the ship was hit numerous times by shrapnel. In many cases, Bruderer could see the shells and the nearby impact points on his radar screen.

Charles Bruderer left the active duty Navy in 1973 as an Operations Specialist, 3rd Class. Bruderer subsequently enrolled at Weber State University in Ogden, Utah to study German, music and accounting, and then joined the Army National Guard in October of 1977. In the National Guard he became a Fire Direction Center Chief with rank of Staff Sergeant.

By 1990, with events heating up in the Middle East, language skills became very valuable and Bruderer, having studied German, was transferred from Artillery to Military Intelligence. Initially he was trained as an interrogator and later assigned to Counter-Intelligence. Bruderer's training caused him to be very upset with the events that recently took place at Abu Ghraib Prison in Iraq.

He commented that he "was very upset by the news of the reported mistreatment of prisoners at Abu Ghraib and that American Soldiers could be involved in this type of activity." He also commented that winning the hearts and minds of the Iraqis was critical to our efforts in Iraq and the events at Abu Ghraib were a very big setback in the War on Terror.

Charles moved to Massachusetts in 1996 when he joined Echo Company, 223 Military Intelligence Battalion, Cambridge, Mass., where he was assigned as a Platoon Sergeant. Shortly thereafter he moved to his present home in Methuen.

Life took a major turn in February of 2003 when Bruderer received a call at the office. The message was, "You're being mobilized. Report immediately to the Armory for Active Duty."

After a few weeks at Ft. Bragg, N.C., Sergeant First Class Bruderer was flown to Kuwait on a C-17. Three weeks later the balloon went up and, only one week after the tip of the spear entered Iraq, Bruderer followed. Life now consisted of tents, dust, wind, heat, and Meals Ready to Eat (MREs). Thirty-plus years after serving in Vietnam, Bruderer was back in a combat theater and living in conditions that in some ways, at least initially, were worse than he had experienced in Vietnam. (Note: Bruderer recommends the Teriyaki Chicken and Chow Mein MREs if you must subsist on them. Avoid Turkey if at all possible.)

After eight months living in tents at various locations, Bruderer was finally stationed at Bakir Army Air Base, known as LSA Anaconda; near the Tigris River in the Sunni Triangle … a location that we know from listening to the news is not very friendly to Americans. Riding in a convoy in the Sunni triangle in an unarmored Humvee while holding an M-16 out an open doorway can be pretty exciting … although you keep hoping it won't be. Note that the Humvee's doors were removed because they provided little protection while restricting the troop's field of fire and much-needed airflow.

The threat of rocket and mortar attacks was always present. Baker Airfield was large and it was shelled frequently … often with rounds landing close enough "to get my attention."

Charles left Iraq in February of last year. When asked about his opinion of the war and our chances for success, he said that he remains convinced of the importance of the mission. "The worst thing we could do is pull out prematurely. It is the worst thing we could do to the memory of the people we lost there", he said. "Once we've gone in, we can't pull out. The job must be completed. If we leave early it will just become a terrorist haven." The key to our success, he says, is that "we must win the hearts and minds of the people and to do that we must convince them we do not intend to stay and that their emerging government is not a puppet of the U.S."

Bruderer is passionate about the contribution of Guardsmen and Reservists to our national defense. He hopes that Americans "recognize that, although Guardsmen and Reservists join to defend our country, they usually have full time jobs or businesses. Their employers and families' lives are disrupted and put on hold when they are called up. In some instances, men I served with actually lost their businesses due to their active duty service. National Guardsmen and Reservists sign up for 'Part Time Service' while trying to maintain a full time civilian life. In this way, they are much like the early Patriots who were called to Lexington Green and the North Bridge in Concord. These Patriots went on to become part of the Continental Army. Guardsmen and Reservists serve in the tradition of these Citizen Soldiers dating back to the beginnings of our Country."

Charles Bruderer, thank you for your service.

Charles Bruderer was awarded the Purple Heart (Vietnam), the Combat Action Ribbon (Vietnam), the Army Reserve Component Achievement Medal, the Vietnam Campaign Medal, the Vietnam Service Medal, the Armed Forces Expeditionary Medal (Korea, USN), the Army Commendation Medal (Iraq), the Global War on Terrorism Medal, and the Meritorious Service Medal.

Bruderer in Iraq, 2003

PHOTO FROM CHARLES BRUDERER

Corporal Joe Bella
Vietnam

By: Tech Sgt. James F. Moore USAF -
September, 2008

METHUEN, MA- There are many
reasons that Joseph G. Bella of Methuen,
is this month's Valley Patriot. He is a
Vietnam Veteran, an advocate of
Veteran's advancement, and a history
buff.

According to the Vietnam service
report of Corporal Joseph Bella:

'Corporal Joseph Bella served in Vietnam from 1966 to 1967, originally
stationed at Dong Ha near the DMZ, with the 1st Battalion, 40th Artillery.
He was transferred six months in country to the 3rd Battalion, 6th Artillery
at Pleiku. The 1st Battalion, 40th Artillery was one of the first mobile
artillery units assigned to Vietnam. Joe was with them when they arrived.

While at Dong Ha with the 1st Battalion, 40th Artillery, Joe's unit took
part in a support action that pinned the Viet Cong down for 14 hours so that
a trapped Marine Recon Platoon could escape.'

The man that has an affinity for History itself has also contributed to
ideals that make our nation Great! Joe's is single and happy. He is also glad

that he has more time to devote to his hobbies, since he's retired and enjoying what he's doing and doing what he loves to do.

Today, his tireless public service continues, even on Labor Day, as his schedule was chock-full of places to go and people to see. Bella, originally from Lawrence, was born in 1946 to Alfred and Connie Bella. He has only one sibling, a sister, Angela.

He was drafted into the United States Army on November 30, 1965 and at age 19, young and green, had never spent more than a week out of the New England area until he went to Basic Military Training at Fort Dix, NJ to begin his service in the Army.

He was then sent to Vietnam after Basic Military Training and training for his primary MOS in Field Artillery. His military service spanned almost 2 years, but he's been serving his country in many other ways since September 1967, when he returned to Methuen.

Returning to Methuen from Vietnam, he says he came back a completely different person. "I was changed for the better," He said, "The training I received was a healthy experience."

Bella was transformed from the young man of little experience to a marketable and able adult. He immediately took advantage of his Veteran's status to enter the civilian workforce enabling him to land a job at Craig Systems in North Andover, MA, a company that specializes in the manufacturing of tankers, fuel oil trucks, fire trucks, buses, and containment shelters.

After about four years of employment there, he spent three years working for the Internal Revenue Service as a batching clerk. Afterward, he moved on to Western Electric out of North Andover and worked as a Reproduction Room Clerk and Stock Inventory Clerk for about seven years.

He then was hired and served as a Local Veteran's Employment Representative, through the Division of Employment and Training (DET). His position was to assist Veterans and to provide counsel for Veterans seeking employment and training. His professionalism and dedication to assisting Veterans was noticed by the American Legion, and as the result of his efforts Joe became a two time winner of the American Legion Local Veteran's Employment Representative of the Year award. This award is given to the individual that had placed the highest number of Veterans back in the workforce in the Commonwealth of Massachusetts.

Bella served from 1975-2002 as a counselor and is now enjoying his retirement. He attended Northern Essex Com-munity College and obtained his Associate's Degree in Liberal Arts with a Major in History, making the Dean's list twice.

Today, Bella is a man of many hats in the community. To name only a few, he served on the Immigrant City Archives as both President and Vice President; a board member of the Methuen Historical Society, serving as Vice President, and President; as Commissioner of the Methuen Historic Commission; and as president of the Friends of Lawrence Heritage State Park. Joe's collection of historical items can be seen and are often on display at the Heritage Park in Lawrence.

"I feel good about explaining stories of the past and it excites me to share them with others and I'm proud of this...it's a rewarding experience," he says. Also, noteworthy is that some of Bella's photos have been used in local historical books.

Joe considers himself an "average Joe, no pun intended" he says. His awards with the American Legion are well deserved and you can sense this with his soft-spoken tone "Veterans (serving) are the most important part of our country's survival and we should try to honor them 24 – 7."

Besides being a history aficionado of sorts, Bella's labor of love is that of collecting newspapers, posters, post cards, and memorabilia – both old and new- of Lawrence, Methuen and American history in general. His love of photography allows him to immortalize those men and remind us of the mortality of the times and the risks they have taken to protect our way of life.

These historical mementos he collects reminds us of how our servicemen have paid the ultimate price for our freedom during the Civil War. Also known as the War Between the States, it is credited as the catalyst of social, political, economic and racial issues that continue to shape and reshape contemporary American thought.

Joe Bella is currently preparing to commemorate these fallen heroes from the 6 Regiment, "I" Company of the Union Army and has taken hundreds of photos of the soldiers' gravestones that served from the cities of Lawrence and Methuen, respectively.

He says that he is compelled to honor this specific group of American heroes in this "special project" of his, which will be his own publication.

Joe is dedicated, he's preparing well in advance for the 150th anniversary of the Civil War, which will be 2011.

What's more, he is a Board member of the Lawrence Civil War Memorial Guard, a re-enactment group which memorializes the 6th Regiment, "I" Company from Lawrence.

Their claim to fame is that they marched through Baltimore on April 19, 1861, and were one of the 1st Regiments called up by President Lincoln to protect Washington D.C. a week after the first shots were fired at Fort Sumter, S.C.

If you would like more information regarding the 6th annual re-enactment, it will be held on September 20th and 21st at the Camp Campagnone Common in Lawrence, MA, contact Beth at 978-686-9881.

An elaborately choreographed re-enactment will be conducted at the place of its origin in Washington, D.C. in 2011.

His overall appreciation of the sacrifices of servicemen and women is evident in his words: "I like to show people that history should not be forgotten...the sacrifices of these men should not be forgotten," he continued. "I can relate... to having served in combat overseas and I feel like I'm a part of them and (I want to) bring history to the forefront."

On any given day, Joe Bella can be seen somewhere running around the Lawrence/Methuen area, serving veterans, volunteering in the community and reaching out to help the people of the Merrimack Valley.

Joe is this month's Valley Patriot and it is well deserved. Joe, the Valley Patriot salutes you. Thank you for your service to our great Nation and to our community, Sir!

Dr. Richard Mooradkanian
U.S. Army, 1953–1953

By: Helen Mooradkanian - June, 2014

NORTH ANDOVER, MA - Dr. Richard Mooradkanian, U.S. Army, 1953-1955, was my trusted military advisor who critiqued each "Hero of the Month" column I wrote before I sent it to press. For the past two-and-a-half years, his wisdom, counsel, and insight guided me in my columns for "The Valley Patriot." When Richard passed away on March 22, 2014, I lost not only my counselor but also my brother and my best friend.

Richard was a student of history. He had the innate ability to put battles, military campaigns, generals, and government leaders into perspective. He saw the Big Picture. The sweep of history. He had a phenomenal memory for details. His anecdotal information made battles and campaigns come alive. He filled in the gaps left by the military textbooks and websites I always used.

Richard left college and entered the service on December 1, 1953. The Korean War had seen some of its bloodiest fighting during those last two months before the armistice was signed on July 27. The armistice ended the fighting but did not end the war. The cease-fire was only temporary, and cease fire negotiations extended for many more years, as Army historian, Andrew Birtle points out.

In the Army, Richard trained with the heavy artillery. His hands were prepared for war.

At Brown University, as a history major, Richard was trained to discern and understand the times.

In studying the rise and fall of nations and empires, he realized that the underlying cause of many wars is the clash of opposing ideologies, conflicting worldviews based on religion. Christianity vs. Islam. Our Creator's inalienable rights given to man vs. a godless society's totalitarian control. The dignity of man vs. the dehumanization of man. Democracy vs. dictatorship. He understood, as only an historian can, that the erosion of freedoms in America stems not from fiscal policies but from the lack of absolutes in moral values and distortion of the Truth. He had seen the pattern all too well in nations where that erosion began with small, imperceptible steps. Below the radar. Until the noose was tightened. "Liberty," he knew, demanded "eternal vigilance."

And so he became a watchman on the wall, a sentry at the gates in the battle for the soul of America. He firmly believed "To be forewarned is to be forearmed." He warned of the influence of the radical Muslim Brotherhood in the Obama administration and the dangers of permitting Sharia law in America. He denounced the shredding of our Constitution by President Obama. "Listen! Listen! Listen to the alarm!" he urged. "The bugle has sounded! Islam says, 'Slay the infidel if he refuses to convert.' Christianity says, 'Love one another.' This is a religious war! Let us stand fast together, for the Truth will always prevail."

PATRIOT COUNSELOR

Richard was a patriot, proud of America and everything she stands for. He was an articulate spokesman for the Truth. A silent warrior. A humble man. His quiet strength came not from himself, which would have failed him—but because he stood firmly on Christ the Solid Rock. And he never wavered.

When I began writing these columns, he became my strongest supporter.

His wise counsel helped me get interviews with several WWII veterans reluctant at first to open up because they had "no heroics" to report. "Tell them," Richard urged me, "they were WILLING to sacrifice their life for our country. Where they eventually ended up, whether in combat or not was something they had no control over. What really mattered was the attitude of their heart."

Some colorful anecdotes came as a result—the hilarious antics of the gooney birds on Midway Island, the carrier pigeons delivering messages on New Guinea, and the infamous "40 and 8" boxcars that transported troops to and from the front lines in Europe. It was gratifying to see the veterans' joy when their contributions were recognized.

For Richard, self-sacrifice had always been paramount. It was the measure of a man. Richard sacrificed himself for others. This grew out of his deep commitment as a follower of Jesus Christ. He generously gave of himself, his time, and his resources to those in need. Without fanfare.

Richard understood the heart. His words brought healing.

"When veterans say, 'I just followed orders. Nothing extraordinary,' tell them: 'In war you see only a small piece of the whole picture. You were given an assignment, and you completed it. Even when you didn't understand. You were faithful.'"

Or invariably, they compared themselves to others. "Tell them, 'You have a story to tell, one unique to you alone—your eyewitness account. Your sacrifice will never be forgotten. You answered the call. You were committed. You played a crucial role in the liberation of Europe.' "

At this, their stories began to flow! The healing had begun!

SHAPING OF A WARRIOR

After Richard finished his training with the heavy artillery, he developed a severe reaction to Army chemicals that was potentially life-threatening. As a result, instead of shipping overseas, he was reassigned to the Medical Corps as a medical-dental specialist, where he discovered his life's profession. Following his Army discharge, he returned to Brown, graduated, and then entered Tufts Graduate School of Dentistry. After receiving his degree, he practiced in Boston's Back Bay and served as a clinical instructor at Tufts Dental for 45 years.

The spirit of freedom runs deep in man's spirit. In Richard's DNA, it was a forceful current. One grandfather barely escaped the Turkish massacres of Armenians when he fled in the middle of the night, with his family, with only the clothes on their backs. Somehow they secretly reached Le Havre, France, where they boarded a ship for America and freedom. Our other grandfather "understood the times" and sent his family, one by one, to America before finally coming himself. Members of our extended family survived Turkish death marches, rescued by American missionaries. Family members served with the U.S. Army in WWI, WWII, and in the Korean War, near the Demilitarized Zone (DMZ).

REPUBLICAN OF THE
YEAR AWARD

On April 23, 2014, in a special ceremony during its annual event, the North Andover Republican Town Committee recognized Richard posthumously for his contributions. Chairman Charles J. Gangi awarded him the "Distinguished Title of 2013 Republican of the Year"

"...for his unselfish dedication to the Republican ideals of individual responsibility and limited government. In his quiet manner, Dr. Mooradkanian generously supported Republican candidates with his time, energy, and resources. Local Republicans in office today can attest to his commitment in advancing a Republican presence in a state long dominated by the opposition party.

"Dr. Mooradkanian was a genuine patriot who served in the U.S. Army during the Korean War and was always proud to express his love for country. He was a true gentleman who promoted his positions with logic and facts and figures that were hard to refute. He was an immensely positive force for Republican principles."

Today, freedom's call rings out loudly as in 1861, when Julia Ward Howe roused a nation with "Battle Hymn of the Republic." She wrote: "He [God] has sounded forth the trumpet that shall never call retreat...Oh, be swift my soul, to answer Him! Be jubilant, my feet!...As He [Christ] died to make men holy, let us die to make men free, While God is marching on. Glory! Glory! Hallelujah!...His truth is marching on."

The Sullivan Family left to right: Former Lawrence Mayor Michael Sullivan, Anne Sullivan, Former Lawrence Mayor Kevin Sullivan, in background with sunglasses, Mark Sullivan. Thomas Sullivan Jr. is behind Kevin.

Corner Named for PFC.
Thomas Sullivan, U.S. Army

By: Tom Duggan, Jr. - June, 2016

LAWRENCE, MA - Last month, the City of Lawrence and the Commonwealth of Massachusetts recognized the heroism of World War II veteran and former Lawrence native, Thomas A. Sullivan of the Army's 338th infantry regiment in 85 Custer Division.

Sullivan was drafted on October 29, 1943, went into training on November 19, 1943, and was shipped to Italy where he arrived on May 4, 1944.

At the corner of South Union and Cambridge Streets in Lawrence, the city unveiled a sign bearing Sullivan's name designating it as Sullivan Corner.

Massachusetts Secretary of Veterans Services, Francisco Urena (who was once the Veterans Services Officer for Lawrence under then, Mayor Michael Sullivan), attended and spoke to more than two dozen veterans and members of the Sullivan family as did Jamie Melendez, the city's Veteran's Services Officer.

"This is so important to honor the services of someone like Thomas Sullivan," Urena told The Valley Patriot after the ceremony. "Especially here on the corner of South Union and Cambridge Street. His family has made such a significant contribution to this city with a business, T.A. Sullivan Insurance, and two of his sons, Kevin and Michael, being former mayors of the city, and such an amazing family." Urena said.

Former Lawrence Mayor Kevin Sullivan, who was elected the city's mayor in 1985, said that he was honored his father's name now stands on South Union Street.

"I hope that people will walk by and see this sign for generations to come and go home and google the name and read about his service. This is wonderful."

20160603_132549 (1)His father, Thomas Sullivan, landed in Italy at 22 years old and fought what was later called the forgotten war because most of the focus in the European Theater was on the invasion of Normandy at D-Day.

"If you think about it, there was really two wars going on, the war against Japan and the one in Europe," former Mayor Kevin Sullivan said.

"Churchill, who had been fighting the war since the mid 1930's, was begging Roosevelt to focus on Europe and win that war first and then focus on the Japanese. Think of 1941, Japan just bombed us so, of course the first inclination is bomb the Japanese with all we have. But, Churchill said you have to help us fight Europe and defeat Hitler. At the time, Churchill was worried that Hitler was going to go into Russia and take Moscow. If that had happened it would have been a whole different war. So, Churchill wanted to keep Hitler busy."

"In 1943, the allies invaded Italy with the hopes of liberating Italy from Mussolini and Hitler."

Sullivan said that since his father never talked about the war after coming home, he had to research the Custer Division to find out about the battles his father fought in.

"So, in May of 1944, they sent a bunch of new troops to help with liberation of Italy and when my father got there, they were almost 12 months into the war in Italy. In the Italian theater were the Apennines Mountains; some of them are more than 9,000 feet high.

The Germans were embedded high up in the mountains and it was up to the allies to climb the mountains and defeat or push back Germans. From 1944 to May of 1945 my father saw vicious and brutal battles almost every single day."

"A month after my father arrived in Italy, the allies invaded Normandy. So, they moved divisions out of Italy to fight the D-Day invasion. That's why the Italian Theater is known as 'the forgotten war.' All eyes were on the D-Day invasion. But, some of those battles in Italy were just as, if not more ferocious as the battles going on in France and then Germany."

"The Germans were in the northern part of Italy, the Balkans were right next door and they have a lot of oil and natural resource that Hitler took over. Churchill felt that if the allies could seize Italy, they could march into the Balkans and from there, they could do an air invasion over Germany."

"Hitler felt that Italy was a stronghold for Nazis, they didn't want to give it up. He ordered his men not to give up an inch of soil to the allies. He ordered them to fight to the death. It just shows how brutal these battles were. It was actually Churchill who was the real architect of how they would wage that war in Italy. At the time, Eisenhower was focused on Normandy and invasion of France.

Sullivan says that his father was wounded near Rome when a grenade hit him in September of 1945.

"He lost most of his hearing and had shrapnel wounds, so he was hospitalized for weeks. But, back then they didn't send you home when you got hurt, they patched you up and sent you back into battle. So, he ended up staying in Italy until the liberation of the country in May of 1945."

Private First Class, Thomas A. Sullivan, US Army came home in January of 1946.

He received the Purple Heart, the Good Conduct Medal, the Victory Medal. Sullivan fought at Po Valley and later fought at Romearno where he was wounded by a grenade.

Haverhill's Mike Buglione

By: Dr. Charles Ormsby - April, 2005

HAVERHILL, MA. – Shortly after his 22nd birthday and nine months before Pearl Harbor, Michael Buglione went to his draft board and requested to be taken in the next round. Heck, he thought, it's just "Goodbye dear, I'll be back in a year." Well, it was over four years before he returned from a Pacific cruise he will never forget.

The first few months of Army duty were routine. Buglione trained at Fort Devens and took part in maneuvers in North Carolina. He recalled with amazement how poorly the US was prepared for conflict. "We were training with wooden rifles and we put signs on trucks that said 'I'm a tank'." Buglione was assigned duty as a machine gunner but he never fired a machine gun until just a few weeks before facing hardened Japanese troops on Guadalcanal.

Buglione was assigned to the 26th Yankee Division at Camp Edwards on Cape Cod when the Japanese struck Pearl Harbor in December of 1941. He was arriving with a truckload of supplies and was told, "Don't unload the trucks … just drive them to the rail yard." – They would be needed more at the front than in a warehouse at Camp Edwards.

Most of the 26th Division was assigned to Europe, but Private Buglione knew he was destined to serve in the Pacific when he was told to get shots for the tropics. Shortly thereafter, he and several of his closest friends from Methuen were assigned to Task Force 6814-C (the "C" represented his first destination: New Caledonia) and were sent to the Brooklyn Navy Yard to board the USS Santa Elena, a cruise ship that had been quickly transformed into a troop carrier.

After passing through the Panama Canal and crossing the equator, the Santa Elena headed for Melbourne, Australia.

At this point, Winston Churchill nearly changed everything for Task Force 6814-C when he requested that Roosevelt send them to Malaysia to help British troops there. Luckily, Admiral King advised against this reassignment. That was fortunate, because shortly thereafter, the British troops on Malaysia were overrun and captured by the Japanese.

Buglione noted that the Japanese treated their British captives horribly. Most of the Brits died at the hands of their captors, some having been subjected to cruel medical experiments similar to those carried out by German "doctors" in European concentration camps. Had Churchill's request not been refused, Mike Buglione's wartime experience might have been very different.

After a short stay in Australia, Buglione was assigned to the Americal Division and put on a troop ship to New Caledonia which, after being there for a few hours, everyone called "Mosquito Hollow". The mosquitoes swarmed all over everyone and you couldn't get away from them. The lotions and mosquito nets helped ... but only a little.

In New Caledonia, Buglione had his first chance to train with the Browning 50 caliber machine gun. Mike remembered that they arrived at camp covered with a cosmolene gel that had to be washed off with gasoline.

Shortly after the Marines landed on Guadalcanal, PFC Buglione was deployed to the island to protect American artillery batteries. One of his more repugnant memories was the stench of bodies (both American and Japanese) that filled the air and the flies that were attracted by the smell. The battles on Guadalcanal were so fierce and constant that neither side had the luxury of burying their dead.

Buglione also remembers the nightly air raids by the Japanese and the time that his unit's howitzer fire gave away their position on Point Cruz to Japanese bombers who responded by dropping three 500 lb. and one 2000 lb. bomb near his position. They thought twice about firing their artillery at night after that!

Air raids weren't their only threats to safety. Japanese artillery routinely lobbed shells at Mike's position on Point Cruz. One Japanese gunner, nicknamed "Pistol Pete" by the American troops, survived the war and later corresponded with members of Buglione's unit. Buglione spent approximately three months on Guadalcanal serving on Bloody Ridge, near Henderson Field, and on Point Cruz. His duty on Guadalcanal was terminated when the jeep he was riding in tipped over, killing one soldier and severely injuring Buglione's shoulder. He was airlifted to the New Hebrides to recover.

Before rejoining his unit, Mike recalled several interesting encounters. While healing his shoulder and struggling with multiple bouts of malaria, he met Joe E. Brown [movie star 1928-1964] who was on a USO tour visiting the troops. Shortly afterwards, Buglione was hiking back from an evening meal with some buddies when a jeep pulled up and they were invited to "jump in" by Admiral William "Bull" Halsey [Commander of the South Pacific Area in 1942/43 and Commander-in-Chief of the Third Fleet in 1944] … quite a treat for a couple of hardscrabble soldiers! Also, during a brief stop on Tonga and Tabu, he encountered local natives who gave him a grass skirt in exchange for an old chino shirt.

In August of 1943, Buglione, still suffering from malaria, rejoined his unit which was now stationed on Fiji. It was during this period that he met Bob Feller, the great Cleveland Indians pitcher, who was serving as a gunner on the USS Alabama, and got his autograph.

After fully recovering (January 1944), Buglione and his unit were deployed to Bouganville. There was heavy fighting on the island with the Japanese 6th Division (the same Division responsible for the infamous Rape of Nanking) dug in on the opposite side. Helping destroy the Japanese 6th Division is something Mike is rightfully proud of.

During this same period, the American forces attacked the Japanese in the Philippines to fulfill Gen. Douglas MacArthur's promise that he would return. The nearby picture of Mike, manning his 50 caliber machine gun on Bouganville, was taken shortly before he was sent to Cebu Island in the Philippines to support the Allied invasion.

Buglione witnessed the immense firepower of the US Navy as they shelled Cebu just prior to his disembarking from an LST on the beach. He recalls the trees being tossed around like matchsticks by the exploding shells.

After taking up his machine gun position to protect American howitzer positions on Cebu, Mike related stories of Japanese soldiers attacking American positions with dynamite strapped to their bodies ... the WW II version of modern suicide bombers.

Probably the scariest threats were the attempts by Japanese soldiers to penetrate the Americal Division's security perimeter at night. One night, the Japanese succeeded in infiltrating the unit's right flank and a fellow soldier in a nearby bunker was killed and two others wounded by the Japanese using sabers. Sabers were used to keep the attack quiet so that the Japanese could make off with several 30 caliber machine guns. Mike was certainly lucky to be in a different bunker that night.

As the fighting subsided in the Philippines, some of the soldiers who had fought from the beginning of the war were able to go home. Those having 100 points or more were sent back to America. Buglione easily met this requirement having served for over three and a half years and in three major battles ... he had 105 points.

As Buglione arrived in Pearl Harbor on his way back, he heard the news of our bombing of Hiroshima and Nagasaki ... and the war was soon concluded. Buglione was discharged on September 1, 1945 ... one day before the Japanese signed the Instruments of Surrender. Of equal importance to Mike Buglione is what happened exactly one year later. He married his wife Mary on September 1, 1946. Shortly thereafter he moved to Haverhill where he worked at the Robbi Shoe Factory for 23 years and Raytheon for 10 years. Mike has been a Haverhill resident ever since.

Corporal Michael Buglione, thank you for your service to your country.

Corporal Michael Buglione was awarded the Good Conduct Medal and The Asiatic Pacific Campaign Medal with Three Battle Stars (Guadalcanal, Bouganville, and Southern Philippines).

IN MEMORY OF
Agnes "Irish" Bresnahan
Vietnam

By: Lawrence "Lonnie" Brennan - April, 2009

"We don't have time, we're running out of time," Retired U.S. Army Captain Agnes "Irish" Bresnahan prophetically whispered as she explained her Vietnam era Agent Orange exposure in an April, 2008 Valley Patriot interview.

PHOTO: COURTESY

"There is no cure, no treatment. It just keeps coming and we are dying," she

explained referring the many former soldiers who shared her illness.

On March 11, 2009, less than a year after honoring the Valley Patriot as our

May 2008 Valley Patriot of the Month, and just two days after providing testimony for her Agent Orange exposure in Washington, D.C., Capt. Bresnahan

passed at George Washington University Hospital.

In our 2008 interview, the frail yet spiritually spunky (then 57-year old) attributed her long illness to state-side Agent Orange exposure during basic

training in the 70s at the U.S. Army's Chemical Center and School at Ft. McClellan in Alabama. Over the years, Capt. Bresnahan has been tireless in her efforts to inform Congress and the Veteran's Administration about the plight of state-side Agent Orange exposure, and the long-term effect of toxins. She has served as a rallying beacon for many, reaching out and creating a network between hundreds of former military men and women who are suffering long-term disabilities due to chemical exposure.

During the past year, the Valley Patriot has followed the plight of Capt. Bresnahan. Reviewed countless e-mails, documents, and testimony from her and others, and have been honored that she chose to include The Valley Patriot in her information network.

Capt. Bresnahan was the beloved daughter of the late John C. Bresnahan and Agnes Scanlan Bresnahan. Born in Methuen, MA, raised in neighboring

Lawrence in a family of 12 children, four brothers, seven sisters, Irish had attended Presentation of Mary Academy in Methuen, Massachusetts and graduated from Trinity College in Burlington, Vermont on the ROTC program in 1972.

She studied at the University of Texas in the post-graduate program.

Irish trained with the U.S. Army at Fort McClellan in Alabama and proudly served her country stateside and in Germany from 1971 until 1977. She earned The Army Commendation Medal four times, twice with the First Oak Leaf Cluster; she also received The National Defense Medal twice. After retiring from the military, she worked at the IRS as a computer systems analyst until 2005. She was a staunch advocate for veterans' rights. She was a member of the Vietnam Veterans of America, the Disabled Veterans of America, the United Female Veterans of America, and the American Legion, among other veterans' groups.

In 1971, "Irish" was commissioned as a 2nd Lieutenant in the U.S. Army, and began Boot-camp training at Ft. McClellan in Alabama. Fort

McClellan was home of the Women's Army Corps School, and the U.S. Army's Chemical Center and School.

In addition to the Chemical School, Fort McClellan hosted the U.S. Army's Combat Developments Command Chemical Biological-Radiological Agency.

It was here, she claims, that her life took an unexpected and unwarranted turn.

"Training exercises involved exposure to various gases which we were told were quote/unquote not in a quantity to inflict permanent harm. We thought it was tear gas" she had told the Valley Patriot.

Following an extreme skin reaction after exposure, Capt. Bresnahan said she began a downward spiral of medical problems.

She was later transferred to Camp Richie in Maryland and from there received her diagnosis at Walter Reed Medical Hospital in D.C. and began a long road back to stability.

Irish is survived by her mother, Agnes J. Bresnahan of Lawrence, Pamela Sullivan of Windham, John and Leslie Bresnahan of North Andover, Michael Bresnahan of York, Maine, Kathleen and Al Augevich of Haverhill, Patricia and Charles Gately of Wareham, Mary Bresnahan of Methuen, Claire Bresnahan of Houston, Texas, James Bresnahan of Pacifica, California, Thomas and Janice Bresnahan of Haverhill, Theresa Bresnahan of Lawrence, Margaret and Ernesto Hernandez of Houston, Texas, Maureen Bresnahan of Lawrence, many nieces and nephews, one great nephew, and many, many friends.

She was predeceased by her father, John C. Bresnahan, a former Massachusetts state representative.

In our 2008 interview, Capt. Bresnahan explained "Agent Orange doesn't care where you were exposed. It's an equal opportunity poison. You could be here or in Vietnam or anywhere," she said.

"People think the baby boomers are going to drain Social Security. We're not. Because we'll be lucky to make it to 60 or 62. You try to get the word out," she explained.

"Everybody has to fight on their own. I have so much documentation through my medical records...what I tell the people is to use my case. Here's my heart break.

How old do I look?" she queried. "It's caught up with me and it's killing me ..I

gave my life to my country," she said.

We at the Valley Patriot, pause to honor and thank Capt. Bresnahan and her service and post-service to the veterans of our Country.

We will miss you "Irish."

Bresnahan's crusade has led to contacts of similar cases throughout the U.S.

Irish Bresnahan
Vietnam

By: Lawrence "Lonnie" Brennan - April, 2008

METHUEN - Her statistics from 1970 are simple: female, 5 foot five inches, 125 pounds, age 19. As she entered her Junior year at the now closed Catholic Trinity College in Burlington, Vermont, Agnes M. Bresnahan was surrounded daily by images of the Vietnam war:

Images of war protests on TV, sounds of protest songs led the Billboard chart. But to spunky "Irish" as she was known, her love of country and dedication to service led her to enlist in the United States Army.

Born in Methuen, MA, raised in neighboring Lawrence in a family of 12 children, four brothers and seven sisters, Irish said she had a simple choice based on her family's makeup: "politics or military" to follow the steps of those family members who came before her.

"The U.S. Army had a special program for Juniors, and three woman from Trinity joined that year," Irish explained.

"The military was recruiting and I became a Corporal when I was 20. One day before graduation, my enlistment contract was finalized." Irish was commissioned as a 2nd Lieutenant in the U.S. Army, and began Boot-camp training at Ft. McClellan in Alabama. Fort McClellan was home of the Women's Army Corps School, and the U.S. Army's Chemical Center and School. In addition to the Chemical School, Fort McClellan hosted the U.S. Army's Combat Developments Command, Chemical Biological Radiological Agency . It was here, she claims, that her life took an unexpected and unwarranted turn.

Unfortunately for Irish, she says, "training exercises involved exposure to various gases which we were told were 'not in a quantity to inflict permanent harm.' We thought it was tear gas," she said.

Following an extreme skin reaction after exposure, Irish says she began a downward spiral of medical problems.

She was later transferred to Camp Richie in Maryland and from there received her diagnosis at Walter Reed Medical Hospital in D.C. Having shrunken from 125 pounds to just 96 pounds, she began a long road back to stability.

After her apparent recovery, she applied and was accepted as an operations officer, and then applied and was assigned to a battalion in southern Germany in the signal corps. Women were not allowed in combat in leadership positions at the time.

It was during her trip to Germany that she was notified of the cessation of action in Vietnam.

She continued to serve, earned medals of commendation and was promoted to Captain. Her service also included the National Defense Service Medal. She was discharged in 1977. Later, under the Vietnam Readjustment Act, she was hired at the IRS in Andover where she worked until 2005. In 2005, complications of her earlier chemical exposure led to a downward spiral of medical problems and she was terminated. "I needed that job, a reason to get out of bed, and a steady routine. I need the structure," she explained.

Today, at age 57, looking back at her time in the military, she proudly displays her medals and speaks with high regard for her fellow veterans. But she remains frustrated and saddened at not being able to help others as much as she would like to help them: to spread the word and let her fellow veterans know that they are not alone.

"I was diagnosed with stateside Agent Orange (exposure) at Walter Reed (hospital) in 1972. And, so I knew it was irreversible, incurable, progressive," she related. "I've suffered brain damage, degenerative bones… my nervous system. I'm told to avoid stress. The only treatment I have is for pain. They can't stop any of it."

"I was able to do well. But the dioxins in my body, they don't go away, and they slowly eat away at you. I was young. I'm still young, but I'm dying. Little by little, for 37 years I've been dying," she said.

Now, Capt. Bresnahan sits beside a map of the United States scattered with pins to show the locations of fellow veterans who she has been in contact with who, she said, have experienced stateside Agent Orange exposure.

"It's something I have been outspoken about" said the now vocal activist and advocate for medical support for her fellow veterans.

"They would throw canisters, they would spray from above. They would spray. They would simulate war exposure," she said. "How many thousands of us are there?" she asked.

"On one of the exercises, they had mustard gas," she explained. "When I came out of the exercise, I blistered up.

Around my mouth, around my neck. I was treated at the hospital."

Since her downward spiral accelerated a few years ago, Capt. Bresnahan says that she has made it "my crusade to try to contact every single person I knew in the military to inform them that if they were sick too, to see my example," she said.

She said she has gone to Washington, D.C. three times to provide testimony regarding state-side chemical exposure.

Capt. Bresnahan is a member of the Vietnam Veterans of America, the Disabled Veterans of America, and the American Legion amongst other veterans organizations.

Initially denied VA medical benefits because her service records did not show service in Vietnam, she appealed and won. She relates cases where others have

been denied entitlements, medical care, and compensation and are still struggling to get the care they need.

Time Is Running Out "We don't have time. We are running out of time," She said. "There is no cure, no treatment. It just keeps coming. We are dying…we don't know how many of us there are. "Agent Orange doesn't care where you were exposed. It's an equal opportunity poison. You could be here or in Vietnam or anywhere," she said.

"People think the baby boomers are going to drain Social Security. We're not, because we'll be lucky to make it to age 60 or 62. You try to get the word out," she explained. "Everybody has to fight on their own. I have so much documentation through my medical records. What I tell the people is to use my case."

"Here's my heart break. How old do I look?" she queried. "It's caught up with

me and it's killing me...I gave me life to my country," she said.

Is there such a thing as a typical Vietnam-era solider? Capt. Bresnahan thinks that every soldier, no matter where or how they served, served their country and she is proud of them. We at the Valley Patriot are equally as proud of our veteran heroes and think our country should do everything possible to help them deal with the aftermath of their service.

Sara Payne Hayden,
WWII WASP

By: Kathleen Corey Rahme - November, 2007

METHUEN, MA - The Massachusetts Women Veterans' Network named Methuen resident, Sara Payne Hayden the Woman's Veteran of the Year at a special ceremony in the State House in Boston this month.

It was a privilege to nominate her for this honor and according to Heidi Kruckenberg the coordinator for Women Veterans' Network, naming Hayden "was a no brainer!" Wearing the 1944 uniform designed by the famous aviatrix Jacqueline Cochran, Hayden received her award in front of numerous veterans and dignitaries.

Sara Payne Hayden, WWII WASP (Women Airforce Service Pilots) was a member of the Class of 1944-10. They were an experimental, non-military group until they finally received veterans' status in 1977 from the federal government. She went to Washington with the WASP's to testify. This was the G.I.Bill Improvement Act of 1977 and it granted these women full military distinction.

During WWII, these women were responsible for testing the aircraft that were shot up during the war and also for ferrying supplies. They were also used for target practice using live ammunition for gunnery trainees; they towed targets for ground to air anti-aircraft gunnery practice and targets for air-to-air gunnery practice.

Her duty station was Randolph AFB, CIS. She was commissioned to the Air Force in July 1949. She served in active duty from August 1951-September 1953 as a Recruiting Officer. Sara Payne Hayden was born and raised in Granite Falls, NC in 1919. She was in a movie theatre in the early 1940's when she saw a reel before the show advertising and recruiting for WASP. She knew instantly that was for her. She did not have the support of her family or friends and against all odds; she borrowed money and entered the WASP program at Avenger Field in Sweetwater, TX. She borrowed money to gain the necessary flight hours before her application and during these lessons many obstacles both financially and socially were overcome in order to complete her fight time.

Sara Payne Hayden has a long history of service and the furtherance of military endeavors. She served as WASP Vice President 1975-1978 "Order of Fifinella" (the mascot designed by Walt Disney for WASP); and the Ways and Means Chair-person; Class Secretary 1965-1975; Military Veterans Affairs Chair, 1994-2007.

For the past 15 years Sara has filled out application forms for WASP's who have not received their discharge or families of WASP's and have helped them with the requirements. She sends them to Randolph Field for processing and the issuance of the DD-214 form.

Hayden was Women Military Pilots, Inc. president from 1980-1983. The Clerk of the Corporation, 1978-present, Officer; WMA, Inc. is a Public Charity of the Commonwealth of Massachusetts, with IRS tax exempt status, whose purpose is to promote and preserve for historical, education and literary purposes the role of military women pilots, navigators and aircrew in the service of their country during times of war and peace.

Hayden is a member of The Ninety-Nines, Inc. She has been a member since 1945 and has served as Treasurer and Secretary of the New England Section, on many Chapter and Section Committees, and current Legislative Chair.

She received the 1994 New England Section Honor Award.

Locally, Hayden is active in the Methuen Women's Post 417 of the American Legion. She is the Past Commander, Life Member just receiving her 50 year, Post Adjutant, Finance Officer and the Boys' State Chair.

Boys' State is an annual one week study of our democratic form of government sponsored by the American Legion. It is open to young men finishing their junior year of high school. Hayden interviews these young men after they have been approved by the high school principal.

Since 2004, Hayden has assisted the families of five of the thirty-eight WASP's killed on active duty who have been buried without a marker on their gravesite. Their memorial services were held in May of 2007 with their Veterans Administration markers in place.

Hayden's activities in the community are well known. They include speaking engagements for various groups especially schools. She was the WASP representative at the opening ceremony of the WWII exhibit at the JFK Museum; Color Guard on women's day at the Viet Nam Moving Wall; and "In Defense of Hanscom" Conference on January 30, 1995. She has been an active contributor at the Woman's Texas University archives. She was featured on MCTV (Methuen Community Television) on the series "Call to Serve" which works with the Veterans' History Project at the Library of Congress. She is part of the permanent exhibit at the Women at Work Museum in Attleboro, Massachusetts where she was also part of the keynote address for the Women Who Fly program at the museum.

Hayden is a pioneer in American military history. She broke through barriers that most can only imagine. She trail-blazed through the skies and her work and sacrifices have made it easier for military women of today. A day doesn't go by that Sara Payne Hayden doesn't celebrate women's role in the U.S. military.

We thank you Sara Payne Hayden for your military service, for your undying loyalty to your country and your community, and we are honored to call you our Valley Patriot of the Month. You are truly a hero in our midst and the people of Methuen and our nation should recognize forever the sacrifices you have made to make life better for the rest of us who have reaped the benefits of your service and sacrifice.

Kathleen Corey Rahme is the former Central District Councilor in Methuen and was elected as a city councilor "at large" in 2005. She is currently the vice-chair of the city council and is the founder of the Methuen Youth Corps. She also hosts "Call to Serve." You can E-mail her at kcoreyrahme@comcast.net

The Woman Veteran

By: Susan Piazza - April, 2010

First I would like to take a moment to congratulate Sara Hayden, WWII Women Air Force Service Pilot (WASP) for receiving the Congressional Gold Medal. This pioneer helped paved the way for me and many other women to join the military during wartime. I will always be grateful to this amazing woman for her actions. My adjutant while at the American Legion, this groundbreaking woman still works tirelessly to inspire and assist women, and men, today. A well-deserved and long overdue honor, I am glad she was able to attend and enjoy this ceremony. Well done Sara! God bless you and keep you active.

Now in keeping with the theme of the woman veteran I would like to give our women veterans some information and resources they might not otherwise be privy to.

The Women Veterans' Network under the MA Dept. of Veterans' Services in Boston is a resource all women should be aware of. This organization regularly holds seminars, speaker luncheons and Wellness Fairs among other events. Woman veterans need to be registered with this office because their events are often publicized only through their e-mails. Case in point, they recently held another Wellness Fair; unfortunately I received their e-mail after the March Valley Patriot went to press and the Fair was held before the April issue of the Valley Patriot hit the newsstands. This event dealt with ways to promote a healthy lifestyle, it offered yoga classes, mixed martial-arts, hands on holistic treatments (acupuncture, Reiki), massage therapy, aroma therapy and nutritional info. Their events are quite comprehensive. To receive their e-mails and newsletters register with Women Veterans' Network by e-mail at:

Panayiota.Bertzikis@state. iiia.aa Or register at the states website www.mass.gov/veterans, This website is not limited to women veterans. This site has information on soldiers' homes, cemeteries, suicide hotlines, etc. It is set up for easy access to information. Another means of registering with

PHOTO: ELIE RAHME

the Women Veterans' Network is by telephone at: (617) 210-5778 or register by fax at: (617) 210-5755. For users of Twitter or Facebook you can follow them at: twitter.com/womenveterans Or friend them at: facebook.com/womenveteransnetwork.

The Bedford VA Hospital has numerous services that they offer for female veterans. Preventative health care procedures such as cervical and breast cancer screening are provided. Contact the Primary Care Women's Health office at: (781) 687-3211. Any questions regarding the Women's Health Program can be addressed to Margaret Russell, LICSW, at: (781) 687-3283.

The Mental Health Clinic & the Center for Psychotherapeutic Change (CPC) at Bedford offers group and individual therapy. For information call: (781) 687-2347. There is also a PTSD & Returning Veterans Program that holds group and individual therapy specifically for PTSD. An ongoing Women's Drop In Group is supposed to be held from 1230-2. However when I called for confirmation and location there was sketchy knowledge of the program and no knowledge of the location. But call the 2347 number anyway. They were embarrassed that they did not have the information I sought. I think that after my inquiry they will do some further checking on this program they offer. I will continue to follow up as well and provide an update to this information in a future article.

As more women serve in the military the number of homeless women veterans has increased nearly doubling over the last decade according to

VA statistics. Many of these women, single mothers, fall through the cracks. (The VA has a good record of reaching out to and helping the male homeless veteran). Women with children have specific needs that need to be addressed. A website, for those who are homeless or are on the verge of becoming homeless, is:

http://www.boston.va.gov/services/social_work/women_home.asp

Another important program is the Women's Integrated Treatment and Recovery Program located at the Brockton VA. This program was specifically designed for female veterans who have problems with PTSD and substance abuse. This medical center can provide a 12 week residential program for those in need. For further information contact the clinical director Dr. Sharon Baker. If you feel that this service may be something you could use I suggest calling prior to urgent need; unless changed, the program takes a total of eight women at any one time. The website for this information   is:

http://www.boston.va.gov/services/women/mental_health_women.asp

The Dept. of Veterans Affairs has a website dedicated to health care for women veterans, you can find further information at their website: http://www.publichealth.va.gov/womenshealth/index.asp If you are not enrolled in the VA Health care system contact the VA at (781) 687-2275 or (781) 687-2597. They will assist you in the necessary paperwork needed to enroll.

If you'd rather enroll in a VA facility, refill VA Prescriptions, or manage your health care online visit www.myhealth.va.gov. One needs to sign up and register prior to using specific sites at My Health Vet. There is a section on this web site for returning service members (OEF -OIF). There is also a section for VA mental health services. I took the virtual tour; it was comprehensive and easy to understand and follow.

I hope this information is of some help. I will continue to make updates as they become available.

As always, I pray all our service men and women, here and abroad, stay safe. May god bless them and may god bless this great democracy, this United States of America. Until later, I remain, Sue Piazza, Past Commander, Chapter 2 Queen City, D.A.V.

Women In Combat

By: Methuen State Rep. Linda Dean Campbell

Over this past summer, we saw two women graduate from the Army's Ranger School, our military's premier course for both leadership and light infantry combat. While there has been a long ongoing debate upon whether American women should fill military occupations associated with close combat, we are now at a point where remaining restrictions will only be based upon an individual's ability to perform a specific job.

My husband always very much objected to the above argument being framed as about "women in combat" because we have actually had women in combat for a very long time.

During the Gulf War in which he served, a female officer my husband knew quite well was abruptly killed in a road accident. The Army also lost two conventional Blackhawk helicopters, which attempted to conduct ad hoc rescues of downed pilots behind enemy lines; one was blasted directly out of the sky with the entire crew, including a teenaged female medic. The other Blackhawk shot down, crashed with two survivors, which included a female flight surgeon who was injured, shot, and then molested after her capture by the Iraqis. There was one other female soldier, a truck driver, who was wounded, captured and also molested by the Iraqis. A further six female soldiers were killed-in-action and many others wounded by the Scud which landed upon a unit's billets on the last day of the Gulf War. And, several other female soldiers were killed or maimed in the many other accidents of the Gulf War.

Finally in our long war on terror, we have had over 150 women service members killed in the conflict, at least seven times that many have been either severely injured or wounded while at war, with many of those impacted suffering life-altering injuries which include traumatic amputation.

So this Veterans Day, let us remember all who have served, especially those of us who have been at war. Let us also remember our women have been in combat as far back as World War II.

Lieutenant Colonel Muriel Katschker U.S. Marine Corps Reserve

By: Ted Tripp – January, 2007

NORTH ANDOVER, MA – Muriel Katschker remembers well where she was on December 7, 1941. She was with her parents listening to the radio when the regular programming was interrupted by an announcer's voice saying the Japanese had just attacked and bombed Pearl Harbor. Instantly, the family knew this meant the country was at war.

At the time, however, Muriel was a young lady and had no idea that years later she would end up with a lifelong commitment to the Marine Corps.

Muriel Katschker was born and raised in Boston. She attended the city's public schools and in high school became head cheerleader on the cheerleading squad. She was also active in the Girl Scouts where she eventually achieved the rank of Mariner. This gave her the delightful opportunity to sail on the Charles River.

In 1945, following high school graduation, Muriel entered Boston University to study nursing. After a year of medical instruction, however, she decided that she wanted to concentrate more on academics and transferred into the biology program. Muriel graduated in 1950 with a bachelor of arts in biology and subsequently went to work in the research department at the Boston University Medical School.

In June of 1952, as the Korean War continued, Muriel decided she wanted to serve her country by joining the armed forces. She chose the Marine Corps Reserve, she says, "because of its high standards." She recalls that her mother cried at the enlistment news but her father, a former member of the Massachusetts National Guard, thought it was wonderful.

Muriel was sent to Quantico, Va. for 12 weeks of Officer Candidate School. Her training included the rigorous physical conditioning typical of the Marine Corps, but she recalls that the most important concept she learned was "the responsibility of being an officer." After completing OCS, Muriel was commissioned a 2nd lieutenant and was given additional training in leadership. In late 1952 Muriel was selected to be a Marine Corps command officer.

From Quantico, Muriel was sent to Parris Island, S.C. and assigned to the Women Marine Battalion, Marine Corp Recruit Depot. Here she was the company officer in charge of training recruits how to march and work together, as well as educate them in the obligations and history of the Marine Corps. After eight months, Muriel received orders to become company commander of Women Marine Permanent Personnel Company, where she was responsible for the quality of work, health and living conditions of 100-150 women Marines. 1953 was also the year she was promoted to 1st lieutenant.

By 1954 Muriel's two years of required active duty was complete. However, she asked for and was granted a three-year extension of service. She was subsequently given orders to become the inspector/instructor of the Women Marine Corps Reserve Platoon at the World-Chamberlain Naval Air Station in Minneapolis, Minn. Her platoon was part of the 4th Infantry Battalion Reserve and consisted of about 40 women.

These women were civilians who had signed up to train one weekend a month with a two-week summer camp, as Organized Marine Reservists. The women had the opportunity to work in most job functions except for combat related duties.

"Muriel's platoon won "outstanding achievement award" for summer camp performance for two consecutive years." Muriel Katschker was also the Women Marine Selection Officer, or recruiter, for Minnesota.

She traveled around the state talking with college women about careers in the Marine Corps, routinely made public appearances and was occasionally on the radio speaking about opportunities for women Marines.

In 1955 Muriel was promoted to captain.

By 1957 Muriel had completed her active duty tour and subsequently became an inactive reservist. In August she entered Harvard University/Radcliffe College to study business administration and the following year she graduated with a one-year graduate certificate.

While studying at Radcliffe, Muriel joined the Marine Corps Reserve 2nd Infantry Battalion in Boston. Here she was commander of the Women Marine Reserve Company.

In 1959 Muriel once again returned to inactive status and now began a civilian career in human resources management, working for high-tech manufacturing and consulting companies. Then, in 1961, Muriel was asked to serve as secretary to the chairman of the 1964 National Conference of the Marine Corps Reserve Officers Association. This involved a three-year planning effort for the first Boston hosting of this important national conference.

In 1962, Muriel also decided to join the Marine Corps Volunteer Training Unit 1-14 in Cambridge, Mass.; she was the unit's administrative officer. The 1-14 met one evening a week to prepare and review reports or studies for the commandant.

By 1965 she was promoted to major and in 1969 to lieutenant colonel.

During the decade of the 1960s, Muriel was always on "mobilization notice orders." In the event of a national emergency, the commandant could activate her and she would have nine days to report to Norfolk, Va. for assignment.

In 1975, 23 years after first joining the Marine Corps Reserve, Muriel Katschker requested that she be transferred to the Retired Marine Corps Reserve. Thirteen years after that, in 1988, Muriel officially retired from the military with a Commandant Certificate of Service.

Muriel Katschker is authorized to wear the National Defense Service Medal because of her military service during the Korean War years.

Muriel now volunteers her time to a number of local charities and organizations in the Merrimack Valley.

Muriel Katschker, we thank you for your years of service to our country.

Don & Linda Dean Campbell

By: Tom Duggan, Jr. - February, 2006

METHUEN, MA - Don Campbell joined the military in 1978. He was commissioned into ROTC at Pittsburgh State University in Pittsburg, Kansas. After serving active duty for his first two years in Kansas, Don was sent to Germany at the height of the cold war and stationed at various bases around the city of Stuttgart, Germany.

At the time, Don says, there were serious problems with terrorism in Europe and on military bases in particular. Explosions on American bases were frequent, Campbell recalls, " it was a big problem even though we were technically in peacetime."

Don served in Germany for about five years and trained on the East/West border between the two Germanys.

Amid the tension and the hostile environment, Campbell says it was there that he met his wife Linda. "I went to the American Express office to exchange currency in December of 1980, and while I was standing in line I met this cute lieutenant named Linda Dean."

"We were both officers," Linda added. "I remember a lot of mud and a lot of cold while we were training there. When we saw the American military spread out all over Germany, it was quite a sight.

It was almost incomprehensible to see the magnitude of the military forces lining up on the border like that. To me it was astonishing to comprehend the things that had to take place to coordinate such a buildup."

Don and Linda hit it off right away and despite their separate duties, they were able to spend a lot of time together, even traveling to the Soviet Union and East Berlin. "The abject poverty was horrible," Linda recounted. "It was just so sad - the conditions those people had to live under. They were literally starving."

"We eventually left Europe in December of 1985 and went our separate ways. The military had other plans for us," Campbell says. "I was stationed at Fort Bragg and Linda was sent to INTEL training and then to college in Arizona for about nine months."

"It gets harder and harder to stay together as you move up in rank when you are both in the military," Linda continued. "So he was back at fort Bragg and I was spending time in Air Force training, specializing in intelligence.

Don also spent time at Airborne School in Fort Benning, Georgia." Eventually, Linda was also assigned to Fort Bragg where, again, they were able to spend time together. "We were split up for a time but then met back at Fort Bragg where we were able to be together for about 2 ½ years," she recalled.

"We flew back to Methuen and were married. When we decided to start a family, that's when I decided to get out of the military because we knew we would be separated again," Linda continued.

Don, however, stayed in the Army and in 1990, during the build up to the first Gulf War, volunteered for active duty. He remembers being told that he would never be sent over to the Middle East in October of 1990, but within a few short months the Army tracked him down and shipped him to Saudi Arabia.

"We were at a family funeral on his side of the family and the Army somehow found out where we were and called us right there on the phone to notify him he was going to the Middle East," recalled Linda. "Our daughter was born about three days after Don left for the war."

"I arrived in the Middle East on the 22nd of December (1990) and I was there until the 19th of July 1991. I ended up flying in on Christmas Eve, just in time to see the Bob Hope show. It was great," he said.

Campbell was assigned to the 10th Personnel Command, which is part of the 3rd Army Division and hand-selected to manage the database at headquarters.

"When I got there they didn't have an automator. The general had to designate someone to do the casualty reporting and personnel management and I was selected.

My duties included managing casualties, tracking people on the battlefield from command headquarters and setting up a data processing installation where we did remote mainframe data entry."

"We set up a database before we were ready to kick off the ground war because we wanted to have the right people in the right places to sustain thirty to sixty days of continual military operations.

Casualty projections were like playing the lottery at the time; it was hit and miss. The low figure was 250 casualties and the high was 20,000. The Iraqis were really inept. Otherwise we would have had more casualties. It all had to be managed by computer at Headquarters.

As an expert in Army strategy, Don worked at the Headquarters of Commanding General John J. General Yeosok. Here, all the logistics for the war were worked out. "Our job was to get the troops the information they needed. We also ran the postal locator which made us very popular," he laughed.

"You are putting people from all different units together for one purpose, coordinating where everyone is supposed to be and where they are going, where the casualties are and where they are being relocated to."

"Basically, I ran the world's biggest computer hacking operation in the Gulf War to synchronize forces, get the mail where it needed to be, get information to the troops - even if it was something like the death of a family member so we could coordinate getting them home. We controlled the troop flow and redeployment system."

Stationed in Riyadh, Saudi Arabia, and then in a major detachment in Darahn, Campbell helped to run a liaison with 7th Corps and 18th Airborne Corps.

He said the possibility of being hit by a scud missile by the Iraqis was always a concern and an immediate danger.

We were always a target because we were at Headquarters. They were shooting at us in Riyadh.

We didn't know what might be attached to the scuds. We knew they had the capability of weaponizing their scuds with chemical agents.

When the ground war kicked off, I was in Daran, and if our guys got hit with chemicals, it was my job to figure out what to do." As it turned out, American forces were lucky not to encounter biological or chemical attacks by the Iraqis.

"We had a lot of operational problems too. There were only two data uplinks in the country. One was in Riyadh and whatever bandwidth they had was at command and control. In Dhahran they installed a satellite uplink and if the Iraqis had taken out that uplink, we would have been in big trouble because the whole war was orchestrated by computer."

Campbell has had several severe health problems since the Gulf War. "Don has gotten very sick from the war. We think it was because they gave him so many shots before they sent him to the Middle East and they gave them all at once.

That's what the military did at the time. I don't think they realized how powerful that stuff was and doing it all at the same time took a toll on him," Linda said.

"After the war, everyone was coming up positive for TB. We knew we didn't have it, but we were testing positive so something was definitely going on," Don added.

Linda says that from the day he got back from the war it was apparent that Don wasn't feeling well. "When he came home he could barely walk. He had written me a letter after getting the shots and at that time he was laid out for a couple of days. The chemical and biological threat was there, so they had to get the shots."

Since Don's daughter was born three days after he arrived in the Middle East, when he returned to the States he wasn't sure if she would even know who he was. "When I came back, I went first to Washington D.C. and then to Indianapolis. On my first week off I came home and was surprised to see that my daughter knew who I was right away. It was very emotional."

"We were at Logan Airport and we had a large sign that said 'WELCOME HOME MAJOR DAD,' Linda fondly recalled. "About a hundred people started gathering at the airport where we were waiting and when he came off the plane, our daughter just jumped into his arms."

Don Campbell retired as a Lt. Colonel in 1999 at 42 years old.

Don and Linda Campbell, thank you so much for your combined service to the people of the United States. We are proud to honor you both as Valley Patriots for your personal sacrifices and endless dedication to the safety of the world.

House Passes Legislation to Honor Women Airforce Service Pilots (WASP) July, 2009

WASHINGTON, DC - June 16, 2009 - The House of Representatives today voted to award the Women Airforce Service Pilots (WASP) with the Congressional Gold Medal, the highest civilian honor given in the United States, in recognition of their service during World War II. Approximately one thousand women served as Women Airforce Service Pilots and performed a variety of missions in support of the war effort including flying aircraft from factories to military bases, towing targets for air-to-air combat practice, and transporting cargo. They were the first women in history trained to fly American military aircraft. The legislation was approved in the Senate last month and will now go to the President for his signature.

Methuen resident Sara Payne Hayden, now 89, was one of the Airforce Service Pilots. Hayden test flew previously damaged aircraft to ensure repairs were successful prior to their reintroduction into combat service, a dangerous, but critical assignment in the war effort.

Hayden also attended Congressional hearings seeking long-delayed recognition for the work of the Women Airforce Service Pilots, who were finally awarded military service status in 1977.

"I was one of the group of women who were trained and then flew military airplanes in World War II, where we were volunteers just doing our job," said Sara Payne Haden. "Now that we are known for our service, I find it amazing that we are recognized with this high honor. It is quite a privilege to say thank you to those honoring us."

"This highly appropriate honor recognizes the contributions of everyday citizens like Sara Payne Hayden whose sacrifices in support of the war effort helped to ensure the preservation of freedom in our time," said Congresswoman Niki Tsongas, a cosponsor of the House bill. "Simultaneously, the Women Airforce Service Pilots paved the way for future generations of women to serve their country."

As the American war effort in World War II expanded, the need for male combat pilots overseas increased. Thousands of women volunteered for the newly created Women Airforce Service Pilots. By the middle of 1942 women pilots began flying U.S. Army Air Forces aircraft within the United States.

The Congressional Gold Medal is the highest civilian honor given in the United States. The medal is an "expression of national appreciation for distinguished achievements and contributions." Each medal is authorized by an Act of Congress, and past recipients include Winston Churchill, Rosa Parks, and Thomas Edison.

Larry Cogswell Pt. 1

By: Sid Smith - May, 2015

When I recently learned that the local chapter of the EAA (Experimental Aircraft Association) was bringing an original flying Boeing B-17 WWII bomber to Lawrence Airport this May 22nd to May 25th, I was reminded of an acquaintance I had formed with a friend in West Newbury: Lawrence "Larry" Cogswell. I often met Larry at the West Newbury Post Office and then sometimes join him Wednesday evenings at the bar in the Park Lunch in Newburyport. Larry, it turned out, was a most enjoyable storyteller with tales of his service in the Eighth Air Force in WWII.

He was also one of the nicest guys I have ever had the outright privilege to meet.

Having since moved from West Newbury, I tried to contact Larry about the forthcoming B-17 fly-in, but was shocked and saddened to learn that he had passed away on February 1st of this year. To me, Larry Cogswell was indeed a more than sterling example of what has come to be termed the "Greatest Generation," and it seemed to me that I had to do something to remind people that the surviving few of these folks are indeed getting fewer every year. They really are heroes, although I doubt you would ever hear them say it, and there are, at best, an ever fewer number of them still living among us. It also seemed to me that Larry was a typical example of the young American kid who answered the call from his nation and "joined up" to fight in WWII.

Larry is gone now but let us see what we might be able to piece together of his and other's stories from the Eighth:

Lawrence H. Cogswell was born in Easton, Maine on March 18th, 1924. He attended school there and then, at Fort Devens, MA, on December 16, 1943 he enlisted in the U.S. Army Air Force "...for the duration of the war plus 6 months" and in the inscrutable manner of armies everywhere he was trained to become an air gunner. Some of the guys went to various aircraft of the period (B-17's, B-24's, B-25's etc.). As fate would have it, Larry was assigned to B-17's and the growing Eighth Air Force. I do not know for certain, but I would guess that he was probably excited about being posted to the 8th AF (which even at that time probably meant England). But I also suspect that most of those young guys did not fully realize what they were getting into since one of the most prevalent signs of youth is their given belief in their own immortality. I suspect that as increasing numbers of new, unknown faces replaced older, known faces in the briefing rooms and familiar aircraft no longer appeared on the hardstands ... that sense of immortality began to slowly fade for most of those young air crews.

In those increasingly distant days, most young "airmen" still believed that the B-17 was the king of bombers and undoubtedly deserved its nickname: the "Flying Fortress." They also believed that the newly minted "Norden" bombsight could place its bombs in a "pickle barrel" from 20,000 ft., or so it was said. Unfortunately the reality was to prove enlightening and hitting that pickle barrel would prove to be a great deal more demanding, difficult, and hazardous than anyone had then imagined.

I had dimly realized this myself, because around early 1944, my mother and I were returning from Pittsfield, MA where my father was working as a welder/steamfitter (and thus an "essential war worker" - so essential in fact that we had a valued "C" sticker for gasoline, and maybe some tires, on the corner of the windshield of our old DeSoto coupe.) My mother and I were probably on the old Boston and Albany Railroad when we made a stop near Springfield to take on a horde of young crewmen from nearby Westover Airfield. They were, to say the least, spirited and were a genuinely rowdy hunch, but I have in the ensuing years often wondered how much of that rowdy spirit was in fact a mask to cover their own deeper, quieter, concerns. They were polite enough toward my mother and I, but I remember being more than chagrined that they filled virtually every space and every seat on that long slow train.

But to a very young kid there was worse to come: I had just received as a gift a truly appreciated new toy: a wooden toy bomber with a red body and blue wings that had a hole drilled through the body lengthwise. At the forward end of the hole there was a small mirror mounted at an angle, so that when you looked into the hole at the tail you could see your feet. Of course it was a pathetic thing by today's standards, but remember that in those days what brought the war home to most adults was the advent of ration cards and family members going off to war while to children the reality was that most toys had changed from cast metal to carved wood or paper. At the front of my little bomber there was a slotted handle which when pulled, would drop two small wooden dowels as "bombs." Now you should remember that all those young men on that train with us were actual bomber crews mostly on their way to Europe.

And then they discovered my "bomber."

Now by the time we arrived at South Station in Boston only the good Lord Himself knows just how many paper cups had been "bombed" and destroyed and how many dollars in wagers had been exchanged, but I can say that somehow, someone remembered just whose toy it was and I eventually did get my "bomber" back. But I was indeed chagrined... and then some. Those trains at that time moved slowly and they had commandeered my "bomber" for hours.

At the time I neither realized nor appreciated what I had experienced... but in the ensuing years I have often wondered just how many of those so very young guys ever made it back home.

The 8th Air Force in England and the 15th Air Force in Italy (combined) lost around 3,200 B-17's and about another 2,500 so badly damaged that they had to be scrapped.

That figure translates to 24,288 aircrew killed in action.

But to a kid of about 7 or 8 years old... even then...

They were all heroes.

NEXT MONTH PART II

PART II

By: Sid Smith - June, 2015

A young kid of 19 years old, like so many of the young guys my mother and I had met, was being assigned to the 8th AF and sent to England; a kid named Larry from Easton, Maine. His orders had to have read something along these lines:

"Cogswell, Lawrence H., PFC,, 8th AF, 45th Combat Wing, 452nd Bomb Group, 730th Bomb Squadron, Captain Hayes, Ralph S., Jr., Commanding Officer, AF Station 142." Once in England, Larry discovered that "Air Force Station 142" was at an airfield in East Anglia known as Deopham Green. It was a somewhat rural place in 1944 and the crew quarters were in what was known at the time as Quonset (or sometimes Nissen) huts. Each hut housed twenty guys and at least most of the huts had poured concrete floors. Heating was by a small British coke-fired stove and given British weather, was never quite adequate.

Firewood was scarce (at that time most Brits did not have much if any). There was no hot water either, but there was a standing (and firm) order that all aircrew were to be clean-shaven. Thus, shaving before missions was always considerably less than pleasant. That order was not through any undue care about personal hygiene and appearance, but rather due to the fact that most missions were to be flown at high altitude ... and oxygen masks had to fit, and fit well, or you were likely to die from anoxia. Missions lasted for hours, and many of them were flown at well over 20,000 feet. It is hard to imagine today a dress requirement, the ignorance of which could result in nothing short of an extremely unpleasant death. And everyone on the aircrew of a B-17 had an essential position. One man down meant one position or weapon unavailable and that drove the odds up against you, odds that were already none too good.

Regardless of what we on the home front were told at the time, the crews considered the food terrible, consisting mostly of powdered eggs and potatoes (and probably sometimes peas). In fact, there grew up a sort of cottage industry, derived from the fine old British tradition of poaching game, as several of the guys would quietly raid the adjoining landowner's game park and poach a few pheasants for the larder. Larry was also to learn that on-board rations during missions consisted solely of hard candy because anything else would probably require a relief call of nature and that the temperatures at altitude made frostbite an all-too-real genuine risk.

Frostbite was almost as serious a threat as the actual enemy! There was one mission where the indicated outside air temperature was -85° F. Imagine an average temperature of around 85 below zero and having to stand near or at an open window for hours with the wind howling by at somewhere around one hundred fifty miles per hour.

Try that for a wind chill factor!

There was often clouds and quite some fog and lots of rain, which meant that too much flying had to be done under considerably less than optimum conditions. In translation, that meant that many missions were flown in which the first genuinely dangerous event consisted of climbing up through the fog and cloud cover without colliding with some other B-17. Those collisions were very nearly always fatal to both airplanes. To this day there are several local churches around East Anglia with windows or plaques dedicated to the memories of aircrews killed before they had even been able to get out of British airspace.

I am certain that, even then, Larry was a quietly affable young guy and he must have seen several of the other B-17's at Deopham Green with their always colorful and imaginative "nose art" such as: "E-Rat-Icator", "Sunrise Serenade", "Dog Breath", "Scrappy Jr.", "Flatbush Floogie", "Now Go!", "3 Cads and a Lad", "Mugwump", "Sack Time Soux", "Our Buddy" (dedicated to the P-47 escort fighters), and many equally colorful others. All of these were marked on the vertical stabilizer with the letter "L" inside a square, which designated that the B-17 was based at Deopham Green.

Some would be around for a few missions.

Some wouldn't.

Most of the East Anglia airfields looked similar to each other. Most had one or two large-ish hangars (although most maintenance was carried out on the hardstands in the open in whatever weather was happening). There were hardstands for the fortresses, taxiways, and the prominent control tower with its little glassed-in room atop the brick and mortar block-like building. There were the always-present Quonset huts and guard shacks, mess halls, ops rooms, weather room, medical hut, vehicle parks, bomb dumps (always located as far as was practical from anything else), and places for the ever present bicycles (if you could get your hands on one). Deopham Green had what they all had: a main runway. Deopham Green's was about 6,000 feet long and considering the bomb and fuel loads the fortresses were too-often required to carry, that was probably just this side of not-quite-long-enough. The runway width often posed a unique challenge, as it was hardly unknown for someone to accidentally slide his "bird" wide and put a landing gear off the runway and into the mud. If that sort of thing had only affected that one aircraft the overall effect might have been minimal, but all too often it would back up and delay the takeoffs, which in turn would delay the join-ups, which in turn would delay the climb outs, which in turn would delay and affect the formation of the combat boxes and ultimately the main columns. All for want of a few feet either side of the runway or one seemingly small misjudgment!

Sometimes those accumulated delays would result in timing problems and because of these, German fighters might be given time between "waves" of bombers for their fighters to land, refuel, rearm, and then....

...you could have something such as the first major attack against Schweinfurt, Germany in which the Eighth lost 60 bombers and 600 aircrew on one mission!

Imagine the feeling within those surviving crews when they were told that they would have to go back and try to finish the job. It is easy to imagine that when those surviving aircrews heard that news there was no universal groan, but rather a slow quiet exhaling combined with a silent sense of inevitability.

Before each individual squadron takeoff it required the efforts of thousands of people involved in intelligence, target selections, weather info including not just surface conditions, but winds aloft at varying altitudes as well as icing conditions, target routes, ordinance required with fusing requirements, squadron aircraft availability, aircrew availability, alternate target choices, decoys and decoy routes, fighter escort range, expected fighter attacks, known flak (anti-aircraft) installations etc.

And it all had to work seamlessly or.... some would pay the ultimate price.

As the old saying goes the ground crews especially knew the absolute necessity of getting it all right because of the all-too-truism: for want of a nail...

It was those ground personnel remaining behind who knew the quiet reality of what was termed "sweating them in" as they waited for the familiar sound of the returning bombers. (To this day if I hear the rare so-distinctive sound of a B-17 it will bring me upright out of a deep sleep. No one of that era will ever forget the unique sound of those four engines.) Everyone among the ground crews back at Deopham Green worried silently about whether or not their crew and their plane would be among the survivors ... and if the landing gear was okay ... and if the flaps were not shot away ...if the brakes were working ...if the rudder was still there .... but, worst of all, if the dreaded colored flare arced upward from a stricken aircraft and then slid over and fell slowly toward the ground indicating that there were wounded, or worse, on board.

Every man knew how many aircraft had been sent, whether there had been any "aborts", and each man silently counted the returning bombers as they did their classic "peel off" to land. Each man hoping that if "his" plane and "his" crew were missing that "ops" would get a call telling them the welcome news that those boys had been forced to land at some other airfield in East Anglia. As each plane taxied slowly to its hardstand with usually only the outboard engines running, the sound slowly died away as props stopped turning, and the entire bomber seemed somehow to sag as if in tired relief. The crews slowly emerged, faces drawn, tired, emotionally exhausted, quietly glad that once more they had survived, and waited for the ride back to the debriefing room. Sometimes they might discuss something that had happened on the mission, but usually they just wanted to get out of their flight gear, get something to eat, and sleep, if sleep could come at all.

They tried not to notice the ambulances, or the fire trucks.

If they were very, very lucky, they might get a pass to go to the railroad station at Attleborough and go to London. In London the most popular destination for the guys was the Red Cross-operated Mostyn Club near the Marble Arch because that was one place that actually had heated baths...

and a guy could just lie there and soak in sheer warm relative luxury. They never knew when they might get another opportunity.

By the way, that railroad station at Attleborough is still there and on the wall is a plaque dedicated by the grateful British to the 452nd Bomb Group.

All of the squadrons had their stories and the 452nd alone had a wealth of them, some of them pleasant, some of them not, but all of them in their own way memorable.

PART III

By: Sid Smith - July, 2015

Before each individual squadron takeoff, it required the efforts of thousands of people involved in intelligence, target selections, weather info including not just surface conditions, but winds aloft at varying altitudes as well as icing conditions, target routes, ordinance required with fusing requirements, squadron aircraft availability, aircrew availability, alternate target choices, decoys and decoy routes, fighter escort range, expected fighter attacks, known flak (anti-aircraft) installations etc.

And it all had to work seamlessly or ... some would pay the ultimate price.

As the old saying goes, the ground crews especially knew the absolute necessity of getting it all right because of the all-too-truism: for want of a nail...

It was those ground personnel remaining behind who knew the quiet reality of what was termed "sweating them in" as they waited for the familiar sound of the returning bombers. (To this day if I hear the rare so-distinctive sound of a B-17, it will bring me upright out of a deep sleep. No one of that era will ever forget the unique sound of those four engines). Everyone among the ground crews back at Deopham Green worried silently about whether or not their crew and their plane would be among the survivors ... and if the landing gear was okay ... and if the flaps were not shot away ... if the brakes were working ... if the rudder was still there ... but, worst of all, if the dreaded colored flare arced upward from a stricken aircraft and then slid over and fell slowly toward the ground indicating that there were wounded, or worse, on board.

Every man knew how many aircraft had been sent, whether there had been any "aborts", and each man silently counted the returning bombers as they did their classic "peel off" to land. Each man hoping that if "his" plane and "his" crew were missing that "ops" would get a call telling them the welcome news that those boys had been forced to land at some other airfield in East Anglia. As each plane taxied slowly to its hardstand with usually only the outboard engines running, the sound slowly died away as props stopped turning, and the entire bomber seemed somehow to sag as if in tired relief. The crews slowly emerged, faces drawn, tired, emotionally exhausted, quietly glad that once more they had survived, and waited for the ride back to the debriefing room. Sometimes they might discuss something that had happened on the mission, but usually they just wanted to get out of their flight gear, get something to eat, and sleep, if sleep could come at all.

They tried not to notice the ambulances, or the fire trucks.

If they were very, very lucky, they might get a pass to go to the railroad station at Attleborough and go to London. In London the most popular destination for the guys was the Red Cross-operated Mostyn Club near the Marble Arch because that was one place that actually had heated baths ... and a guy could just lie there and soak in sheer warm relative luxury. They never knew when they might get another opportunity.

By the way, that railroad station at Attleborough is still there and on the wall is a plaque dedicated by the grateful British to the 452nd Bomb Group.

All of the squadrons had their stories and the 452nd alone had a wealth of them, some of them pleasant, some of them not, but all of them in their own way memorable.

One of the unusual ones concerned a B-17 from Deopham Green named "Sunrise Serenade" after the popular song of the period. "Sunrise Serenade" was hit hard on a mission and had been hit so hard that several of the crew decided the time had come to leave. A few were able to use their parachutes and get out, but "Sunrise Serenade" was damaged so badly that it broke apart and crashed. Part of the bomber crashed onto the lands of a castle in Belgium and the tail nearly hit the castle itself. What was left of

"Sunrise" then lay nearly forgotten for half a century until a Belgian group decided to attempt to recover whatever might be left.

Back in the states, one of the survivors who had jumped from the falling bomber heard about the recovery effort and made the cryptic remark, "If they find a pair of boots, they're mine!" When questioned about why he had not been wearing his boots, he explained that at altitude it was so cold that the G.I. boots were not adequate protection against the cold so many of the guys would bring along a pair of boots to use on the ground in place of their flying boots in case they were shot down. Flying boots were not built to endure walking. The damage to "Sunrise" had been so sudden and so drastic that the gunner had had no time to do anything except make certain his parachute was strapped on and then jump.

Yes, the search group found his boots!

It is unknown if they gave them back ... but it would have been one hell of a souvenir!

Another story concerned a young lieutenant who was the co-pilot of a B-17. He and his crew were jumped by a pair of Luftwaffe Ju-88 fighter-bombers and shot up badly with both of their left engines so badly damaged that they had to stop them and feather the props. (Note: actually it was a good thing for the allies that some "genius" in Germany had decided that the Ju-88 had to be redesigned to have dive-bombing capabilities with the result that it was built much heavier than it needed to be with resulting lower performance. Had they left it as originally designed it would have been an even more fearsome opponent.) The two pilots realized that it was going to be a truly daunting task to keep a loaded B-17 airborne on only two engines, and even more so, on only the two right engines; they realized they would have to "go for the deck" and lighten the bomber as much as possible. They jettisoned their bomb load and began to throw out every piece of non-essential equipment as they traded about twenty-five thousand feet for additional range.

Carefully looking at their briefing maps, they plotted a return to England that avoided all of the known flak installations. Or so they thought.

But even at their lightened weight, flying their B-17 at minimum altitude on only the two right engines was a nearly herculean task and the two pilots had to help each other with all they had to keep it in the air. At one point they almost lost it when they had to climb a few feet to miss some high-tension wires and they must have had to virtually stand on the rudders to keep the stricken bomber flying anywhere near straight.

Seeing a farmhouse below them, they barely missed the roof and discovered that, masked by the house, there was a flak gun installation in the back yard! The surprised gunners opened up on them and tore up the right inboard engine setting it on fire and thereby making moot the point of trying to keep their B-17 in the air.

Choosing a nearby field they put their Boeing down as lightly as they could and when the smoke settled found that the crew were basically unhurt. However as they climbed out they saw German troops from the nearby flak gun running toward them and firing in the air to frighten off the few Belgians who had run over in an attempt to help the Americans. The two pilots later reported that they were "roughed up" by the Germans and as they were marched off, they saw two young Belgian boys on their bicycles who had witnessed the entire crash landing and subsequent events from a road adjacent to the field. They did not notice that one of them was writing something on a scrap of paper.

As an interesting aside, because the pilot was Jewish, his dog tags were stamped with the letter "H" (for Hebrew) but it was a common practice for Jewish aircrew to have a second set of dog tags stamped with a "P" (for Protestant) which they wore on missions. The Germans often asked if there were any Jews among their POW's; but no one ever talked.

They were eventually sent to Stalag Luft 3 in Poland (which was the location about which the actor Steve McQueen later made the subject of his film The Great Escape), and it was not nearly as habitable a place as the film portrayed. Our two pilots also endured what became known to a few as the Stalag Luft 3 death march as the Germans force-marched the camp several hundred miles away in deep winter to keep the valuable American aircrews from being captured by the advancing Russians. More than a few Americans died from cold and starvation. Our co-pilot saw and experienced it.

Greg Page
THE WAR ON TERROR

By: Gary Mannion, Jr. - September, 2010

LOWELL, MA - Greg Page sat on his couch waiting to leave for Newark International Airport to catch his plane to San Francisco; he was about to embark on his senior year at Stanford University.

Whatever it was that seemed important to him as he sat there was, although he didn't know it yet, about to become insignificant. Most seniors heading off for their last year of college are worried about finding jobs and making their place in the real world. This senior in college was about to join the real world very fast and before he knew quite what had happened.

Greg was distractedly watching TV while he waited for the time to leave. Suddenly a news bulletin flashed across the screen; a plane had hit one of the towers of the World Trade Center in New York. Greg called his mother to warn her that she would be hearing the news, but not to worry because it was not Dad's tower.

In 1993, when the World Trade Center was bombed, Greg's father made it all the way down the stairs -- covered in soot but, thankfully, all in one piece. So, Greg figured that this was just like that last time and he decided to believe that he had nothing to worry about. Like so many watching, he assumed that this was some sort of horrible accident and that, like last time, his father would escape unharmed.

But mere moments later he and the rest of the world witnessed actions that made it clear that this was no fluke; this was a part of a deliberate attack on the United States of America. More importantly to Greg, a plane had just crashed into his father's building. In fact, the plane seemed close to his father's office on the 72nd floor. For Greg the next few hours were, as they were for a lot of Americans, very long hours indeed. Terrified and confused, Greg had no idea if his father was dead or alive.

Greg was one of the lucky ones waiting for news of a loved one that day. For some reason unknown to him, his father had taken a later train that morning and had only just arrived in the lobby of his building when the first plane hit.

Horrified and confused, his father decided not to attend work that day. Not sure just what was happening, he left the tower and headed for St. Paul's Episcopal chapel, which is where he was when each of the towers collapsed. He called Greg to let him know that he was alright and Greg spread the word throughout the family.

Greg felt like he had just survived a game of Russian roulette. His father escaped an unimaginably horrific death thanks to the happy accident of taking a later train than usual. And Greg, by not choosing Flight 93 to San Francisco, had avoided being aboard the flight now famous for those heroic passengers who overpowered their hijackers and diverted an intended attack on the Capitol or White House. Naturally, all of this had a huge impact on Greg. He remembers sitting there in shock that night, thankful that his and his father's lives had been spared, grieving for all those innocent lives that had been lost and, beyond that, not really knowing what to think.

Not knowing when air travel would resume, Greg decided to take a cross-country bus from Newark to San Francisco. He noticed, to his surprise, that as he traveled further west people seemed less affected by the recent events. When he finally got to Stanford, he had begun to feel like he was experiencing 9/11 and its aftermath in a very different way from many of his peers.

While the demonstrations and discussions around him seemed very critical of the U.S., implying, if not saying straight out, that the United

States had no right to invade Afghanistan, Greg felt quite difficulty. He, along with many Americans, felt that nothing could justify the attacks of 9/11.

When he thinks back on this time, Greg recalls: "I could see a double standard that some people were applying to domestic versus foreign terrorists. In some people's eyes, it was okay to label a Timothy McVeigh or a Ted Kaczinski a "wacko" and dismiss them outright, but if a group of people from another country attacked us, then there must be some justification. I personally felt pretty strongly against all terrorists."

During that year, Greg was the Opinions Editor of the Stanford Daily and wrote several editorials stating his belief that the military incursion in Afghanistan was the right course of action, and that the attacks could never be justified. He then followed through on his original post-college plan to get a Master's in Education and get into teaching. He enrolled at the Harvard Graduate School of Education, doing his student teaching in 9th and 10th grade history in Cambridge.

With the Afghanistan War going on and the Iraq War starting, Greg began to feel a tug towards the military. He decided that it wasn't enough for him to just teach about history or write about what others did; he felt compelled to be a doer, to take part in history. Greg followed his heart and decided to enlist in either the Army or Navy Reserve while still pursuing full-time teaching.

In 2004, he began Officer Candidate School in Pensacola, FL. After being commissioned he then moved on to the Naval Intelligence Officer basic course. He soon graduated in 2005, winning the Admiral Porterfield prize as the #1 overall Excellent student in his graduating class.

From 2006-2008 Greg did some work overseas, due to security purposes we have chosen not to describe exactly what he was involved in.

The time that Greg spent in Iraq working made him want to transfer over to one of the ground services, where he could have a more direct, long-term role in the Global War on Terror.

He knew he wanted to get back to Massachusetts, where he attended graduate school so he contacted the Mass Guard, where he would later take employment at the end of his stint in the Navy. He found an opportunity in Groton, CT as the Intel Officer for the Admiral's staff at Submarine Group TWO.

Greg would soon meet his future wife, Ratriey, in July of 2008 they were soon engaged in August of 2009, and just got married this past July.

He is currently serving in a full-time capacity with the Mass Army Guard. He is now serving as the Brigade Assistant Intelligence Officer. He was part of those mobilized to support two State Active Duty missions: Operation RISING WATER and Operation BROKEN PIPE. The first was flood related, the second was after the pipe burst in Weston. Although in both cases, he was restricted to administrative work he did have a hand in the operations.

Like the dedicated military man he is Greg is dedicated to improving his community and staying involved as much as he can. He is a life member of Walker-Rogers VFW post in Lowell, Treasurer of Lowell Downtown Neighborhood Association, Senior Vice Chair of Lowell Global War Veterans. Member of Lowell Mission Church on Andover St and recently has volunteered with the Sam Meas campaign.

Greg is a prime example of an American hero. From that day on his couch in 2001 to his recent work with the National Guard Greg has always kept his country close to his heart.

Although he may not of known it that day but the attacks he and the rest of the world witnessed inspired him to take action and to stand up for his country.

We as Americans can be thankful that we have people like Greg willing to answer the call of courage and be that hero. We are proud to name him our Valley Patriot of the month.

Sgt. Charles P. Sarantos
U.S. Army
112th Allied Division

By: Helen Mooradkanian - January, 2014

NORTH ANDOVER, MA - "We were the second largest convoy to leave for Europe—5,000 of us aboard the U.S. Army troopship George Washington— when we left New York in early 1944, bound for Liverpool, England. By the time we arrived in England in April, two months before the D-Day invasion of June 6, our ranks had swelled enormously," recalls Sergeant Charles P. Sarantos, 112th Allied Airborne division, then an 18-year old Lowell native who now lives in North Andover.

"On the way, we were attacked by a fleet of German warships, submarines, and aircraft. The cannons' deep boom reverberated non-stop. Bombs exploded. Ships caught fire. We rescued a great many survivors from the ocean, bringing them on board our ship." Charlie still remembers the thunderous booming of cannon that resonated deep in the bowels of the ship's galley, where he was on duty slicing huge slabs of bacon during that long voyage. His unit had been assigned to KP duty.

Once he reached England, Charlie advanced across Europe serving in five major campaigns of WWII. The 112th Allied Airborne Division—

comprised of Americans, British, and French—saw combat at Rome-Arno in Italy... in southern France—where they repelled the German counteroffensive in the Battle of the Bulge (December 1944-January 1945) and Operation "Varsity" in March 1945...then advanced through the Rhineland, Ardennes-Alsace, and Central Europe, and ultimately reached Berlin.

First assigned to the 512th Airborne Signal Corps, which later became part of the 112th Signal Battalion (Special Operations) (Airborne) and the 112th Allied Airborne Division, Charlie set up critical communications networks, working with the American Waco CG-4A combat gliders that had been introduced in February 1941 to transport troops and equipment. Behind enemy lines. In stealth. Under cover of darkness. To shock and confuse the enemy.

American combat gliders were shipped, unassembled, in huge wooden crates by cargo vessels to England, where they were assembled and then flight-tested. A single CG-4A glider required five enormous crates. In Manchester, England, Charlie saw them being assembled by untrained British civilians before the Ninth Air Force took over their assembly.

These gliders were towed across the skies by C-47 military transports, and relied on two-way radios to communicate with the C-47 pilot. Charlie set up the communications system, including a 10-volt generator on a trailer loaded into the glider. He also reinforced the CG-4A's honeycombed plywood floors to prevent heavy equipment from crashing through (which sometimes happened).

Charlie remembers seeing American glider pilots being trained in England. Many were civilians with only a pilot's license who had been allowed to volunteer because of the shortage of trained operators.

Germany had been effectively using gliders in WWII since 1940 and by 1941 had 300,000 trained glider pilots, produced by their numerous national glider clubs. Great Britain began their program in 1940, followed by the U.S. in 1941 after entering the war.

Four American glider missions flew as part of the D-Day invasion of Normandy, two with extensive fighter escort, although Charlie's unit was not involved. His unit did see their first action on August 15, 1944, when their combat gliders infiltrated France in Operation "Dragoon," dropping troops and equipment near Le Muy, France. After setting up a command post there, five days later they moved the post to Valescuic, France, to support combat teams attacking a front along the northeast from the northernmost end to the Mediterranean coast 20 kilometers south.

Charlie himself flew on a number of glider missions to test the effectiveness of the radio communications. He had many close brushes with death, more than he wishes to recall.

Yet always, always, underneath he sensed the everlasting arms of the eternal God.

GLIDERS: "FLYING COFFINS"

These combat gliders were dubbed "silent wings" or, more aptly, "flying coffins." A 300-foot long nylon rope, about 1-inch in diameter, attached the glider to the C-47's tail via a D-ring coupler. Once they approached the drop zone, the glider was released to float silently to the ground with its cargo of troops and equipment.

The pilot had virtually no control over where he landed. No engine. No propeller. No weapons. In the midst of combat, the gliders were targets before they even landed, so a fast descent was crucial, preferably from altitudes as low as 400 to 600 feet. When under enemy fire, they had to crash-land in trees or other obstacles set up by the Germans. The pilot had only seconds to zero in on his landing spot.

As General William Westmoreland, U.S. Army, Retired, said, "Every landing was a genuine do-or-die situation...They were the only aviators during WWII who had no motors, no parachutes, and no second chances."

The CG-4A glider could carry a load of more than 4,000 pounds—the pilot and co-pilot plus 13 troops, or various combinations of troops with a jeep, or a 75mm howitzer along with 18 rounds of ammunition and gun crew, or a 1/4-ton truck, or a small bulldozer, as well as ammunition and other supplies. They provided backup for the paratroopers who had arrived earlier.

As the Americans advanced toward Berlin, wire and radio communications became extremely difficult as the supported combat teams moved rapidly over mountains in southern France. Charlie's unit commandeered the local wire networks to support the forward teams, some as far as 100 miles from the command post. They not only set up direct lines from the command post to each team but they also installed lines between the teams and provided teletype and wire communications to the Sixth Army Group Headquarters.

"BIG THREE" Postdam Conference

With Germany's unconditional surrender, Charlie, as part of the 112th Army Airborne Signal Battalion, was with the first American troops that entered Berlin for the Allied occupation of that city. The Brandenburg Gate insignia indicates their service in Berlin.

There in Berlin Charlie was present at an historic event that climaxed the end of WWII: the Potsdam Conference, July 16–August 2, 1945, that brought together the "Big Three" heads of state—U.S. President Harry Truman, British Prime Minister Winston Churchill, and Soviet Premier Josef Stalin. Charlie was assigned to set up and work communications during the conference, sending and receiving messages, because of his expertise in electronics and his seniority in the military.

At Potsdam, the "Big Three" discussed post-war arrangements in Europe and the portioning of the postwar world. One result was a joint proclamation by the U.S., Great Britain, and China that mandated the terms of Japan's surrender, ending with the ultimatum that Japan must immediately agree to unconditionally surrender, or else face "prompt and utter destruction."

"ON A WING AND A PRAYER"

Charlie grew up in a Christian family committed to God and to prayer. "We lived next door to the Greek Orthodox Church, and I literally spent most of my growing up years in the church. I believe in God. I believe in the power of prayer. During the war, I had many close calls with death but I survived miraculously. I always felt God's protection during the war, and I still feel His protection to this day. I know God answers prayer. He has blessed me abundantly."

The psalmist wrote, "The Lord is my rock and my fortress and my deliverer; my God, my strength, in whom I will trust...I will call upon the Lord, who is worthy to be praised, so shall I be saved from my enemies" (Psalm 18:2-3).

Sgt. Thomas Siopes
U.S. Army

By: Helen Mooradkanian - December, 2013

In the early dawn hours of March 25, 1969, in the rice paddies of South Vietnam, near Bong Son, in the province of Binh Dinh, 22-year old Sergeant Thomas F. Siopes, Company A, 2nd Battalion, 503d Infantry, 173d Airborne Brigade (separate), was leading a patrol on a "search and destroy" mission to clear out "Charlie," the Viet Cong, before his entire platoon advanced into the area.

Tom led his men swiftly through the rice paddies. If ambushed, they would have no cover. Tom knew the enemy's hit-and-run tactics, their surprise attacks that never let up, day or night.

Suddenly a massive volume of small-arms fire shattered the silence, pinning Tom and his squad to the ground. The volley of gunfire was intense. It lasted what seemed like an eternity.

Tom Siopes saw his point man, Franklin Aquino, go down. As bullets whizzed past his head, Tom half-crawled, half-ran to the front of the column to help him. He hit the ground several times, dodging the bullets.

On reaching the wounded paratrooper, Siopes found him having difficulty breathing. A bullet had penetrated the man's chest and exited through his back, causing one lung to collapse. Blood was flowing out. The "sucking chest wound" was life-threatening. After quickly applying first aid, Siopes then shielded his wounded comrade with his own body and dragged him about 100 yards to the nearest combat medic. As the enemy began retreating, he prepared a landing zone for a chopper to airlift the soldier to an aid station. Aquino's life was saved. The entire squad survived.

For this act of heroism and sacrifice, Tom Siopes was awarded the Bronze Star Medal with "V" device for "Valor".

Three weeks later, he put his life on the line again in yet another firefight, characteristic of the guerrilla warfare that marked the Vietnam War.

Ambush on the An Lao River

On the morning of April 13, 1969, Siopes, as a platoon sergeant in Company A, was leading a combat patrol along the An Lao River. Around mid-morning, his squad was ordered to cross the An Lao River and defend the ford so the rest of the company could cross over.

Above the riverbank, covered with jungle growth, three or four Viet Cong were lying in wait. Completely concealed in "spider holes" they had dug into the ground. As Tom's squad was leaving the sandbar in the middle of the river, the Viet Cong opened fire with automatic small arms. Taken by surprise, Tom's men at first froze, and then became disorganized. Completely exposed—surrounded only by water—they had no cover, not even a sandbar.

Quickly sizing up the situation, Tom knew they couldn't stay there in the kill zone. Shouting encouragement to his men, he charged up the riverbank alone—100 yards ahead of his men—deliberately drawing enemy fire on himself to distract the enemy so his men could cross the river to safety. As he raced headlong up the riverbank toward the Viet Cong, bullets cracked over his head and around his feet. The Viet Cong kept firing at Tom, but could not stop him. A grenade exploded at his feet as he climbed the riverbank, injuring his leg and knocking him down. Still he jumped back up and kept going, charging at the enemy, firing at them continuously with his M-16. The wounded Viet Cong ran for their lives.

Tom Siopes was awarded the Silver Star for his valor that day, and also the Purple Heart. However, it was 38 years before he actually received the

Silver Star. The original paperwork, submitted by his company commander, Captain Vance Forpaugh, had become lost in the system. When Forpaugh realized what had happened, he worked with platoon leader Lieutenant Joe Weker to resubmit everything again. Finally, in 2007, in a special ceremony at the VFW in North Andover, Tom Siopes was presented his Medal.

Vietnam—ambushes and firefights

Tom Siopes arrived in Vietnam in November 1968, after a year of training Stateside and one week of jungle training at the 173d's base camp in An Khe. He was assigned to Company A, 2nd Battalion, 503d Infantry, 173d Airborne Brigade, a separate brigade formed in 1964 as a strike force for all of Southeast Asia.

The 2nd Battalion penetrated into the most inaccessible enemy strongholds over a wide area—in the four densely populated districts of Binh Dinh Province, in the Central Highlands military region (II Corps Tactical Zone). They were so successful in throwing the Viet Cong and the North Vietnamese Army into confusion that the expected January 1969 TET Offensive never took place in Binh Dinh.

The 173d Airborne Brigade's chief focus was keeping the Viet Cong disorganized and on the run. Search-and-destroy missions routed the enemy from their hiding places, destroyed their forces, equipment, and base camps.

In January 1969, the 173d discovered two of the largest enemy caches ever found by the Brigade. The 2nd Battalion found the biggest weapons cache of the operation in Binh Dinh—including a recoilless rifle, mortar, rounds for both, a stash of grenades, mines, small arms and ammunition. One week earlier another battalion had found a medical cache of 300 pounds of surgical instruments, drugs, plasma, and a microscope.

Wide-scale guerrilla warfare. Ambushes and firefights. Surprise attacks by day and night. An elusive, invisible enemy that used hit-and-run tactics—and knew the terrain well. U.S. troops could not see the enemy but knew he was there. An extensive intelligence network helped to accurately pinpoint where the enemy was, how large his force was, and what he was doing. "Snoopy" readings detected human odors. Red Haze, using heat-sensors, discovered the heat from enemy campfires. Yet when paratroopers entered these areas, the enemy often fled after light skirmishes, leaving behind caches of rice and medical supplies.

Redeeming the past

After his discharge from the military on August 29, 1969, Tom Siopes went on to serve with the Andover Police force for 37 years, retiring as a Lieutenant in 2011.

He still keeps in touch with Aquino, whose life he saved, and his CO Vance Forpaugh. As a Vietnam veteran, he knows full well how these returning heroes were vilified and shunned by the general public. Now he is determined that this will not happen to today's returning veterans who lost limbs in combat during the War on Terror following September 11, 2001. Tom is active in a national, all-volunteer organization that builds custom-designed homes for these severely disabled veterans. Homes for Our Troops has already built 146 homes so far—with another 31 in progress—providing veterans with homes at no cost.

"I'm so happy these veterans are being welcomed home as the heroes they truly are, that they are not abandoned and forgotten," he says. "Although we cannot change the past, we can learn from the mistakes of the past. And we can choose to make a difference and help those who have gone through the fire for us."

In the Scriptures, the Lord promises: " 'Fear not, for I have redeemed you...When you pass through the waters, I will be with you; and through the rivers they shall not overflow you. When you walk through the fire, you shall not be burned, nor shall the flame scorch you...I will make the Valley of Achor [trouble] a door of hope' " (Isaiah 43:1-2, Hosea 2:15).

SSGT. Dudley Farquhar
U.S. Army, 1st Cav - Americal
(23RD Infantry)

By: Helen Mooradkanian - February, 2014

They called it "the Valley of Death"—the dreaded Hiep Duc Valley in Vietnam. The enemy's stronghold. A major battleground. One where American units were nearly annihilated. Sergeant Dudley H. Farquhar, A Troop, 1/1st Cav, Americal Division (23d Infantry), as a member of Americal's Reactionary Forces was sent in with their mobility and firepower to aid embattled troops.

He served in Vietnam from January through December 1970. "Handwritten on our helmets were: 'Yea, though I walk through the valley of death, I will fear no evil...' I will overcome evil!' But truthfully, the enemy controlled that valley," he said.

"More than once we got trapped inside and had to shoot our way out. One time we nearly ran out of ammunition! If it hadn't been for the heavy air strikes by Air Force and Navy bombers, we wouldn't have made it out!"

said the Newburyport native who has lived in several Merrimack Valley towns, and now lives in Winthrop.

"The Hiep Duc Valley was the perfect kill zone. The U-shaped valley has only one entrance—the one way in is the only way out. Steep, heavily forested mountains surround the valley on three sides— covered with triple-canopied jungles. The enemy's heavily reinforced bunkers, dug deep in the mountainsides, are totally camouflaged. Invisible from land or air. They would lure our armored personnel carrier and tank units into this valley, then seal off the one escape route as we tried to leave, attacking us with mortars and rocket-propelled grenades. You could not see them—but they saw you! We were caught in a cross-fire."

Dudley was stationed at American's base in Chu Lai in I Corps, the northernmost tactical military zone in South Vietnam. Strategically, I Corps was the most important zone. It bordered the Demilitarized Zone (DMZ) separating South Vietnam from Communist North Vietnam. It was close to the Ho Chi Minh Trail.

It was also the most difficult to protect not only because of its size (10,000 square miles) but also its terrain. On the west lay Laos, where jungle-covered mountains hid supply bases of the North Vietnamese Army (NVA) and Viet Cong guerrillas. On the east were the flat, wet coastal plains covered by rice paddies extending to the beaches and the South China Sea.

"We would cover all of I Corps, park our track vehicle and then send out foot patrols. Our search and destroy missions usually lasted from 30 to 45 days—routing the enemy, searching for rice and weapons caches. Our only outside contact was through airdrops by choppers that brought in needed supplies and "medevac-ed" the wounded and KIA."

The Americal, the Army largest division in Vietnam, fought side by side with the Marines in I Corps, later taking over after the Marines left the area.

Warriors–close calls with death

When Dudley drove the "point" track or lead armored personnel carrier, his "Kit Carson" scout, named Cau, was an NVA defector who knew exactly where the NVA had planted land mines, and warned Dudley in advance—as a result, saving a great number of American lives. He had deserted the North Vietnamese Army and rallied to the Americans through the program "Open Arms" ("Chieu Hoi"). Formerly the paymaster for an entire NVA division, he defected when the NVA killed his whole family after denying him leave for the birth of his first child.

"Not all our men trusted him but I did. He earned my trust. For three months, he sat on top of the track next to me and warned me in advance of land mines. Our demolition teams would then go out and explode them. The secondary explosions confirmed his word.

"As sergeant, you must discern not only whom you can trust, but with what. Survival in combat means focusing on the present moment. If you get distracted, that's when the will enemy get you."

Descended from a Scottish clan known as warriors, Dudley Farquhar got bored when stationed in Germany, and volunteered, at first unsuccessfully, for Vietnam—finally writing to then-Senator Ted Kennedy for his help. His great grandfather, Ira Dudley Farquhar, U.S. vice-consul in Barcelona, Spain, during WWI served in WWII as Major, U.S. Army, Military Intelligence. His uncle, Michael Farquhar, served as Company Commander of a 101st Airborne unit in Vietnam.

From earliest childhood, Dudley has been an "overcomer." Raised by 15 different foster families, he finally found a loving home with Buddy and Joyce Clark, of Merrimac, who shaped his values and modeled a life of giving and service to others.

While in Vietnam, Dudley contracted malaria, his fever spiking to 106.5 degrees. Direct exposure to Agent Orange penetrated his system through open sores and wounds and lay dormant until it resulted in end-stage liver disease, diagnosed in March 2011. He received a liver transplant in September 2012, after 15 months on the wait list.

A promise to God—a vow fulfilled

One horrific memory still sticks in Dudley's mind. "It was March 18, 1970. We were out on patrol. Four of our men were blown to bits. Totally unidentifiable. I had to go out with a few others to gather their remains into body bags. I'll never forget that date…

"It was in Vietnam that I found myself talking to God," says Dudley. "I promised Him, 'God, get me through this, and when I go home I will become a changed man. I will serve others.' "

The Lord answered his prayer. And Dudley kept his promise.

In the more than 40 years he's been home, he has worked tirelessly as a national advocate for veterans—POW/MIAs and families, homeless veterans, veterans in VA hospitals, soldiers in Afghanistan—and children in shelters. During his 34 years with Lucent Technologies, North Andover (formerly Western Electric and AT&T), he was one of the youngest elected chapter presidents of the Telephone Pioneers, the prestigious charitable group founded by Alexander Graham Bell. Through his tireless efforts he has touched numerous lives for the good. For him, it's purely a labor of love. A few of his projects since returning home:

• Operation TRIUMPH ("To-Return-Immediately-Unauthorized-MIAs-and-POWs-Homeward"), to raise public awareness and pressure government officials for a full accounting of the nearly 2500 yet unaccounted for, and specifically the 64 missing Massachusetts men...

• POW/MIA Bracelets, his first project in the 1970s, gave hope to then-POWs that America had not forgotten them...

• "Three-Flag" Pins (American, POW/MIA, state) for all 50 states, all service branches, took 10 years to complete...

• POW/MIA Postage Stamp issued in 1995, a 12-year effort, with Lowell Post Office (opening on Sunday!) issuing the first!...

• Mass. law signed in 1986 mandated that every city, town fly one POW/MIA flag, and was signed by Governor Michael Dukakis...• First New England Shelter for Homeless Veterans in Haverhill, association with Mass. Vigil Society...

• Operation Platoon Mom, by AT&T Telephone Pioneers, that sends coffee to ground troops in Iraq and Afghanistan...

• Northeast Family Institute's shelter for troubled boys, where Dudley, as project chairman for 27 years, brings joy and hope into their lives.

Dudley survived for a purpose. He has turned every misfortune into an opportunity to serve and bless others.

Jesus said: "...whoever desires to become great among you, let him be your servant...just as the Son of Man did not come to be served, but to serve, and to give His life a ransom for many" (Matthew 20:26, 28).

LTJG. Gerald Halterman
USN- Pearl Harbor Survivor

By: Helen Mooradkanian - November, 2013

At 6:54 a.m. Sunday, December 7, 1941, the quiet midnight watch was about to end for 20-year old Gerald L. Halterman, U.S. Navy, Yeoman 3rd Class. An urgent message came in on the teletype in the communications office at Pearl Harbor, 14th Naval District, where he was on duty for the entire Pacific Fleet. The destroyer the USS Ward had spotted an unidentified submarine in a restricted area, at the harbor's entrance. "We have attacked, fired upon, and dropped depth charges."

Immediately below Jerry's office, in a room he didn't even know existed, Jerry sensed, from the flurry of activity, the Japanese code was being broken. It was! Japan had ordered all existing codes to be destroyed at once—an ominous sign.

Jerry typed the Ward's message and handed it to the on-duty officer, unaware he had just typed the message that would plunge America into

WWII. One hour later, Japan attacked Pearl Harbor. The next day, President Franklin Roosevelt and Congress declared war.

When relieved of duty early, Jerry headed to the receiving station for breakfast, shower, and sleep.

"At 7:55 a.m., I had just turned into my bunk on the third (top) floor when low-flying Japanese torpedo planes began swooping down over the harbor, attacking our ships," says Halterman, now 92 and living in Sudbury. "I heard a terrible noise. My bunk was near a front window. When I looked out, I saw the planes coming toward our building—I was directly in their flight path—and flying as low as 50 to 100 feet. As they flew toward my window, then made a sharp right-angle turn, I stared right into the faces of two Japanese pilots, wearing goggles, in open cockpits. The huge red ball, Japan's symbol, was plainly visible. Forty planes dropped their torpedoes, their wakes going into our ships.

"The first to be hit was my former ship, the USS Oklahoma, taking nine torpedoes. It capsized in 8 to 12 minutes, taking 429 men to their graves, including my three closest buddies. When I ran to a back window, I saw the USS Arizona explode in a ball of flame, a blazing inferno, as bombs hit its ammunition supply—1,777 men aboard died.

"The Japanese attacked in two waves. The first wave began at 7:55 a.m., with low-flying planes dropping torpedoes on Battleship Row. Because of Pearl Harbor's shallow 30 to 40-foot waters, no one had expected torpedoes to be launched from altitudes below 100 feet. Yet the Japanese achieved this, replacing the heavy steel fins with lightweight wooden fins.

"The second wave began at 8:55 a.m. High-altitude bombers and dive bombers flew back and forth across the harbor, attacking more ships. They left untouched my building, used as a marshalling point, and also the repair facilities and oil storage tanks. They expected to return to Pearl Harbor and use this fuel six months later to seize Midway Island, on their way down to Australia."

By 9:45 a.m. it was over. The Japanese left Pearl Harbor to begin a day-long attack on American bases in the Philippines.

More than 2,400 Americans lost their lives at Pearl Harbor on the "Day that will live in infamy," and 1,778 were hospitalized.

"In the midst of the horror, I always knew God was with me. I felt my mother's prayers. They carried me safely through the war," Jerry said.

The high cost of freedom

Jerry grieves deeply for the black-oil-soaked survivors, only the whites of their eyes and teeth showing. For those burned beyond recognition. For the lives cut short. For the terror his former shipmates suffered on the Oklahoma, trampling in the dark on oil-slicked linoleum decks...water gushing through doors left unfastened for an Admiral's inspection...a single ladder for radiomen stationed three decks below...the 32 men trapped inside until rescued the next day.

"The attack on Pearl Harbor was a turning point for America," says Halterman, a member of the Pearl Harbor Survivors Association, Boston Chapter, and one of the incorporators. "It united our nation to declare war against Japan and the Nazis, supporting our ally Great Britain, who stood alone after the fall of France. It saved Great Britain. It saved Australia. It saved America and our freedoms."

Six months later, June 1942, Jerry typed a crucial message addressed to Admiral Chester Nimitz, Commander of the Pacific Fleet. U.S. planes had spotted four Japanese aircraft carriers near Midway. Admiral Nimitz' reply, which Jerry also typed, was: "Sink the b---s!" The Battle of Midway, June 4–7, was a decisive victory for America and the Allies, and a turning point in the war.

Jerry cherishes President Ronald Reagan's words: "Freedom is a fragile thing and is never more than one generation away from extinction. It is not ours by inheritance; it must be fought for and defended constantly by each generation, for it comes only once to a people. Those who have known freedom and then lost it have never known it again."

Miracles—and a mother's prayers

Before Jerry Halterman left home for the Navy in 1939, after graduating from high school in Carbondale, Illinois (population 3,000), his mother took him aside and said, "Get down on your knees. We're going to pray together for your safety."

"To this day, I vividly remember that time of prayer. It saved my life. I always felt the presence of the Lord with me. She did the same for my two brothers, who served at Okinawa and Iwo Jima. We all came home without a scratch. I firmly believe it was my mother's fervent prayers, throughout the war, that carried us all through."

As a child, he remembers lying on the hard wooden pews of Grace Methodist Church each Sunday, the youth groups later on. He chose his companions carefully. In the Navy, he preferred to play baseball and tennis instead of going on shore leave with others. He sees "the hand of God" in the choices he made throughout his life. "In the Navy, I was at the right place at the right time, and my superiors helped me achieve my goals."

As yeoman 3rd class, he was offered the unheard of privilege of shore duty at Pearl Harbor's communications office. Despite the "pull" of his friends on the Oklahoma, he felt strongly led to accept it, knowing God was with him.

When Japan attacked, his building was left standing. He ran to grab a gun to fire at the planes but they were all locked up, so he took refuge in a ditch.

He chose Harvard Business School for Naval Supply Corps training rather than amphibious training in Florida, and this prepared him for his 35-year career at Raytheon Missiles Systems Division, in engineering and public relations. The Atomic Bomb ended the war just as he was preparing to take part in the invasion of Japan.

"Each one of us has a purpose in life," says Jerry. A son born with Down's Syndrome, now 53, "has been a blessing to our family."

In the wake of Pearl Harbor's unspeakable horror and tragedy, we can draw comfort from the Scriptures: "He who dwells in the shelter of the Most High will rest in the shadow of the Almighty. I will say of the Lord, 'He is my refuge and my fortress, my God, in whom I trust'...and under His wings you will find refuge" (Psalm 91:1-2, 4).

Corporal George A. Flibotte
U.S. Army Air Corps

By: Helen Mooradkanian - October, 2013

Nineteen-year old George A. Flibotte, U.S. Army Air Corps, now of Tewksbury, was with the Ninth Air Force stationed across the English Channel from Omaha Beach on D-Day, June 6, 1944. As part of the 1925th Ordnance Ammunition Company, he was loading bombs onto convoys of trucks to supply the B-25s and B-26s. These medium bombers provided support to the amphibious landings and ground troops during the invasion of Normandy, while the Eighth Air Force heavy bombers, B-17s and B-24s, flew bombing raids into Germany.

Early on the morning of June 6, the skies filled with thousands of paratroopers dropping behind enemy lines. A massive naval armada continuously bombarded the beaches. Loaded "Higgins boats"—LCVP or landing crafts, vehicle and personnel—carried thousands of troops who would hit Omaha Beach in multiple assault waves. The Ninth Air Force medium bombers—B-25s, B-26s, and Douglas A-26 Invaders—flying as low as 12,000 to 15,000 feet—strafed the enemy gun emplacements and coastal areas. Fighter planes swept beyond the beaches to flush out enemy planes.

"How our men scaled those cliffs at Omaha Beach, I'll never know, with the Germans hidden on the cliff tops, waiting for them, ready with machine guns and mortar," George recalled. "On the second day after the invasion, the medics ran out of plasma and sent out an urgent call for blood donors. At the time, we were in the mess hall. We immediately volunteered, gave blood, put away our mess kits, and rushed back to the bomb dump, where we loaded bombs onto truck convoys for delivery to planes."

The air cover was massive. The U.S. Army Air Force reported it alone had "dispatched more than 8,000 planes on missions directly related to the invasion."

George had entered the Army Air Corps in June 1943, at the age of 18, from North Reading. While training as a radio technician at Scott Field, Illinois, his plans were changed abruptly. Two weeks shy of completing his course, he was ordered to leave for England at once. "On May 13, 1944, we boarded the SS Brazil, a converted ocean liner, and arrived at Liverpool, England on May 24, assigned to the Ninth's 1925th Ordnance Ammo. Less than two weeks later, the D-Day invasion began."

Constantly on the ready as the Allies raced to Berlin, and the bombing attacks intensified, there was no opportunity for a furlough until George was discharged in 1946.

A new type of air war

The Normandy invasion opened up a new type of warfare for the Ninth Air Force. "We were constantly moving, moving, moving from one site to another throughout Europe."

While the Eighth Air Force with its heavy bombers flew from semi-permanent installations directly into the heart of Germany, the Ninth's medium bombers followed the advancing troops as they moved swiftly across France, Belgium, and Germany, following General George Patton's Third Army.

As the 1925th Ordnance Ammunition Company moved, George spent a couple of months at various sites in England from May through July 1944 while the Ninth sent out bombers and fighter-bombers during the Normandy Campaign, including the Battle of the Bulge.

By the end of September 1944, the Ninth Air Force had moved bases from England to the continent. "We flew in a C-47 from England to Nazi-occupied northern France: Fall 1944 (Senlis), December 1944 (Le Nouvion), January and February 1945 (Bohain and Vaux, north of Paris), April 1945 (Sillery, near Reims, 80 miles northeast of Paris), May 1945

(Saint Dizier and Liesse), June 1945 (Bucy). In 1945 he was in Belgium and then in Germany.

Bombs delivered on-time!

With the Ninth moving quickly across Europe, bombs were stockpiled outdoors, off-site from an air base—in case the airfield were hit—yet centrally located so as to be within a few mile radius of several airfields, accessible either by truck convoys or railcars.

"We had a dozen crews in my company, with four to six men in each. We received, stacked, stored, and shipped. Get 'em in—get 'em out! That was our slogan."

After the bombs came in by ship from the States, they were distributed by rail to various points. "Each day we went down to the rail yards to receive incoming shipments, using fork lift trucks, mobile cranes, and crawler tractors to unload bombs from railcars onto trucks, which then hauled them to the bomb dump. There we uncrated the bombs and stacked them by type and size: fragmentation cluster bombs (20- or 25-lb in a "bird cage"). These bombs were effective against ground troops, spraying a 120-foot area. We also stored 100-lb bombs, 250-lb bombs, 500-lb bombs, as well as 1,000- and 2,000-lb bombs. Our bombers attacked railroad equipment, ammo dumps, planes on the ground, rail terminals, marshalling yards, railroad bridges, concrete docks, and piers, as well as massive suspension bridges.

With the Ninth's bombing missions accelerating in Europe, the 1925th Ordnance Ammo Company played a crucial role in on-time delivery.

Chateaux—and "40 and 8" boxcars

As the German Army was being pushed back, George's ordnance company often slept in abandoned chateaux in France and Belgium for a month or so at a time as they moved from site to site. In December 1944 they moved into a vacant chateau outside the town of Le Nouvion in northern France, once under Nazi occupation. "It was a cold winter but we brought in a generator, hooked up some electrical wiring, made the necessary changes, and ended up with heat and electricity. The following April of 1945, we stayed for a month in another abandoned chateau not far from Reims, outside the town of Sillery, 'the champagne capital of the world' at that time, while we closed down two bomb dumps and shipped the bombs to Germany. Outside Frankfurt, Germany, we took over a partially bombed-out airbase and fixed it up to make some pretty decent living quarters."

Far removed from the abandoned chateaux George used as temporary living quarters was his three-day ride between France and Belgium in the infamous "40 and 8" boxcars. The "40 and 8" originated in France during World War I. Half the size of U.S. railcars, these boxcars measured only 20.5 feet long and 8.5 feet wide. During WWII, they transported troops to and from the front lines in Europe and North Africa. The Nazis used them to transport POWs.

Stories are told of how soldiers, in these unheated boxcars, nearly froze to death in the winter despite attempts to light fires. In the summer, the heat was unbearable. In many cases, they were known to start-and-stop, start-and-stop every 50 yards or so. Fortunately, for George, the three-day journey took place in the springtime. "Although the interior was primitive," he said, "at least the boxcars kept moving. Our mattress was a bale of hay spread out on the floor. Our pillow, the duffle bag we carried."

George Flibotte answered the call. He played a crucial role in supporting the Ninth Air Force in the liberation of Europe. Although distance separated him from his earthly father, his heavenly Father was watching over him wherever he went. As Jesus said in His parable of the talents, "Well done, good and faithful servant! You have been faithful with a few things, I will put you in charge of many things" (Matthew 25:14ff).

Frank Yount
U.S. Navy Seabees

By: Helen Mooradkanian - September, 2013

It was January 1, 1945 as the convoy of 556 ships filled the horizon—LSTs, troop ships, aircraft carriers, submarines, destroyers, cruisers, and warships equipped with the largest guns, 16-inch diameter. They were sailing from Dutch New Guinea to Lingayen Gulf on the island of Luzon, in the Southern Philippines—where the Allied invasion of the Philippines was about to begin. On January 9, General Douglas MacArthur launched the massive land-sea-and-air battle that caught the 287,000 Japanese defenders by surprise. They had not expected the invasion for another few weeks.

Frank Yount, 115th Naval Construction Battalion (Seabees), now of North Andover, was in that huge convoy. "We had been building the Navy's advance base at Hollandia, on Humboldt Bay, in Dutch New Guinea, when we received orders to depart for Lingayen Gulf.

"As we approached Lingayen Gulf, the sky lit up from exploding fire. Aircraft dropping bombs. Navy guns ablaze. Mortar fire. Japanese "kamikaze" suicide bombers diving into our warships.

It was a strategic victory for the U.S. and its allies, one that military historians say no one had anticipated when the U.S. Sixth Army stormed the beaches of Lingayen Gulf on January 9. U.S. troops far outnumbered those used in North Africa, Italy, or southern France. Some 68,000 troops from ten U.S. divisions and five independent regiments made amphibious assault landings and secured a 20-mile beachhead by nightfall. Several hundred thousand more followed.

This decisive victory set the stage for the liberation of Manila and the Philippines. It was due, in part, to the Navy's advance bases constructed by the Seabees far out into the Southwest Pacific. Without them, combat troops and ships would not have had the vital support services close to their theater of operation.

"As soon as we arrived at Lingayen Gulf on Luzon, January 21, 1945, we began building an airfield for the Marines and roads for heavy vehicles, even while under enemy fire," Frank said.

Frank Yount was 17 years old when he left the family farm in rural North Carolina (Granite Falls, population 4,000) to join the Navy. Assigned to the 115th Seabee Battalion, heavy equipment section, he helped build naval advance bases to support combat troops in the New Guinea and Philippine campaigns, and also the planned assault on the Japanese mainland. The 115th Seabees went in and cleared the land, built roads and huge parts depots, constructed airstrips and landing fields, staging areas for troops, and repair and refueling bases for ships.

"I had never seen a bulldozer until I joined the Navy," says Frank. Yet the first time he saw one, during training at Davisville, RI, he climbed up into the cab and began test driving it. Very quickly he was charged with training others. At the age of 17, he became captain of the bulldozer squad.

Milne Bay, New Guinea

On December 10, 1943, Frank Yount had departed from Davisville, RI, on an old cargo vessel, "The Alcoa Patriot," along with 1600 other Navy Seabees. Destination: Milne Bay, on the southeastern point of Papua New Guinea, in the Southwest Pacific.

The 69-day voyage was slow and torturous, at 6 knots an hour (about 7 miles). No escort. Buffeted by wild Atlantic storms. German subs off the coast of Cuba in the Caribbean. "Before we reached the Panama Canal, we were held up five times while U.S. destroyers from the naval base at Guantanamo Bay chased off the enemy subs."

When they finally debarked at Gamadodo (Frank was the first to go ashore with his bulldozer), they "battled a sea of knee-deep mud...torrential downpours that never let up... thick clouds of mosquitoes (it's one of the worst malaria spots in the world)...jungle rot that literally dissolved our boots...and the occasional python that slithered across our path...

"We operated those bulldozers seven days a week, around the clock, and cleared several hundred acres of jungle. We uprooted and knocked down gigantic trees, built sawmills and parts depots, ammunition magazines (storage). We pushed aside layers of mud, hauled coral from the beach, crushed and surfaced it, added gravel 2-feet thick in order to build and grade roads. We built airfields and landing strips, adding an additional sub-layer of interlocking metal plates, each 12 feet long, pouring concrete over them."

Milne Bay's harbor stretched along 20 miles of coral and mud beaches that turned into dense, swampy jungles extending all the way to the mountains. Given a tropical rainfall of 125 inches a year and muddy, sandy soil, it was hardly suitable for heavy construction. Yet the Seabees did the impossible.

"Before we left, we had built a huge replacement center that became one of the principle staging areas for the transfer of Army, Navy, and Marine troops in the New Guinea and Philippine campaigns. By mid-1944, we had put up barracks for housing 40,000 men. We also built a huge two-story, 120,000-square-foot spare-parts warehouse, with concrete floors—probably the largest building in New Guinea—that stored everything from ships' engines to the smallest warship components." Other structures included a pontoon assembly depot, and staging area where ships could anchor, refuel, and be refitted.

After completing their assignment at Milne Bay, the 115th Seabees boarded LSTs on December 1, 1944, and departed, in a five-ship flotilla, up the northeast coast of New Guinea to another advance base, Hollandia, on

Humboldt Bay in Dutch New Guinea, arriving there December 18. Hollandia became the advance headquarters of the Seventh Fleet, a logistics base for the Navy, as well as a supply base for General MacArthur during the liberation of the Philippines.

Preparing for assault on Japan

On February 8, 1945, the 115th became the first Seabees to debark at Subic Bay naval base on the west coast of Luzon, to prepare the base for the planned invasion of Japan. "At Subic Bay, we constructed facilities and camps, a pontoon pier, and docks. We also rebuilt the adjoining small naval base at Olongapo, which the Japanese had completely destroyed a few days before the U.S. invasion, systematically burning down churches, homes, buildings, and breaching the dike to flood the lowlands. We constructed new facilities for port director, communications, repair base for destroyers and submarines, dispensary, and housing for 1200 men in 32 two-story Quonset huts. We built roads, six steel warehouses (160 by 200 feet), and supervised completion of an amphibious training center where Army and Marines could practice all stages of assault landings on beaches.

Built on rock—or sinking sand?

After Japan surrendered, they remained in Luzon for a few months and built roads through the mountains for the Filipinos, hauling rocks from streambeds and crushing them. As a civil engineer and former operating manager of a sand and gravel company, Frank Yount knows the importance of building on rock, not sinking sand.

Jesus also talked about building. "Anyone who listens to My teaching and obeys Me is wise, like a person who builds a house on solid rock. Though the rain comes in torrents and the floodwaters rise and the winds beat against that house, it won't collapse, because it is built on rock. But anyone who hears My teaching and ignores it is foolish, like a person who builds a house on sand. When the rains and floods come and the winds beat against that house, it will fall with a mighty crash" (Matthew 7:24-27).

Corporal William T. Poulios U.S. Army

By: Helen Mooradkanian - August, 2013

Nineteen-year old Corporal William T. Poulios, of Chelmsford, 87th Infantry Division, 347th Regiment, swept across France, Belgium, Luxembourg, central Germany, to Czechoslovakia—in 154 days of combat! From December 6, 1944, to May 8, 1945 (when Germany unconditionally surrendered), the 87th drove relentlessly from Metz, France, to Plauen on the Czech border in the liberation of Europe.

They captured fortress-like cities...crashed the Siegfried Line with its "dragon's teeth"...crossed rivers at flood stage, including the treacherous Rhine...slogged through knee-deep mud, heavy snow, sleet, and fog in the Ardennes Forest...survived sub-zero temperatures during record cold waves that winter of 1944–1945...endured pneumonia and frostbite...escaped the deadly accurate 88mm artillery, which swiveled and fired in any direction. Bill Poulios called it "the finest in the world."

For the Lowell-born youth who had never traveled beyond Dracut, it was a baptism of fire. "My parents, who came here from Greece, gave full allegiance to America. My mother told the judge, when applying for U.S. citizenship, 'If Greece and America were at war, I would fight for

America!' " All four brothers fought for the U.S. in Europe, Guadalcanal, and Korea.

Fortresses of Metz

When he enlisted in 1943, Bill Poulios trained for the U.S. Army Air Force but was transferred to the 87th Infantry Division when General Eisenhower called for more ground troops in Europe. He landed in France on Dec. 1-3, 1944. The 87th, barely tested in combat, was rushed into mop-up operations at the Battle of Metz, France, eliminating the last pockets of Nazi resistance.

Metz was highly fortified, surrounded by two perimeters of 18 forts and observation posts, interconnected by tunnels. Two weeks earlier it had fallen to U.S. forces, yet the Nazis clung stubbornly to the remaining isolated forts, surrendering them one by one. One of the last, Fort Driant, fell to the 87th on December 8, 1944.

Bill was leading a night patrol outside Metz when a German general, with 150 of his men, surrendered to Bill and gave Bill his saber.

On December 10, 1944, the 87th Division moved near the Saar–German border, at Gross Rederching. In quick succession, they captured Rimling, Obergailbach, and Guiderkirch despite fierce resistance.

The Bulge, race across Europe

Then followed a 300-mile road march in open trucks from Germany's Saar Valley to the vicinity of Bastogne, Belgium. When Hitler launched the Ardennes Offensive in mid-December, the 87th Infantry was plunged into defending Bastogne and its environs on December 29, against Hitler's advance.

It was a long, brutally cold winter. "We nearly froze to death as we raced across Belgium to the Siegfried Line—with hardly a chance to clean up or rest," Bill recalls.

The 87th captured the Belgium towns of Moircy on December 30 and Remagne on December 31. On New Year's Day, 1945, they withstood the bloodiest German counterattack of the Ardennes Salient or Battle of the Bulge. They broke through the impregnable German defense around the main supply route connecting Bastogne and St. Hubert.

On January 2, 1945, they freed Gerimont, Belgium. On January 10, they flushed out the enemy, house by house in Tillet.

On January 13, they reached the Ourthe River in the Ardennes. On January 15, they moved to the Luxembourg-Germany border on the steep banks of the Sauer River. Through constant night patrols, they broke through the German side's elaborate warning system of trip wires rigged up to flares and explosives.

On January 23, they seized Wasserbillig, Luxembourg, and then advanced toward the Siegfried Line.

On January 28, 1945, outside St. Vith, Belgium, near the Schnee Eifel Mountains, the 87th Division secured the high ground west of the Our River. By the end of January, they captured three more towns: Schlierbach, Selz, and Hogden.

By February 5, 1945, they seized the last town near the Siegfried Line, Roth. By February 9, they captured the key city of Neuendorf. In two days, they had advanced so rapidly that food and ammunition had to be hand-carried to the front over miles of snow-covered trails.

Siegfried Line's "dragon's teeth"

The Siegfried Line was a formidable barrier built by Hitler to protect Germany. Multiple fronts blocked infantry and tanks. The first line of defense consisted of landmines and barbed wire laid between "dragon's teeth" - pyramid-shaped, reinforced concrete blocks 3 to 4 feet tall that could rip treads off the heaviest tanks. Between the "dragon's teeth" were diagonally-placed steel beams. Behind them rose a series of massive steel and concrete pillboxes, heavily fortified, with interlocking fields of fire. Connecting the whole were wire communications and tunnels.

Yet it fell! American forces cleared the landmines, smoked the pillboxes, cut the communications cable—and our infantry and tank destroyers rolled through!

Moving on roads loaded with landmines, booby-traps, and pillboxes, the 347th Regiment, in night attacks, captured Ormont (in 20 minutes) on February 26, and Hallschlagg, then crashed through the Siegfried Line's highest point, "Gold Brick Hill."

On March 6, 1945, they crossed the Kyll River and advanced rapidly to the Ahr River, 25 miles inside Germany. On March 8, they seized Dollendorf.

Un March 16 they began crossing the Moselle River in assault boats and established a beachhead, under a barrage of heavy fire.

By nightfall, they had successfully crossed the Moselle, gained control of the ground between the Moselle and the Rhine, and captured more than 200 German prisoners. Then they pushed toward the Rhine.

On March 18-19, the Division captured Koblenz, Germany, at the junction of the Moselle and Rhine Rivers.

On March 25-26, they successfully crossed the Rhine in assault waves—fighting the treacherous, swift-moving current, dodging heavy enemy fire all along the riverbanks and bluffs, including the deadly accurate 88mm artillery. "It was pure hell!" Yet they did it—totally defeating the surprised Germans, who withdrew rapidly, completely disorganized. They secured the east bank, cleared the towns of Oberlahnstein and Braubach, and advanced east.

In one month, March 1945, the 87th Infantry had advanced nearly 103 miles inside Germany, captured 225 pillboxes, taken some 10,300 prisoners, and cut off the German Army's main withdrawal route! They had crashed through the Siegfried Line, crossed the Kyll and Ahr Rivers, assaulted the Moselle and Rhine Rivers, captured Koblenz, and spearheaded the Division's race 45 miles into Germany that last week. On March 31, the 87th set up its command post deep inside Germany.

Bill recalls one poignant story about POWs liberated in Plauen—20 Greek nationals who had spent two years in slave labor, manufacturing airplane parts in an underground factory. "They couldn't speak English so I served as their interpreter. The men, all skin and bones, had not eaten for days. As our guests, I took them to our mess hall where we fed them until they could eat no more. When they tearfully pleaded with me to take them to America, I was very sad, very sad, I could not do this."

Amazing stories beyond human endurance and strength, physical and emotional. Bill Poulios, a man of prayer raised in the Greek Orthodox Church, knows where his strength lies. The cross he has worn around his neck all his life witnesses to the everlasting God who "gives strength to the weary and increases the power of the weak...those who hope in the Lord will renew their strength, they will soar on wings like eagles; they will run and not grow weary, they will walk and not be faint" (Isaiah 40:29-31).

2nd Lt. Walter Hedlund
U.S. Army, WWII

By: Helen Mooradkanian - July, 2013

CHELMSFORD, MA - On D-Day, June 6, 1944, Walter Hedlund, then a sergeant, U.S. Army, 29th Infantry Division, 3rd Battalion, 115th Regiment, Company I, stormed Omaha Beach in Normandy—part of the second assault wave.

"The first assault wave, our own 116th Regiment, was slaughtered by the Germans. They never got beyond the beach," said the Lowell-born native now living in Chelmsford.

"When we waded ashore through chest-high surf, the beach was lined with the dead, the wounded, and floating vehicles. There was mass confusion. We had to go through them—unable to stop and help—because we had to get off that beach, climb steep cliffs, and secure the beach. That was our mission. The wounded urged us on, shouting, 'Keep going! Keep going!'

"Continuous fire pounded us. From above, German aircraft strafed us. From the cliff tops, enemy machine guns shelled us. As we inched forward through the sand dunes, land mines exploded. We didn't get very far. The night of June 6th we were still on the beach. I was on the front line, just on top of the ridge. I could have thrown a rock into the ocean."

Miraculously, the 29th Division scaled the cliffs and secured Omaha Beach.

Walter led a 40-man platoon, of whom all but four were lost. "Some of my men froze-only 17, 18, 19-year olds, with very little training. I'm alive today because of my Ranger training with the British Commandos."

BRITISH COMMANDOS:

"In war, kill—or be killed"

"You either kill—or be killed! Make up your mind."

This was the mindset instilled by the British Commandos, the elite shock troops known for their daring exploits of stealth behind enemy lines. Walter Hedlund was one of a highly select group who trained with the Commandos for three months at a secret mountain base in the Highlands of Scotland, and then served with the No. 10 Commandos for another three. He trained at zero-degree temperatures, stripped to the waist. He became skilled in surprise attacks by night, infiltrating deep behind enemy lines on foot. He became expert at amphibious landings, climbing sheer cliffs and mountains, surviving combat unarmed. He developed endurance through 25-mile speed marches, alternately running then walking.

"By night we sailed on dangerous reconnaissance raids from Dover, England, to the shores of German-occupied France. We didn't know it then but we were gathering data for the D-Day invasion. One night we were sent to bring back beach sand. The purpose: to learn if the beach could support heavy tanks."

THE NORMANDY HEDGEROWS

"We were not prepared for the hedgerows of Normandy—4 to 6-foot high mounds of dirt covered on top with heavy hedges that marked farmland boundaries. Their unusual height didn't show up in aerial reconnaissance photos, yet they formed an impenetrable barrier. We could not go through them but had to climb over them—something no tank could do without exposing its unarmored belly to gunfire.

"At the top of the hedgerows, German machine guns lay hidden. Through the only opening, an invisible gap at the top, the Germans fired at us. We never saw them."

"In a few weeks, we solved the problem. We welded two iron prongs to the front end of a Sherman tank, drove the tank into the hedgerows. Dynamite blasted the hedgerows wide open."

After six weeks of continuous combat, the 29th advanced from Omaha Beach through the hedgerows to Saint-Lo, a critical crossroads city, which they secured July 18, 1944.

During July and August 1944, Walter Hedlund was wounded three times. The first two times at Saint-Lo and its general environs. Both times he was sent to a field hospital. Both times he "got bored," slipped out of bed and walked away, rejoining his company.

The third time, he was wounded severely in a fierce battle against a garrison of Nazi fanatics at Brest, France. He was shipped to a hospital in England where he spent nearly four months, nearly losing a leg to gangrene. "Major Green saved my leg. I'll always remember him." On release, he rejoined his company in western Germany in their assault across the Roer River and the drive toward the Rhine.

Battlefield Commission, Silver Star

On the morning of August 26, 1944, Company I, 115th Regiment, attacked the German garrison on Hill 81, near Brest, an important French port and submarine pen on the Brittany peninsular. It was heavily defended by a garrison of 50,000 German troops. "But first we had to cross an open field and a big ravine, continuously raked by German machine guns."

Walter led his platoon of 40 men to spearhead the attack. In lead position, he was pinned down at the ravine. "My radio stopped working. So I made my way back to the rest of the company to make communications." Finding his commander severely wounded and unable to lead, Walter immediately took command.

The official report states: "In the midst of fierce enemy fire and mass confusion, he reorganized the company, arranged for a field artillery unit to provide white smoke barrage so his platoon could withdraw safely, then established defensive lines that withstood the very powerful German thrust. His leadership and bravery were nothing short of sensational under extremely confusing circumstances. So outstanding was his leadership that he was left in command until wounded in action two days later."

For his action on Hill 81, Walter Hedlund received the Silver Star and the rare, highly coveted Battlefield Commission to 2nd Lieutenant. He was recommended for a Medal of Honor.

CROSSING A SWOLLEN RIVER

After returning to Company I, in January 1945, Walter took part in the 29th Division's daring frontal assault across the swollen Roer (Ruhr) River February 23, 1945—and capture of the key fortress city of Julich, Germany. Crossing the Roer was crucial in the drive toward Germany's Rhine River. But when the Germans opened the dams and flooded the valley, crossing the Roer became a violent struggle against both German troops and the turbulence of the swift, strong current.

Less than an hour after the Germans had launched their deadly night barrage of machine gun and mortar fire, assault boats and amphibious tractors began crossing in a great wave.

Once again, when his CO was wounded, Walter Hedlund took command. He was awarded a second Bronze Star for his outstanding valor in securing the bridgehead and for his "high standards of initiative and leadership" in organizing and deploying troops as they reached the enemy side.

SERVANT-LEADER

Before the Army, Walter had preached a few sermons at his Baptist Church in Lowell and, throughout WWII, he carried a pocket New Testament. During 60 years as a funeral director in Lowell, he conducted many services and became widely known for his compassion. The Greater Lowell Salvation Army honored him with the "Exceptional Service Award" plaque (37 years of service), as did the Greater Lowell American Red Cross (40 years). Chelmsford erected a plaque in the town center, by the flagpole, for his dedicated service as Homeland Security Director (1973-2012), director of patriotic parades and celebrations (45 years), and volunteer firefighter (1955-1970).

Walter's guiding philosophy is: "J-O-Y. 'J'—Jesus is first; Jesus guides me through prayer. 'O'—others; 'Do unto others as you would have them do unto you.' 'Y'—put yourself last." A true servant-leader, he exemplifies "the joy of the Lord is your strength" (Nehemiah 8:10).

Walter Hedlund for all you have done for our community and our country, thank you for being a Hero in our Midst.

Corporal Robert Bailey
U.S. Army

By: Helen Mooradkanian - June, 2013

On September 15, 1944, at 8:30 a.m., 20-year-old Robert F. Bailey, of Lowell, U.S. Army, 31st Infantry Division ("Dixie Division"), 155th Infantry Regiment, Cannon Company, stormed the beach on Morotai Island, off the New Guinea coast in the southwest Pacific. Morotai would become a crucial air and naval base and a key part of General Douglas MacArthur's strategy for the liberation of the Philippines. Located north of Australia and part of the Dutch East Indies, Morotai was the final landing point between New Guinea and the Japanese-occupied Philippines.

In that assault landing on Morotai, 45 LSTs (landing ship, tank) lined the shore. Offshore coral reefs and boulders caught landing craft. Troops, vehicles, and supplies were unloaded onto the beach—with no opposition from the 500 or more Japanese caught there by surprise. But the calf-deep mud and chest-high surf were "the worst ever seen," General Krueger reported. Deep holes and fissures nearly submerged vehicles and men, causing delays.

While Bob was sitting on the beach waiting to move out with his platoon, he saw General Douglas MacArthur wading through the surf to come ashore! "We quickly put on our helmets and stood up," he said, recalling that scene vividly.

By noon of September 15, the Americans had seized Pitoe Airdrome. With the capture and occupation of Morotai, the U.S. now had control of the Halmahera Sea, cutting off 35,000 Japanese soldiers garrisoned at Halmahera Island.

Robert Bailey was awarded the Purple Heart for combat on Morotai. On the evening of October 4, 1944, Bob and his friends returned to their tent after watching the movie "Johnny Eager," starring Lana Turner and Robert Taylor. Suddenly the Japanese bombed their tent. Bailey and others were wounded—but Bob's friends, on either side of him, were killed instantly.

Morotai was the staging area for Mindanao. Bob took part in that invasion the following April 1945 when the 31st joined the Eighth Army in the final drive to liberate the Philippines.

Jungle warfare - from "ducks" to carrier pigeons

Before engaging in combat, Bob trained in jungle warfare and amphibious landings at Oro Bay, New Guinea, arriving there April 22, 1944. In the mountains and jungles of the Southwest Pacific islands, American forces relied heavily on:

• DUKWs or "Ducks"—six-wheel amphibious vehicles with a payload capacity of 2.5 tons that transported ammunition, supplies, equipment and troops over rough seas and onto the islands. Bob rode in his first DUKW at Oro Bay. Amphibious landings were vital to General MacArthur's mission in the Southwest Pacific.

• Self-propelled 105mm howitzers—designed specifically to travel and maneuver over the rough jungle terrain and through heavy mud. "We had six in our Cannon Company," said Bob, "and they provided immediate support of the infantry wherever our regiment went."

• Carrier or homing pigeons—that carried messages from reconnaissance patrols behind enemy lines, flying over the dense, impenetrable jungle that blocked radio airwaves. Bob first used them in Sarmi-Wadke, New Guinea.

New Guinea is the second largest island in the world (after Greenland), with a northern coastline that extends nearly 1,600 miles. Mountains as high as 15,000 feet and dense tropical rainforests cover the area. A major mountain range runs through the center of the island, from east to west, with many sections impassable. "We saw a yearly rainfall totaling 240 inches," said Bob. Other areas got up to 300 inches. "In one 24-hour period, we would get up to 27 inches of rain. Then the monsoon season would begin."

In July 1944, Bob Bailey and most of the Dixie Division relieved the 6th Infantry Division at Maffin Bay in the Wakde-Sarmi Campaign. They landed on Sarmi, on the New Guinea coast, as U.S. forces seized Wakde Island—two miles away on Maffin Bay—from the Japanese. Wakde had a good airstrip for the B-24 Liberator heavy bombers, critical for freedom in the Philippines.

While the Division's 124th Regimental Combat Team (RCT) went to Aitape, New Guinea, and fought in the bloody battle along the Drinumor River, other elements built bridges, roads, and docks, and engaged small units of the enemy (killing more than 1,000 Japanese), without provoking large-scale counterattacks.

Aggressive patrolling kept the Japanese at bay. "I remember the first time I used carrier pigeons for communication in Sarmi," said Bob, a radio operator. "Our 20-man recon patrol had gone behind enemy lines. We used trained pigeons to send back news of the enemy's location, troop strength, and gun positions. We inserted the message in a tiny capsule fastened to one of the pigeon's legs. Pigeons were so dependable we did not need to code messages.

"We set off on patrol, carrying the pigeons in a wire-mesh crate. The steaming tropical heat. Dense jungle growth. Chest-high swollen rivers we had to wade through, where crocodiles lay hidden. All this took their toll. We took turns carrying the crate of pigeons on our shoulders. But when one of our men stumbled and fell from exhaustion, the crate crashed to the ground, the door flew open—and the pigeons vanished forever! We never saw them again. Fortunately, we did not run into the enemy that time."

Mindanao: 72,000 enemy troops

On April 22, 1945, the 31st Infantry began landing on Mindanao, the southernmost island in the Philippines. The largest Japanese force was amassed in eastern Mindanao—more than 43,000 armed troops plus 29,000 combat and service troops—far outnumbering the Allies. The Japanese were entrenched along the north-south Sayre Highway (about 250 miles long). The highway's northern stretch lay in total disrepair while the southern portion was nothing but a dirt road that ran from Kabacan across unchartered mountains.

The 31st Division drove north along the Sayre Highway, toward Kibawe, to block the enemy's retreat from the east. They captured Kibawe and its airstrip by May 3 and then took Kabakan, at the junction of the east-west and north-south routes, thus gaining control of the supply routes.

Destroyed bridges, impassable trails, unforeseen obstacles slowed them down. "At one point we had to take a small landing craft up the Mindanao River," Bailey said. "On reaching camp, when unloading, one of our 105mm howitzers toppled into the river and sank. It took us 10 days to retrieve it, haul it out, and then dig a path to tow it to land. During that time, we traded with the Filipinos: one T-shirt for two chickens. We had chicken and eggs every day. It was the best we ever ate."

As the 31st advanced north, they successfully wiped out a Japanese "banzai" (suicide) attack—the last major Japanese offensive on the Sayre Highway. From then on, the chief obstacle became the torrential rains. On May 23rd, Bailey's regiment met up with the 108th RCT. The Sayre Highway was finally cleared. Strong patrols flushed out Japanese who had fled to the mountains. By July 1st, all organized Japanese resistance had ended. On August 15, 1945, Japan finally surrendered.

The 31st slogged courageously through the unknown, overcoming insurmountable odds. Each patrol had a point man—the leader who showed the way. Whom do you trust?

Jesus said, "I am the Way, the Truth, and the Life." That's why the apostle Paul could write: "We are hard pressed on every side, but not crushed; perplexed, but not in despair ... struck down, but not destroyed ... Therefore we do not lose heart" (John 14:6; 2 Corinthians 4:8-9, 16).

Thank you Robert Bailey for being a Hero in Our Midst.

Bataan Hero: Sgt. Victor Cote
USAF. Army, 1920-2013

By: Helen Mooradkanian - May, 2013

In this Memorial Day issue, we honor a local WWII veteran who survived the brutality of the Japanese POW camps and the "Hell Ships." Although he passed away February 3, 2013, shortly before his 93rd birthday, his story of courage and endurance lives on.

***

Sergeant Victor Cote, U.S. Army Air Corps, was a POW in Japan's Camp 17 near Omata, Kyushu, when he heard B-29 Superfortresses thundering overhead. Looking up, he saw a large mushroom cloud rising over Nagasaki, 40 miles across the bay. It was 11:01 a.m. on August 9, 1945. The B-29, "Bock's Car," and its escort planes had flown directly over his camp on their way to Nagasaki to drop the second atomic bomb, ending WWII.

"I didn't know what the bomb was, only that it was something new and powerful," the Tewksbury native recalled. After 40 months as a POW—with the last twelve spent in slave labor at Camp 17's coal mines—his ordeal was finally ending.

Ten hours earlier Victor's first cousin, Philip Cote, had witnessed "Bock's Car" take off from Tinian Island in the Pacific with its escort planes, one of which he had just serviced. Philip was crew chief of maintenance for the B-29 bombers on Tinian, where he had served exactly one year to the day. (For Philip's story, see "Hero in our Midst," September 2012.)

The atomic bomb saved Victor's life. The Japanese had a standing order to "eliminate" all evidence of POWs as soon as the first Americans landed on their mainland.

Victor Cote cheated death repeatedly. At the age of 22, he narrowly escaped the Bataan Death March—lying in a makeshift field hospital with dysentery. Later captured by the Japanese, he was sent to several notorious POW camps in the Philippines: O'Donnell, Bilibid, and Cabanatuan, where "Americans died like flies." He also endured three months stuffed in the dark, unventilated hold of a "Hell Ship" bound for Japan—and the infamous Camp 17, reputedly the worst.

Despite 25 attacks of malaria, scurvy, pellagra, dry beriberi, and cerebral malaria (seizures, coma), Victor Cote survived and lived a long, healthy life.

His cousin Philip Cote, now 97, still lives in Dracut—not far from the Cote family compound on Trull Road, Tewksbury, Mass., where Victor and Philip were raised together.

When asked how he managed to survive, Victor said, "I just wanted to live." Miraculously he did, by the grace of God.

DECEMBER 1941—WAR!

Victor was stationed at Nichols Field, Manila, when it was bombed within days after Pearl Harbor. "My barracks went up in flames. Japanese dive-bombers filled the entire sky, destroying every American plane. Not one got airborne."

Victor was handed a rifle pulled out of storage, but it jammed—it had not been cleaned. "Japanese dive-bombers swooped down relentlessly all day long. This hell lasted a week before we boarded a barge to cross the bay to the Bataan peninsula. That trip was a nightmare. A low-flying Japanese plane strafed us throughout the trip."

Finally reaching Bataan, he was pressed into combat on the front lines near Parsay—without prior infantry training. "Only a field separated us from the advancing Japanese Army. Every day planes flew over, bombing and strafing. I saw legs blown off my friend—men dying all around me."

One week before his 22nd birthday on April 7, Victor was told! "You'll never live to see your birthday." Dysentery put him in the hospital where the doctor confirmed, "There's nothing we can do for you." So he lay on the ground, waiting for death.

In a twist of irony, because of this, Victor escaped the 85-mile Bataan Death March, April 10 16, 1942, that ended at Camp O'Donnell. He survived the hospital, but the Japanese captured him anyway when he left his jungle hideout to catch a monkey for dinner. He was trucked to Camp O'Donnell, arriving just after the Death March survivors staggered in.

"The entire front gate area of Camp O'Donnell was covered with the dead and dying, "boys dying at the rate of 60 a day." (Military reports state 1500 Americans died at Camp O'Donnell, most of them Death March survivors.)

Victor was assigned to burying up to 150 men a day, in a shallow pit 18 inches deep, 20 feet wide by 40 feet long. Monsoon rains would wash away the topsoil, exposing a protruding arm or leg.

Most POWs died of starvation, polluted drinking water, malaria or dysentery. "We got one small ball of rice a day. One spigot of water supplied the entire camp of 7,000 Americans. You had to stand in line for three hours."

After two weeks at Camp O'Donnell, Victor was sent back to Bataan to collect old anti-aircraft guns and ammunition left behind by American forces. A month later, he was sent to Bilibid prison in Manila, a transfer point to other camps. "Men were dying here faster than at Camp O'Donnell—all skin and bones, vomiting uncontrollably." From Bilibid he was transferred to Cabanatuan, a Japanese slave labor camp.

At Cabanatuan, Victor leveled 3 to 4-foot high anthills with a long-handled hoe and planted camotes (sweet potatoes). His weight dropped from 150 to 100 lb. Many times he thought he would die, especially after very severe dysentery and malaria hospitalized him for six months. The dysentery section had an unnumbered "Zero Ward." No one ever left there alive. "Death surrounded me constantly. I'd go to sleep next to a POW and wake up next to a corpse. While waiting for death, we played macabre games: who would be the next to die?"

Japanese brutality was savage. "They beheaded POWs. They buried them alive. They made them dig their own grave and then would shoot them in the head. They forced men to kneel in submission at the front gate, hands tied behind their knees, 24 hours a day, and beat them. They beat one POW all day long for picking up a bar of soap. We were forced to watch these executions."

THE "HELL SHIP" AND THE CROSS

Then Victor was thrown into a "Hell Ship" bound for Japan—where 500 to 1900 POWs would be crammed into the dark, unventilated hold, with virtually no food or water, for a three-month trip from Manila to Japan—which normally took five days. Victor slept on bags of grain infested with lice, lived on one cup each of rice and water a day.

He arrived in Japan a skeleton in rags, assigned to Camp 17's coal mines. "We had to build stone walls to shore up crumbling ceilings. Cave-ins killed many POWs. A 5-ton rock crashed, narrowly missing me. I saw men beaten to death for stealing food, or for no reason at all. Some 200 died the year I was there.

"Each morning outside the gate, we saw two to four Americans tied to a wooden cross, where they knelt until they died."

The cross, symbol of suffering and death—yet also symbol of the ultimate triumph of good over evil, eternal life over death. At the cross, Christ conquered Satan and the grave. Jesus said He came "to destroy the works of the devil" (I John 3:8). He promised, "I am the resurrection and the life. He who believes in me, though he may die, yet shall he live" (John 11:25). "Where, O death is your victory?"

Sgt. Robert A. Hunter
U.S. Marines

By: Helen Mooradkanian - April, 2013

In late summer of 1944, an aircraft carrier filled with Marines sailed from San Diego for Peleliu Island in the Pacific—and a mid-September invasion. On board was 18-year old Robert A. Hunter, of Tewksbury. "We were all pumped up and ready for action after training together for one year."

The "island hopping" strategy in the Pacific had proved successful as the Marines secured one island after another in their advance toward the Japanese mainland: Roi and Namur in the Marshall Islands (February 1944), Los Negros (March 1944), Wake Island (May 1944), Saipan and Guam (July 1944), and Tinian (August 1944).

But instead of Peleliu, Bob and half his group ended up on Midway Island that September with the 3rd Marine Aircraft Wing, VMF-324 (fighter bombers). Their job: retrain land-based Corsair F4U fighter pilots to operate from aircraft carrier decks—even more urgent since Japanese "kamikaze" (suicide) pilots began attacking U.S. ships.

Bob was bitterly disappointed. He requested a transfer to Peleliu with the ground troops. His commanding officer grew livid. "Rising slowly from behind his desk—he looked 7 feet tall!—the veins in his neck and arms bulged. A deep red flush crept up his neck and spread across his face. Clenched knuckles gripped the desk. Finally, he barked, 'Get back to your barrack! Get down on your knees and pray you'll eventually make it Stateside!' "

Bob's CO, it turned out, had been a fighter pilot at Guadalcanal when he was captured by the Japanese and tortured as a POW. He finally managed to escape. The CO's decision probably saved Bob's life. The Battle of Peleliu in September 1944 turned out to be one of the bloodiest battles in the Pacific War, with reportedly the highest casualty rate of any amphibious invasion. Some 80% of the Marines who had trained with Bob died in that battle.

Bob's life was spared for a purpose. Like many veterans, he wondered why. The answer, in part, would come decades later.

Midway—Where "Gooney Bird" Meets "Bent-Wing Gull"

Since April 1944, when the Corsair F4U was finally cleared for carrier-based takeoff and landing, there had been a scramble to retrain land-based fighter pilots. Since existing carriers could not be spared, and were also subject to submarine attacks, one solution was to convert the paddle-wheel steamers on the Great Lakes into training vessels—in the safety of Lake Michigan. Their decks, however, were only two-thirds the length of a fleet carrier's.

Midway Island, half-way between San Francisco and Tokyo, had access to complete aircraft facilities since Pan-Am World Airways used it as a stopover and refueling station. Its paved runways were marked off to the precise dimensions of a carrier deck.

It was there on Midway that the "Bent-Wing Gull"—the Corsair F4U fighter-bomber with folding wings—met the Albatross or "Gooney Bird," so-called because of its hilarious 25-step courtship dance, shrill whistle, and comical antics.

The Japanese called the Corsair F4U "Whistling Death" because of its speed (more than 400 mph), maneuverability, 4,000-pound-bomb payload capacity, and kill ratio of 11:1. American troops called it the "Sweetheart of Okinawa." The F4U became one of the more popular, although controversial, fighter planes.

Since Midway was nesting home to the Albatross and dozens of other species of birds—including the bo'sun bird that can fly backward—paving the runways helped drive the Albatross to relocate. Inevitably, however, flocks would return, flying onto the runway.

"We were very careful, very protective of those birds," Bob Hunter recalls. "They loved to perform by dancing together. They strutted and pranced around, whistling or making gurgling noises in their throat." Whenever the "Gooney Bird" met a man or a 10-ton truck, it would bow low but refuse to get out of the way. They had absolutely no fear of man.

The island's rats were another matter. "We slept next to the aircraft in revetments—tent-shaped dugouts covered with sandbags. Rats crawled over us at night, gnawing on our fingers if our hands were exposed," he recalls.

Dive-bombing on Wake Island

Although a land-based telephone communications specialist, Bob went on one surprise "bombing mission." It's one he will never forget.

On Midway he ran into an old friend from Tewksbury High, a Marine pilot of the Dauntless SBD-2 dive bomber. SBD-2 fighter pilots trained by dropping bombs on Wake Island after the Japanese had reclaimed it. "C'mon. I'll take you for a spin," he said. Bob couldn't resist the offer.

The SBD-2 was the chief Allied dive bomber in the Pacific Theater. From an altitude of 25,500 feet, the pilot literally dove at a steep angle over the target—dropping up to 2,250 pounds of bombs. It sank more enemy ships than any other aircraft in the Pacific.

Little did Bob know that he was in for the ride of his life. "Now when I drop my bomb and pull out of my dive," his friend said, "you yell as loud as you can and open the canopy above your head. That will help me regain altitude…" Of course, it was a joke, and the force of gravity left Bob totally speechless and unable to lift a finger!

Saving lives one at a time

After the war, Bob joined the family business as an orchardist, caring for acres of fruit orchards. A powerful truth came alive for him. Good trees, like good people, bear good fruit. Bad trees bear bad fruit. Bob knows his life was spared for a purpose and he reached out to help others, counseling teenagers and visiting the elderly in nursing homes.

Along the way he learned some lessons.

At the age of 30, Bob returned to finish college, got his Master's, then earned an advanced certificate toward a doctorate in education and counseling. All the while he worked several jobs to support his growing family. "I became a workaholic. I focused on making money. I even accumulated quite a tidy sum—only to lose it all virtually overnight. Since then I counsel young men, 'Spend quality time with your family. Don't let ambition or the love of money consume you.' "

A former school guidance counselor who practices "active listening," Bob has seen lives transformed. A struggling young girl, later diagnosed as a schizophrenic, was directed to the therapist who helped her. An 18-year old boy, a high school dropout hooked on alcohol and drugs—who looked on Bob as the father he never had—took Bob's counsel. He got help, then entered a special high school diploma program (higher than a GED) that Bob had helped to establish at Middlesex Community College. He graduated as class valedictorian, received a $500 college scholarship, and studied culinary arts for a future in restaurant management.

Recently, Bob took in a destitute man—without money, job, or place to live— who had spent his life savings caring for his elderly, terminally ill father. He found the man a home, a job, and soon the man will be baptized at First Baptist Church of Tewksbury, where Bob is a trustee.

New life. New hope. Jesus said, "Do not lay up for yourselves treasures on earth, where moth and rust destroy and where thieves break in and steal; but lay up for yourselves treasures in heaven, where neither moth nor rust destroys and where thieves do not break in and steal. For where your treasure is, there your heart will be also" (Matthew 6:19–21).

Thank you Sgt. Hunter for all you have done for our country and being a Hero in Our Midst.

Sean McLaughlin
Citizen Patriots Support
Soldier's Family - A "Thank You"

By: Tech Sgt. James Moore USAF -February, 2009

HAVERHILL, MA - This month's Valley Patriot of the Month is Army Major Sean McLaughlin of Haverhill.

The military family is a resilient institution. While serving in the Armed Forces takes its toll on the member serving, military service permeates through to the core of the family. From long hours and deployments, to having to relocate upon receiving orders, to moving on to the next assignment and uprooting from a location that you just spent four years together as a family, the loved ones of the ones that serve pay the

PHOTO: COURTESY

price. With all of the dynamics that it entails, the day to-day routine wouldn't be possible if it weren't for good friends and neighbors.

Army Reserve Major Sean McLaughlin wants to express his gratification for those who have helped his family and he would like to create a heighten awareness of the presence of military families in your local community.

Major McLaughlin has lived in the Merrimack Valley for most of his life and is originally from Manchester, NH. He has lived in Haverhill for over 10 years. He and his wife Cynthia have known each other since their high school days at Manchester Central High School; they began dating while in college. Now, they have two beautiful children, Jack (9) and Emily (6) and it is Cynthia that has had to sacrifice for her husband's service, as has many countless spouses throughout the years.

She was a teacher and track coach at Haverhill HS at on time, but since Major McLaughlin's mobilizations have taken him away so much over last few years, she has become a stay at home mother in an effort to maintain a sense of stability in Jack and Emily's lives. We commend you Cynthia!

Major McLaughlin has served honorably with the Army Reserves since when he earned his commission from UNH in 1990. His service has taken him from his home in Haverhill, Massachusetts to Fort Bragg, North Carolina, to Iraq as well as other locations abroad to defend the United States on the Global War on Terror.

"Being mobilized to perform duty here in the states has obviously been less stressful on my family then my previous deployment to a war zone. But the family separation is still difficult and seeing dad only on infrequent visits can be hard on my children", says the Major.

"I was deployed to Baghdad, Iraq where I served as the military liaison to the Governor of Baghdad. From that experience, I have gained a great deal of respect for the Iraqi's that believe in the democratic process and are willing to hold elected office."

"During my time in Baghdad, Governor Ali al Haidri, the first Baghdad Governor I worked with, was assassinated by insurgents. He was a good man and his loss is deeply felt."

"The man who replaced him, Governor Ali Fadel, also faced multiple and frequent attempts on his life. Despite that, he worked tirelessly for Baghdad citizens without fear for his personal safety. I found the bravery of the Iraqi's who stand against the insurgents and try to make their country a better place truly inspiring."

He's currently at Fort Bragg, NC and serves as the Course Manager for the Civil Affairs mobilized officer qualification course. He says that almost all the officer students in the course are reservists on a battle roster for either Iraq or Afghanistan.

All of the students will work in Civil Affairs once they get in theater.

The Major comments on how his employers have helped, he says, "my employers at Salem High School in Salem, MA, have been very supportive and accommodating. I really couldn't ask for a more supportive employer".

This is also an additional concern on a Guardsman or Reservist and one that Major McLaughlin can rest easy with.

Well, this is a little break from the norm, friends. Major Sean McLaughlin wanted The Valley Patriot to give him a forum to express his gratitude to those in Haverhill that have been supportive and helpful to his family during his deployments. He also warns that there are those in the community that aren't so patriotic.

The following words are from the heart of a Patriot, whose duties dictate that he stay almost permanently geographically separated from his family. Words of endearment for Haverhill's "True Patriots", also words of concern, as told by Major Sean McLaughlin:

Haverhill's True Patriots "Americans are a patriotic people. As a soldier, I see this almost every day when I wear the uniform. Strangers will come up to me and thank me for my service.

People will sometimes offer to buy my coffee when I'm in line at the donut shop or just wave and give a thumbs up as they drive by me when I'm walking down the street.

I'm always grateful when people show these small acts of appreciation, but I feel a bit guilty as well. Guilty because I know the people who are making some of the greatest sacrifices of this war don't get any acknowledgement at all. Soldiers receive all the awards, ribbons and applause from the crowd while our spouses take on the burden of raising a family alone and our children get an absentee parent.

"Since the global war terror began, I've been mobilized twice. First, I was sent to Baghdad Iraq and now I'm winding down a second tour at Ft Bragg North Carolina training my fellow reservist for deployment. All added up, it's been twenty five months so far that I've been back on active duty. Over two years of my wife running a house alone and trying her best to raise a son and daughter. Over two years of dad missing holidays, kid's baseball practices, dance recitals, and soccer games.

The experience would have been much harder for my family and I to bear if it weren't for the support and understanding of the Haverhill community.

We've been lucky to have good friends, in the area and neighbors up the street who understand the strains that the military puts on a family. My children's teachers at both Pentucket Lake School where my son is in fourth grade and

Walnut Square where my daughter is in kindergarten have been extremely helpful.

They have gone out of their way to be accommodating and sympathetic to children whose Dad is away in the service.

Sure, not everyone is thoughtful or considerate of what a military family goes through. Like everyone we've got our share of petty neighbors and had more than one dishonest tradesman has tried to exploit the fact that my wife isn't an expert on home construction. Some folks will never really appreciate the fact that the freedoms they enjoy as Americans are paid for with the sacrifices of military families.

But thankfully, those people are the minority. In general, the Haverhill community has been terrific to my family and I during both my army mobilizations.

For a soldier, knowing that your family is being supported by the people back home is a great relief. A pat on the back in the airport or thumbs up from a stranger is great, but treating our families with kindness and empathy while we are away means much more. It is an act of true patriotism that every soldier appreciates.

When asked why he decided to serve, he replied, "Honestly, it's tough to recall. It was always something I intended to do".

A verbal salutation or greeting and a "thank you for your service", or "thanks for what you do" is welcome and appreciated. Displaying an American flag on a vehicle or on a window is too, and a yellow magnetic ribbon, is an excellent show of support. Better yet, a centerpiece in the front yard of a random home in the Merrimack Valley, landscaped with pristine freshly cut grass, with fresh mulching in a circle and cobblestone border, with a 25 foot-tall flagpole that hoists up and proudly displays our Flag, as the sound that Old Glory makes as the wind moves her about, whipping and clacking and when the sun reveals the crimson, white, and blue; it is a symbol of strength, honor and valor.

All of these are great examples of support and patriotism that is uncommonly shown throughout the community.

Folks, what hits home the most for the Soldier, Marine, Airman, or Seaman, is how their loved ones are faring while we serve, whether, near or far. Thank you!

Lt. Colonel Don Sheehan
USAF

By: Helen Mooradkanian - February, 2013

When 6,000 Marines were trapped at their base during the 77-day siege of Khe Sanh—a surprise attack by 40,000 heavily armored North Vietnamese and Viet Cong during the infamous 1968 Tet Offensive —it was "the longest and deadliest battle" of the Vietnam War. West Point graduate Lieutenant Colonel Don Sheehan, USAF (Retired), of Tewksbury, flew into Khe Sanh with a C-130 Hercules cargo plane. Dodging a gauntlet of enemy ground fire, he flew in low enough to airdrop, from an altitude of 1500 feet, tons of supplies directly onto the Marine drop zone. Each pallet load, with built-in parachute, weighed several thousand pounds and carried food, ammunition, and fuel. Don was serving with the 773rd Tactical Airlift Squadron out of Clark AB, Philippines.

Not only was the task challenging—the Marines needed 185 tons daily of supplies, as well as troop reinforcements. But the ground fire was intense; it never stopped. "It prevented our C-130s from landing. Earlier one of our planes had been hit on the ground and had exploded into flames. So to avoid gunfire, we flew in as low as possible—ideally within cloud cover— guided by our skilled navigators who calculated airspeed and wind drift, and our loadmasters who released the pallets at the proper time. We dropped our loads by parachute onto the drop zone. Although we took minor hits, I felt no fear. I knew the Lord held me in the palm of His hand," Don said.

Khe Sanh sits on a plateau in a remote section of South Vietnam, near the Laotian border, overlooking the Ho Chi Minh Trail. "The North Vietnamese owned the night. You couldn't drive a truck anywhere without being ambushed." But through aggressive air power, the Americans took back the night.

Throughout his tour of duty in Vietnam, 1967–1969, Don Sheehan flew 15-day shuttles to other bases—Cam Ranh Bay, Nha Trang, Da Nang, the smaller dirt airstrips of Song Be, and throughout Southeast Asia.

Once he evacuated a small village, an isolated outpost in the remote central highlands of South Vietnam that was being harassed and threatened by the Viet Cong. All 40 South Vietnamese soldiers and their families were flown to safety for relocation.

They were like sheep without a shepherd, abandoned by their leaders— "soldiers, some in mismatched uniforms, with rifles on their shoulders. Their wives were laden down with black garbage bags, holding all they owned, slung over the shoulder, while carrying one or two babies with children trailing behind, clutching a teddy bear or a loaf of bread."

For his "extraordinary achievement" while serving in Vietnam, Don was awarded the Distinguished Flying Cross.

C-130s on skis at North Pole

As perilous as it was to fly in combat in Vietnam with the huge C-130, little compared with the challenge of landing and taking off on Greenland's polar ice cap near the Arctic Circle. The 10,000-foot thick ice cap is covered by a flat, expanse of ice and snow extending as far as the eye can see. There are no ground control navigational aids to guide the planes.

Don flew the only aircraft equipped with skis, the C-130D-6, jet-powered turboprops, to supply the men who manned the remote, isolated radar sites (DYE 1, 2, and 3) on Greenland's DEW line—the Distant Early Warning line. These powerful radar sites monitored the skies constantly for any Russian planes approaching North America. The C-130D-6 had two main skis (20 feet long by 6 feet wide) and a nose ski (10 feet by 6 feet).

Don served with the 17th Tactical Airlift Squadron out of Elmendorf AFB, Alaska, which maintained two planes at all times at Sondrestrom AB, Greenland.

Persevering toward the goal

At the age of 14, Don had read the book "West Point Today" by Kendall Banning. "That book changed my life," he says. "From that moment on, I wanted to go to West Point, with all my heart and soul. It became my driving passion." Although he had to wait three years, these were years of preparation. It was well worth the wait," he said. Don graduated from West Point with the class of 1956. His was an illustrious class: 30 became generals (including General Norman Schwarzkopf), with a total of 77 stars.

The military discipline, both physical and mental, helped shape the man Don is today. He realized his dreams. He graduated from West Point. He became a pilot. He taught and mentored Air Force cadets in love of God and country, duty and honor. On invitation, he spent two tours of duty teaching English at the U.S. Air Force Academy, 1963–1967 and 1969–1973, beginning as an instructor and ultimately promoted to associate professor).

While attending West Point, Don met Dorrie Sidener and was swept off his feet. He pursued her for four years. Today, after 54 years of marriage, he says, "She still holds the mortgage on my soul."

As a West Pointer, Don knows what it means to be "a man under authority." He knows whom he can trust. Today he is waiting for that one word, in perhaps his greatest hour of testing…

Trusting for a miracle

A year ago Dorrie suffered a stroke and became bedridden.

In the midst of this trial, Don waits patiently and expectantly, with hope, for a miracle.

"I've always believed that the Lord holds us in the palm of His hand. He brought Dorrie and me together. We trust Him. Throughout each day of our marriage, we prayed the Rosary, the Stations of the Cross, and meditated on the events in Christ's life. I can never thank God enough for all He's done for us. As our children were growing up, we prayed the Rosary together as a family each day, with all seven of our children. Today, I continue to pray with Dorrie each afternoon."

"The Lord is at the center of our lives, the foundation of our marriage. Dorrie and I both saved ourselves for each other before our marriage. In fact, because Dorrie refused to compromise her faith, she left Hollywood after starring in three films—two Westerns, with Jock Mahoney and Gene Autry, and a comedy co-starring with Mickey Rooney."

Don believes in the power of prayer and miracles. "Jesus came to heal the sick," he says. In answer to prayer, he saw his daughter healed of post-chicken pox encephalitis, a dangerous swelling of the brain against the skull. She later graduated magna cum laude from Fitchburg State College.

"Each day I pray for a miracle, that Dorrie will be healed. I know nothing is impossible with God. I give thanks to Him every day. He's been so good to us. I trust Him completely. Whatever God has in store for us, I accept. Both Dorrie and I put our trust in the Lord."

A love story for Valentine's Day…Of God who is faithful…of a man and woman faithful to God…and to each other.

The Bible records the story of a Roman military officer who asked Jesus to heal his paralyzed servant. "Only speak a word, and my servant will be healed. For I too am a man under authority." Jesus "marveled" at his "great faith." He said, " 'As you have believed, so let it be done for you.' And his servant was healed that same hour" (Matthew 8:5-13).

Thank you Don Sheehan for all your bravery and sacrifice. You are truly a Hero in Our Midst.

Cpl. George Seddon
USA
Phyllis Seddon, USN

By: Helen Mooradkanian - May, 2012

WESTFORD, MA - Corporal George Seddon, U.S. Army, 10th Mountain Division, fought in the mountains of Italy while his wife Phyllis, then-fiancée, U.S. Navy, cared for the severely wounded returning from the Pacific Theater during World War II. Together, the couple from Westford, MA, epitomize "The Greatest Generation."

The 10th Mountain was an elite, highly specialized division created in 1943 to fight and survive under the most brutal mountain conditions—50-deg below zero winter blizzards—in Italy's Alps and Apennines. The infantry moved on skis, the artillery on snowshoes. Sled dogs and Missouri mules were the only means of transporting 75mm Howitzers and supplies through the mountains.

These men were pioneers, unique in the annals of American military history. They fought on the mountain peaks. They fought in the valleys. They endured the rigors of sub-zero mountain warfare while training in the Colorado Rockies. They endured the heat of the Texas flat lands in preparation for the Po Valley offensive.

They were renowned for their courage, daring—and stealth attacks. They routed the experienced mountain divisions of Germany.

Olympic skiers and seasoned mountain climbers were turned into hardened infantrymen. Recruited by the National Ski Patrol, not the Army, they patrolled mountain slopes. They scaled cliffs of sheer rock with toboggans strapped to their backs. On reaching the summit, they engaged the enemy with only empty rifles and bayonets—without the cover of artillery fire. Surprise attacks were their forte. They won victory after victory, but not without cost. The 10th Mountain suffered one of the highest casualty rates in the war. Of the 13,000 soldiers deployed to Italy, nearly a thousand died.

The 10th Mountain entered combat at the 11th hour in Italy's Apennines on January 28, 1945. They captured Riva Ridge, Mount Belvedere, and led in the Po Valley offensive that cut off the Germans from reaching the Brenner Pass.

In three short months of intensive, bloody battles, they liberated Italy. It was one of the fastest advances through enemy territory of any division in WWII. The German Army surrendered Italy on May 2, 1945.

Prepared at "Camp Hell"...

George Seddon, with the 85th Mountain Infantry Regiment, 604th Field Artillery Battalion, received his initial training with the 87th Regiment, high in the Colorado Rockies, on the continental divide. They began at Camp Carson in Colorado Springs and continued another 10 months at Camp Hale in Pando, near Leadville—elevation 9,480 ft. above sea level. "It was 200 miles from Camp Carson to Camp Hale," he said, "and we trekked the entire distance in 10 days, covering 20 to 25 miles a day on snowshoes over deep snow, leading our mule pack trains with all our equipment and supplies."

Camp Hale was dubbed "Camp Hell." Only the very hardy could endure the rigorous training. Steep slopes, 12-ft deep snow, 50-deg-below-zero temperatures, climbing and rappelling down sheer cliffs. At night they slept in caves carved out of the snow. "Food on mess trays froze solid in seconds unless we first dipped the metal trays in boiling water."

In the Artillery, George loaded and unloaded pack mules with 300-lb equipment, led them on 25-mile-a-day treks through the mountains. It took three mules to carry one 75mm Howitzer, disassembled. He had charge of three mules named "Hitler," "John," and "Mary." "I don't know who named them but I made sure "Hitler" was always in the lead," he laughed.

"You have to approach mules carefully, let them first get used to your presence. Gradually we moved closer and closer. Then we walked around him, eventually patted him on the back. Finally, we gave him food and water. Only then could we safely secure a load on his back."

Before deployment to Italy, George got a foretaste of mountain warfare in the foggy, wind-swept Japanese-occupied islands of Kiska and Attu in the Aleutians, off Alaska. "Although the Japanese had already evacuated when we arrived, they left behind equipment, mines, booby traps, and underwater foxholes."

…For victory on Mount Belvedere

"Camp Hell" was good preparation for Mount Belvedere.

In late January 1945, the Tenth finally entered combat in the North Apennine Mountains of Italy. They faced German positions along the 5-mile long Mount Belvedere-Mount della Torraccia ridge. Other divisions had tried to take Mount Belvedere three times but had failed.

To get to Mount Belvedere, they first had to capture Riva Ridge, a 4,600-ft high escarpment, used by the Germans as a lookout for guarding all approaches to Belvedere. A 1,500-ft vertical ascent was the only way to the summit. The Germans, with their experienced mountain troops, believed no one could scale Riva Ridge so they left only one mountain battalion to defend it. But in the middle of the night, the 10th Mountain's 86th scaled the escarpment and took the Germans by surprise!

Mount Belvedere followed. The 85th and 87th Regiments scaled Belvedere, which was heavily protected by troops and minefields. In the bloody battle to capture the summit—again executed in secret at night—the 10th Mountain attacked with bayonets, without the cover of artillery fire. Again the surprise assault brought victory!

The Germans made seven counterattacks over two days but were roundly defeated. The Tenth were fearless fighters. In three days, they took nearly 1,200 prisoners and occupied 35 square miles of enemy territory. By March 5, the 10th Mountain Division had occupied a solid line of ridges and mountains. They were now in a position to break through the Germans' Apennine Mountain line and open the way to the Po Valley.

Seddon, also a combat medic, narrowly escaped death in "Purple Heart Valley," so named because the one way "in" was also the only way "out." In the Po Valley, the Germans had blown up all the tunnels so the 85th loaded their artillery on amphibious vehicles and "ducked" them across the storm-tossed waves of Lake Garda—under the constant barrage of enemy fire from the other side of the lake. They finally reached Torbole, which they captured after a fierce battle. Here Seddon saved his commander's life and received the Bronze Star.

The singing warriors

Both George and Phyllis Seddon come from a long line of Salvation Army officers. Phyllis' father, John Valentine, traveled with the founder, General William Booth. Both her parents, and an uncle and aunt were officers (pastors) in the Salvation Army. George's parents were also officers (his father a Brigadier General), as were his mother's whole family.

George Seddon also faced his own personal "Mount Belvedere" when battling several types of cancers. He has been healed of them all. Today, he and Phyllis, true to their Salvation Army background, brighten the local Dunkin Donuts where a crowd always joins them in singing old Gospel songs. Through this, they have been able to encourage others facing "Mount Belvederes" of cancer and fear. True to their faith, the Seddons have their feet firmly planted on Christ the Solid Rock, who has made their feet like hinds' feet to scale the mountains of adversity (Habakkuk 3:19).

The commander of the 10th Mountain Division, General George Hays, told his men: "When you go home, no one will believe you when you start telling of the spectacular things you have done. There have been more heroic deeds and experiences crammed into these days than I have ever heard of. The Lord had us by the hand."

Fred Pietrowski
U.S. Navy

By: Helen Mooradkanian - January, 2013

LAWRENCE, MA - It was early 1961 during the Cold War. The United States had just closed its embassy in Havana, Cuba. The Cuban Missile Crisis would not come to a head until one year later, in October 1962—the closest the U.S. and the Soviet Union ever came to a global nuclear war.

Fred Pietrowski, U.S. Navy, of Lawrence, Mass., was an electrician aboard the submarine USS Angler (SS240) when a goodwill tour to New York suddenly turned into a chase to drive off two Soviet diesel subs and capture a Soviet nuclear sub. Few know about that incident in early 1961 when Pietrowski discovered three submarines hiding near the Statue of Liberty, long before any major confrontation between the two world powers.

From the port lookout, Fred had focused his binoculars on the Statue of Liberty, only 800 feet away. Suddenly he saw a Soviet periscope pop up out of the water only 300 yards from the Statue. When reported to their New London, Conn., base, the order came: "Chase him!"

Minutes later, Fred saw a second Soviet submarine hiding only a half-mile from Wall Street! Again the order: "Chase him!"

Then they heard the turbine whine of a nuclear sub. The unmarked sub refused to identify itself! This time, they were told: "Ram him!"

Instantly, five U.S. submarines sped to the scene. All six American subs spent three days, 24/7, trying to capture the Soviet nuclear sub for its technology. "We chased it all the way down the coast to Virginia, where it took off."

Three Soviet subs hiding, undetected, in New York harbor! "Each missile on a submarine has 157 nuclear warheads—enough to blow up the East Coast from DC to Boston," Pietrowski points out. "Surely, God was protecting us."

Fred joined the Navy in 1959, after graduating from Central Catholic. His life in the Navy and civilian life has been a series of miraculous escapes from the jaws of death, literally.

"Shark!"

In October 1962, Fred was deployed to the Mediterranean on a three-week patrol, a secret mission, aboard the submarine USS Entemedor (SS340). Under Sealed Orders.

"Not even our captain knew where we were heading or our destination. If anything happened to us, we were told, 'You were never there!' "

Unknown to them, it was the beginning of the Cuban Missile Crisis.

"We went into 'ultra quiet mode'—like a ghost ship floating through the ocean depths. No air conditioners. No unnecessary movement. I took only twenty-one steps from my bunk to my workplace, and only seven steps to eat. No emptying garbage at sea (the enemy could track us).

"For three weeks we endured suffocating heat without a shower—140 degrees where I worked, 125 degrees in the rest of the boat. It hurt to breathe though my nose. The stench of rotting garbage filled our nostrils.

"After two weeks, our main electric propulsion motors began to overheat. Now at 179 degrees, they would automatically shut off at 180 degrees, forcing us to float to the surface—like a "sitting duck!"

"We took photos through the periscope for intelligence gathering—without any idea of what we were photographing—missile sites, installations, or vessels. We laid 36 mines at a time. Finally, mission accomplished, we left the area undetected and surfaced.

"Once far removed from our mission zone, the captain stopped our sub and with engines running let us cool off with a swim. Two men were posted on shark-watch, armed with M-1 rifles. We splashed around, playing basketball with the five officers."

Suddenly, someone screamed, "SHARK!"

"I saw a gigantic black fin, over a foot high, moving swiftly toward us! It was a 35-foot long Great White Shark, our captain later told us. At the slightest movement in the water, it will attack at speeds to 15 mph.

"A football field away lay our submarine..."

"To the torpedo-shaped shark, our submarine looked, and smelled, like its prey, a large black whale: round, with wide black diving 'fins' in the front and back. The exhaust of our diesel engines sprayed fishy-smelling bilge water along with smoke." The Great White, naturally curious, swam up alongside the sub and kept taking sample bites of the submarine—first circling one way, then the other—hour after hour. "Whenever the shark swam to the other side, we would swim toward the sub. Whenever he came toward us, we formed a tight group and floated, holding still."

One hour went by. Two. Three...After six hours, with the hungry shark still circling the sub, the captain yelled, "It'll be dark soon. Come in, or I'll have to leave you here..."

"We had no choice but to swim toward our sub—and the hungry shark.

"When we were 100 feet from our boat, we made a dash for it. But there was only one set of foot holes leading up to the deck—and sixty-five men in the water!"

Fred was among the last twelve remaining in the water when he heard, "Here he comes!"

"Swim forward and stand on the diving planes," yelled the captain. Twelve men squeezed together on the diving plane—no bigger than a kitchen table—while knee-deep in water.

"The Great White headed straight for me, passing right under my bare feet! His mouth opened wide—exposing multiple rows of 300 serrated teeth!

"At one point he was only 8 feet away, staring at my chest!

"Miraculously, we all made it to safety."

Hurricane Ella

Leaving the Mediterranean from that mission, the Entemedor headed straight into the North Atlantic Ocean and into the teeth of Hurricane Ella, with its 115-mph winds that tossed them like a toy boat for days. "With less than one day's air supply, we could not submerge. We had to ride out the hurricane."

"On day four, a 120-ft high rogue wave—an almost vertical wall of water—slammed us broadside. I was tossed 20 feet through the air. Our sub rolled radically to the right—stopping at a 57-degree angle (a 54-degree angle is the point of no return). All oil drained out of engines. We lost power. There we hung, in total darkness!

At that radical angle, over a thousand gallons of sulfuric acid would spill out from batteries. If mixed with salt water, it would form a deadly chlorine gas that spelled instant death.

"In that darkness, with hydraulic oil flowing all over the tiled deck, I crawled over pipes and cables, feeling my way to the main battery switch, finally found it and turned it on. Immediately the lights and power came on, the engine propellers began to turn. Slowly the submarine rose to a vertical position. The fact that we survived is a miracle."

It took them eleven days to cross the Atlantic.

"Before arriving in New London, we posted armed guards. This was unusual. Waiting at the gate were Marines, standing shoulder to shoulder, armed with machine guns. The Cuban Missile Crisis, we learned later, had begun."

Fred's escapes from death also include: Almost falling on the back of a 16-foot shark. Being trapped in a sealed compartment filled with 12 feet of water. Submarine rammed, cut in half, and sunk—twice. A head-long fall that split open his skull, with doctors giving him up for dead.

Fred bears witness to the Navy hymn, "Eternal Father, Strong to Save." From experience, he knows the Biblical truth: "The eternal God is your refuge, And underneath are the everlasting arms" (Deuteronomy 33:27).

Thank you Fred for your service to our country. You are truly a Valley Patriot and a Hero in Our Midst.

Army Capt. John Loving

By: Helen Mooradkanian - November, 2012

On October 22, 1969, three U.S. choppers flew down into a "hot" landing zone in the southwest corner of Vietnam, in Tay Ninh Province, on the Cambodian border. Their mission: sweep out the nest of Viet Cong hiding in Cambodia, officially neutral at the time.

As the two American combat advisers, the South Vietnamese commander, and 80 South Vietnamese soldiers hit the ground, the Viet Cong opened fire with machine guns, mortar, and small arms.

Cambodia was sanctuary to the Viet Cong, who hid there in their jungle base and routinely made forays across the border into South Vietnam —attacking, terrorizing, and killing soldiers and civilians—without fear of retaliation. No U.S. troops were allowed to fight in Cambodia nor fly into the country.

First Lieutenant John Loving, Raleigh, North Carolina, U.S. Army, 24-year old commander of a six-man U.S. Mobile Advisory Team to the South Vietnamese Army, was used to leading with minimal supervision from superiors. They had to go behind enemy lines. They were in an open field, completely exposed. They had no support from U.S. gunships. He was glad his trusted friend, Sergeant First Class Mack Rice, was with him.

When two South Vietnamese received critical head and neck injuries, Loving called in a medevac helicopter. The red smoke grenade showed the helicopter where to land. It also made the others sitting ducks for the enemy. At the height of the firefight, with mortar rounds dropping all around them, Rice loaded the wounded onto the chopper. Amid the deafening roar of gunfire kicking up dirt all around them, all the South Vietnamese fled.

Now the two Americans stood alone facing the enemy—John Loving and Mack Rice—along with their radio operator. "The radio operator would have probably run too but I was holding onto the microphone," Loving said.

When Loving called in gunships to open fire on the Viet Cong, the pilot of the assault helicopter balked. "Sorry, that's in Cambodia, sir," he said.

Loving was furious. "Red Dog," I yelled to the pilot. "This is Sassy Cat SIX. By emphasizing the word 'six,' I clearly indicated I was a commander. The pilot didn't know I was only a first lieutenant," he writes in his book, "A Soldier's Faith" (Anomalos Publishing House, Crane).

"I'm the commander of this operation, and I'm telling you this is Vietnam, not Cambodia. I want you to shoot up that target and anything else you see that looks like the bad guys."

After a long pause, the pilot replied. "Roger. This is Red Dog and I'm attacking this target based on your order, and I note your call sign is Sassy Cat Six."

Almost immediately, the pilot unleashed a tremendous volume of rocket fire onto the Viet Cong machinegun emplacement, completely knocking it out. Further attacks completely destroyed the mortar and wiped out the enemy. The battle had lasted all morning.

Loving, Rice, and the radio operator dashed across a field under heavy fire and found two more critically wounded. Again Loving called in a chopper, and helped load the wounded himself, as mortar rounds exploded around them.

For his valor that day, Lieutenant Loving received the Silver Star. Sergeant Rice received the Bronze Star with V.

Three life lessons learned

On the battlefields of Vietnam, John Loving learned three key lessons about life that turned his life around and made him an overcomer.

"Wake Up Call #1: I suddenly realized I was not in control." While setting up an ambush along a riverbank, Loving and his platoon were fired on by powerful 50-caliber machine guns and red tracers from an approaching boat. Their only cover was a muddy rice paddy, with a thin layer of water. Unknown to them at the time, this was a U.S. boat that had detected Viet Cong slipping in secretly and lurking on the shore. "We couldn't get up and run because the gunner would see us and mow us down. There we lay in the mud helpless, nearly 20 U.S. and South Vietnamese soldiers. I was directly responsible for them all. Yet there was nothing I could do to save them . . ."

This crisis led John Loving to question: Did he really believe God existed? And if so, was He a loving God to whom he could pray? "I decided "yes" to both questions. Then, for the first time in my life, I surrendered my will to God. Our platoon was miraculously saved."

"Wake Up Call #2: The imposter—appearances are deceiving." After a trip up the river to Tay Ninh City, Loving and a group of American soldiers were returning to base when suddenly Loving saw something moving in the water, about 200 meters away. It was a man, obviously Vietnamese— bobbing in the waves! His head and shoulders were visible, his right arm rose as if waving to them. Was this a Viet Cong trick to lure the Americans into an ambush? Was it a civilian needing help?

As they came closer, Loving realized the young man was dead, his open eyes rolled back into his head, his right arm frozen in death. As the waves lapped against the shore, the corpse swayed back and forth, almost as if to warn, "Be careful. I didn't think I would end up like this, but it could happen to you."

The man was dead yet he "seemed" alive.

That bobbing image crystallized for Loving all the trauma of Vietnam. Memories may be suppressed for many years but had not been erased. Like that corpse bobbing in the water, the flashbacks would pop to the surface, unexpectedly. So he tried to hide the pain of deep wounds behind a façade, what John Eldridge calls the "false self." The manly response, Loving thought, was to shut down his emotions. . . Then he came upon the words of St. Irenaeus, "The glory of God is man fully alive." One day he experienced the truth of Jesus' promise: "The thief comes to steal, and to kill, and to destroy. I have come that they may have life, and have it more abundantly" (John 10:10).

"Wake Up Call #3: I am not invincible." Although Loving had escaped death many times in Vietnam, one close call really shook him up. He had flown into provincial headquarters with a few men to pick up supplies. "Thirty minutes before our return to Ben Cau, I went to the bar at the NCO Club. My two companions finished their business and, anxious to get back, they returned on the chopper as scheduled. I decided to stay and finish my drink and catch the next one 30 minutes later. The first chopper was shot down, and all three men died instantly. That night I couldn't sleep. I dreamt Death was stalking me. Then the words of one of my men pierced the darkness: 'Our mothers are praying for us.' I came to realize I had been spared because I still had a purpose to fulfill here on earth. My work was not yet finished."

John Loving found peace—not in psychiatric therapies that are only partially effective—but in the Person of Jesus Christ who said, "Peace I leave with you, My peace I give to you; not as the world gives do I give to you. Let not your heart be troubled. . ." (John 14:27).

Angelo Giambusso
USAAF, USA

By: Helen Mooradkanian - October, 2012

One month before his 21st birthday, 1st Lieutenant Angelo Giambusso, U.S. Army Air Force, North Andover, Mass., had flown five extremely hazardous combat missions—into Hitler's oil fields in Ploesti, Romania—plus another 40 strategic bombing attacks in 10 countries across Europe. Yet nothing compared to the dangers of Ploesti, for which he received double credit.

Angie was navigator on the B-24 Liberator heavy bomber, the "Belle of the Orchard," attached to the 720th Squadron, 450th Bombardment Group (H), 47th Wing, 15th Air Force. Stationed in Manduria Italy, a large air base 242 miles southeast of Naples, he was engaged in the saturation bombing of Ploesti's oil fields, tanks, refineries, and marshalling yards—which supplied one-third of Hitler's petroleum needs during World War II. Saturation bombing eventually slashed Ploesti's oil production to 7% of capacity.

Ploesti seemed impenetrable. It had one of the best integrated air defense networks in Europe: several hundred 88mm and 105mm anti-aircraft guns secured the widespread area, while smaller caliber guns were hidden in haystacks, rail cars, and mock buildings. Three fighter groups were always on standby. Unknown to Giambusso and his crew, a signals-intelligence station in Athens was continually monitoring and relaying the Allies' planned bomb runs to Ploesti, picking up signals as far away as North Africa.

Germans warn: Americans coming

On one of Angie's missions, his bombardier, who understood German, had picked up the Luftwaffe's message that Americans were headed to Ploesti...

"We flew in formation so we had lots of fire power. But if a plane got separated or disabled, it became a sitting duck for German ME 109 fighter planes. You either got crippled or shot down. Our plane was badly shot up many times, crash landed a few. We were grateful for our fighter-plane escorts."

Angie especially remembers one successful bomb run to Ploesti, probably their fiercest fighter attack encountered—and one that earned them a Unit Citation. It was April 5, 1944. A formation of forty B-24 heavy bombers, carrying the maximum payload of 8,000 lb., set course for Ploesti's marshalling yards and refineries. Nearing target, the B-24s were aggressively attacked by 40 to 60 enemy aircraft firing rockets, cannon and heavy machine guns—trying to destroy the formation before they reached their target. Angie's squadron, being in the lead, took the brunt of the attack. First the Germans attacked in pairs, threes, and fours—diving through the B-24s' formation and up under the second attack unit. Then they attacked from all angles—many from the 6 o'clock position in formations of six abreast. Planes at the 10 o'clock position fired a volley of rockets. The battle raged about an hour. Through it all, the B-24s severely wiped out Ploesti's oil supplies and marshalling yards, destroyed at least 27 enemy fighters, and damaged many more.

"Our plane was badly shot up and crippled. If it weren't for the Tuskegee Airmen (the famed all-black unit) who came to our rescue, we would have been dead. We had to make an emergency landing but came through OK. I tell you, were we grateful! We had barely touched ground when one of our crew literally flew out the cabin door and spontaneously grabbed the biggest, tallest Tuskegee guy and locked him in a huge bear hug. That's a sight I'll always remember—that rural boy from the deep South will never forget who saved his life!

Giambusso also flew on strategic bombing missions to Yugoslavia, Romania, northern Italy, Germany, Poland, Czechoslovakia, Austria, Hungary, and the Balkans. In southern France, they supported the Allied landings on the coast under very difficult circumstances, with night take-offs and rendezvous executed with exceptional precision and skill. They often engaged in "shuttle bombing," going from one target to another.

The heartbeat of a patriot

Angie Giambusso loves America. It's a fire burning in his heart. He openly talks about love of country with youth (he was a substitute teacher at North Andover High). "I love my country. I love the military life. When I see the American flag flying or recite the Pledge of Allegiance or sing "The Star Spangled Banner" or hear a bugler play taps or a military band playing, it stirs my heart," he says with emotion. In high school, he enrolled in the Cadet Corps, the Citizens Military Training Corps in Boston, where he trained one month a year for four years before entering the service.

Angie's military career spanned two wars—WWII and the Korean War—and two branches of the service. He went from flying on B-24 Liberator bombers in Europe to clearing land mines and building roads for the infantry and tanks in the mountains of Korea. The latter, he says, was far more grueling.

After his discharge in 1945 from the USAAF, he entered the reserves and was called up during the Korean War. By then an MIT graduate working as a mechanical engineer, he wanted to stay in his field so, after overcoming many hurdles, he transferred into the Army. He went before a board of three generals and was commissioned a 2nd Lieutenant in the U.S. Army. He later rose to Captain with the 13th Combat Engineer Battalion, Company A, which supported the 17th Infantry "Buffalo" Regiment, 7th Infantry Division.

From B-24s to land mines

From September 1951 to September 1952, Angelo Giambusso served in Korea where he cleared both anti-personnel and anti-vehicle land mines. Early in the Korean War, the U.S. had set anti-personnel mines to protect the borders. These followed a specific pattern and were set with trip wires, making them easier to find. Far more dangerous and difficult were the "shoebox" mines laid by the Chinese Communists. These rectangular wooden boxes, about 1 ft. long, held a tiny explosive inside. They lay hidden under a thin layer of soil. "You had to push a prong to find them." Most dangerous of all were the anti-tank or anti-vehicle mines. Much larger and often booby-trapped, they had to be exploded first.

Giambusso also did "lots of road work"—maintaining existing roads and building dirt roads on mountain ridges for Sherman tanks and the infantry.

He was awarded the Bronze Star for his "outstanding engineering achievements" during October 21, 1951, to August 20, 1952, in constructing a ridge-line tank road in the mountains during mid-winter despite the "tremendous hardships of weather and terrain." He laid mines "under enemy observation and fire." He "maintained supply lines despite landslides and washouts during the winter months and the spring thaw." Nothing "thwarted the firm resolution of Captain Giambusso...(whose) determination and leadership...inspired his men..."

Angie Giambusso also received a Letter of Commendation as commanding officer for "outstanding performance of duty," November 21, 1951 to January 6, 1952, in building a road through the mountains, needed for the supply and evacuation of troops, under "the most adverse conditions." He not only stabilized existing roadbeds but also built roads closer to battle lines and a tramway that hauled supplies close to Hill 1243, near Kumhwa.

Angie Giambusso knows what it means to go through the fire, protected. Aerial battles over Europe. Crash landings. Enemy fire on mountains in Korea. Hidden explosives and land mines.

As the Lord promises: "Fear not...I have called you by your name; You are Mine...When you walk through the fire, you shall not be burned, Nor shall the flame scorch you...Fear not, for I am with you..." (Isaiah 43:1-2, 5).

Corporal Philip Cote

USAAF

By: Helen Mooradkanian - September, 2012

Corporal Philip Cote, U.S. Army Air Force—who will celebrate his 96th birthday on October 31—was an eyewitness to history on Tinian Island in the Pacific during World War II. Raised in a log cabin in Tewksbury, Mass., and now living in Dracut, he witnessed two momentous events: two B-29s—the "Enola Gay" and "Bock's Car"—taking off for Japan on top-secret missions.

Philip served as master mechanic and crew chief for the revolutionary Boeing B-29 Superfortresses that first landed on Tinian in January 1945 and, by February 1945, were regularly flying bombing missions over Japan. He was assigned to a specific B-29 and, as crew chief, was responsible for its safe operating condition before it took off for the 10-hour flight over water to the Japanese mainland. He literally memorized the entire service manual to do his job, thanks to his extraordinary memory, knowledge and skill in mechanics, and ingenious mind. (He has eight inventions to his credit.)

Tinian Island is one of the three largest islands in the Marianas—along with Saipan and Guam—and is located 1500 miles south of Tokyo. From December 1944 to September 1945, Tinian played a crucial role in the final months of the war in the Pacific. It was the largest—and the busiest—airbase in the world. It had six 8,500-foot runways built specifically for the B-29s—four at North Field and another two at West Field. The B-29s brought WWII to an end just two-and-one-half months before the planned invasion of the Japanese homeland—an invasion that had cost America 5 million casualties.

Two events stand out in particular for Philip.

In the middle of the night at 2:45 a.m. on August 6, 1945, a huge B-29 Super fortress, the "Enola Gay," piloted by Lt. Col Paul Tibbets, Jr., took off from North Field on Tinian Island. Only hours earlier, the heavy bomber had been towed very slowly over pit No. 1, where a 9,000-lb uranium bomb, "Little Boy," 28-inches diameter and 120 in. long, had been hydraulically lifted into its specially designed bomb bay. Destination: Hiroshima.

It was an incredible sight. Philip remembers the two huge bomb pits that had been dug for the two atomic bombs: one to be loaded into the "Enola Gay" destined for Hiroshima, and the other—a 10,000-lb plutonium bomb named "Fat Man," 60-inches diameter—to be loaded into "Bock's Car," destined for Nagasaki. He saw them take off on August 6 and August 9, respectively. In fact, he serviced one of the two bombers that followed the "Enola Gay."

When Philip enlisted in the USAAF in 1942, he had his heart set on becoming an aircraft mechanic. Much to his chagrin, however, he was assigned to serve as a medic in the regular Army. "I couldn't stand the smell of hospitals," he said of his one-year tour of duty in Pensacola, Florida. With dogged determination, he took his appeal all the way to Washington. His persistence paid off, and he was reassigned to the Army Air Force and sent to Tinian.

"The heat was oppressive," he recalls of the broiling semi-tropical sun that beat down on Tinian. "Temperatures climbed well over 100 degrees every day the whole time I was there. And I was there exactly one year to the day. During that time, it rained only one day!"

The ground crews on Tinian were recognized as the hardest workers on the base. "We worked around-the-clock, day and night, to get our B-29s ready for their next mission, sometimes fixing the plane's engine from one raid while preparing it for its next mission. Our only rest came when the aircraft was away on a mission." Philip was responsible for the engines, controls, and accessory systems. At best, he may at times have one assistant and perhaps a mechanic. He could call on specialists from the Service Groups for help whenever needed. Often working 24-hour shifts with little time for meals, Philip dropped in weight from 164 to 124 lb. The sun also turned his skin a deep mahogany color. "It took me two years before I lost my suntan," he smiles.

B-29 master mechanic/inventor

As the premier heavy bomber of World War II, the B-29 was developed for long-range, high altitude combat missions. It had a range of over 3,500 miles and flew at altitudes of 27,000 to 34,000 feet. Payload capacity was 20,000 lbs. of bombs.

It featured many "firsts" in American aviation. It was the first bomber to feature pressurized sections (separate sections for flight crew, gunners, and tail gunners).

It was the first to feature remote-controlled guns, the first to use radar units to navigate and locate the target in bad weather. It was the first to use four giant engines (each 2200 hp).

As a result, the crew chief had a heavy responsibility. "We often faced problems never faced before," Philip said. Engines would overheat, catch fire, and crack—a tendency made much worse by the 100-plus degree heat on Tinian. Engine overhaul took more than a day to complete. Some engines almost never made it to the 100-hour mark. "We constantly had to change those big engines when they developed problems."

In order to get at the giant engines, Philip had to remove the cowling (outer metal cover) by unscrewing numerous "quarter-turn" fasteners. He found a simpler, faster way to do this by modifying the design of the existing tool then had the machine shop on the base produce it to specifications. When the supervisor saw Philip using the new tool, he took it away. But a few months later, all mechanics on Tinian were using Philip's new tool.

After the war, Philip and his wife Cecile raised their family—Tom (a Vietnam veteran), Carl and Philip Jr. who passed away at 10.

Philip worked for a Lowell textile mill. There he developed an air distribution system to clean textile looms still in use today, although by law his employer holds the patent. Other inventions include: a suction device for a hand-held auto vacuum using compressed air available at any gas station; a zippered vacuum cleaner bag. He even cut a 1939 Buick in half with a hacksaw, attached a plow to the back and used it to plow his farm.

Doctors call him "amazing"

Philip has escaped many close calls with death. Once while he was working on a B-29, and the co-pilot was sitting in the cockpit, a couple of bombs were accidentally released and rolled out near him. Fortunately, they were not "armed" and did not explode.

The long hours of exposure to the tropical sun on Tinian did wreak havoc. After his discharge from the military, Philip developed melanoma or skin cancer on his arms and back. He's had 41 surgeries to remove these tumors. "Every single doctor told me, 'you are an amazing man to survive all this.' "

When asked how he managed to overcome these trials, Philip points heavenward, to the Lord. His long, productive life is a testimony to his faith, work ethic, sense of duty and honor. "I've never sworn in my life," he says proudly.

As the psalmist wrote: "He will call upon Me, and I will answer him; I will be with him in trouble, I will deliver him and honor him. With long life will I satisfy him and show him My salvation" (Psalm 91:15-16).

Helen Mooradkanian is our new Valley Patriot Hero columnist and a former business writer. She is also a member of the Merrimack Valley Tea Party, You can email her at hsmoor@verizon.net

Corporal
Samuel Blumenfeld

By: Helen Mooradkanian - August, 2012

On March 3, 1945, in Italy's northern Apennines, storm clouds gathered as Private Samuel L. Blumenfeld, now of Littleton, Mass., first entered combat in WWII with the 10th Mountain Division, Field Artillery Battalion. For one born and raised in New York City, mountain warfare in winter was a new experience. But Sam was trained and prepared. His unit fired 155-mm howitzers to support the Tenth's second major assault on Germany's heavily fortified Gothic Line—the last line of defense against the advancing Allied armies. Through accurate, constant, and devastating artillery fire they softened the newly reinforced German lines. As a result, in only two days, by March 5, the 10th Mountain infantry had advanced further northeast beyond the already captured Riva Ridge, Mount Belvedere, and Mount della Torraccia—taking 1,200 prisoners and occupying 35 square miles across a solid line of ridges and mountain crests. Now they controlled a 120-mile front across the crest of the Apennines to southeast of Bologna. This placed them, and the Allies, in a strategic position for their major spring offensive into the Po Valley.

In April they advanced into the Po Valley and routed the Germans. Germany surrendered May 2, 1945.

This persistent, intensive campaign prepared Sam for another kind of warfare in later years: the culture wars.

Pressing through Apennines

The Italian Campaign was one of the hardest fought campaigns of the war. The northern Apennines form an unbroken barrier 140 miles long and 40 miles deep—from the Mediterranean to the Adriatic Sea. Some peaks have crests that rise 7,000 feet high. The Gothic Line, built on those heights, was embedded with 88-mm Panther gun turrets, steel shelters, bunkers dug into mountainsides, and minefields. The Line stretched east from the Ligurian Sea through Pisa, Florence, and beyond. A fortified stronghold. Forbidding. Formidable. Not easily broken. But through perseverance, it fell.

On April 9, 1945, the U.S. Fifth started its offensive toward the Po Valley through Bologna. From April 13 to 18, the attacks escalated: 2,000 piece artillery barrage, aerial bombing, and intensified ground fighting routed the Germans, and drove the enemy out of Mount Pigna, Mount Mantino, Mount Mosca, Mount Pero, and Reno River Valley. The Americans moved from ridgeline to ridgeline, from valley town to valley town, slowly pushing back the Germans. The enemy fought stubbornly, but could not prevail. By nightfall on April 17, the 10th Mountain Division had broken through what remained of the Germans' defensive line. Other victories soon followed.

The Allies reached the Po Valley on April 19, 1945, The 10th Mountain took 2,900 prisoners and captured Mount San Michele.

The turning point came the next day, April 20, when the Allies quickly surged forward through the Po Valley's flat terrain and excellent network of roads. They destroyed surviving enemy forces. It now became a race as to who would reach the Po River first, and the Alpine foothills beyond— the Allies or the Germans.

On April 21, 1945, Bologna fell to the Allies. By dawn on April 22, the entire Fifth Army was in the Po Valley. That same evening, the 10th Mountain reached the Po River at San Benedetto, 30 miles north. By midnight, the rest of the division arrived, and large amphibious DUKWs transported troops across the river. The rapid American advance left many pockets of Axis soldiers, and special task forces mopped up these areas.

By April 24, the entire U.S. Fifth Army front had reached the Po.

Ultimately, more than 100,000 Axis troops surrendered south of the Po River. Germany surrendered May 2, 1945.

Post-war mop-up and occupation

After the war ended, Sam, now a technical corporal, was transferred to an Infantry unit with the Occupation forces in Tarcento, Friuli province, to complete the orderly surrender of German forces, maintain security, and help the Italians begin their postwar reconstruction. Relations between American troops and native Italians were especially warm and cooperative. But near Trieste and the Yugoslav border, there was great unrest because of border disputes between Italy and Yugoslavia. Stationed in Trieste were troops of Communist dictator Marshall Tito. The 10th Mountain patrols prevented armed conflicts. Later, during U.N. negotiations to resolve the border dispute, Sam served as clerk recorder at the meetings.

The war between good and evil

The long, arduous warfare to rout the enemy from strongholds in the Apennines and Po Valley prepared Sam Blumenfeld for future work in another arena. What was the source of evil? How did it operate? How do you fight it? It led Sam to a decision that transformed his life.

Born of Jewish parents who had left Poland in the 1920s to escape poverty and persecution, Sam was raised in his family's faith. He was unfamiliar with the English Bible until introduced to it in a New York City public elementary school, where his principal recited the Twenty-Third Psalm at every school assembly.

"The words of this Psalm impressed me deeply," he said. "'The Lord is my Shepherd, I shall not want . . .Yea, though I walk through the valley of the shadow of death, I will fear no evil: for Thou art with me' (Psalm 23: 1, 4).

"These words carried me all through my military service. I felt safe, knowing I was continually protected, that God had a plan for my future. To this day, I sense God's protection."

In the 1980s, while during research on public education, Sam began reading the New Testament and became "a follower of Christ the Jewish Messiah, Yeshu'a." He says: "I believe Christ is Who He says He is, the

Son of God. He is The Truth. No one has influenced Western civilization the way Christ has. Regimes based on lies all crumble and fall: Nazism, Marxism, Communism. But Christianity is based on Jesus Christ, the Truth. Yet we have allowed atheists to take over in the public schools and destroy a child's belief in the God of the Bible, a moral crime that leads children into atheism, nihilism, and even Satanism. This can result in self-destructive, murderous behavior."

Today Sam Blumenfeld has the courage and boldness to stand in the gap for Christians and focus on exposing a public education system that is "promoting an atheist, pro-socialist educational agenda that is destroying our children." He has gained renown as a prolific author of conservative books, a bold advocate for biblical and conservative moral values in public education. He now writes articles for The New American online (www.thenewamerican.com). His first book "How to Start Your Own Private School" was written at the request of the Conservative Book Club. Others quickly followed, including "The New Illiterates." Best-known is his reading program, "Alpha-Phonics," written to help parents teach their children to read at home. It has been used by thousands of home-schooling parents, especially Christians. His expose of the National Education Association, "NEA: Trojan Horse in American Education," sold over 60,000 copies and persuaded many parents to home-school their children. He has also written a book on the Shakespeare authorship controversy, "The Marlowe-Shakespeare Connection."

Engaged in spiritual warfare for years, Sam can attest to the apostle Paul's words: "For the weapons of our warfare are not carnal but mighty in God for pulling down strongholds, casting down arguments and everything that exalts itself against the knowledge of God"

(2 Corinthians 10:4-5).

PFC. Edwin Fraser

By: Helen Mooradkanian - July, 2012

WESTFORD - On February 16, 1945, at 8:30 a.m.—three days before the Marines stormed ashore on Iwo Jima— PFC Edwin Fraser, Westford, Mass., a combat medic, was among the 503rd Airborne's Regimental Combat Team (RCT) of 1,800 paratroopers who made a surprise assault on the island of Corregidor in the Philippines. The skies filled with fifty-one C-47 "Gooney Birds," as the men jumped six to eight at a time. Landing zones were small. Winds high, up to 35 mph. Split-second timing was crucial—only a 6-second "window."

This was one of the very few airborne assaults during WWII in the Southwest Pacific—and probably the most difficult. It was Ed's third combat jump.

"We expected only a few hundred Japanese on Corregidor, most wiped out by the heavy naval and aerial bombardment. The island was a mass of rubble," Fraser said. "Instead, more than 6,500 Japanese soldiers and elite Imperial Special Naval Landing Forces (Marines) were waiting for us, hidden in the intricate underground network of caves and tunnels—caves also storing high-powered explosives. At Corregidor, we saw our most vicious combat action."

Ed's chute got caught on the side of a 500-ft cliff on Topside, the high ground of the tadpole-shaped island (Topside was also where the Imperial

Japanese naval commander had his post, on the side of a cliff, for total surveillance.) "I looked up and saw a Jap directly above me, his gun aimed at me . . . He shot me in both legs, but I was able to join the others in cleaning out Topside. We carried a 110-lb load, including a heavy Thompson submachine gun strapped to the body, carbine and knife tied around the leg for hand-to-hand combat, and hand grenades."

Corregidor. Gateway to Manila Bay. "The Fortress." "The Rock." Impregnable. Impenetrable. Or so the Japanese believed. Sheer cliffs rising 500 ft. above sea level encircled the island. To surprise the Japanese, the first paratroopers had to land within a few hundred yards of the enemy's command post, on landing zones measuring only 300-350 by 200-250 yd.

The Americans succeeded! One group of 30 paratroopers overshot their target, landing instead on top of the Japanese commander's post! They killed him within minutes. Already the heavy bombing had destroyed phone lines. Now their leader was dead too. Within one hour after the first paratrooper had landed, Americans had Topside under control.

Around 2:00 p.m. on February 16, 1945, the 503rd raised the American flag on a telegraph pole. Two weeks later they moved it to the parade ground for the official flag raising.

The 503rd Airborne had come to recapture "The Rock," after its surrender to Japan on May 5, 1942. They helped General Douglas MacArthur fulfill his promise to the Philippines: "I shall return."

A god falls—a rock shatters

The Japanese were "savage fighters," Ed Fraser recalls, "vicious, with no concern for human life. They committed atrocities on our wounded and on civilians. We knew they were going to blow the island out of the water."

As Time wrote in a cover story, "the U.S. came face to face with a startling fact—it was waging war against a god...to 70 million Japanese he [Emperor Hirohito] was divine." To die for him was their greatest honor.

At midnight on February 17, the day after the airborne assault, the Japanese retaliated with a 50-man suicide charge or "banzai" attack. They were quickly wiped out. Two larger "banzai" attacks followed on February 18, at 3:00 a.m. and again at 6:00 a.m., when nearly 600 shrieking Japanese attacked the 503rd RCT on Topside, in heavy hand-to-hand combat. More than 500 enemies were killed; survivors committed suicide rather than surrender. Still 2,000 Japanese remained in Malinta Tunnel, many sealed in by earlier bombings.

On February 21, Malinta Hill erupted like a volcano—split asunder by a series of detonations in quick succession. The Japanese, trapped inside, chose suicide and had blown themselves up. Two nights later, on February 23, more suicide explosions ripped through Malinta Tunnel.

For days afterwards, Corregidor reverberated with underground explosions.

By February 27, after two weeks of vicious fighting, the 503rd had secured Corregidor. More than 4,500 enemies had been killed, with thousands more buried in tunnels or cave-ins. Thirty POWs were taken.

A false god had fallen. "The rock" lay smashed. A fortress was no more.

On March 2, 1945, General MacArthur returned to Corregidor for the official surrender and flag raising ceremony.

Liberating the Philippines

During three years in the Southwest Pacific, Ed Fraser fought in several major offensives including:

• Markham Valley, New Guinea—September 5, 1943. The first U.S. airborne operation in the Pacific Theater and Ed's first combat jump. Its success led to future airborne operations. After two weeks of combat, they forced the Japanese to evacuate a major base at Lae.

• Noemfoor, off the Dutch New Guinea coast—July 3, 1944. On Ed's second combat jump, they destroyed the enemy's garrison and helped build airfields crucial to the Allies' advance to the Philippines.

• Leyte, Philippines—November 18, 1944. Preparation for Corregidor. Ed was also assigned to a large hospital there, after the Battle of Leyte Gulf, October 23-26, the largest naval battle in history. The Gulf was strewn with sunken destroyers and battleships, some with "kamikaze" suicide planes (loaded with explosives) protruding from their bow.

• Mindoro, central Philippines—December 15, 1944. Land-based "kamikaze" planes threatened the 503rd amphibious assault. "We came under intense air and naval attack here, at one point shelled for 25 minutes by an enemy naval task force." The RCT secured sites for airstrips for planes destined for Luzon.

• Negros, central Philippines—April 7–September 1945. Transported by landing craft to this island, the 503rd battled the Japanese alone for more than five months in the mountains. (The 40th Infantry Division had suddenly been redirected to Mindanao.) The battles were fierce. Patrols never returned. "Bouncing Betty" grenades, shooting 6 ft. in the air before exploding, sprayed a wide area and killed large numbers at one time.

When the Japanese government surrendered on August 15, 1945, the 503rd took 7,500 POWs, total, on Negros, including a high ranking general.

Ed was placed in charge of POWs. Among them were Japanese Marine officers, medically trained in the U.S. Grateful for the care they received, these officers presented Ed with four pen-and-pencil sketches they had made of him, autographed in both English and Japanese.

On September 2, 1945, Japan formally surrendered to Supreme Allied Commander General MacArthur.

Afflicted—but not crushed

Ed Fraser lived through "banzai" charges, "kamikaze" pilots, lack of water, a fortress that crumbled a typhoon's 30-ft swells in the South China Sea.

During WWII, the U.S. government issued all the military a pocket New Testament with protective brass cover, which most carried in the pocket over their heart. In the inscription, President Franklin Delano Roosevelt had written that as Commander-in-Chief he "commended the reading of the Bible...the Sacred Book...[with its] words of wisdom, counsel and inspiration ... a fountain of strength..."

As those who fought on Corregidor can affirm, "The Lord is my rock and my fortress and my deliverer, My God, my strength, in whom I will trust" (Psalm 18:2). For He has promised: "Never will I leave you. Never will I forsake you, no not ever" (Hebrews 13:5).

SSG. A. Robert Fairburn, III
173rd Airborne U.S. Army

By: Helen Mooradkanian - June, 2012

November 11, 1967, Veterans Day, on Hill 823 in the remote forested jungles of Vietnam's Central Highlands. During the 33-day "Battle of Dak To." It's a date that Staff Sergeant Bob Fairbairn, Boston, and others from 1st battalion, 503rd Airborne Infantry, 173rd Airborne Brigade, will long remember. "Task Force Black" was trapped in a deadly ambush—199 men from 1-503rd Companies C and D overrun by two battalions of the North Vietnamese Army (NVA). Within the first 15 minutes of battle, nearly every man was either killed or wounded.

"Everyone out front was dead," Fairbairn said. Severely wounded himself, he first destroyed all the radios and machineguns before pulling out, dragging machine gunner Jerry Kelley's body with him up the slope. Fairbairn was the last paratrooper out.

No sooner had he joined the wounded being treated when he heard the cry "frag" amid the battle's din. A Chicom hand grenade! PFC John Barnes, Dedham, Mass., threw himself on the grenade—saving the lives of Fairbairn and 15 other wounded troopers. Barnes died almost instantly and, for this act of heroism above and beyond the call of duty, he received the Congressional Medal of Honor.

Fifty years earlier, exactly to the day, November 11, 1917, during WWI in France, Fairbairn's grandfather, an officer with the 26th Yankee Division, was wounded in combat and decorated for heroism.

Now his grandson Bob Fairbairn was awarded four Purple Hearts and a number of other awards for valor and service in Vietnam. Fairbairn cherishes the Purple Hearts most of all. They bond him to all his fallen brothers.

November 11. A day of tragedy and triumph. Of death and life. Of destruction and hope. Both are inextricably linked. For out of the ashes of despair rises the gift of new life, as Bob's life today testifies to.

SSG Bob Fairbairn comes from a long line of courageous patriots who have fought valiantly for freedom and America.

His great-great grandfather, Albion Parris Howe, a major general in the Civil War, commanded the 2nd Division, VI Corps, at the battle of Fredericksburg and later was Commander of Artillery, Washington D.C. He served in the Honor Guard at Lincoln's casket and internment, and on the military commission that tried the Lincoln conspirators. His grandfather, a Colonel in WWI, served in France. His father, a Lieutenant Colonel in the Marines, served in WWII. His nephew received the Silver Star for service in Fallujah, Iraq, and is now fighting in Afghanistan. His godson is a combat-wounded Marine.

"Into the jaws of Death"

Bob served in Vietnam from 1966 to 1970, fighting in the bloodiest, deadliest, longest-running battles of that war. He literally went "into the jaws of Death, into the mouth of Hell"—then came out fighting. His men consider him a legend.

Among the Decisive Battles Bob fought in:

• "The Iron Triangle" in "Operation Big Springs" (January 30 to February 16, 1967), in deadly War Zone "D," site of the thickest jungles, where the 173rd discovered and destroyed 26 base camps and more than 1,000 underground bunkers.

• "Junction City I and II" (February 22 to April 13, 1967), where Bob was among the 780 Sky Soldiers who parachuted into War Zone "C" and destroyed the enemy's central headquarters churning out psychological propaganda throughout South Vietnam. This was the first major U.S. airborne assault since the Korean War.

• "The Battle of the Slopes" (June 18 to 22, 1967), in Dak To, which began as a routine search-and-destroy mission and ended up being the deadliest ambush of American lone rifle companies attacked by waves of NVA battalions.

• "The Battle of Dak To" (November 1 to December 14, 1967), a series of battles in "Operation MacArthur" that lasted 33 days and 110 continuous hours. It ended when the Americans captured Hill 875, after suffering horrific losses and the deadliest "friendly fire" incident since WWII. U.S. forces devastated three NVA regiments, preventing them from taking part in the Communists' Tet Offensive launched in late January 1968.

A part of Bob still remains on Hill 875 at Dak To, where his three closest buddies received the Medal of Honor posthumously: Pfc. John Barnes III, Sp 4 Carlos Lozada, his best friend from jump school, and his Chaplain (Major) Charles Watters.

General Westmoreland called the 173rd Airborne "my fire brigade."

Infamous Battle of Dak To

The Sky Soldiers, as the 173rd Airborne Brigade was known, were one of the first army units sent to Vietnam. They were the first to go into the jungles to search and destroy enemy base camps and the first to use small, long-range patrols. They remained in combat longer than any other American military unit since the Revolutionary War. They earned four Presidential Unit Citations and had 12 Medal of Honor recipients.

Initially headquartered in Bien Hoa, the 173rd operated in provinces around Saigon. When intelligence revealed the NVA was planning a massive attack against the U.S. Special Forces' camps in Dak To, in the Central Highlands, the 173rd was deployed there—to the wildest jungles in South Vietnam, if not in all of Southeast Asia, where the borders of South Vietnam, Cambodia, and Laos meet. These camps at Ben Het, in

Kontum Province, provided surveillance and a major roadblock to the enemy at the southern end of the Ho Chi Minh Trail. They also supported and trained the isolated Montagnard villagers.

Dak To is surrounded by steep, muddy ridges rising to 4,000 ft., forested with 100-ft tall jungles of double- and triple-canopy rain forests and dense, low foliage—infested with leeches, diverse snakes, and half the world's mosquitoes. It's a land of "perpetual twilight." Guerrillas hid in jungle lairs and fortresses of reinforced underground bunkers, tunnels, and fortified trench lines. By night they set ambushes and attacked in "human waves."

"The Battle of Dak To" included the Battle of Hill 823, Hill 1338, and climaxed in the decisive Battle of Hill 875.

On Hill 875, the NVA had built a massive complex of fortified bunkers and trenches connected by tunnels and had amassed 7,000 soldiers in four regiments.

On November 19, the 503rd Airborne Infantry began climbing Hill 875. After some of the bloodiest fighting of the war, the survivors finally reached the summit and captured Hill 875 on Thanksgiving Day.

When the battle finally ended on December 14, the jungle had turned into a barren landscape, devoid of life.

From ashes, new life springs up

In a forest fire, the intense heat that kills trees also brings forth new life—releasing seeds that sprout. New saplings spring up.

From 1990 to 2001, Bob lived in Saigon with his wife and daughter. He built medical clinics at Dak Pek, Dak Seang-Dak Sut, and Dak To-Ben Het. Bob and his brothers from the 173rd support the Omni Y Deo Orphanage at the Catholic Cathedral in Kontum for the mountain people of the Central Highlands, an ethnic minority regarded as second-class citizens by the Vietnamese government.

Fairbairn, with other Vietnam veterans in "Veterans Assisting Veterans," has also raised tens of thousands of dollars with motorcycle runs to support the widows and children of U.S. veterans who died in Iraq and Afghanistan, and to aid our brain-injured combat veterans. His gifts continue to give life and hope.

"Every good tree bears good fruit...By their fruits you will know them" (Matthew 7:17, 20).

Cpl. Tony Lutz
& George Lutz

By: Helen Mooradkanian - April, 2012

When 25-year-old Corporal George A. (Tony) Lutz, II, U.S. Army, of Virginia Beach, VA, was killed by a sniper's bullet outside Fallujah on December 29, 2005, only six weeks into his deployment in "Operation Iraqi Freedom," his tragic death set in motion a series of events nationwide that no one could have foreseen. Least of all his heartbroken family.

This is, in part, the story of Tony and his legacy, his passion for God, America and family. It is also the story of Tony's father, George A. Lutz, Sr., who, in his grief, reached out to comfort other military families with the comfort he himself received.

Above all, it is a compelling story of healing—and hope. Of death swallowed up in victory.

The father's journey began simply. Soon it turned into a mission. Now it's become a nationwide movement. On Memorial Day 2008 George Lutz launched the national non-profit Honor and Remember Inc. (www.honorandremember.org), and unveiled publicly the Honor and Remember Flag, designed to be a national symbol of remembrance for all military who died in defense of our nation's freedoms, whether in combat or not. It pays tribute to heroes from all wars, even as the POW-MIA flag honors those captured and missing.

George Lutz took his mission to all 50 states (2010), to Congress (2011) where 153 members co-sponsored HR 546 in its support. (You can sign a petition of support on the website.) Several Congressional offices display the flag. Lutz also appeared on Fox News, CBN, CNN and Dennis Miller's radio show.

"Today we have the largest number of living veterans of any time in our history," George Lutz says. "These fallen are among the least honored in our history, from Vietnam and Korea. We cannot let them be forgotten."

Growing movement across U.S.

Two years ago, George Lutz drove cross-country visiting each state capital and meeting with governors, state legislators, businessmen and citizens to establish support for the flag. He covered 29,000 miles in 5 and one-half months. His journey began June 7 at CBN, with first stop Dover, Delaware. It ended November 11, Veterans Day, in Arlington National Cemetery, where his son Tony is laid to rest. Last year, he took his mission to Congress, visiting all 541 offices. Today he continues to travel around the country presenting personalized flags.

Already 11 states have adopted the Honor and Remember flag. Another 12 have pending legislation. It is adopted by: Pennsylvania, Delaware, Maryland, Virginia, North Carolina, Oklahoma, Louisiana, Oregon, Utah, Arizona and Kansas. Pending states include: Alaska, Colorado, South Dakota, Texas, Ohio, New Hampshire, Connecticut, Rhode Island and others.

Twelve state chapters, including New Hampshire, now promote the flag and its mission.

The flag flies at professional sporting events, including NASCAR. The newest sponsor, American Majority, a leading national conservative grassroots movement, displayed the flag for the first time at the nationwide series Bristol, Tennessee, race on its #81 MacDonald motorsports car. The flag now flies at several tracks across the country.

National endorsements include: Vietnam Veterans of America, Associations of the U.S. Army, Navy, and Air Force, American Gold Star Mothers, Blue Star Mothers of America, Gold Star Wives of America, Sons of The American Revolution. Corporate sponsors include Amerigroup, General Dynamics, Geico, and Regent University

This movement has captured the heart of the nation and is well on its way to becoming a national symbol of remembrance.

"Lest we forget"

"Tony was a fearless soldier who supported the war in Iraq 100%," George Lutz told us. "He looked forward to his mission, which he felt was his calling from God." He told his dad, "God is literally my shield." The day before he was shot, Tony said, 'I'm not afraid to die. I know where I'm going.' And he talked openly about his faith and heaven."

As a psychological operations specialist with the Army's 9th Psychological Operations Battalion, 4th Psychological Operations Group, Tony engaged both enemy forces and Iraqi civilians in a battle to "win their mind" through broadcast messages, dropped leaflets, and "face-to-face" communications. Because of his valuable skills-set, he was accompanying Marines in volatile Fallujah when felled by a single snipers bullet.

An Army comrade said of Tony, "He laid down his life for us. He laid down his life for his family. He laid down his life for the people in Iraq, who deserve the same freedoms we have."

For Tony's dad, George Lutz, the loss was devastating. "For months I was numb with grief. Until one day the Lord broke through to me with the words, 'Your son is with Me.' That was the turning point.

"I was grieving as a father grieves on losing his son. Then I thought about God sending Jesus to die for us. And I felt as if God were saying to me, 'I know what it feels like because I did it. I sent My Son, and it hurts. I know it hurts but I did it.' This just gave me a peace."

From then on, George Lutz began attending funerals of veterans from WWII, Korea, Vietnam, Iraq and Afghanistan. He visited with their families, giving comfort and hope. Invariably, two questions repeatedly cropped up:

"Did my son (husband, father) die in vain?"

"Will people forget the sacrifice made for freedom?"

"Those words 'in vain' bring a lot of hurt to a lot of people, especially from wars like Vietnam and Korea," Lutz said. "I thought about that a lot. The American flag symbolizes the price of freedom and unites us as a nation. The POW-MIA flag honors a very special group. Yet we have no official national symbol of public gratitude for those who died defending our freedoms."

The flag's symbolism

This led George to design a unique flag for this forgotten group, using military symbolism. The red stands for the blood shed by our military throughout our nation's history. The white recognizes the purity of that sacrifice. The blue star recalls the World War I symbol hung in windows indicating a family member away at war. The gold star symbolizes the ultimate sacrifice of the fallen hero who will never return. The folded flag signifies the final tribute given the family. The flame reminds us of the hero's eternal spirit living on in the memory of loved ones.

Lutz has presented more than 700 personalized flags to veterans' families from WWII to Afghanistan, with nearly another 1,000 waiting. Each personalized flag bears the veteran's name, date and country where he was KIA. Each presentation is always a public ceremony to honor the fallen. Last April the Louisiana Governor publicly presented 60.

Healing has begun for families once imprisoned in grief: the widow who had tried to commit suicide, the elderly couple whose only son died in Vietnam unacknowledged in 40 years, the five Navajo Indian families on a remote reservation. George Lutz reached out to others with the love of God, and found healing himself. Hymn writer F.M. Lehman wrote, "The love of God is greater far than tongue or pen can ever tell. It goes beyond the highest star and reaches to the lowest hell." Scripture records, "God so loved the world that He gave His only begotten Son…" (John 3:16). The apostle Paul declared, "Who shall separate us from the love of Christ?" Neither "tribulation…death nor life" (Romans 8:35-39).

Lt. Clebe McClary

By: Helen Mooradkanian - January, 2012

Heavy rain and fog shrouded the jungles of Vietnam like a canopy on March 3, 1968. Shortly after midnight, a 26-year old Marine, Second Lieutenant Clebe McClary, Pawleys Island, SC, lay dying on Hill #46. He had been leading his 13-man patrol on reconnaissance deep into uncharted territory behind enemy lines before a planned attack involving several thousand troops. They were in the Quan Duc Valley, southwest of An Hoa, an American base for helicopters and planes.

Suddenly the 13 Marines were ambushed by more than 200 North Vietnamese armed with mortars, automatic weapons, and hand grenades.

McClary, a platoon leader in the 1st Marine Division's 1st Reconnaissance Battalion, had successfully completed 18 patrols, more than any other lieutenant in his battalion, without losing a man. Now his team was nearly wiped out on this, his 19th patrol since arriving in Nam the previous October.

McClary himself was virtually dead. At least that's what the North Vietnamese soldier thought as he aimed a final bullet to McClary's head. That's also what the chopper crew thought when they finally got through the fog to pick up the wounded on Hill #46.

Delivered from death

Three grenades had ripped through McClary's body. Another explosive device had hurled him through the air. His left eye was torn from its socket. Blood covered his face completely. Left arm ripped off below the elbow. Both eardrums shattered. Right hand mutilated. Legs shredded like hamburger. Severe trauma to the head.

Yet he would not surrender. Between the rounds of grenades that hit him, McClary had picked up his shotgun and engaged in fierce hand-to-hand combat with the enemy. Despite excruciating pain, he resolutely moved among his men, from one position to another, encouraging them and directing their fire. Until he fell to the ground, unconscious.

For his inspiring leadership and bravery, McClary was awarded three Purple Hearts, the Silver Star and the Bronze Star.

Before that fateful night had ended, Clebe McClary was to cheat death three more times. At the end, a Navy corpsman refused to leave him for dead. Risking his own life, he dragged Clebe 50 yards into an awaiting chopper then held onto him, legs dangled outside, as the chopper took off. A moment later 150 North Vietnamese stormed Hill #46…

Broken body but spirit strong

As traumatic as that night and his combat wounds were, McClary was severely tested even more during his recovery. He spent more than two years in military hospitals, going through 30 to 40 critical surgeries, followed by intensive rounds of physical therapy that never ended.

"When I returned home from Vietnam, I faced at least 40 major surgeries. The doctors told me I would never walk again. I could not feed or dress myself, and my mental wounds were even more serious than my physical wounds."

At times he got discouraged. At times he got depressed. And yes, he thought, "Why me, Lord?" Yet he never stopped there. He always looked beyond his limitations to what he had the ability to do. Most of all, he grew impatient. A former athlete, he never lost his will to overcome adversity. And he never became bitter.

His faith played a key role in his recovery. As he writes in his book "Living Proof" (foreword by Tom Landry), he persevered, believing that God had a purpose for his life. Miraculously, he recovered from his injuries. Although doctors had told him he would never stand up or walk on his own, McClary was able to recover full use of his legs—and walk.

"I never thought I'd be hit in Vietnam. It wasn't arrogance but rather confidence in myself, my men, and in God who had seen us safely through danger time and time again."

"While in Nam, I sensed that God was leading me and my men for a special reason. When our chopper safely straddled mines that should have blown us away, I knew we were in divine custody. Family and friends bombarded Heaven with prayers for my safekeeping. More than one church had me on its prayer list.

"I did what was expected of a Christian—attended chapel services when near the base, filled in if a chaplain was unavailable." But later, during his time of severe testing, he realized something was missing. There was something more to life.

Two life-changing moments

Two key events changed the course of his life. The first occurred just after he had begun coaching football at the University of South Carolina, a long-standing dream. One day he witnessed student demonstrators on a college campus burn the American flag to protest the Vietnam War. Deeply angered by this desecration, McClary immediately resigned his coaching position and enlisted in the U.S. Marine Corps.

The second occurred during his recovery. While on leave from a hospital in South Carolina, he attended an evangelistic crusade at the football stadium where he had starred in many games and coached several teams. It was sponsored by the Fellowship of Christian Athletes, and featured former New York Yankee second baseman Bobby Richardson, who gave his testimony.

Deeply touched by both the message and Richardson's testimony, McClary suddenly realized he was doing all the "right things" for the "wrong reasons." He writes, "I never drank or smoked in order to become a good athlete and impress people. I was a good person, playing the role people expected of me. I grew up in the church and believed in the Bible, tithing, good morals but I had never invited Jesus

Christ into my heart as Savior and the Lord of my life." That night, both Clebe and his wife went forward to make their commitment.

"Now," he says, "I've joined the greatest Army that has ever marched, the Army of Jesus Christ. God's purpose for my life has now become clear."

Adversity births new beginning

Today Lieutenant Clebe McClary, U.S. Marine Corps (ret.) has a whole new career as one of the nation's most sought-after motivational speakers. He is using his powerful story of courage, determination and inner strength to inspire audiences around the world. His more than 7,500 speaking engagements have taken him to all 50 states and 30 nations.

He has addressed professional athletes, corporations, military bases and professional associations. Baseball teams include: Boston Red Sox, New York Yankees, Atlanta Braves, Cincinnati Reds, Houston Astros, San Diego Padres, San Francisco Giants, Los Angeles Dodgers, Cleveland Indians, and Milwaukee Brewers. Football teams include: New England Patriots, Dallas Cowboys, Miami Dolphins, Atlanta Falcons, Buffalo Bills and Minnesota Vikings.

Through his Wounded Warrior Ministry, part of the Clebe McClary Evangelistic Association, he ministers to combat veterans and their families, at a beautiful facility he built in Pawleys Island, SC.

From nightmares to hope

"The nightmare of Vietnam is not easily forgotten," he says. "The horror of that midnight on Hill #46 will never be erased." Yet three mottos help him. FIDO: "Forget It and Drive On." PRIDE: "Personal Responsibility in Daily Effort." PATCH: "Positive Attitude that Characterizes Hope."

"Life's tough. Are you going to get bitter, or are you going to get better?

"Remember, God has a purpose and plan for your life." As it is written: "He will transform the Valley of Trouble into a gateway of hope."

Admiral Jeremiah Denton
U.S. Navy Retired

By: Helen Mooradkanian - December, 2011

On Christmas Eve 1967, in the darkness of a POW camp in Communist North Vietnam, a soft, low voice began singing carols. "Silent night, Holy night, all is calm, all is bright."

The haunting strains came from the cell of a lone POW, locked in solitary confinement. He was shackled in leg irons with a 5-ft, cement-filled iron bar linking ankle cuffs together. Elbows tied behind his back, cutting off circulation.

Yet his spirit remained unbroken. His voice penetrated the deep silence, bringing comfort, hope and cheer to the other Americans.

The POW camp was "Alcatraz," known for its unspeakable brutality.

The POW was Jeremiah A. Denton, Jr., U.S. Navy, later promoted to Admiral, who endured nearly eight years of excruciating torture as a prisoner, more than four of them in solitary confinement where he was viciously tortured, beaten until unconscious, starved and threatened 18 hours a day, every day from 1965 to October 1969. He stands as a symbol of the indomitable American spirit of a man devoted to God, country, duty and honor.

On July 18, 1965, the 41-year old Denton, Commanding Officer of Attack Squadron Seventy-Five, was shot down in his Navy A-6E Intruder jet while leading a group of 28 aircraft on Thanh Hoa. Captured, he was imprisoned in the "Hanoi Hilton."

A hero and patriot of epic proportions, Denton described his experiences in his memorable book, "When Hell Was in Session," now updated and reissued (WND Books).

Famous 1966 televised interview

Millions of Americans came to know Denton on May 17, 1966, during a televised interview arranged by North Vietnam. Tortured before the interview, he was threatened with greater torture if he didn't respond properly. Yet Denton looked straight into the TV camera and blinked his eyes in Morse code repeatedly to spell out the word "t-o-r-t-u-r-e." Naval intelligence immediately picked it up, the first confirmation that American POWs were being tortured.

In response to allegations of U.S. "war atrocities," Denton boldly proclaimed: "Whatever the position of my government is, I believe in it, I support it, and I will support it as long as I live."

He paid dearly for his courage. "During the all night torture that followed," he wrote, "I prayed to die."

Not by might—but by moral strength

"The North Vietnamese had one objective: break our will." In any war, as the Prussian military strategist Carl von Clausewitz wrote, "It is principally the moral forces which decide" victory.

"Since my principal battle with the North Vietnamese was a moral one, prayer was my prime source of strength. Another source was my country; no sacrifice was too great on her behalf," Denton wrote.

"The strength of our nation is more than material strength. We are a strongly moral people, and our country is based on spiritual strength. Lose that and we lose everything," he said.

"Founded on faith in God, the United States has been blessed as no other nation. God is denied by the Communists, and this denial is reflected by the way they treat their own subjects.

"We learned to outwit our captors although they held all the cards because our will was superior to theirs."

As senior officer in command, Denton instructed POWs: "We will die before we give them classified military information."

"Since communications are at the heart of any resistance, we increased ours through taps, scrapes, coughs, sneezes and hacks. We spent all Christmas Eve 1967 sending Christmas greetings to each other."

The North Vietnamese were incredulous. "Although we were completely under their physical control, we flatly refused to cooperate with them.

"They wanted to subdue us. They failed. We increased our tapping."

As a result, "our captors became our prisoners."

Going from strength to strength

Determined to resist at all costs, Denton knew he must do two things. "Build my physical strength, by running in place and most important, build a reservoir of psychological strength first through prayer and meditation, and then through communication with other POWs."

He developed a daily routine. "I would pray, exercise, plan escape, eat, nap, communicate with the POW in the next cell, and then start the cycle again.

"On Sundays I would shout the Lord's Prayer at the top of my lungs after asking everyone to join in.

"I became known as president of the Optimist Club. The presence of God was very real to most of us. Our taped conversations almost always ended with GBU (God bless you), and at night GNGBU (Good night, God bless you). Most of us lived with the awareness of God's love," he wrote.

"We held Sunday church services, despite orders to stop. On February 7, 1971, we had a showdown. Guards stormed our service and ordered the choir to stop singing. We totally ignored them and continued. One POW gave the sermon. Another quoted from Scripture. A third gave the benediction. These three 'church leaders' were pinned with backs against the building. One man began singing 'The Star-Spangled Banner.' As his hoarse voice rose in triumph, we all joined in, our voices rising in full, joyous crescendo that rolled through the courtyard and over the walls. A hundred guns couldn't stop us," Denton recalled.

"Patriotism can motivate men to perform heroic acts for their country," said Denton, "but only prayer to God can provide the moral strength needed to resist your captors and endure torture."

"Jesus was with me in the cell"

One morning, after five days and nights of horrific torture, Denton told the Lord he could take no more. "Tears ran down my face. 'Lord, I surrender all to You.' Immediately, a deep feeling of peace settled into my tortured mind and pain-wracked body. I felt zero pain. It was the most profound moment of my life."

When confined to solitary in "Alcatraz," in a 47 by 47-inch cell with no window, a 10-watt bulb, and tiny air holes, "I really panicked. I said, 'Jesus, I'll go nuts. You know I'm claustrophobic.' " Yet during his years in that cell, his legs in irons 18 hours a day, "Jesus was with me in that cell all the time. I enjoyed an inner serenity that would boggle your mind. I prayed. God answered in amazing, miraculous ways, as He always does to desperate prayers."

Songs in the night

One POW wove a cross for Denton of bamboo strips taken from a broom. This touched him deeply. When guards found the cross and destroyed it, he was devastated. Yet a work crew, brought in to make ventilation holes smaller, secretly collaborated to fashion a more intricate cross for Denton, beautifully woven from straws.

"Before solitary," he said, "I had faith in God. After solitary, I knew God in a personal way. If we have everything and don't have Jesus, we have nothing."

Many times, guards ran out weeping, refusing to torture Denton anymore. Once a guard, returning to resume the torture, found the iron bar already halfway through Denton's Achilles' tendons. Seeing the look of total peace on Denton's face, he left screaming, "No more! He won't break!"

Dedicated servant

Denton set up a foundation that supports One Nation under God, national security, humanitarian affairs. He served as U.S. Senator (R-Alabama), 1981-1987. As Peter Marshall said, "Only when you have something to die for, have you something to live for."

Louis Heliotis
Francis "Gunner" Hayes
Lenny Enaire
Michael Wilson

By: Tom Duggan, Jr. - April, 2011

The North Andover Republican Town Committee held their annual Spring Fling last month and as they do each year the committee honored some of our local veterans in town. Selectmen Rosemary Smedile and Dan Lanen presided over the honors and presented each veteran with a certificate of appreciation. Here are the four heroes they honored that night.

PFC LOUIS N. HELIOTIS
Drafted July 1943 * Discharged October 1945, Company B, 87th Chemical Mortar Battalion. Purple Heart with Oak Leaf - Wounded January & November 1944.

Combat Infantryman Badge -During War; Bronze Star - After War
Prisoner of War —Winter 1944/45
French Legion d'Honneur awarded April 2006

Louis Heliotis was drafted in August 1943 following his sophomore year at Lowell High School. He was processed at Fort Devens and sent to Camp Rucker (now Fort Rucker), Alabama. Assigned to the 8th Chemical Mortar Battalion, Company B, as a member of a heavy mortar gun crew, his initial training lasted two to three months and was followed by maneuvers at Camp McClellan, Tennessee. In the spring of 1944, he and his company were loaded onto first class Pullman cars for a trip to New York City where he boarded the "Queen Elizabeth," which had been commandeered as a troop ship, for his journey to Grenock, Scotland.

Upon arrival in the spring, Louis was transferred to Tiverton, the 'waiting place" for the 87th Chemical Mortar Battalion. He trained and lived with British troops, attached to the 4th Infantry Division, until late spring 1944 when they were transported to the port of Southampton. He crossed the English Channel on the USS Barnette, a troop ship proceeded down rope ladders onto a landing craft to arrive on Utah Red Beach on June 6, 1944; this landing point was selected as they had heavy mortars to bring ashore with them. The Company worked their way inland amongst the hedgerows under periodic attack of the Germans, mostly artillery fire, the continued advance brought them to and over the German/Belgium border; by then, it was into the winter of 1944/45. His combat experience during this advance merited him the European African Middle Eastern Ribbon with six Service Stars and the Distinguished Unit Badge.

One night, in November/December 1944, while in the Hurtgen Forest, Louis and several of his unit were overrun by German troops and taken prisoners. Louis' account of his prisoner of war time identified continual marching during the days and camping at night; they were properly fed. One day he was isolated into a small group and, while they were marching, were attacked and strafed by an American fighter plane. He was hit by "friendly fire" in the left leg and lower back, they were serious wounds, but not sufficient enough to make him unable to get up and about. He managed to get to a German aid station where he was treated and transported to what he described as a hospital manned by British and Scottish medics under German control. At some point in the January/February 1945 time frame, he was liberated by American forces, having been a POW for four to six weeks. Spring 1945 found him in France, transported back to New York, on to Lake Placid, New York, and subsequently to a VA hospital in

Augusta, Maine, to recuperate. He was sent home to Lowell in the spring on leave and finally discharged at Camp Edwards, Massachusetts, in October 1945. On April 28, 2006, Louis Heliotis was one of twelve American veterans who received the insignia of Chevalier in the French National; Order of the Leg/on d'honneur. This award was presented to the recipients at Norwich University, Northfield, Vermont, by Monsieur Francois Gauthier, Consul General of France in Boston, for their bravery exhibited during the 0-Day battles in Normandy at the Omaha and Utah Beaches. Following his discharge, Louis utilized the Cl Bill to become a machinist and starting in 1950, spent thirty seven years working for Raytheon at various sites in Massachusetts.

FRANCIS "GUNNER" HAYES
Branch of Service: U.S. Army
When Enlisted: 1943
What Conflict: WWII
Stationed: August 1944, spent two weeks in Britain. Went to Europe theatre and was attached to the 4th Armored, 37th Tank Battalion. Pushed through Europe.

Mission/Job: Was a Cannoneer/Gunn in a M4 Sherman tank, under General Patton. During the Battle of the Bulge went into Bastone to support the 101st Airbourne who were surrounded by Nazi Forces.

Awards: EAM (European-African-Middle) Eastern campaign medal, with 4 battle stars, WWII Victory medal.

LENNY ENAIRE
Branch of Service: U.S. Army
Enlisted: 1948
Occupation of Japan/Korean War
Stationed: Yokohama Signal Depot, Japan/Korea
Mission/Job: Attached to the casualty section of headquarters. Tracked the wounded, missing and killed in action personnel.

Served: 1949-1950 Japan
    1950-1951 Korea
(Forced to extend 2 year contract "Truman year")
Awards: Korean Service, Japanese Occupation, National Defense, Korean Unit Citation

MICHAEL WILSON

Branch of Service: U.S. Marine Corp

When Enlisted: August 2003

What Conflict: Iraqi Campaign

Stationed: Naval Sub-base Bangor, WA 2003-2005

Twenty Nine Palm CA 2005-2006

Camp Gannon, Hussaba, Al Anbar Iraq

Mission: Marine Security Guard – Protecting Vital National Assets

Recapture Team Member

Camp Gannon Sgt. of the Guard

In charge of supervising camp security and personnel

Squad Leader – Patrol the streets daily and carry out various missions

Time Served: August 2003 – August 2007

Awards: Good Conduct Medal, National Defense, Iraqi Campaign, Global War on Terrorism, Sea Service Deployment Ribbon, Navy Merit Unit Award.

Assistant Coach to North Andover winning Wrestling Team, North Andover High School State Champs.

Joe Costa - Desert Storm
THE WAR ON TERROR

By: Gary Mannion, Jr. - August, 2010

"No Shore Too Distant, Alone and Unafraid" the motto of the USS Shreveport, LPD-12 this was the slogan for the seamen that served aboard her, in her over 30 years of commission.

The ship was commissioned in the early 1970's and since has been the home to many sailors in the U.S. Navy, Joseph Costa was one of them. Born and raised in Lawrence MA, Joe served his country in the United States Navy from February of 1988 to April of 1992.

Joe attended St. Mary's grammar school and graduated from Lawrence High School in 1985.

Joe's father Joseph Costa Jr. was a veteran of the U.S. Army in WW II, and although Joe had no initial desire to join the Army, he would soon take a leap of faith that would change his life forever.

A couple years after graduating high school, Joe found himself in a whirlwind of a rut.

He did not have a steady job, nor did he have a car. He felt as though he was stuck in a state of nothingness and going absolutely nowhere with his life. In the mid-eighties, at the height of drugs and rock and roll, Joe decided that he would make something of himself, even at the age of 21.

He took a journey to the U.S. Army recruiting office. However, as much as he wanted to serve his country, the Army was very pushy and so anxious to have him enlist that it actually turned him away from joining the Army all together.

He decided, after some consideration, that he would take a chance with the Navy. They, on the other hand, made it obvious to him that although they wanted him to enlist they would take him tomorrow, in a week, or in a month. The recruiter was slow paced and relaxed.

He sat with Joe and showed him his excellent test scores. Then without any more consideration, Joe enlisted. His mother originally thought his decision not to join the Army was a result of his girlfriend at the time, Leslie, convincing him not to join.

He however did join, and did so, without consultation with anyone.

Costa soon found out that he would be leaving only a week later. Once he finally got home and sat in his room and looked around, it finally sank in and as he thought about it, the fear of what he was about to embark on brought tears to his eyes.

Nonetheless, alone and unafraid he left for boot camp in February of 1988 and headed to Great Lakes Illinois. He was then sent to Operations Specialist or "A" school in Dam Neck, Virginia where he spent four months. He then boarded The Amphibious Assault ship USS Shreveport LPD-12. He would serve on this ship until 1991.

The ship was the Primary Control ship for all amphibious assaults. His duty on the ship was located in the heart and soul of the vessel. He was a radar monitor and used the ships scope to guard it from any buoys or land masses that might cause harm to the ship. He embarked on a Mediterranean cruise in 1989 stopping in France, Italy, Turkey, Portugal, Spain, and Egypt.

Like most sailors Joe would have gone crazy without any recreation. He decided to use his talents to help entertain his fellow sailors.

He posted a flyer, mentioning the prospects of starting a band, and before he knew it a few sailors and a couple of marines decided to join him and they became known as the Pelicans. They played shows while at sea and also performed in France and Italy.

In August of 1990 Joe and the crew aboard the ship were deployed to the Persian Gulf for the start of the Persian Gulf War. For the next eight months, Joe was involved in Desert Shield/Desert Storm. In April of 1991, Joe severely sprained his ankle and was assigned to shore duty.

This was a result of much manual labor and many injuries to his ankle. He had a history of weak ankles in his family and once the Navy doctors realized that this was a reoccurring thing, they put a cast on his ankle and he was sent to the fleet area and surveillance facility in the Virginia capes.

He was given a two week leave and it was then that Joe decided to marry Leslie. After his leave, he reported back to Virginia and Leslie soon followed and moved down there with him.

In 1992 the USS Shreveport received the Arleigh Burke Fleet Trophy for outstanding readiness and performance. Although Joe was not onboard at the time the award was given, his eight months of dedication and hard work helped the ship receive the award. In April of 1992, Joe was discharged and he headed back home to Lawrence.

One cannot assume that they would know what it is like to serve his or her country at a time of war. They cannot assume they know what it feels like to defend and protect the freedom for which its countries ideals are built on. Joe and many other Americans do know what that feels like.

It is with them and them alone that the idea of putting their lives on the line for all Americans ideals and freedoms can rest. As the motto of the USS Shreveport goes "No Shore Too Distant, Alone and Unafraid", Joe answered that calling when he joined our Nation's Armed Forces. Heroes like Joe take this call to arms every day. Nothing we do will ever be enough to thank people like this.

In Joe's case, the Military was a chance to make something of himself. Going into the service during wartime is something no 21 year old should have to do.

But Joe insists that "It truly turned out to be a much needed life experience and made me grow up fast and become the positive thinker I am today".

The Valley Patriot is proud to call Joseph M. Costa its Valley Patriot of the Month and a hero in our midst.

Fred Kuehn - WWII

By: Gary Mannion, Jr. - July, 2010

During WW II, many young men and women answered the call to serve their country. They did so whole heartedly, never dreaming the impact their generation would have on the future of the world. Fred Kuehn was one of them.

His generation was a different kind of generation; it has been called the "greatest generation". Fred claims that "perhaps we were a great generation, but other generations have been also, and so will other generations to come." In 1943, Fred Kuehn joined many of his fellow Americans in the armed services. He was drafted and eventually became a member of the U.S. Army Corps of Engineers. Although Fred had previously tried to enlist with the Army Air Corps, his hopes were crushed when it was determined that he was color blind. In all of his disappointment and anger, he said: "If they don't want me, then they can come and get me." And they did; soon after he was drafted into the United States military.

Born in Lawrence, MA, Fred grew up in the Prospect Hill district of the city. He attended Lawrence High and was a member of Christ Presbyterian

Church. The grandson of German immigrants, Fred practiced his prayers in German every week at Sunday school. This would later become important while Fred was serving overseas. After graduating from Lawrence High, he attended the University of New Hampshire and became a member of the ROTC, realizing that being drafted could not be far away. Sure enough, he was drafted, but was given a three month deferment until he turned 18. When those three months were up, he was sent to Fort Belvoir in Virginia for basic training and, because of his studies in engineering at UNH, for combat engineer training as well.

He was qualified for the Army Specialized Training Program. This meant that instead of being shipped overseas right away, he would attend Brooklyn College to study engineering.

Shortly after he started classes at Brooklyn College, the plans for the invasion of Normandy were being put into place and the program at the college was discontinued. The need for man power in Europe was growing and Fred was assigned to Camp Polk to join the 75th infantry Division as a rifleman. He took part in maneuvers and was then transferred again. In April of 1944, he returned to the corps of engineers and joined the 289th Engineer Combat Battalion at Camp Robinson, AR. In October of 1944, Fred and his battalion were sent overseas. His battalion shipped out to Europe from New York Harbor, part of a large convoy of ships numbering over 80 vessels. Along the way, while off the coast of Ireland, one of the ships was torpedoed by an enemy submarine. That ship just happened to be their supply boat. The rest of the ships were forced to dock in Bristol, England, in November of 1944.

Fred's battalion was then ordered to proceed to the continent in December of 1944 on high alert. This was around the time that the last two major German offensives were to take place. On December 31st 1944, they crossed the English Channel and landed on the southern front. They had started their journey at the time the renowned Battle of the Bulge had started, and they wouldn't finish till the end of January.

However, Fred was in the middle of one of the lesser known battles during this time, the second of the last two German offensives known as Operation Nordwind. Although the battle may have been overshadowed by others that claimed the pages in history books, it was still one of the most important battles of the war.

The German objective was to divide the French and the American armies. They did manage to push the Americans back but, in the end, General Eisenhower had ordered the 7th Army, which contained the 21st Engineer Corps, to which Fred belonged, to push forward. And push forward is just what they did. They were successful in April of 1945, only 5 months after Fred had entered combat.

Fred spent the closing months after hostilities in Europe ceased stationed just west of Heidelberg. Fred's battalion had a group of German prisoners of war under their control whom they supervised on work details. One Sunday, while Fred was on guard duty, a few prisoners wanted to attend church. Fred sought and was given permission to do so.

He marched the prisoners to a nearby village with a church. He led the men inside and followed, taking a seat in the last pew. Fred took off his steel helmet, set aside his rifle and joined the congregation. Fred's eyes, as he speaks of this time, grow unfocused and it seems as if he is transported back to that time, so many years ago. At that Mass in a little town in Germany, as the congregation and the POW's stood at one point to recite the Lord's Prayer, Fred himself stood up and repeated the prayer with them.

At only 19, Fred saw things that most in this generation or any other could hardly imagine. He talks about the cold winters overseas and the action that he saw like it was yesterday, with the matter-of-fact tone more commonly associated with reports of a typical day at work. Those years across the ocean are etched in his mind with the clarity reserved for the very intense. When asked if he had the choice to do it all over again, Fred says, with a simplicity that belies the magnitude of the statement, that he imagines he would. This is the perfect example of the generosity of men and women like Fred who have made it possible for Americans today to call their country the land of the free and, as embodied by people like Fred, the home of the brave. We are honored to have Fred Kuehn as our Valley Patriot of the Month for July.

Sgt. Dan Cotnoir, U.S. Marines

Ordnance Maintenance Company, 4th Maintenance Battalion, Devens, MA

By: Tom Duggan, Jr. - January, 2010

LAWRENCE, MA - In 2005, Sergeant Daniel Cotnoir of Lawrence was named Marine of the Year by the Marine Corps Times for his outstanding bravery and service to the United States.

Sgt. Dan Cotnoir began his military career in 1999 when he joined the Marine Corps. He was trained as an armorer (small arms repairman). But his military career took a big turn when his civilian career as  the funeral home director became his military assignment in Iraq.

Sgt. Cotnoir's became a mortuary affairs specialist whose job consisted of retrieving the remains of fallen Marines from the battlefield so they could be prepared and brought home to their families for a proper funeral and burial. In 2004, Cotnoir and his unit of 20 men were deployed to Camp Taqaddum, Iraq for Operation Iraqi Freedom.

During Cotnoir's service to this nation he was responsible for returning 182 fallen heroes back to their families here at home.

The grueling task of recovering fallen Marines often included sacrificing his own safety to retrieve these hero soldiers. More often than not, Cotnoir had to endure heavy enemy fire.

Dan even helped cut down the burned bodies of civilian contractors hanging from a bridge in Fallujah, the shocking scene that was broadcast via satellite all over the world.

Cotnoir was promoted to Sergeant while in Iraq.

Because of his service in the Marines as a mortuary affairs specialist, Cotnoir earned the title of Marine of the Year in 2005. In the Citation it states "For Sgt. Cotnoir was called upon to do what no other Marine really wants to do, but what must be done: take charge of bringing fallen Marines home to their final resting place, from the battlefield. This he has done with a tremendous sense of honor and dignity befitting the memory, sacrifice and integrity of those who have given their lives for our country...His selflessness and dedication to fallen Marines and to their families back home is truly inspiring.. It is truly our honor to recognize this outstanding, unsung hero."

Dan Cotnoir's family has owned Racicot for over 19 years. He went to Camp Pendleton in California where he was assigned to help train Marines in mortuary affairs. The assignment involved teaching Marines how to clean and recompose bloodied bodies of soldiers killed in combat. Cotnoir helped pioneer a new mortuary affairs occupational specialty for the Marine Corps. He trained 40 Marines in mortuary and remains-recovery skills. He wrote a manual and designed a specialty training package.

Cotnoir continues to give back to the community. He organizes an annual Marine Corps golf tournament that raises money for Toys for Tots and volunteers for military funeral details. He is a member of the Lawrence Exchange Club, life member of VFW post 8349 and life member of AMVETS post MA29. Cotnoir is also a member of the Marine Corps League and American Legion Post 122.

Cotnoir also ran for mayor of Lawrence in 2009 and has volunteered his time on numerous boards and civic organizations.

For his bravery and sacrifice to his country as a Marine and his continued activism and service to his community here at home, The Valley Patriot is proud to honor Sergeant Daniel Cotnoir of Lawrence as our Valley Patriot of the Month.

Thank you Dan for making our country and community a better place and being a role model to young men and women everywhere. We will never be able to repay you for your heroism!

Sgt. Major Eric Nelson
1983-2007

December, 2009

LAWRENCE, MA - While attending the North Andover Veteran's Day observances, I was privileged to listen to guest speaker Sgt. Major Eric Nelson.

Nelson is a retired U.S. Army officer of 24 years. he spent his first career in the U.S. Army and is now spending his second career working for Valley Works in Lawrence helping other veterans find jobs. During his speech to the North Andover residents, Nelson talked about honor, bravery, commitment, sacrifice and what it means to be a soldier. These are the values that make up a "Valley Patriot of the Month" and that is why we chose Sgt. Major Eric Nelson.

Eric Nelson was born on May 31, 1965 in Lowell and attended University of Massachusetts in Lowell. He graduated in 2011. Prior to enrolling at UMass Lowell, Sgt. Major Nelson had a distinguished military career beginning in 1983 when he enlisted in the U.S. Army. He joined the Army as a Field Artillery Fire Support Specialist and trained at Fort Sill, Oklahoma.

Upon completion of his training, Nelson attended Airborne School at Fort Benning, Georgia. He then joined the 82d Airborne Division at Fort Bragg, NC from 1884 to 1987. From 1988 to 1999 he was part of the 56th

Medical Evacuation Battalion, Air Ambulance at Fort Bragg and the 3rd Military Intelligence Battalion. During that time Nelson also flew numerous combat missions in Saudi Arabia and Iraq as an Aeroscout Observer Section Sergeant during Operation Desert Shield and Desert Storm.

In 2003, Sergeant Major Nelson was an Aviation Mission Operations Manager for the 4th Aviation Brigade stationed in Baghdad, Iraq. During that mission, he trained over 300 personnel on convoy operations with no combat accidents or injuries. He also led and managed a team of 15 staff in an Operations Center responsible for assigning missions and tracking aircraft and ground vehicles throughout area of responsibility, 24 hours per day.

He developed, planned, and implemented training to track the movement of 2,000 personnel, 50 helicopters, and over 300 ground vehicles daily. Because of his outstanding contribution during this time, most notably through developing realistic training that directly influenced the combat success of the organization, Nelson was awarded the Bronze Star Medal.

In 2004 Sergeant Major Nelson became a Senior Aviation Trainer and Performance Coach stationed at the Joint Multinational Readiness Center in Europe until 2007. During that time, he facilitated workshops in community leadership, led a team of 45 trainers and experts and coached senior leadership.

For his contributions, Nelson was awarded the Army Aviation Association of America's Order of Saint Michael Medal for contributions in training and developing future Army aviation leadership. He was also recognized for the collaboration with multi-national forces.

In 2007, Nelson received an honorable discharge from the military and began working at Valley Works Career Center in Lawrence to help other veterans. He continues to work there as the Local Veterans Employment Representative assisting veterans to find employment.

During his military career, Nelson received numerous awards and decorations that include: Air Medal (#2), Army Commendation Medal (4 OLC), Army Achievement Medal (3 OLC), Good Conduct Medal (6th Award), National Defense Service Medal (2), Southwest Asia Service

Medal (2 Bronze Service Stars), Humanitarian Service Medal (#2), NCO Professional Development Ribbon (#3), Army Service Ribbon, Overseas Service Ribbon (#2), Kuwait Liberation Medal (Saudi Arabia), Kuwait Liberation Medal (Kuwait), Meritorious Unit Commendation, Army Superior Unit Award, Drivers Badge, Master Parachutist Badge, Senior Aircraft Crewman Badge, and the Turkish Parachutist Badge.

Nelson is married to the former Juliet Elisa Wilson from the Canal Zone, Republic of Panama. Juliet is also a veteran.

The Valley Patriot is proud to be able to honor such a man who was so willing to sacrifice his life and the future happiness of his family to defend this country.

Thank you Eric Nelson for your service to this nation and for the countless contributions you have made to your community. The debt that we owe you and the men and women you served with is immeasurable and can never be repaid.

James H. Derby

WWII

This is the second in the three-part series of "Heroes in Our Midst ~ The Mt. Vernon Neighborhood."

By: Lawrence "Lonnie" Brennan - September, 2009

"I was 18 and 4 months (of age) when I joined the Air Corps," Valley Patriot of the Month James H. Derby began, "I was a navigator. I got 24 missions in then I was in the hospital." The missions were B-17 bombing runs during WWII when "Jim" and his squadron flew daring daytime bombing runs from their base in England against heavy German defenses.

Now a sprite, 84 year old, the former WWII B-17 navigator had joined Mt. Vernon neighbors Ed Hickey and George and Helen Haynes at Joe's Landing Café at Lawrence Municipal Airport following a Summer open house and tour of a restored B-17 bomber. Mr. Hickey and Mr. Haynes are also Valley Patriots of the Month (see note). Mr. Derby is now a retired engineer, married to Kathryn (Wills) Derby.

"Yes, we got hit. I remember when we got hit on our second mission, engine blown out, when we got close to Holland and the pilot asked, should we go to Sweden, or can we make it home. I asked how much gas we got. I

293

said O.K., we can make it. Keep this course but throw everything out that's not nailed down. Guns, ammunition," he explained.

"If you can't keep up with the group, you're on your own. All the way over I kept taking drift readings on the clouds, which was not good, but I was looking to see if there was any difference in wind direction... and ah, when I thought we were close (to England), I said John (our pilot), go down. He said, if we go down below this cloud level we'll never get back up, because we didn't have the power. He said I'm not going down. I said John, go down, I feel we're five to six miles off the coast. And he went down and right in front of us was an airfield. We lucked out."

"On another mission, we had the hydraulics shot out, and we didn't realize it. So therefore we had no brakes. So when we landed, we headed down the runway. So what happened is when after we hit the emergency brakes, the plane nosed over and the framework joined the runway. Here I have this photo," he said as he referred to his package of photos and handwritten notes. "Four engines in the ground. I grabbed and held onto the largest thing near me. The only thing that saved me from becoming part of the runway was that: the Norden Bombsite. I hugged it for my life," Mr. Derby exclaimed.

"I flew 95% of my raids when I was 19. They sent us in over Berlin. We were the lead of the entire air force coming in at 11,000 feet over Berlin. They (the Germans) were throwing rocks at us, slingshots, peashooters, oh my God. Anyone who was hit headed straight for Russia," Mr. Derby said as he related the altitude and heavy anti-aircraft bursts that his plane experienced during their mission, flying so low "it seemed any gun could hit".

"And if they were close, as George (V.P. of the month, August. 2009 George Haynes) will tell you, the 88s they burst black. The 105s they burst white. The 105s they would burst above you and shoot down. The 88s they burst below you and shoot up. Shrapnel. Flack. You could see the red of the 88s, you knew they were close. There were concussions sometimes when they were close."

In another mission which he termed "the worst I was ever on", he read some of his notes and explained that the target was the Zejas-Ichon Works in Leipzig. "They made precision instruments including radar and pre-coded detonation devices. Our squadron was the false leader of the attacking B17s and our target was the town of Bohlen, a suburb where the anti-aircraft guns were located. We were loaded with bundles of 20 pound anti-personnel bombs," he explained.

As the false leader, Mr. Derby joined a small group of planes which diverted directly towards the flack batteries, in an attempt to consume, confuse, distract, and also destroy the anti-aircraft defenses with their special bombs and numerous anti-personnel bombs. Meanwhile, the main force of B17s went on to direct their heavy bombs on the precision instruments factory.

"We spun off to hit the flack batteries, and the minute they saw what we were doing they zeroed in on us. Twelve of us (planes) went in, four of us got out. We lost 80 men that day. Forty of us survived. I was one of them, that's when I thought I was invincible," Mr. Derby half-chuckled as he related his luck that day.

"Capt. Ten Eyke was the pilot on the lead plane on the last raid of his second tour and an 'observer'…We were flying the #10 position in the 'box' formation…when Ten Eyke took a direct hit in the gas tank – burst of orange then black smoke. He dropped off on his left wing and John (our pilot) almost stood our plane on its tail to avoid going down with him."

"After the war, we did what was called the Casey Jones project, which was to map the world. The maps were not accurate at all. We did Norway and Sweden, then we moved over to Belgium, we did Europe. We were told to not fly over Russia if we did we would be shot down," he said.

"In 1951 I was asked to go over to Korea. And I spent four days down in New Jersey, I forget the base. They got my shots up to date, and they wanted me to go over," Mr. Derby related, but in the end, his dispatch to another war area was cancelled. "I do not have a discharge to this day. They could legally call me over today. I had a separation," the 84 year old chuckled.

The Valley Patriot is proud to be able to share a bit of the service that Mr. Derby gave to our nation. We ask that you please forward your Valley Patriot of the Month nomination to the editor so that we may honor more of our service men and women.

Edmund "Ed" Hickey
U.S. Navy - Korea

This is the third in the three-part series of "Heroes in Our Midst ~ The Mt. Vernon Neighborhood."

By: Lawrence "Lonnie" Brennan - October, 2009

The year was 1951 when a youth from Lawrence named Edmund "Ed" Hickey joined the Navy. The previous year North Korean troops invaded the Republic of South Korea and fighting men and women from the United States and several other nations were embroiled in a horrific conflict defending South Korea from the communist North.

"I was 18, well, almost 19 when I joined in 1951 during the Korean War," Ed Hickey, the now 77 year-old retired Navy veteran and October 2009 Valley Patriot of the Month explained. "I volunteered."

"My family was a Navy family. When I joined, I already had three brothers in the Navy. Two had been in World War II and got called back as reservists when the Korean War broke out," Mr. Hickey said.

Mr. Hickey gathered this summer with Mt. Vernon neighbors and Valley Patriots of the Month Jim Derby and George Haynes, along with George's wife Mary at Joe's Landing Café at Lawrence Municipal Airport. They recently observed an open house and tour of a restored B-17 bomber. Both Mr. Derby and Mr. Haynes served in WWII and had many stories to share with their neighbors (see August and September '09 editions).

"I remember one storm," Mr. Hickey related about his travels as he explained life at sea. "We were on our return trip from Northern Europe and the Mediterranean Sea when we encountered a winter storm with waves 50' or more, all the way across the Atlantic. We used up so much fuel going up one wave after another and making slow progress that we had to make an unplanned stop in Bermuda for fuel. That delayed our arrival in Norfolk Virginia until February 10, 1952. Eight days later, two oil tankers broke apart in the same storm system off Cape Cod and sunk. They weren't built like our ship. That storm is worth reading about," he said as he recommended the book The Finest Hours by Michael J. Tougias.

"My mother had four sons in the Navy during the Korean War and I managed to meet or at least see all three of my brothers at some point," he said. "I met Jim in San Juan Puerto Rico just after our U.S. Navy fleet exercise training for A.S.W. (anti-submarine warfare). We had two aircraft carriers and 20 destroyers involved in that exercise," he said. "And I passed one in Japan. Our ship, a destroyer called the U.S.S. Waldron was arriving at our Naval base in Yokosuka, Japan when my brother Bill's ship, an electronic supply ship, was headed to Sasebo, a base in southern Japan. We passed at sea about a half mile apart. I sent him a signal, because I was the Quartermaster up on the bridge, running the signal light. So I sent him a brief message saying. sorry I missed you and hope to see you sometime, but I didn't see him until I was discharged from the Navy years later."

He would occasionally meet his other brother, Jack in Norfolk, VA where Jack served on the U.S.S. Mississippi testing experimental rockets.

"I finished up as Quartermaster Second Class. Not bad for four years of service," he related. As a Quartermaster in the Navy, Mr. Hickey was responsible for navigation and visual communication. During his service, he was responsible for steering his ship in and out of port, working with being refueled from refueling ships and aircraft carriers which would come alongside, as well as navigating through the locks at the Panama Canal and the Suez Canal amongst other duties.

"Steering the ship through the Panama Canal and seeing the ship go 30-40 feet in height from one level to another, then to the lake, and then stepping back down into the Pacific Ocean was one of the most interesting events, I must say."

Join the Navy, See the World – How True

During his tour, Mr. Hickey visited more than 24 countries on the U.S.S. Waldron, DD-699.

"I had the opportunity to transfer to other ships, but decided to stay on the Waldron, continuing service to my country and I got to see the world."

"Out at sea, we were always there for a reason," he explained. "Honing our skills or showing the flag. We were always active. The purpose of a destroyer is to hunt, detect, and if necessary, kill submarines," he explained. The U.S.S. Waldron carried six 5" guns, 16 40mm guns, five torpedo launchers, and multiple depth charges. The crew of the Waldron would also perform other tasks.

"I remember one rescue we performed at sea in 1952. It was the pilot from an old propeller plane who came flying in about 50' above the flight deck then nosedived into the water. They were still using some propeller planes back then. We had to retrieve him and return him to the carrier. They gave us five gallons of ice cream for our efforts, the standard reward from an aircraft carrier for delivering one pilot."

Fortunately, his ship avoided direct active action in Korea. "My ship was preparing to go to Korea but the shooting had stopped," he said.

Upon leaving the Navy, Mr. Hickey sought employment at Western Electric (later AT&T and Lucent Technologies) where he met his bride Helen. Mr. Hickey retired from Western Electric in 1994, working mostly as a scheduler for fiber optic products at the time. After 48 years of marriage, Mr. Hickey lost his wife Helen two years ago. "I didn't leave her side for the year after she was diagnosed, except to go to the store or fetch the paper."

His four children are all living locally: Edmund Jr, of Amherst N.H.; Paul, of Haverhill; Kenneth, of Framingham, and daughter Patricia, of Newburyport. He has two grandsons, Matthew and Alex, and a granddaughter Mikayla.

Mr. Hickey, a life-long Lawrencian, keeps active, walking two miles, three-to-four times each week. He recently volunteered as an adult altar server for funerals at St. Patrick's Church. His hobbies include his tomato garden where he grows 24 tomato plants and 24 pepper plants.

His other interests include reading and photography. "You have to keep your mind active as well as your body," he explained.

It was Mr. Hickey who introduced the Valley Patriot to his neighbors Jim Derby, and George and Mary Haynes from the Mt. Vernon neighborhood association, and we owe him a debt of gratitude for taking the time to share his own personal story with our readers.

The Valley Patriot is proud to highlight the service of our men and women in uniform, united to protect and defend our nation.

House Passes Legislation to Honor Women Airforce Service Pilots (WASP) July, 2009

WASHINGTON, DC - June 16, 2009 - The House of Representatives today voted to award the Women Airforce Service Pilots (WASP) with the Congressional Gold Medal, the highest civilian honor given in the United States, in recognition of their service during World War II. Approximately one thousand women served as Women Airforce Service Pilots and performed a variety of missions in support of the war effort including flying aircraft from factories to military bases, towing targets for air-to-air combat practice, and transporting cargo. They were the first women in history trained to fly American military aircraft. The legislation was approved in the Senate last month and will now go to the President for his signature.

Methuen resident Sara Payne Hayden, now 89, was one of the Airforce Service Pilots. Hayden test flew previously damaged aircraft to ensure repairs were successful prior to their reintroduction into combat service, a dangerous, but critical assignment in the war effort.

Hayden also attended Congressional hearings seeking long-delayed recognition for the work of the Women Airforce Service Pilots, who were finally awarded military service status in 1977.

"I was one of the group of women who were trained and then flew military airplanes in World War II, where we were volunteers just doing our job," said Sara Payne Haden. "Now that we are known for our service, I find it amazing that we are recognized with this high honor. It is quite a privilege to say thank you to those honoring us."

"This highly appropriate honor recognizes the contributions of everyday citizens like Sara Payne Hayden whose sacrifices in support of the war effort helped to ensure the preservation of freedom in our time," said Congresswoman Niki Tsongas, a cosponsor of the House bill. "Simultaneously, the Women Airforce Service Pilots paved the way for future generations of women to serve their country."

As the American war effort in World War II expanded, the need for male combat pilots overseas increased. Thousands of women volunteered for the newly created Women Airforce Service Pilots. By the middle of 1942 women pilots began flying U.S. Army Air Forces aircraft within the United States.

The Congressional Gold Medal is the highest civilian honor given in the United States. The medal is an "expression of national appreciation for distinguished achievements and contributions." Each medal is authorized by an Act of Congress, and past recipients include Winston Churchill, Rosa Parks, and Thomas Edison.

Paul B. Thompson

By: Lawrence "Lonnie" Brennan - June, 2009

"There are a lot more (people) who are much more worthy than I am" the humble 'gentle giant' softly responded when notified that he had been nominated as a Valley Patriot Hero of the Month. "We have a lot of guys, so many. I thank you. I'm honored," said Paul Thompson, the Commander of the American Legion Rene J. Gagnon Post 211, Georgetown.

On Monday, May 25, 2009, countless Georgetown residents filled the streets for a grand Memorial Day parade and ceremonies at the newly dedicated Harry Murch Memorial Park. Mr. Thompson, the 76 year old post commander and master of ceremonies for the event explained afterwards that "When I turned the corner and saw the new flag poles with all of the services represented, I have to admit it was a bit emotional."

For years, Commander Thompson has joined a dedicated group of American Legion and VFW members and many others in town to commemorate major events, including Veterans Day and Memorial Day.

A familiar prominent figure in town, having won 8 elections, served on the board of selectmen for 17 years, served on the school committee for two terms, and served on the finance committee and the board of health, more than one parade patron nodded and smiled when noting that in uniform Commander Thompson gives the familiar look of John Wayne in the movie 'Green Berets'.

"This is the best event I have attended in all my years" he remarked. But with some sadness, he noted during the ceremony that Armond J. Soucy, age 92 would be stepping down from leading the rifle firing squad. "He's served for 65 years. Incredible. Absolutely incredible," the commander said.

Married for 52 years to Catherine B. "Buffy" Thompson, the commander and his wife have six children, 3 boys, 3 girls "and two redheads, two blondes, and two brunettes," he noted, "the gene distribution was kind to us."

In 1950 Mr. Thompson entered the Coast Guard and was trained at Cape May, New Jersey, the Coast Guard's boot camp. He later attended the Navy's Sonar school in Key West "because the Coast Guard didn't have their own sonar school at that time, we joined with the Navy for advanced trainings and such. I went there and became a 'sonar man" he said.

Deployed predominately in the mid-Atlantic, the young Thompson could take up to 5 days sea voyage to "reach station." From there, a typical tour lasted approximately a month of monitoring at sea, as well as weather and instrumentation relays to government as well as commercial aircraft.

"I learned a lot and spent a lot of time at sea," he explained.

After serving he "figured I would take more classes, high dreams and such, then by chance, I met my future bride at a restaurant in Woburn. The rest is, how we say, history. Fifty two years of marriage, it's been incredible," he said about the new direction of community service that began after marriage.

"What makes me tick? I don't know. I just love Georgetown. This is where we've been since oh '62. We've raised our children here. I, well, I just have tried to help" he said.

"I served with 13 different selectmen and women over the years. When I won my first election, I got some advice from Joe Soucy. He said he had some advice, and if you want to take it, fine, if not O.K. The first year you should spend learning the position and the board and town operations, the second year contributing more and more, the third year you are a full board member and that's when you'll do the heavy lifting. Basically his message was to get to know the job," he said. "I've always told that to other selectmen. I've served with some guys that were very good, and some that, well, needed some learning."

"It's never easy, you know, being an elected official you try to please folks, you try to get consensus. It's not always easy you know.

Like most former military men, Commander Thompson continued his service through community involvement, and passed along the tradition of service to his family.

"I was the chairman of the school committee in 1975, so I had the distinct pleasure of presenting the diplomas to the graduates. My daughter graduated and she went into the Army shortly after and stayed there for 30 years. Suzanne just retired a while ago as a Sergeant Major" he said.

"I don't really like to talk about myself that much. I have a great sense of pride in this community. Ah, when we were marching down East Main Street yesterday, and we were going towards Harry Murch Park, and as soon as I saw the (new) flags up there, I got emotional. The veteran's group and me, we all got to see our own service flag up there," he said. "What a project for the town. I've penned a letter to Peter Durkee (Highway Surveyor) thanking him and others for their tremendous work on this project," the American Legion Post Commander said as he related the re-dedication of the memorial park.

The Valley Patriot highlights veterans and veteran support groups and organizations that have contributed to our communities. Please send your nomination for future profiles to the editor.

William Gallagher
U.S. Navy Seabees, WWII

By: Kathleen Corey Rahme - May, 2009

Service is no stranger to Bill Gallagher. He served as the Town Manager and as a City Councilor of Methuen for many years. Prior to that, Bill served in the US Navy Sea Bees in WWII. Bill answered the 'call to serve' in 1943 and again in 1946 when he was in the reserves. Gallagher served in both theatres of operation and we are grateful for his service.

PHOTO: TOM DUGGAN

Gallagher did his boot camp in the USNTC Camp Peary, Williamsburg, VA and joined the 114th Battalion which was commanded by Commander Earl G. Katlenback, CEC, USNR. He was then given orders to report to USNCTC, Camp Endicott in Davisville, RI. He received his advanced training in heavy equipment operation and simulated jungle fighting.

As part of that experience, he was involved in going into the woods where wooden figures would pop up out of nowhere and represent the enemy. There was an Ensign who would give the trainees a hard time. He would stay behind a mound of dirt and observe the trainees as they shot at the targets. The young trainees would deliberately fire into the mound so it would spray all over them. While the Ensign thought they were a poor shot, there was a more experienced Warrant Officer who knew what they were doing. He told the Ensign that he would never stay in the same trench with him during any future exercises!

Gallagher would continue his training in Lido Beach, Long Island, NY when in October of 1943 he was assigned to a new base. He received training in landing crafts for beach assaults. His group set up a tent city in order to simulate an actual field base with a motor generator for power and field kitchens. They even had a desalinated water supply. The group would use this base to train Navy shore parties for overseas assignments. Equipped with sand bars, these beaches proved beneficial for training. Often the landing crafts would find their way onto a sand bar and when the gate would open and extend, it would be over deeper water. Men in full combat gear would disembark and disappear below the waves. Bill and others would have to pull them out of the drink. This was great training because the same thing would later occur in actual landings.

On July 26, 1944 Gallagher would leave for Europe on the USS Lejeune, a former German supply ship that was converted into a troop carrier. He arrived in Bosneath, Scotland on August 5, 1944 where he boarded a truck and went to Helensboro, Scotland. A few days later, he went to Southampton, England where he would board a Canadian Landing Ship (LCI) that would take him to France.

The Germans were attacking in the area so the ship was delayed. They

circled the English Channel and there were reports that it was probably sunk because it did not arrive as scheduled. The U-boats were everywhere and they were forced to observe radio silence so they were unable to communicate.

Finally, on August 11, 1944 he arrived in Cherbourg, France. Pup tents were set up and they worked on Omaha, Utah, Juno and other beaches constructing facilities that would allow troops and supplies to come directly ashore without the use of the landing craft. Additionally, the Sea

Bees built large pontoon barges equipped with outboard engines to go to retrieve supplies from the bigger ships that were unable to enter the harbor. This often proved to be a difficult and dangerous operation due to the severe weather conditions in the English Channel.

The Sea Bees were always constructing new and temporary bases during the war effort. With their "can do" spirit, they constructed one in Cherbourg, France which consisted of Quonset huts, a mess hall, hot showers, laundry facility, and a recreation area. It was one of the best bases in France.

Gallagher's group left Cherbourg and arrived in Nantes, France. They set up tents in an open field and on one of his first nights there, a guard heard noises in the bushes nearby. He gave the command to halt. The noise continued so he opened fire. Gallagher and others emerged from their tents in their skivvies carrying their rifles and ammunition. It turned out to be two cows that he killed and the farmer was none too happy. While in Nantes, the men all acquired dysentery from drinking the water from a well.

The French Free Soldiers were a force to be reckoned with. They were executing German collaborators at night and it was in ear-shot of Gallagher's group. One night when he was on guard duty, he heard the shots.

Gallagher's tour of Europe would soon end. He left Nantes and traveled to Le Harve, France and to Salcombe, England on December 12, 1944. They arrived in Plymouth, England to wait for another ship to transport them back to the USA. Would you believe it was actually the USS Lejeune that took him to Europe in the first place? What a coincidence! They arrived on December 27, 1944. After having some leave, and allowing for some time for the 114th Battalion to regroup, he eventually received orders to go to the Pacific.

In March of 1945, Gallagher, having the new rank of Coxswain, left Port Hueneme, California on the S.S. Sea Bass. The ship arrived in New Hebrides and New Caledonia. Half of the battalion disembarked to do construction work, but primarily they were to load and unload supplies. His group loaded a complete Army division along with their tanks, artillery, ammunition and other supplies for the invasion of Okinawa. This invasion was to preclude the invasion of Japan itself. After the successful Okinawa operation, he was scheduled to be part of the invasion of Japan.

The first atomic bomb was dropped on Hiroshima on August 6, 1945 and the second on Nagasaki on August 9, 1945. The Japanese surrendered unconditionally on August 14, 1945; the actual surrender being on September 2. Gallagher and his group received this information as they were preparing to leave for the Philippines. They were elated since the casualties were estimated in the millions on both sides had an invasion actually taken place.

Discharged in May of 1946, he was assigned to the Navy Reserves where he served until May of 1953. Thanks Bill and others like you for honorably serving your country.

Tom Hargreaves

By: Tom Duggan, Jr. - January, 2009

METHUEN, MA - This month's Valley Patriot of the month is well known to Veterans and their families in the City of Methuen. He is Tom Hargreaves the city's Veteran's services director.

Hargreaves went into the army in September of 1969 and served until September of 1972.

Hargreaves was trained at Fort Dix in New Jersey, then stationed at Fort Devens for a short time before being stationed at Fort Gordon in Georgia. Hargreaves was then shipped to Frankfurt Germany for 22 months and performed his duties as a trained intelligence communication officer.

"My duties were in classified teletype operations," Hargreaves said. "I was also the traffic control supervisor for my shift.

But the teletypes we used were nothing like the technology we have today, it was basically using phone line, sort of a glorified fax line to relay classified communications."

"Any time there was flair up in the Middle East we were point of contact where initial communications came in and we would pass them off the appropriate destinations."

Hargreaves had a direct line to the Pentagon and the White House and was tasked with relaying classified intelligence communications to other military personnel and then back up through the chain of command.

Hargreaves married his wife Barbara Perkins just before leaving for Germany in 1970. Barbara followed him to Germany shortly after he left the states and stayed with him until he was honorably discharged. Barbara and Tom in celebrated their 30th wedding anniversary last month.

When he came home to the U.S. Tom got involved in The Masonic order and is still deeply involved with the Masonic Temple today. He credits his love of his country and the military to his father, Pickles Hargreaves who served in the Navy. He also had an uncle who served in the navy and his brother, David was stationed at Cameron Bay in Vietnam from '71 to '72.

Tom is the senior warden of his church at Saint John's the Evangelist Anglican Episcopal Church in Salem New Hampshire.

Hargreaves was appointed as the Veteran's Services Director for the City of Methuen by Mayor Manzi on October 15, 2007 and confirmed by the city council on November 8, 2007. He worked for the Valley Works Career Center in Haverhill and Lawrence helping veterans obtain employment and is a life time member of the American Legion Post 122. This year he started his first term on the executive board of the Legion.

Tom grew up in Methuen, is a product of the Methuen Public School where he graduated with Barbara from the Tenny High School in 1967.

Tom volunteers his time with the Shriners and the Masons, running blood drives and helping parents with CHIPS (Child Identification Program); where they do DNA cheek swabs of children, take pictures and videos and give them to parents to keep on file in case a child goes missing. The program is no cost to parents. He also helps run programs for children with Dyslexia, also at no cost to children.

While many of the military heroes we honor in the pages of the Valley Patriot have amazing stories of battle and glory to tell, the support those men in battled receive from men like Tom Hargreaves are just as notable and just as vital to our military success in campaigns around the world.

We believe that every man and woman who has served our nation in the armed forces, whether they be army, navy, air force, marines, national guard (and even merchant marines) truly deserve our undying loyalty and respect. We are proud this month to honor Tom Hargreaves as our Valley Patriot of the month for not only his service while in the US Army but also the incredible work he has done to make our country and our community a better place once he returned home.

The work he has done and continues to do in helping our veterans every day is immeasurable and the dent we owe you can never be repaid.

Civilian: Jim Wareing

By: Tom Duggan, Jr. - December, 2008

METHUEN, MA - For the last five years The Valley Patriot has reserved this space for honoring military heroes in the Merrimack Valley. It is, and

has always been our mission to publicly thank the men and women who honorably serve our nation, answer the call to put themselves in harm's way and continue contributing to the betterment of our nation when they returned home.

This month, we honor a non-veteran as our first ever, honorary Valley Patriot of the Month.

Methuen resident Jim Wareing, while never having served in the military has dedicated his life to helping our men and women in the armed forces fighting abroad.

Wareing has spent thousands dollars of his own money purchasing and collecting items for care packages to send to our troops in Iraq and Afghanistan, paying the postage, keeping in contact with soldiers in the field and calling attention to their needs here at home.

Wareing is also single handedly responsible for the patriotic displays, flags, and welcome home messages to returning troops posted on highway overpasses and bridges across the state.

With no personal interest or gain for himself, Wareing has designed and lobbied for a "Support the Troops" license plate in the Commonwealth of Massachusetts, the proceeds of which will go towards additional care packages to service men and women in the Middle East.

Wareing also established New England Caring for Our Military an organization established to network with military families, help the families of deceased military personnel and raise awareness of the needs of returning vets.

Last summer, Wareing volunteered his time, efforts and energies to help the family of slain American Hero Sgt. Alex Jiminez who was killed by terrorists in Iraq. Wareing spent countless hours with the grieving family of Sgt. Jiminez, organized the funeral and public services and served as the family spokesman with the press, shielding them from the onslaught of publicity associated with those services.

If all this wasn't enough, Jim Wareing suffers from Multiple Sclerosis, a debilitating and painful disease that makes ordinary daily tasks difficult if not impossible for some.

Given his personal limitations it is nothing short of amazing that Jim Wareing has been able to accomplish all that he has to honor the men and women in our armed forces putting their lives on the line for our country.

With his health failing, Jim is now embarking on a new endeavor in the name of our troops and their families by lobbying congress and the public to defeat the cleverly named Fallen Heroes Commemoration Act (HR6662).

If passed, this bill would give the press unrestricted access to military bases when the bodies of fallen soldiers are returned home for burial services. Currently, the decision to allow or restrict the media is left to the grieving families, many of whom prefer to have private time alone with their loved one when they arrive back in the states.

Jim Wareing has been honored by President George W. Bush and former Secretary of State Don Rumsfeld for his unending dedication to our servicemen and his efforts to make their and their families lives a little more comfortable.

For these reasons and so much more the Valley Patriot is proud to name Jim Wareing as our very first (and possibly last) Honorary Valley Patriot of the Month. The amount of care and compassion Mr. Wareing has provided to our brave troops can never be measured.

Scott Dempsey

By: Tech. Sgt. James Moore, USAF - November, 2008

LAWRENCE, MA - Scott Dempsey and his contributions to his country are nothing short of noteworthy. They have been honorable and just. He has been brave and steadfast. The Valley Patriot is delighted to showcase his service as November's Valley Patriot of the month.

Scott Dempsey was born in Lynn in 1982 to the late Brian survived by his mother, Laurie. Scott has one sibling, sister, Lindsay. He pretty much lived a normal life in the suburb of Boston where he played little league baseball and Pop Warner football with dreams of playing for the Red Sox and the beloved Pats. He was also raised in Lynn where he attended Lynn Vocational and Technical Institute, studying the Electrical Program as well as lettered in Varsity Football.

Shortly after his 20th birthday, he enlisted in the United States Army to become a "19 Delta", or also known as a Calvary Scout. He left for basic training on Apr 14, 2003 and earned his stripes with the 5/15 Calvary, Bravo troop, second platoon and graduated from Basic Military Training. His Military Occupational Specialty (MOS) was trained to be a 19 Delta, Armored Reconnaissance Specialist. After 17 weeks of total training, called OSUT, one stop unit training, he graduated on August 15, 2003.

He traveled home to take some leave after Basic Training and prior to going to Germany for his first assignment and boarded a flight to Germany.

He reported to Friedberg, home of the 1-37 ARBN (1st Battalion, 37th Regimen Armored Battalion), the Bandits.

Immediately upon his arrival to Friedberg, he was informed that most of his post was already deployed and he, too, would soon be heading in that direction. The foreshadowing of the story was very obvious for Dempsey and he soon left for Baghdad at the end of September to join his scout platoon.

Since his unit was deployed and he was the new guy, he had to work twice as hard to be "squared away". It was a light scout platoon, or a platoon of Hummvees. During the day, the scout platoon would provide gun truck security to convoys, conduct route clearance missions, special operations, and sometimes, humanitarian missions. Scouts wear many hats on the battlefield including providing personal security for the battalion commander as well as the Command Sergeant Major. Dempsey, took his responsibilities as a driver and scout, "very seriously".

By "very seriously", he says, a driver held the truck together, making sure that it was up and running, every day. Requiring it to be mission capable at a moment's notice-being a good scout meant being a good mechanic and very good at "acquisition" he said tongue-and-cheek. Making sure the job got done.

In April, 2004, Dempsey was promoted to Private First Class and soon learned that the tour had been extended indefinitely. They moved from Baghdad to Karbala, where intense door-to-door fighting took place as well as heightened awareness for UXOs (unexploded ordnance) and IED's (improvised explosive devices), since this was new territory for the unit. For the unit's work in Karbala, they were awarded the Presidential Unit Citation. Additionally, Dempsey was awarded Combat Spurs and Stetson. This is the HIGHEST honor for a Calvaryman. By the Order of the Combat Spur, he was dubbed a Knight and entered in the rolls of the grand and noble, Order of the Spur. He was also awarded the Army Commendation Medal for his actions in Karbala.

After his time in Karbala and in late August of 2004, he redeployed with his unit to Germany. After a year and a half there, he was honorably discharged.

When asked the simple question of why he joined the Army, Dempsey answered in a manner with such resolve and fortitude that it can only come from a war-weary veteran himself: "to sum it up, my favorite subject is (American History) the American Revolution. I love the principles this country was founded on. In the Battle of Lexington, four men from Lynn were killed and two wounded. Men from my city had a huge impact on the formation of this country."

He continues, "Also a long tradition, as the Pine Grove Cemetery in Lynn will show of great men giving their lives for this great country." "...I came from a long line of soldiers including a great grandfather who stormed the beaches of Normandy, winning the Bronze Star and Purple Heart...a cousin served in Bosnia and another in Somalia."

In regard to his passion and love for our wonderful nation and what it means to benefit from being an American, he humbly states:

"All these men that have come before me...(have) given me this country that I enjoy today. They passed the torch to me, and it was my turn to have the honor of defending my country-the honor of carrying my nation's flag into battle."

Dempsey, 26, is currently attending Northern Essex Community College in hopes of finishing his degree in Education and becoming a high school History teacher.

"[I would like to] show tomorrow's young people how great this country is and how it is worth defending and show them how important the past is and its relationship to the future."

He is also battling another war within himself due to his selfless service in the Middle-East. He wants people to be aware of and to not turn a blind-eye to the effects of war.

"I would like to get involved with Veterans and to help them navigate the Veteran's Affairs (VA) system. In a sense, "a way of keeping a brotherhood together even after service is complete."

He vows that, "the best way for a Veteran to learn about the VA system is through Veterans, not a teleprompt." So stay tuned for next month's issue of the Valley Patriot as we'll learn of PFC Dempsey's struggles to obtain assistance through the VA system, in his words....

Scott, you are no doubt a Patriot. We commend you for your service and look forward to reading about your story, next month-same place.

Tech. Sergeant James Moore is a recruiter for the United States Air Force and our Valley Patriot Hero Columnist.

Alex Jiminez
WAR ON TERROR
August, 2008

Since the very first edition of The Valley Patriot in March of 2004, this space has been reserved for honoring local veterans who have either performed heroically in battle or made a significant difference in their community.

This month we honor Spc. Alex Jimenez of Lawrence whose remains were found last month in Iraq after a 15 month search for the captured soldier.

Jimenez is the second veteran to be honored posthumously as a Valley Patriot of the Month. His bravery and his service to the United States Army, his family and community are a model of patriotism for young people across the country.

The death of Alex Jimenez brought an entire community together in sorrow and healing.

We at The Valley Patriot continue to pray for the friends, family and fellow military men and women who served with Alex in Iraq.

He is a true American hero and we only hope that the cowards who took his life receive the justice they deserve.

Tech. Sergeant
Jeremiah Sullivan

By: Dr. Charles Ormsby - January, 2005

A boyhood attraction to trains, electronic gadgets, and Morse code earned Jeremiah (Jerry) Sullivan a ticket to see Europe by air. Actually, it was numerous tickets; they were for a B-17, and the reception wasn't very friendly.

Jerry was born and grew up in Lawrence. He graduated from Lawrence High School in 1943, knowing that the Army had plans for him. First, the Army sent him to basic training in Biloxi, Mississippi. After Jerry acclimated himself to the oppressive heat, the Army decided (based on Jerry's aptitude for electrical systems and Morse code) that he would enjoy wintering in Sioux Falls, South Dakota while attending Radio School. Jerry said that not very much snow fell that winter ... it just blew horizontally, first in one direction and then back in the other direction.

After his blood thickened sufficiently to withstand the bitter cold, it was time to head off to Yuma, Arizona for the summer to attend Gunnery School. Jerry says he wasn't very good at recognizing aircraft (friend, foe, or type) in the tests that were given. When faced with either being assigned to artillery as a radio operator or as an aircraft gunner, he decided he wanted to get a good score on the aircraft recognition test. Recruiting a fellow gunner, who had just passed the test with flying colors, to stand in for him on the exam, Jerry "earned" a perfect score! His perfect score opened up an option for him to stay stateside as an instructor and avoid going into combat, but Jerry opted to go to war. In mid-1944 Jerry was put on a troop ship (with the other members of his B-17 crew) and headed for Naples where he was assigned to the US airbase at Foggia, Italy.

Jerry recalls the process of checking the bulletin board each day to see if you were scheduled for a mission the following day. Those of us who have never experienced the horrors of war can probably never appreciate the experience of looking at that bulletin board and wondering, every day, if you were about to be assigned to your last mission.

I asked Jerry to describe his feelings before his first mission over enemy territory. He hesitated and then said he would tell me about that day.

When you have a mission assigned, you get a 4:30AM wakeup call. You dress for the flight ... long johns, sweater, heated suit, and heavy uniform ... the knitted hat, helmet, gloves, and oxygen system came later. This was high altitude flying in an unheated, unpressurized, tin can ... it was COLD at over 30,000 feet! Next it was breakfast. The cooks were especially good to the aircrews. Jerry recalls the breakfast before his first mission: his stomach was so cramped and tense he couldn't eat. This wasn't just another day at the office.

After breakfast, while still dark out, you were driven to the flight line to pick up your equipment bag and parachute. On that first day, Jerry was fitted for his parachute harness ... something he hoped he would never have to use. Finally, it was time for the aircraft pre-flight checks (engineer and gunners) and pre-mission briefings. After the radio operator was given the secret radio codes and all crewmen synchronized their watches, it was time to fly.

Who makes up a B-17 crew? Jerry gave a brief lesson: The crew was made up of 10 men (starting from the front): the bombardier and navigator in the nose, a pilot and co-pilot in the cockpit, the engineer between and directly behind them, the radio operator who also was a gunner on the upward firing gun (this was Jerry), the ball-turret gunner (hanging beneath the plane), the left and right gunners, and, finally, the tail gunner.

The missions were flown by squadrons of 7 to 9 planes with fighter escorts that were not typically in formation. The fighters often had their own missions and were on-call nearby if the squadron was attacked. Late in the war the capacity of the German Luftwaffe was significantly reduced and fighters did not often attack the squadrons. The biggest threat in 1944/45 was from flack. If a B-17 was hit by flack and forced to leave the main squadron, German fighters, who wouldn't attack a combined squadron, would rush to finish off a wounded bomber.

Jerry vividly recalls the heavy flack encountered on many missions. The sky was often black with the residue from exploding shells. "We had to just cruise through it," he said. "You couldn't hear it, not because it wasn't loud, but because the aircraft was so noisy". Flack often exploded very close to the plane and holes were patched in the airplane after nearly every mission.

Jerry received weather reports for the target area every 15 minutes en route. The mission called for them to fly to the IP (initial point) and from the IP to the target area (the "bomb run"). During the bomb run, the altitude, airspeed and heading were prescribed … no maneuvering to avoid flack or the bombardier would never be able to hit the target (as advanced as the Norden bomb site was, it couldn't handle anything other than straight and level flight over the target).

After the bombs were released, Jerry checked the bomb bay and announced over the interphone, "Bombs are gone" or "Bombs are still there". Once, when the bombs were stuck and nothing else would release them, the engineer had to go into the bomb bay and dislodge them with his foot.

There is much more to tell, but you'll have to talk to Jerry to hear the rest.

I always thought it was "25 missions and you go home" for B-17 crews… but this was not true late in the war. Jerry finished his flying career just about when Germany surrendered … after an unbelievable 50 missions! Actually, it was a few less than 50 because, after really bad missions, the crew was credited with two missions. Jerry recalls this may have been awarded to his crew three times, so his mission total is probably around 47; with 44 of those as lead bomber. Jerry flew in many B-17s on those missions. His favorite was one was named "Vaudeville" because it had a subtitle, "Coming Home".

Jerry, who still lives in Lawrence, has recently been diagnosed with cancer and is beginning chemotherapy. We pray for his successful recovery.

Jerry, thank you for your brave service.

PHOTO: PROVIDED BY JEREMIAH SULLIVAN

Bob McCann
U.S. Marines

By: Tom Duggan, Jr. - June, 2008

METHUEN, MA - This month, The Valley Patriot honors Methuen resident and former Veterans' Services Director for the City of Lawrence, Robert "Bob" McCann. He was Director for the City of Lawrence for over 20 years, from 1983-2004.

As with most veterans we interview, McCann humbly resisted being interviewed as a Hero in our Midst, because, he says, "I didn't do anything heroic, like some of the servicemen you've highlighted. I really don't deserve a recognition like that."

McCann's heroism may not have come on the battlefield while serving in the U.S. Marines, but since being honorably discharged in 1955, he has been a stalwart advocate for military families and honoring our deceased military veterans.

McCann was 23 years old when he joined the Marines. He trained at Paris Island, was then stationed at Camp Lejeune, where he worked in the motor pool, and was then transferred to Camp Pendleton where he worked in the warehouse. McCann served from 1952-1955.

McCann, who has been married for 52 years, not only served as the City of Lawrence's Veteran's Services Director, helping military families obtain medical and education benefits, but McCann has volunteered on dozens of city projects and spearheaded the erection of at least three war monuments on the Campagnone Common in Lawrence.

Lawrence resident William Lord, who served as a drummer with the 40th Massachusetts Infantry carried Union Colonel Eldridge G. Floyd of the 3rd New York Infantry to safety from behind enemy lines. He was awarded the Medal of Honor by Congress. Bob McCann, knowing the history of William Lord, formed a committee and began fund raising to erect a monument in honor of Lord.

McCann raised more than $10,000 from private businesses and local citizens, working with City Attorney Charles Boddy and Lawrence Mayor Michael Sullivan to have the labor provided by the city and securing the site on the Common where the memorial stands today.

On June 14th 2004, the day the William Lord Monument was unveiled on the Campagnone Common, the program that day read: "We join today to celebrate the support of the unified community that brought one man's dream to reality. The Lord monument does much more than memorialize William Lord, it celebrates Lawrence's ability to unite behind a cause, as it has so often done over its 150 year history, and to accomplish its goals. This monument symbolizes through the efforts of William Lord and Bob McCann, that we can achieve our visions, if we set our hearts and wills to the task."

McCann was also instrumental in the erection of the Korean War Monument on the Common and a Monument Honoring All Women who served in the military during all wars.

McCann may be best known as president of the South Lawrence West Little League, where he was also a business administrator, putting in 25 years helping the children of the Mount Vernon area of Lawrence to have a baseball league each summer.@

McCann served as President of Lawrence Veteran's Council, was the State Commandant of the Massachusetts Marine Corps League, and Commandant of the Merrimack Valley Marine Corps.

In short, though he may not think he is deserving of being named as a Hero in our Midst, Bob McCann is and has always been a man who has given of himself for his family, his country and his community. Whether it is delivering flags to the wakes and funerals of military servicemen and women or working with veteran's services agencies and organizations to honor those who have offered and sometimes given their lives in service of their country, Bob McCann is always there to make a difference.

We at The Valley Patriot are pleased this month to honor Robert "Bob" McCann as out Valley Patriot of the Month, Hero in Our Midst.

Above Left, a monument honoring all military women who served in war, above right, the Korean War Monument. At right, the William Lord Monument. All three of these monuments were erected on the Lawrence Common as the result of the efforts of former Veteran's Services Director Bob McCann.

Natasha Young

Staff Sgt. Natasha Young with the Commandant, General Conway, while forward deployed to Iraq.

By Tech. Sgt. James Moore, USAF - May, 2008.

LAWRENCE , MA -- A patriot, as defined by the Merriam-Webster Dictionary, is "One who loves his or her country and supports its authority and interests." The word is sometimes overused or even misused, but not when we use it to describe Natasha Young, make that Staff Sergeant Young, United States Marine Corps, who is this month's Valley Patriot of the Month.

Staff Sergeant Young hails from Lawrence, MA and joined the United States Marine Corps in 1999. This October will mark her 9-year anniversary as a marine. When I asked her whether she plans to make the Marine Corps a career, she said in an earnest tone, "Absolutely!"

Staff Sergeant Young is a Marine first and foremost, but also a Bulk Fuel Specialist currently serving as an Enlisted Accessions Recruiter in

Plymouth, MA. Her 8 year career has taken her to Ft. Lee, Va., Okinawa, Japan, the Humvee Detachment in Londonderry, NH, New River, NC, Cherry Point, NC, Camp Lejeune, SC, Iraq, and now to The United States Marine Corps Recruiting Substation, Plymouth, MA.

She always sets the pace in whatever position she holds and is doing many great things with her new position as an Enlisted Accessions Recruiter. She has been awarded a Navy Commendation Medal, 4 Navy and Marine Corps Medals, the Navy Unit Citation, 2 Meritorious Unit Service Medals, an Iraqi Campaign Medal, and Expeditionary and Service Medals in the Global War on Terror.

When I asked her which awards and/or decorations are the most important to her she replied, "Do you want me to be completely honest?" and then continued, "I don't wear them because they look nice, but the one that is the most important to me is my Navy Commendation Medal..." Staff Sergeant Young earned this award while she was deployed for a year in support of Operation Iraqi Freedom.

While stationed at Camp Lejeune, Staff Sergeant Young was tasked with the 2nd EOD Company (Explosive Ordnance Disposal) and was attached to that Company for two years. She was hand-picked by the Company Commander of the 2nd EOD Company to accompany them to Iraq due to her organizational skills and her attention to detail.

She went on to say that some of the men and women she was deployed with from the 2nd EOD Company paid the ultimate price and did not return with her.

"They are an, awesome, awesome group of men and women and for the first time in my career, I felt that I was amongst heroes."

She continued by saying that this particular deployment was the toughest, and at the same time the most gratifying, deployment she has ever participated in. "I worked with extraordinary men working under extraordinary conditions. They were GREAT! It was the hardest work I've ever done. They should get all the credit in the world."

When I first spoke to Staff Sergeant Young, I was really impressed with her professionalism and demeanor as she spoke of her service and commitment to the Marine Corps. Her enthusiasm and sincere appreciation for being a part of the Corps was ever present during our conversation.

She loves the fact that the Marine Corps has taught her many things, but what she cherishes the most about her service in the Marine Corps is her fellow Marines and the friendships that she has developed over the years.

These are people that have come from all walks of life. The one thing they have in common is that they are Marines. She admits, "I don't take no for an answer, and I don't ever lay my head down at night and wonder if I made a difference on any given day. I gave it all. I love what I do."

Staff Sergeant Young is pursuing an Associate's Degree in Liberal Arts at this time and, in the future, she would like to earn a Bachelor's degree in Social Work/Youth Counseling. She has aspirations of setting up her own "Boot Camp" for youngsters in the future.

Staff Sergeant Young has a very big soft spot for the youngsters generally, and for Lawrence youth in particular. She says, "If they can dream it, they can do it!" She attributes her strong-willed, can-do attitude to living and growing up in Lawrence.

As for the way she feels bout serving in the United States Marine Corps, she says, "To do things that you thought weren't possible ... to be able to do them...it's very gratifying."

This local heroine is aware of some of the ways that women in the Marines (maybe all military women) are often portrayed. "I'm a Marine and a lady first," she declares, "I'm class. We're still women, but we just wear cammies to work because of the nature of our job. We are Marines, but still moms, still wives and still homemakers. Some of the best moms are Marines...."

She is truly a Patriot and no doubt a top-notch, quality individual that exudes enthusiasm and is fervently proud to serve her country.

She describes herself as "colorful" and "vibrant" and I would have to say that that is an apt description after speaking with her. You may see Staff Sergeant Natasha Young on her brand-new 2008 Harley Nightster somewhere on I-495. If you do, say, "Hi" and "Semper Fi".

Staff Sergeant Natasha Young, thank you for your dedicated service!

Tech. Sergeant James Moore is a member of the United States Air Force and our Hero columnist. You can e-mail Sgt. Moore at moore.jr5@verizon.net

Lawrence Latinos Contributing to Our Nation's Defense

By: Tech Sgt. James Moore, USAF - June, 2008

The great city of Lawrence has had a rich history of sending its finest men and women to serve in the United States Armed Forces. Just like any city in the Union, Lawrence is proud of its veterans and has gone to great lengths to honor them. One obvious example of the pride people in Lawrence have for our servicemen and women is the Lawrence Veteran's Memorial Stadium which we all adore and love.

Lawrence is proud of her past and present veterans and is now sending three more of its finest residents to serve in the United States Air Force. This goes without saying that The Valley Patriot is honored to showcase these individuals. They are Hispanic-American Airman trainees preparing to enter the United States Air Force.

So, June's Air Force Corner (which will be a mainstay for the Valley Patriot for months to come), would like to introduce three people in the Delayed Enlistment

Program at the United States Air Force Recruiting office in Lawrence for we believe it is important to shine the spotlight on them and celebrate their going off to do great things while making invaluable contributions to our nation's Air Force.

In the City of Lawrence, many Hispanic Americans have been drawn to military service in one way or another: looking for job skills, obtaining an education, providing for their families, fulfilling a conviction to serve, just to mention a few. The qualifications needed to enlist in the United State Air

Force are amongst the most stringent of all military services, in short not just anyone can qualify.

Darliny Ayala

Conversely, there are those individuals who were born to serve, such as Darliny Ayala, Francisco Castro, and Hector Vega, who all hail from Lawrence, Massachusetts. They have made a commitment and taken the Oath of Enlistment for the United States Air Force. They've also been accepted into the Community College of the Air Force.

For Ayala, Castro, and Vega their reasons for joining are each different, but their resolve to succeed in the future is very much similar. Ayala epitomizes the spirit of a Lawrencian and that of a future leader in the Air Force. Ayala, 18, was born in the Dominican Republic and became a U.S. citizen at the age of 11. She wanted to join the Air Force for everything that it has to offer and to serve as an Intelligence Specialist, possibly serving as a Cryptologic Linguist.

Ayala is a 2007 graduate of Greater Lawrence Technical High School. Two young people she holds very near and dear to her are her younger twin brothers, who both have Autism. Their names are Andy and Ariel.

They have become her inspirations for joining the Air Force. "(I want to)...be able to provide for them in the future," Ayala says, adding that she would like to be a role model for them by earning her Bachelor's Degree while serving in the Air Force.

Ayala is full of the American Spirit and is a versatile individual. Some of her accolades include: Honor Roll student, National Honor Society student, Student Athlete in Cross-Country, Outside Track & Field, Varsity Basketball. She was also a member of the Drama Club.

There's a big heart in the 5' 1" young lady from Lawrence, she says that she's going to miss her city but, according to Ayala, "I'm very enthused to start a new life as an Airman in the Air Force and I can't wait to travel and see different countries." Also, her father, Jose Ayala, is a mainstay and is very active in the Hispanic in the community. He also has his own radio program every morning from 6-8 am on AM1490 WCEC and is the Merrimack Valley's ONLY Hispanic News/Talk radio station.

Hector Vega

A very enthusiastic and outgoing addition to the Air Force is Hector Vega, 21, of Lawrence. He is also a 2004 graduate of Greater Lawrence Technical High School in Andover and entered the Air Force on June 3rd. He's originally from Puerto Rico and lives with his mother, Rachel. He's been working in the electronics field for the past two years and is applying his knowledge and skills and aims to be an Avionics Apprentice working on Aircraft Computers and Crossing into the Blue. Vega explains, "I need to have a new start in life and do something positive and I know that I can do all this in the Air Force." Vega, is a very outgoing individual and brings a plethora of qualities to the Air Force. He's always good with a joke and enjoys Hip-Hop music and love cars.

Francisco Castro

Finally and also from Lawrence is Francisco Castro who departed for San Antonio, Texas on June 3rd along with Vega.

Francisco and his family immigrated to the United States from the Dominican Republic in 2003. He was inspired to join the Air Force by his father's influence

and with his grandmother's support, whom he spends most of his time with, along with his 2 year old little brother.

At age 22, Castro loves baseball and is always good with a statistic on any game, especially his favorite player, Ken Griffey, Jr. Castro is very diligent and

obtained more than 24 semester hours of college since he's been in the United States while attending ITT Technical and Northern Essex Community College in

Lawrence. He has earned advanced rank by having earned these college credits. He will enter as an E-2, or the rank of Airman. Once he's completed Basic Military Training and Technical School, Castro will be able to transfer these credits and apply them to our Community College of the Air Force Associate's Degree in Applied Science. The CCAF is degree granting institution and one is accepted once they've qualified for the Air Force.

I'm proud to have these fine individuals in "my" Air Force. They are exactly what we are looking for in a prospective Airman. They are mentally, morally, physically, and academically qualified and prepared for the task at hand. They bring diversity to the Air Force, which is what the Air Force strives to achieve, mirroring today's society and providing opportunities for advancement and marketability for all that qualify. But as far as accepting challenges, embracing change, and achieving great things, well it appears that they will achieve more than they ever imagined by applying the same principles and values they've already instilled within themselves and taking advantage of what all the Air Force will provide.

To serve in our Nation's military is a privilege and not a right, and a privilege that is held in the highest regard. These three outstanding individuals will develop in to outstanding, Airmen, leaders, and will be are the future of our nation's Air Force.

Also, a Latino patriot, who was also a Medal of Honor recipient was Army Master Sgt. Roy Benavidez In his book Medal of Honor: One Man's Journey from Poverty to Prejudice, he wrote these memorable words: "we have an extraordinary opportunity, an opportunity to be better than we were yesterday. We must all strive to improve ourselves to be the best we can be. That's how we can honor the memory of those who have given their lives to fight and defeat terrorism and ensure their sacrifices are not in vain. When opportunity knocks, we must be ready to answer the door." He also adds: "...Opportunity, combined with education, is a key to success; and the military is a great place to seek it, find it and achieve success from it."

Unfortunately, Benavidez passed in 2001, but was solely responsible for saving 8 lives during Vietnam in Loch Ninh, 2 May 1968.

Stephen Label

By: Tech Sgt. James Moore, USAF - June, 2008

METHUEN, MA - For the past four years The Valley Patriot has used this space on our front page to honor and thank those men and women who have served in the U.S. military as our "Valley Patriot of the Month."

This month, however, on our four year anniversary we decided to reach out to some of the young people in our community and let them know that we truly appreciate and admire their decision to join the military, (especially in the current political climate). We believe that for a young person to forgo the freedoms of college life and the comforts of living here in the US to put their lives on the line for our nation makes them heroes too.

One such example is Methuen resident Stephen Lebel. On March 4, 2008, Label left home to enter the United States Air Force as an Air Force Aircraft Armament Systems Apprentice. He will be continuing his family's tradition of service to our great Nation by serving in the United States Air Force.

Both of his parents have served in the Air Force and his stepfather spent some years in the United States Army. His mother, Kristine Williams, served as an Aerospace Ground Equipment Technician and met Stephen's father while serving in Germany. It was her influence and guidance that led Stephen to aspire to be an Airman.

Lebel's younger brother Alex, attends Marsh Grammar School in Methuen and his Language Arts class is now learning how to properly address, place postage, and seal an envelope to be mailed.

Susan Ginchereau, Lebel's Kindergarten teacher and now the Fifth Grade Language Arts teacher at Marsh Grammar School in Methuen, saw an opportunity to provide her students with a heart-felt lesson in learning how to properly send a piece of mail.

This is something that is essential to learn as a youngster, but the quality of Mrs. Ginchereau's teaching put a warm touch to this subject.

As Stephen's recruiter, I was invited by both Stephen and Mrs. Ginchereau to speak to her class about what Stephen's Air Force Specialty would entail and what his average day at Basic Military Training would be like to the Fifth Grade class.

On an aside, I have to say this is the part of my job that I love the most in the Air Force Recruiting Service, but this was not a recruiting venture.

As I introduced myself and made the youngsters feel comfortable, the Fifth Graders at Marsh Grammar proceeded to ask many well thought out questions, such as: "Why do you have to get your haircut?"

"How long is boot camp?"

(and) "What kind of airplane do you (I) fly?"… just to mention a few. I answered their questions to the best of my ability and even though I wished I had been a pilot, I eventually explained that he would have a complex mailing address that would have up to six lines.

I let them know also that he wouldn't be able to let us all know what that address would be until his first Saturday there.

Now Lebel, 19, was once a student of Mrs. Ginchereau's when he was in Kindergarten at Marsh Grammar School. Coincidentally, his sister Nicole was once a student of hers and now Stephen's little brother, Alex, is a current pupil of Ginchereau's.

Mrs. Ginchereau's Fifth Grade Language Arts class and Stephen will be pen-pals while he's at Basic Military Training.

"This is going to be great for Alex," says Lebel's mother, Kristine of her younger son Alex. As you could imagine, the thought of Stephen not being there for Alex now is something that Stephen and Alex have talked about a lot since Stephen's commitment to join the United States Air Force's Delayed Enlistment Program (DEP).

This is often the dynamic of an Airman leaving for boot camp. To Alex, his big brother as his class' Pen Pal makes him even more proud than he already is. I'm sure that even after Basic Military Training and on in to Stephen's Technical Training, Alex will be the best in his class at sending the old-fashioned letter. Mrs. Ginchereau's class is also going to be a pen pal with a Soldier that is stationed near Basra, Iraq. His name is Sergeant First Class Michael Kulikowski, of Philadelphia, PA.

The Valley Patriot is grateful to Stephen for your willingness as a young person to step up to the plate, and help your country at a time when there is so much uncertainty around the world. We are happy this month to tell your story in hopes that it will inspire other young men and women to join the armed forces and help protect America. Good luck at boot camp and we'll see you in six and a half weeks.

Christopher Fantasia

By Tech Sgt. James Moore, USAF - February, 2008

SALEM, NH - Airman First Class Christopher Fantasia, home on Recruiting Assistance Duty at the Air Force Recruiting Office in Lawrence, Ma., is making a difference in the world.

He is a patriot and has a genuine enthusiasm for his work. Airman First Class Fantasia joined the Air Force in 2005 and plans on making a career of the Air Force. He's just returned from Baghdad, Iraq, in support of Operation Iraqi Freedom 5.

His Air Force specialty, TAC-P (Tactical Air Control Party) allows him to work almost exclusively with the United States Army.

TAC-P personnel provide close air support (CAS) for all conventional and all Special Operation Forces missions within an area of responsibility.

TAC-P is considered a part of Air Force Special Tactics and is somewhat of an atypical Air Force Specialty Code (AFSC) since most Airmen aren't categorized as "Battlefield Airmen".

TAC-P is one of only five Battlefield Airman Careers in the Air Force, meaning that the Airman must be combat mission ready (CMR) at all times. AFSC is to the Air Force as what is commonly known in the United

States Marine Corps and Army as "MOS", or Military Occupational Specialty.

Airman First Class Fantasia is originally from Everett, MA, and graduated from Everett High School in 2001.

He joined the United States Air Force as a resident of Salem, NH, where he spends most of his time at his mother's house while home on leave. He is currently stationed at the Army Post, Fort Stewart, Georgia and is a proud father of a beautiful baby girl, Alexa Fantasia who was born in December, 2007.

Airman First Class Fantasia says he chose TAC-P because of its uniqueness and excitement. According to Airman Fantasia, "I wanted an exciting job that would uphold me to the highest standard and challenge me physically, mentally, and technically."

"I get to do, all that an adrenaline junkie like me gets to do, and serve a great cause that I get paid well to do!" An adrenaline junkie, he is.

"If I had to do it all over again, I wouldn't change my decision to join the Air Force", says Airman First Class Fantasia.

Working exclusively with the Army affords Fantasia the opportunity to wear distinctive unit and combat patches that your average Airman wouldn't be able to wear.

Airman First Class Fantasia just recently returned home from an eight month deployment in Iraq, which he started five months earlier than anticipated to meet the requirements of the increased American troop surge in Baghdad.

Fantasia deployed from Fort Stewart, Georgia with the 3rd Infantry Division (3ID). He was deployed with the 3rd Infantry Division/7th Cavalry Unit which fell under the 82nd Airborne Paratrooper Brigade during his time in Baghdad.

The distinguished service patches he wears proudly on his uniform raises some eyebrows with his fellow Airmen, current and former veterans from all other services.

Since joining the Air Force in 2005, Fantasia has earned multiple certificates and college credits by virtue of his Air Force training and is applying these credits towards his Associate's Degree at the Community College of the Air Force.

He has earned awards and decorations while in the Air Force and for his time and service in Baghdad, Iraq, Operation Iraqi Freedom 5 (OIF 5). Most notably, Fantasia was awarded the Air Force Commendation Medal and an Army Achievement Medal for his distinguished service.

Airman First Class Fantasia graduated Basic Military Training (BMT) in San Antonio, Texas in September of 2005. After he completed BMT and prior to being fully qualified in his career field, he moved on to his required technical training at Hurlburt Field, Florida home of the Air Force Special Operations Command.

Airman First Class Fantasia spent 18 weeks learning small unit tactics, close air support procedures, radio etiquette, and troubleshooting. Additionally, he went through convoy training, day/night land navigation, HMMWV (aka. High-Mobility, Multi-Wheeled Vehicle, also known as Humvee) training with night vision devices and visible and non-visible lasers as well as stealth tactics.

When I asked him how he felt doing this type of work, day in and day out, he says with enthusiasm, "I have a blast!"

The physical demand for TAC-P is grueling, requiring trainees to complete, for example, 12 mile "ruck" marches, 2-10 mile runs, and "smoke" sessions.

"Smoke" sessions are what Airman Fantasia affectionately refers to as a combination of all physical training aspects in a circuit training-type of session, all of which is done before 8 a.m. He also had to endure S. E. R. E. training, at Fairchild AFB, Spokane, WA, SERE is an abbreviation for Survival, Evasion, Resistance, and Escape.

All Air Force members that are considered on "Flying Status" are required to undergo this training. This is known also known as survival training.

This is a unique Air Force Specialty, so there are always questions to be asked, even from myself.

I have had the pleasure of getting to know Airman First Class Fantasia on a personal level and have gained a level of respect for the good job he had done in his two and a half year of service.

As for myself, well, I have had the pleasure of serving in the United States Air Force for a little over twelve years at this point and I haven't had the opportunity to do half of the exciting things that Airman Fantasia has had the opportunity to do.

Since he's been home, Fantasia has been spending his free time with friends and family, especially quality time with his little Alexa.

He will be on Recruiting Assistance Duty until the 8th of February and will be heading back to Fort Stewart, Georgia, soon thereafter.

The Valley Patriot wishes to thank Airman First Class Fantasia of the United States Air Force for his service to our country and we are proud to honor him as our Valley Patriot of the Month, Hero in our Midst. He is clearly a shining example of what a true patriot is and does.

Airman First Class Christopher Fantasia, The Valley Patriot Thanks you, the air force thanks you and the people of the Valley also thank you. Be safe in your next assignment!

Technical Sergeant, James F. Moore, Jr. has been in the United States Air Force for more than 14 years and is The Valley Patriot's new Hero reporter. If you would like more information on how you can be a part of the World's Greatest Air Force, please contact Technical Sergeant, James F. Moore, Jr. 160 Winthrop Ave., Stadium Plaza, Lawrence, MA 01841, 978-686-1464 or via e-mail: james.moore@rs.af.mil

Arthur Rauseo

By: Lonnie Brennan - December, 2007

GEORGETOWN, MA - Quietly, peacefully, a former naval seaman makes his way to a local coffee shop. He takes his seat on a short stool at a curved counter, smiles to a familiar server, shares quips and views on the past day's events and the morning papers. As he sips his coffee he banters with friends, cupping his ear and leaning forward to hear.

Everyone knows the man, George-town's former Fire Chief and current Electric Light Commissioner. The proprietor of a small clothing store. A familiar face, a friend to many. Another day for Arthur Rauseo, age 82.

Peeling away the years, one stands in awe at the simplicity, the determination, the sincerity, the energy, the Americanism of this gentleman citizen. At age sixteen and a half (although his photos from the era make him look more like age 14), Mr. Rauseo enlisted in the armed forces. We were at war, and, like so many in our Country, this young lad stepped forward with deliberate eyes to serve our country. He kissed his mother goodbye, and that was the last time he would ever see her. She died before he could return from the war. "I never saw my mother again."

Mr. Rauseo sports his familiar cap: U.S.S. LOWNDES A.P.A. 154, IWO JIMA - OKINAWA. A reminder of challenging times as he related the events of a long-ago journey to bring an end to hostilities.

His brother Joe was a U.S. Marine. "A miserable bastard when they wouldn't let him fight!" Mr. Rauseo said. "My brother George, he flew.

We were all fighting. There were seven, seven of us kids, Georgie" his eyes began to well up a bit, "Georgie was, well, we, my brothers, we all, we did, we all served." His siblings: Nicholas, Angelo, Joseph, Michael, Mary, and George. Arthur was the youngest. One sister, five brothers. Mother Marian Maringello, father Pasquale, Italian immigrants.

On board the U.S.S. Lowndes, Mr. Rauseo served as an electrician's mate. "I fixed things, and sometimes I shot things. We did whatever we needed to do. They trained. We served." He received medals. He received a Combat Action Ribbon. He lived war.

"Saipan. I was there," he said with a big long, drawn sigh as he pointing to old photographs showing staging areas. "That was just one place. We were preparing, you know, for assaults. Assaults. You know, supplies," he said. "Lowndes' a transport ship. I served on two ships. See. Supplies, soldiers, thousands of them. Okinawa. You know. They shot at us. From the sky, from the sky."

Boxing gloves? "Yeah, in the navy. Those are mine," he offered as I turned them over. "In those days, they would keep you for training, you know, until, until you know, you're supposed to be 17, O.K., so I get into Boston, and I was supposed to be, well, we were in war, they just sent me (to active duty)," he explained.

Medals. Medals in boxes, dusty in a basement. Photographs. Folders. Aerial photos, scrubbings. Treasured memories hidden away. "Yeah, some of this stuff, I guess I should show" he said.

Decades of service on the Georgetown Light Commission, past chairman of the Cable T.V. Advisory Board, past member of the finance committee, a former water commissioner, former real estate broker, construction supervisor, electrician, and having served in many other capacities within the town, Mr. Rauseo is a life member of V.F.W. 7608, and the American Legion.

He helped start little league baseball in town. A former president of the Georgetown Student Athletic Fund, the Georgetown Fire Dept. Inc., and Georgetown Shoe Sales, Inc,. Retired from the Georgetown Savings Bank board of directors this past June, after serving as a bank director since 1991. He was a member of the Massachusetts 100 club, a charity organization that provided thousands to children ... a lifetime of work and volunteerism. His proudest involvement is his 55 years with the Georgetown Fire Department's Central Fire Company.

Everyone who's been in Georgetown for more than a handful of years seems to know Mr. Rauseo. He's seemingly done every position except selectmen. "I wouldn't do it. They put me up to it. I said no. I can't do it. You know what you get. I run a store. I don't want it. I don't want it. So I killed it, and said no. I wouldn't take it. And still, they voted for me. I can't have it with the business. People. You know. It's too much," he explained as why he avoided that one position.

Ah, the smile as he shuffled and lifted the heavy old fireman's coat. A big grin. "This was mine. Chief. When I was chief" he said. "Original. These, they protected you. Heavy like this. You know" he said. Wife Marjorie, son Jim, daughter Sharon. Four grandchildren, all girls: Catherine (16), Alex (15), Megan (14), and Sarah (12).

Pouring through more photographs and old documents, he showed one of small ships around larger ships. "See, we were the small guys, we went in here," he said pointing towards some unidentified shoreline. "I don't want a kid to see a photo like this," he said showing wounded soldiers. "You see we were getting the s*** kicked out of us. How can I show that to a kid? I don't want to." Again, you could see history scanning across his face. A mix of dedication, sorrow, and energy. Good energy. Friends and service. Service to his country, a patriot. A hero.

"This is the hardest thing you had to do," he said relating to a photo of sea burial. We paused.

Mr. Rauseo returned from the war and did what many others have done. Raised his children. He seldom spoke of the war even when prodded his daughter Sharon said. "He didn't, most of them. That generation, they didn't want to talk about it too much. Look, he has so much. I tell him, people should see this," she said. A loving daughter. "Dad, this really should be someplace," she said holding another memento. "Ten years ago, they wouldn't talk" she said about the war heroes. "I saw a documentary they're doing. Now, they're starting to talk. They're at that point. They know they have to. I never heard some things when I grew up. Now, I see these, and he tells more now."

Turning over another package of photos, Mr. Rauseo exclaimed "everything but the kitchen sink," his ship delivered to the front. "That's going in. I kept these in pretty damn good shape," he said" showing yet another set of photos.

The Valley Patriot is proud of the heroes in our midst. And we are especially proud of those who served in war, and then continued to serve in our communities, adding to the fabric of our lives, helping in whatever way they could to help others. Engaged in the community, serving, helping. Working with others. "Enjoying life," he said. As the long-time proprietor of Georgetown Clothing, his shop, now manned by his son Jim, serves yet another generation. Long gone is his cobbler's shop. And long-ago memories from Sharon's sewing lessons at dad's store. "I used to take a shoe box cover and run that in the sewing machine. That's one of my earliest memories," she related.

Mornings at Theo's coffee shop. 'Arthur' gets called out by many, raising their voices so he can hear them, deaf in one ear now. Talking of the day's events, he shuffles a paper. Just another day in a small town. Sitting alongside a hero. A hero in our midst.

By: Ted Tripp - June, 2007

Joe Edward Smith
Korea

By: Ted Tripp – June, 2007

NORTH ANDOVER, MA - The year was 1962. At the height of the Cold War, a young Pfc. Joe Ed Smith of the U.S. Army 7th Cavalry was assigned to guard duty along the demilitarized zone (DMZ) separating North Korea from South Korea.

The DMZ was a no man's land of observation posts, fences, barbed wire and thousands of land mines dividing the Korean peninsula. It was created as a direct result of the truce signed after the 1950-53 Korean War. On one dark night, Joe's unit got word to look out for a high-level North Korean defector who would be attempting to cross the DMZ into the south.

Intelligence services in those days provided defectors with safe routes through the minefields and booby traps. Joe's observation post was also warned to watch for any North Korean soldiers following or chasing the defector. One of Joe's more enterprising squad members decided to go out and try to help the defector make it across. He found the defector, tackled him, and then managed to hide him in a hole - dug specifically for the purpose - from enemy soldiers tracking him into the DMZ.

At dawn, Joe was relieved to see his buddy return unharmed with the valuable defector in tow.

This was just another small but important victory for our side in the great 20th century struggle between the freedom-loving countries of the West and the communist bloc dictatorships of the East.

After Korea, Joe came back to the states for 50 days before being shipped off to the 11th Armored Cavalry in West Germany. He was stationed at an

Army base near Straubing in Bavaria to patrol the Czech border against incursions by the Soviets.

One of Joe's more interesting stints during this deployment was as a military guard at the Dachau Prison. A portion of this infamous Nazi death camp of World War II was being used as a U.S. Army military prison in the 1960s. After Joe completed his military commitments in November of 1964, he returned to Boston and found employment as a mail carrier. He also kept in touch with fellow veterans through various VFW and American Legion posts over the years, although he didn't officially join any. He just enjoyed the camaraderie.

Then, about five years ago, he met Commander Jim Cassidy and Adjutant Ted Eaton of American Legion Post 219 in North Andover. They convinced him to join the Legion and become an active participant. In just three short years after joining, the membership of Post 219 installed Joe as its new commander.

Besides Joe's involvement with the veterans, he has become well known around North Andover by volunteering his time and talents for both charitable and civic causes.

Perhaps this can best be explained by his background and family history.

Born in 1944, Joe grew up in Everett and Boston as one of fifteen children. His parents, Susan and Noah Smith, instilled in all their children an appreciation for the future. When finishing up high school, they gave their children a choice: either further your education or join the military. Military service was considered an honorable profession as well as a way to develop important skills. One of Joe's brothers, Thomas Alonzo, also joined the Army and ended up serving as a communications specialist during the Vietnam War.

So at the age of 17, Joe volunteered to join the Army and was sent to Fort Dix, New Jersey for basic training. After completing basic, the Army tried to make Joe a clerk, but he would have none of it. He wanted to be in the infantry with all the excitement and outdoors activity that it entailed. He got plenty of what he wanted with 16-hour days in the bitter winter cold and stifling summer heat on the Korean DMZ near Panmunjon.

After Joe finished his military commitment and settled into civilian life, part of his mail route included the Franklin Institute of Boston on Berkeley Street. One day while delivering the mail, he started chatting with Frank

Malazola in front of the school. Unknown to Joe, Malazola was the Dean of Students and he would eventually persuade Joe to use some of his veteran benefits to apply to the Institute.

Joe was accepted and enrolled in the school's evening "Institute Preparatory Course" so that he could continue to work during the day. He was subsequently awarded an Alfred P. Sloan Scholarship, which enabled him to switch to full-time day study. In 1972 he graduated with an Associate's Degree in Civil Engineering.

Then he went on to Lowell Tech – now UMass Lowell – and received his B.Sc. in Civil Engineering in 1976.

Joe's first job out of school was with the Greater Lawrence Sanitary District (GLSD), which had just opened a brand new, state-of-the-art sewage treatment plant. At that time, to be an employee of the GLSD, you had to live in one of the towns served by the district.

And so Joe moved from Lowell to North Andover in 1977 and has lived in town ever since.

After a few years, Joe left the GLSD and went to work for the state where he continues to this day. He is a Principal Civil Engineer for the Division of Capital Asset Management and Maintenance, Office of Planning, Design and Construction, out of Boston. Joe is also a director and steward of the Massachusetts Organization of State Engineers & Scientists Union (MOSES).

Joe has been active in North Andover in many ways. He is a charter member and former director of the North Andover Rotary Club. One of the projects he especially likes is the Wednesday morning before-school class where he, along with other Rotarians and parent volunteers, teach chess to about 40 students at the Franklin School. Chess has been one of Joe's passions since his youth and he loves teaching it to newcomers. Joe also helps the Rotary raise funds to support the N.A.

Athletic Association, High School Scholarships, the Boy Scouts and the Trinitarian Church plays. In addition, Joe is a trustee and treasurer of his Heritage Green Condominium Trust.

Joe is a member of St. Michael Parish where he is an usher, a Eucharistic Minister, belongs to the Men's Prayer Group, sings in the adult choir, and is a member of both the Holy Name Society and the Parish Pastoral Council. While not originally a Catholic, he says he couldn't resist the spirit of Pastor Paul Keyes and was finally baptized into the faith by Father Keyes about seven years ago.

As the Legion Commander, Joe is striving to reinvigorate one of the Legion's major community projects. This involves working with the high school to help nominate deserving and talented students to attend Boys State, Girls State and the Student Trooper Program. Once students are selected, the Legion raises funds to send them to weeklong conferences at a cost of about $300 each. These programs help inspire our youth to leadership positions in both government and law enforcement.

Joe's sense of community service has also extended to local North Andover municipal boards. He has served on the Zoning Board of Appeals and was appointed as the ZBA representative to study town zoning issues on a special Task Force Committee. However, Joe is perhaps best known for his perennial March campaigns for selectman. He has now run for this office seven times and has yet to be victorious.

When asked if he plans to run again, Joe proclaims loudly, "Absolutely. I am going to run again next year."

Joe Smith, thank you for your service to our country.

Chief Master Sgt.
Michael Ingham
U.S. Air Force

By: Ted Tripp - December, 2006

HAVERHILL, MA – Next month Mike Ingham will retire after 33 years of service in the Air Force, both on active duty and in the reserves. His assignments have taken him all over the world: Germany, Italy, Spain, England, Alaska and Central America.

Born in Haverhill in 1953, Mike grew up in the city and attended Haverhill High School. He graduated in 1971 and at the time had no interest in joining the military, particularly since the Vietnam War was still being fought.

His mother urged him to continue his education and signed him up at the Montserrat College of Visual Art in Beverly. She told him that if he didn't pursue educational opportunities, he would end up "driving a truck."

Mike went off to school and studied fine art, photography and sculpture, among other pursuits. But after two years, Mike was looking for something else. So in December of 1973, Mike Ingham went down to see the Air Force recruiter in Haverhill and enlisted.

Mike was sent to Lackland Air Force Base in Texas for what was supposed to be eight weeks of basic training. He had been told that this was the best time of the year to go because there were two weeks during Christmas and New Year's that didn't count. However, he remembers that when he got there he found out that he still had to train during those two weeks that "didn't count" - so he ended up with a total of 10 weeks of basic training.

On New Year's Day, 1974, during training, Mike met Shirley Lawrence from the small town of Alger, Ohio. After a short courtship, the two were married on February 23, 1974.

After basic, Mike was sent to Sheppard Air Force Base, also in Texas, for further training. Shirley was initially assigned to Chanute Air Force Base, Ill. for schooling as a jet mechanic, but was later reassigned to Sheppard Air Base where the two were reunited. After a short courtship, the two were married on February 23, 1974.

Mike had decided he wanted to be a loadmaster, one who loads equipment and supplies onto airplanes. But that particular school was not open at the time, so he ended up at the "heavy equipment" school. Here, Mike learned to operate front-end loaders, bulldozers, cranes, graders, forklifts and large tractor-trailers. He chuckles when he recalls his mother's warning about ending up "driving a truck."

Mike was asked to stay on as an instructor, but he and Shirley decided to accept an assignment to Bitburg Air Base in Germany as part of the 36th Tactical Fighter Wing. Mike was now a heavy equipment operator and spent his time maintaining/constructing roads and buildings at the base. One of his critical jobs was training for the emergency repair of runways.

This was during a period of the Cold War when the threat from an invasion of Soviet and Warsaw Pact forces was always present and the U.S. had to be prepared. If the Soviets ever attacked, the route would be through Germany. Bitburg was a major defensive position and once its fighters took off to oppose the invading force, they would need undamaged runways to land on, refuel and continue combat operations.

Meanwhile, Shirley had been trained to service F4 Phantom jets and in Bitburg became the first female crew chief to maintain F4 fighter planes.

After two years in Germany, Mike and Shirley were transferred to Little Rock Air Force Base, Ark. Mike continued to operate heavy equipment in maintaining the base infrastructure, but occasionally got to load the giant C-5A Galaxy cargo plane.

Near the end of the two years in Little Rock, Mike and Shirley decided it was time to leave the Air Force and return to civilian life. They came back to Haverhill and Mike got a job with J & A Construction, and later with Toreneo Trucking, both in Methuen.

Then, in 1978, Shirley decided she wanted to join the Air Force Reserves. However, shortly afterwards she changed her mind and told Mike she was signing him up instead. The next weekend Mike reported to the 905th Civil Engineering Squadron at Westover Air Force Base in western Massachusetts. Shortly afterwards, the squadron was reorganized to become the 439th Civil Engineering Squadron.

He remembers the first thing he was told when reporting for duty – get a haircut!

This would be the beginning of Mike Ingham's life-long commitment to the Air Force Reserves.

Reservists train one weekend a month and have a two-week deployment once a year. It was during these two-week deployments that Mike got to travel the world.

He remembers well his first assignment, in 1978, to Lakenheath Air Base in England. Mike's main job was to build revetments on the base, but at one point he was given the keys to a tractor-trailer and told to deliver some material. He recalls the harrowing experience of quickly learning how to drive a big rig on the left-hand side of the road without creating an accident!

In 1989, about 50 members of the 439th spent two weeks at the Soto Cano Air Base in Honduras. Mike, who was a master sergeant by now, unfortunately was not allowed off base because there was a lot of unrest at the time. The Contras were still fighting the Sandinistas in Nicaragua and General Manuel Noriega, as the leader of Panama, was suspected of being a drug kingpin. Mike remembers that the base was crawling with Special Forces troops and, while the 439th was at the base, the U.S. actually sent forces into Panama to capture Noriega.

In the early 1990s, after the region had settled down, Mike and the 439th were sent to Howard Air Force Base in Panama to renovate buildings for housing units. Mike vividly remembers his fascinating tour of the Panama Canal and its huge locks and ship-towing trams.

Mike Ingham takes a break while on a two-week deployment

He also recalls his experience in Panama City. There was a great disparity between the rich and the poor and it showed. Mike says there were occasionally dead bodies in the streets with buzzards nearby. He had never seen buzzards in a city before.

In the late 1990s, after Hurricane Mitch devastated Honduras, Mike and his squadron were again sent to that Central American country, this time to rebuild a school destroyed by the storm. In the area where they were to work, over 2000 people had died and thousands more were still missing. Even with all this hardship, the Hondurans were delighted to see the 439th.

The mayor and a large number of locals turned out to help the Air Force squadron build the new school. With everybody pitching in, the school was completed within the two-week period the 439th was on site.

Twice while Mike was with the 439th, the unit was activated. The first time was in 1990 for operations Desert Shield and Desert Storm. The 439th spent seven months at Westover, helping to keep the base running during the massive buildup of troops being sent to defend Saudi Arabia and eventually liberate Kuwait. Westover was a launching point for troops from all across the country on their way over to the Middle East.

The second time the 439th was activated was after the Iraq War in August of 2004. The squadron spent four months at the Al Dhafra Air Base in the United Arab Emirates (UAE). This base was a support hub for our troops fighting the terrorists and insurgents in various parts of Iraq.

The base operated with KC-135 tankers and U-2 spy planes, as well as several of the new Northrop Grumman Global Hawk Unmanned Aerial Vehicles.

Mike worked directly for the base commander, a colonel, on managing construction/maintenance projects as well helping with security for the base and its personnel.

During most of Mike Ingham's association with the 439th, there were about 100 reservists in the squadron. Approximately 10 percent of these were women. In recent years, the 439th has been reorganized by adding other units and now numbers about 150 reservists.

When the 439th was first organized into a squadron, Mike offered his art school training and proudly designed the unit's emblem.

Since Mike has belonged to the squadron, the 439th has received several "outstanding unit" awards and Mike is quick to add that he feels privileged to work with what he calls "the finest group of electricians, carpenters, contractors and maintenance people that you could ever imagine."

The 439th Civil Engineering Squadron is part of what is called the Air Force Expeditionary Force.

The Expeditionary Force coordinates the various Air Force Reserve units from around the country so that when one unit leaves an assignment, another seamlessly takes its place. This provides continuity until the task is completed.

During much of Mike's time in the reserves, he used his specialized training and expertise to Haverhill's benefit.

He has worked at the city's wastewater plant, in the highway department, at the water department, and for the past 11 years he has been Director of Veterans' Services.

Mike and Shirley have two children: Michael Robert Ingham and Joseph Aldan Ingham; and two grandchildren.

Michael Robert followed in his parent's footsteps and spent five years in the Air Force as a helicopter mechanic, servicing the H-60 Black Hawk transport helicopters used by the Special Forces. Joseph is currently a police officer in Haverhill.

Michael Ingham, we thank you for your 33 years of service to our country. Shirley and Michael Robert, we also thank you for your years of Air Force service.

Corporal Frank Sanzi, Paratrooper, Korean War

By: Ted Tripp - November, 2006

NORTH AND - OVER, MA - On June 25, 1950 the North Korean Army, bolstered by Soviet tanks and aircraft, invaded South Korea.

Immediately, President Harry Truman ordered General Douglas MacArthur to transfer ammunition and supplies from Japan to the ROK (Republic of Korea) Army and provide limited air support. On June 27th, Truman authorized the use of U.S. land, sea and air forces in South Korea. The newly formed United Nations also condemned this "act of aggression" and a week later placed the forces of 15 member nations under U.S. command to oppose the North Korean Army. President Truman appointed MacArthur as the Supreme Commander.

The U.S. 8th Army, stationed in Beppu, Japan, was rushed to South Korea to stem the invasion and assist ROK forces retreating to the southern tip of the peninsula. One member of the 8th Army's 24th Division, 19th Infantry, was Frank Sanzi's brother, Sergeant First Class Robert D. Sanzi. Sergeant Sanzi was a World War II infantryman who had decided to stay in the Army at the conclusion of the war. Now he was being sent into battle in a new war.

Shortly after Robert was sent to Korea, the Sanzi family received a telegram from the Army dated July 17, 1950 stating that their son was "missing in action" somewhere on the South Korean peninsula. The news devastated the Sanzis, but one member of the family decided to take action and do something about it. Frank Sanzi, Robert's close brother, immediately told his father that he was going to join the service, get sent to Korea and look for his brother. The following day Frank went down to the Marine recruiter to sign up, but the Marines would not guarantee that Frank would be sent to paratrooper school, a requirement that Frank had strongly stipulated. But the Army was more than accommodating and promised Frank paratrooper training. And that's where he signed his enlistment papers.

Within three days of the telegram's arrival, Frank Sanzi had been sworn in and was on his way to Ft. Dix, N.J. for twelve weeks of basic training. From here he was sent to jump school at Ft. Benning, Ga. to train as a paratrooper. After three weeks of grueling physical instruction and jumping out of airplanes, Frank received his parachutist wings and was sent to Ft. Campbell, Ky. for further training as a member of C Company, 1st Battalion, 187th Airborne Regimental Combat Team (ARCT) of the 11th Airborne Division.

It was here at Ft. Campbell, in the late fall of 1950 that Frank volunteered to go to Korea. Two days later, while Frank was undergoing airborne training, a staff car pulled up and out stepped General James Gavin. The general approached Frank and explained to him that there was no further news about his brother. He then told Frank that he didn't have to go to Korea because of his brother's status as MIA. Frank simply told the general, "I want to find my brother."

Two weeks later Frank Sanzi received orders to Korea with the 187th ARCT. After a brief leave to go home, Frank was sent to Ft. Lewis, Wash. and then was put on a plane to Honshu, Japan. This was the first time the military had used airplanes instead of transport ships to get its troops to a battlefield thousands of miles away. Frank remembers that the trip over was "first class."

In late November of 1950, before Frank arrived in Korea, the Chinese had joined the North Koreans to counterattack General MacArthur's brilliant amphibious landing at Inchon. The Chinese knew that the North Koreans would be quickly defeated without their help. The rejuvenated enemy forces began to push MacArthur's forces back towards the 38th Parallel.

The paratroopers of the 187th ARCT had already made one combat jump on October 20, 1950 at Sukchan–Sunchon, about 20 miles northwest of Seoul. Frank Sanzi had arrived too late to participate in that jump, but was prepared for the next one.

That came on Good Friday, March 23, 1951 into an area known as Munsan-Ni near the 38th Parallel. This was to be part of "Operation Tomahawk."

The 4000 troops of the 187th were crowded into C46, C47 and the C119 "Flying Boxcar" transports for the jump.

All went well until after the landing when Frank's unit was ordered to take one of the nearby villages. At that point, Frank says, "All Hell broke loose!" Enemy soldiers poured into the area, backed up by mortars. The fighting was heavy with hand-to-hand combat as the G.I.s fought their way up a hillside. Frank Sanzi was right in the thick of the battle. As he moved forward, a North Korean or Chinese soldier caught Frank off guard and bayoneted him in the inner thigh. Frank recalls that the enemy had much longer bayonets on their rifles than did the Americans.

The enemy soldier took a step backwards and proceeded to finish Frank off with his bayonet. Wounded, Frank couldn't get to his .45 side arm, but he was able - just barely - to raise his M-2 "sniper rifle" and fired off a burst that stopped the enemy soldier dead in his tracks.

Sometime later, after medics had initially treated Frank's wounds – he also had picked up some shrapnel during the fighting – Frank was rushed by helicopter to an Army MASH unit behind the lines for emergency surgery to stabilize his injuries. From there he was transferred to a hospital in Sasebo, Japan for further care and recovery. He would eventually spend two months in the hospital, much of it to recover from some gangrene which had set in after the first operation.

At this point in his life, Frank was only 19 years old. But he was a battle-hardened soldier. So he was sent back to the 187th to fight once again.

Several months later in September of 1952, with only one night's notice, Frank Sanzi was asked to jump again into a combat situation. The target drop was Taegu.

Frank landed without incident and was proceeding along with the rest of the troops to the unit's objective when Frank's bayonet wound started to bleed. It had not healed completely as the doctors had thought. At this point, Frank's commanding officer removed him from combat and sent him back for further medical treatment. Shortly afterwards, Frank was "permanently disqualified" from any further military jumps.

Because of the wound, Frank's C.O. told him he could go back to the states and be discharged. But Frank wasn't done looking for his brother yet. When the C.O. told him that he needed a truck driver to take ammo and supplies to the troops at the front, Frank quickly volunteered. Based out of Uijongbu, Frank started driving ammo and supply trucks up and around winding mountain roads seven days a week to bring the needed goods to American troops.

Frank would continue driving supply trucks until shortly before the end of the war when, in June of 1953, he was finally sent home. This time Frank traveled back to Seattle by slow troop transport, the USS Marine Adder (AP-193). Frank chuckles when he notes that the military was quick to send him over to Korea by airplane when it needed him most, but was just as quick to put him onto a slow boat back home when it no longer needed him.

The first thing that Frank did after getting home was go to the North End for spaghetti and meatballs. He sorely missed that old-fashioned Italian cooking.

Frank had spent two years in Korea and was no closer to finding out what happened to his brother than when he had left. That is, until he got home. When he arrived back home after the war, his father told him for the first time that his brother's body had been located by the Army approximately a year after he was listed as missing in action. Robert's body was subsequently sent back to Boston and he was buried in Forest Hills Cemetery in Jamaica Plain. During the entire time Frank was in Korea, his parents had never told him that his brother had been found. His father explained to Frank that with all the stress he was under in Korea, the family didn't want to burden him with the news that his brother had been located. Frank still regrets to this day that he was not at his brother's funeral.

Sergeant First Class Robert D. Sanzi would eventually have a VFW post in the South End named in his honor and to this day Castle Square in Boston is also sometimes referred to as Sanzi Square.

Frank settled back into civilian life after the war and went to work for his father in the furniture antiquing business, eventually starting his own similar business. That lasted until 1967 when Frank decided he wanted a little more excitement in his life and joined the Merchant Marine. After only three weeks of training, Frank was certified as a mariner on Group 4 fuel ships. As one who is now used to danger, it is not surprising that his first assignment was on a gasoline tanker delivering fuel to Vung Tau, Vietnam during the Vietnam War. Shortly after that harrowing trip, he switched to tugboats out of East Boston. He worked on the tugboats for 13 years until he retired in 1991.

In the early 1960s, Frank was introduced to Suzie Bouchard by a family member in Charlestown. Frank asked her for a date the following night, but on his way over to her place his car broke down and he never made it. He called her the next day and fortunately she forgave him and they rescheduled the date. On November 11, 1961, Frank and Suzie were married at St. Catherine of Siena church in Charlestown. This Veterans Day will mark their 45th wedding anniversary.

The Sanzis have three grown children: Dianne, Daniel and Francesca; and five grandchildren. Daniel would eventually follow close in his father's footsteps. He became a Marine and as part of the 2nd Marine Division fought in Operation Desert Storm in Iraq in 1991. He is currently a firefighter in Lawrence, after having worked previously as a firefighter in North Andover.

Frank is a lifetime member of the Disabled American Veterans. Frank was awarded the Purple Heart and other campaign medals from the Korean War. However, he never accepted or received them, explaining that the Purple Heart reminded him too much of his brother's tragic death on the battlefield.

Corporal Frank Sanzi, we thank you for your service to our country.

Final note: Frank would like to dedicate this column to "All the boys who are overseas in Iraq." He adds, "I think about them often."

Joe Messina
Aviation Radioman 3rd Class

By: Ted Tripp - July, 2006

METHUEN, MA - Joe Messina was taking a shower below decks on the aircraft carrier USS Hancock after his Curtis SB2C Hell-diver returned from another grueling mission attacking Japanese shipping in Manila Bay.

Shortly after the ship's General Quarters sounded, there was a tremendous explosion just over his head and men were yelling "fire." The engine and remnants of a Kamikaze had just hit the flight deck after being struck by one of the carrier's 5-inch anti-aircraft shells.

Joe got out of the shower in a hurry and went up to see what was going on.

There were Japanese planes everywhere attacking the U.S. Fleet. About a half-mile behind the Hancock and off to the right was the carrier USS Intrepid. A Zero, damaged by guns from the Hancock, veered towards the Intrepid and Joe watched as it hit the ship near the side elevator with a big explosion. Seconds later another plane dove into her followed by more explosions. The Intrepid burned for hours and started to list, but eventually recovered from the attack.

While all this was going on, Joe Messina's parents back in Lawrence thought he was stationed in Pearl Harbor, far from the dangers of battle in the China Sea. Joe could not tell them where he actually was and what he was doing, so it was easy to write home that he was enjoying himself in Hawaii.

It was November of 1944 and Joe Messina was fighting the war as a radioman and gunner in a Navy Helldiver somewhere in the Pacific. He was part of Flight 1, a squadron of 12 planes assigned to Air Group 7 in Carrier Task Group 38.1, which consisted of four carriers, two battleships, and various cruisers and destroyers. He would go on to complete 12 missions, earning the Distinguished Flying Cross and two Air Medals before it was all over.

Joe was born in Lawrence in 1923 and attended the Leonard and Oliver schools, graduating from Lawrence High in June of 1941. On December 7th that year, Joe was watching a movie at the Victoria Theater when an announcement was made that the Japanese had just bombed Pearl Harbor. He ran home to tell his parents that the country was at war. At this time, Joe was working as a welder at Bethlehem Steel's Quincy Shipyard and was subsequently declared exempt from the draft. Even so, in 1942 Joe tried to enlist in the Navy Seabees but was turned away because of the critical nature of his job.

In March of 1943 the Army decided it needed Joe regardless of his job and tried to draft him. While in high school, Joe had spent a year in the Citizens' Military Training Camps – a predecessor to ROTC - and the Army wanted men with experience. He reported to the Boston Army Base and promptly told the recruiter: "I'm not going in the Army. Put me in the Navy or put me in jail." Joe had learned through a friend that the food in the Navy was much better than in the Army and he was determined to eat well while serving his country. Fortunately, the Army recruiter relented and handed Joe over to a Navy officer who signed him up.

Joe was then sent to the Newport, R.I. Naval Training Station for four months of boot camp. Upon finishing, he signed up for the "Cooks and Bakers School" — still thinking about his stomach — but the Navy sent him instead to Radio School at the Naval Air Station in Jacksonville, Fla. This was followed up with Radar School training, and then in December Joe was sent to Naval Air Gunnery School in nearby Yellowater, Fla. Here Joe learned how to operate .30-caliber machine guns in the Douglas SBD

Dauntless dive-bomber. He finished the three months of training with 62 hours of flight time and an appreciation for naval aircraft.

In January of 1943 Joe Messina was sent to the Naval Air Station in Wildwood, N.J. to await orders. At this time the Navy was forming Air Group 7 with the new Curtis SB2C Helldiver, a far superior plane to the Dauntless. In April he was assigned to Air Group 7 and was sent to Quonset Point, R.I. for further training. This is where Joe met his pilot, Lt. Dan Kalus, whom he would fly with on all future missions.

The new air group practiced formation flying, navigation, gunnery and dive-bombing while waiting for deployment. That came several months later when the aircraft carrier USS Hancock was launched from the Quincy Shipyard. Incredibly, Joe had worked on the Hancock as a shipyard welder before he entered the Navy. While serving on the ship, he could proudly point out sections he had helped to build.

The Hancock was an 888-ft long, 27,000-ton fast carrier with 36 bombers, 36 fighters and 18 torpedo planes. It had a top speed of 33 knots and a complement of 3000 to 4000 crew and officers.

By August of 1944, the Hancock, with Joe Messina aboard, had completed a shakedown cruise and was headed to the Pacific war zone via the Panama Canal, San Diego and Pearl Harbor. The Hancock would

eventually become part of Rear Admiral Bogan's Carrier Task Group containing the carriers USS Wasp, USS Hornet and USS Intrepid.

On October 10, 1944, Joe saw his first action. He was part of a formation of six Helldivers which attacked three Japanese cargo ships.

They sank one and set the remaining two on fire. After Joe returned to the ship, he checked out a .50-caliber bullet hole in the plane less than three feet from where he was sitting. The war was now personal.

The next day the Hancock headed for the island of Formosa. On October 12th, the Helldivers took off to attack a chemical factory at Karenko, which was unknowingly defended by hidden 20 mm and 40 mm anti-aircraft guns. At 500 feet, Joe's plane dropped its bombs when all of a sudden the left wing "blew up in our face." A 40 mm shell had ripped a three-foot by three-foot hole in the wing, tearing away the altimeter, radio and flaps.

The crippled plane shuddered and immediately turned back towards the Hancock. Reaching the ship, the landing signal officer noted the plane's predicament and called for the fire fighters and crash crews to be alert. The Helldiver came in fast and caught the third wire. As soon as the plane stopped, Joe was out quickly and moved to help Pilot Kalus get away from the plane. Fear of fire was always a great motivator.

On October 25th, the U.S. Fleet located a large Japanese task force of 3-5 battleships, 4-6 cruisers, and at least 10 destroyers. Fifty-five fighters, fifty-five bombers and seventeen torpedo planes took off from the Wasp, Hornet and Hancock to attack the ships. At 1310 hours Joe's flight sighted the enemy.

From 12000 feet Joe's Helldiver started its decent through withering anti-aircraft fire towards a heavy cruiser. At 5000 feet, with the dive flaps closed, the plane hurtled downwards and was doing close to 400 miles/hr. when it finally released its bomb. This was followed by a huge explosion on the fantail of the ship. Joe's Helldiver had scored a direct hit. A moment later, Joe was able to get a spectacular picture of the damaged cruiser.

It was this mission which earned Joe the Distinguished Flying Cross. But the battle was costly for U.S. Forces. Out of Joe's original squadron of 12 planes, only three made it back to the Hancock that afternoon. Some went down in the attack, some had to ditch in the sea because they were out of fuel, and some ended up landing on other carriers. The next day, fortunately, four planes that had landed elsewhere made it back to the Hancock.

Joe Messina went on to complete 12 missions in the Helldiver. Then, on November 30, 1944 the Navy decided that half of the squadron of dive-bombers would be sent home and the pilots would be retrained to fly fighters. Kamikazes were becoming such a menace that the Navy needed more fighter pilots to confront the threat. This meant that Joe's combat flying days were probably over.

He was sent back to the states where he tried to hook up with some Navy B-24s and later on with another dive-bomber squadron. But by then the war was winding down, and Joe was finally discharged in September of 1945. He returned to Lawrence where he took up the floor covering and carpet trade. For many years he had his own business, the J.M. Carpet Service.

Several years after the war Joe was introduced to Marilyn Gallant at a dance held at St. Mary's in Lawrence. They were married in 1950 and the two recently celebrated their 56th wedding anniversary. Joe and Marilyn have three children, Jay, Richard and Marie, seven grandchildren and one great granddaughter.

Joe Messina, we proudly thank you for your service to our country.

Final Note: Joe would like us to know that throughout his Navy career the food was always great.

He had made the right choice.

Christian Farnham
Daniel Leary
Philip Brooks

By: Tom Duggan, Jr. - June 2006

NORTH ANDOVER, MA - From the 2006 Memorial Day Services in North Andover.

*Specialist Christian Farnham

Spc. Christian Farnham began his military career in 1992 when he decided to follow the family tradition of enlisting in the Marines. His father and brother both served in the Marine Corps. Farnham said it was very important to him that he follow in their footsteps and serve his country.

As a resident of Methuen, Farnham went to the United States Marine Corps Recruiting Station in Lawrence, signed up for the Marines, and was immediately shipped off to Parris Island, South Carolina for basic training. He was 20 years old at the time.

Following the completion of Marine recruit training, Farnham was given orders to report to Camp Edwards on Cape Cod. He was stationed there from 1992-1994 and eventually received an honorable discharge in 1994. However, he didn't feel that he had completed his work with the military or his service to the United States.

So, in 2001, while living in Allenstown, New Hampshire, Farnham enlisted in the U.S. Army National Guard. He became part of the 744th Transportation Company out of Hillsboro, N.H., which also contained units from Claremont and Somersworth. The three units had between 90 and 120 Guard troops.

The 744th was activated in December of 2003 and Farnham was deployed to Iraq to assist our nation's mission of fighting terrorists in the Middle East, and to prevent them from taking over a free, democratic Iraq.

Stationed at Camp Anaconda, about 35 miles north of Baghdad, Farnham's mission was to operate a gun -truck vehicle for fire support through convoy escorts.

Farnham's convoy route went from Kuwait to Camp Anaconda. His unit also provided security details guarding Iraqi workers.

Farnham says that life was very difficult in the Middle East, and that they were being mortared all the time. They were also hit with RPG's (rocket propelled grenades) and small arms fire on a regular basis. His first week in Iraq, Farnham says, the 744th lost one of their men when a convoy was hit by an IED (improvised explosive devise) and a truck flipped over.

Farnham says his most memorable moment was when he was in the lead truck in a convoy of fire support vehicles. When the convoy reached Baghdad, he looked back and realized that the rest of his convoy had taken a wrong turn and was no longer be-hind him, leaving him alone and vulnerable to attack.

When he finally found the convoy heading down a different road, Farnham says he was able to backtrack and meet up with them once again. "I was very nervous," he recalled.

Farnham served in Iraq until May of 2004 when he sustained severe hip injuries and was medivaced to Walter Reed Hospital. He underwent two hip operations that left him unable to continue his duties on the battlefield. Farnham received an honorable discharge in March of 2006.

Farnham now lives in North Andover with his wife and two small children. He says that the Iraqis seemed to appreciate the work of the U.S. solders and he was proud to serve his country.

Captain Daniel Leary

Captain Daniel Leary is a lifelong North Andover resident who was deployed to Kuwait as part of Operation Iraqi Freedom.

Leary began his military career when he joined the ROTC program while he was a student at Cornell University. He was commissioned in 1999 at the age of 22 and had been on active duty until February of 2006.

Leary's first assignment was in South Korea. He was stationed in the Demilitarized Zone (DMZ), where he was the Platoon leader of the 2nd Infantry Division of the Medical Service Corp.

He was stationed there from December of 1999 through May of 2001.

Leary was then transferred to Walter Reed Medical Center in Washington, D.C., where he received training in Health Facility planning. He was there from May of 2001 to October of 2002.

Leary subsequently became the Company Commander of the U.S. Army Medical Research Institute of Infectious Diseases (USAMRIID) in Fort Detrick, Md.

He was in charge of all troops and the administrative command. The job came with a great deal of responsibility, preparing troops for deployment to Iraq.

Leary was Commander of the Institute until February of 2002, when he was deployed to Kuwait for Operation Iraqi Freedom.

He was stationed there until December of 2005, and eventually left active duty in February 2006.

While in Kuwait, Leary was responsible for building medical clinics to support the coalition forces.

He designed and provided construction management for the clinics and managed contracts with foreign nationals who performed the actual construction. While there, Leary oversaw the building of 6-8 clinics.

Leary now lives with his wife in North Andover.

*Specialist Philip Brooks

Spc. Philip Brooks also served in Iraq. Brooks enlisted in the U.S. Army National Guard in Danvers in 2005. His unit was deployed to Iraq in August of 2005, where he served until December of that year. Brooks served in the 1/102nd Field Artillery just south of Baghdad. This was a 150 member unit.

He was assigned to a security force at a prisoner detainment facility. Brooks could not say where the detainment facility was located. He also said he did not see much combat on his assignment, but knew that at any time he could be thrust into battle and had to be ready at a moment's notice.

During training for the assignment, Brooks injured his right hand but refused to quit and went on to Iraq to serve his country despite the injury. He has since had surgery to repair his hand.

Brooks says that he's glad he went to Iraq and that the Iraqi people, despite American media reports to the contrary, were grateful for the U.S. military presence and protection. Brooks said he supports the mission to secure Iraq from terrorists and so-called insurgents, adding that he saw many acts of kindness by American troops. He cited one example of U.S. military troops giving toys to the Iraqi children. "They were so happy. The expressions on their faces really said it all," Brooks related.

Brooks is 26 years old and now lives in North Andover with his fiancée.

The Valley Patriot is proud to honor these Heroes In Our Midst for their service to our country and their dedication to combating terrorism in Iraq.

Captain Leary, Spc. Brooks and Spc. Farnham have shown by example the critical work that is needed to keep the United States safe by fighting the war on terrorism abroad.

Thank you, Captain Leary, Spc. Brooks and Spc. Farnham for putting your lives on the line to protect the American people. Americans appreciate the sacrifices you have made.

Chief Petty Officer Ed Mitchell

By: Ted Tripp - May, 2006

NORTH ANDOVER, MA - An electrical short circuit had forced early termination of the dive of the Navy's Deep Submergence Research Vehicle, Turtle. As the Turtle returned to its support ship and was loaded on board, the electrical problem turned into a raging fire that threatened the sub, the support ship and the entire crew.

The fire was dangerously close to several tanks of flammable ballast liquid and was also approaching the sub's batteries where hydrogen was present. If the fire reached either of these areas, the resulting explosion would have sunk both vessels and killed all aboard.

The crew quickly determined that the only way to fight the fire was to get the Turtle back into the water. As young Petty Officer 3rd class Ed Mitchell fought the fire with a 4" fire hose, his crewmates sealed the Turtle's hatch, unfastened the tie-downs and released the research sub off the stern of the boat into the water. The sea quickly put out the fire to the relief of all. Although the Turtle was almost completely destroyed, there were thankfully no injuries during the harrowing ordeal.

The life of a submariner is filled with challenges and dangers as these Navy elites patrol the oceans of the world keeping the U.S. safe from its enemies.

Ed Mitchell, Veterans Agent for North Andover and Boxford, spent 18 years on various submarines, much of it during the cold war with the Soviet Union.

Ed grew up in Franklin, Mass. and graduated from Tri-County Vocational School in 1980. Ed had no real plans for the future and when a buddy of his called and said, "I'm picking up a case of beer and then think I'll go down and join the Navy. Want to come?" Ed said, "Sure," and that was the start of his long career.

The Navy recruiter was a submariner and talked the two of them into applying for submarine school. The extra $135/month in pay also seemed attractive to two young single guys. After eight weeks of boot camp at the Great Lakes Naval Training Center in Illinois, the pair were sent to the U.S. Naval Submarine School in Groton, Conn. Here they were taught the fundamentals of submarines, the basic operational systems, safety and survival in emergencies. Part of the training included a visit aboard an actual submarine and, after that, Ed's buddy decided he wasn't cut out for the close quarters of submarine service. Ed was now on his own.

Ed Mitchell's first orders were to report to the nuclear-powered USS Will Rogers, a fleet ballistic missile submarine carrying 16 nuclear-tipped Poseidon missiles. These subs are nicknamed "Boomers" and patrol the seas to deter an enemy's nuclear attack on U.S. soil. Their main objective is to patrol undetected from other navies.

The Will Rogers had two crews of about 120 men each. There was a Blue crew and a Gold crew, and they alternated operating the submarine at about 3-month intervals. Ed was part of the Blue crew. This schedule gives crew 3-months of shore duty between deployments, so that they can live a somewhat normal life. While on patrol, the sub would typically spend at least two months at sea somewhere in the North Atlantic. Ed went on four patrols with the Will Rogers and recalls that at one point they were submerged for 72 days.

Ed started off on the sub as a Seaman Apprentice and, as was typical, was assigned to galley duty. Here he worked 14 hours a day preparing food and keeping the area clean. Next to fire, one of the worst fears on board a sub is a sickness which could disable an entire crew. Cleanliness was paramount to safety.

Here Ed learned that one of the most important components on a sub was the ice cream machine. No sub would leave port without a fully functioning ice cream machine. "It's critical for crew morale," he says. Although the machine only produced vanilla, Ed decided to see what would happen if he added coffee to the ingredients. His coffee ice cream was a big hit and he went on to try blueberry pie filling, orange and chocolate to the crew's delight.

During Ed's assignment on the Will Rogers, his first priority was to get his "Dolphins." This is a pin similar to the wings that aviators earn, but is reserved for the submarine service. It takes a year of hard work and a lot of studying to have the Dolphins pinned on your uniform.

Besides the galley work, Ed's primary battle station was as the Missile Compensator. This required him to shift ballast around the sub to keep it level while missiles were being launched and seawater filling the now empty tubes. A stable and level firing platform is critical to the safe operation of a submarine in missile launch mode.

After two years on the Will Rogers, Ed was sent to San Diego and assigned to the Turtle. This experimental deep dive submarine was part of the Navy's Submarine Rescue Unit and had a crew of 13 specialists that operated and supported the vessel. Its major function was to search, locate and recover disabled submarine sections.at great depth. Ed and the crew practiced constantly and also worked closely with scientists exploring the ocean's seafloor. Ed is proud to report that his deepest dive was 9,994 feet. It's safe to say that not many people in the world have been that far below the surface of the ocean.

After five years with the Turtle program, Ed was assigned to shore duty at the Naval Ocean Systems Center in San Diego where he was responsible for six torpedo recovery boats involved in torpedo research and development. Although Ed had been promoted several times during his career, it was here that Ed decided he wanted to become a Chief Petty

Officer. As he explained, there is an old saying, "The Chiefs run the Navy." The modern version is, "The Chiefs make the Navy run."

So Ed cut his shore duty short and in 1990 he returned to the East Coast where he was assigned to the USS George C. Mar-shall, another Boomer. After two primary deterrent patrols, the submarine was ordered decommissioned as a result of military cutbacks after the end of the cold war. The sub was sent to Washington State to be cut up and scrapped. Ed still has the original nuclear missile launch trigger from the Marshall as a souvenir from its active days.

It was during Ed's duty on the George C. Marshall that he was reacquainted with and married North Andover native, Diana Koebrick. As children, Diana and Ed had spent summer vacations at their grandparents' cottages on Little Island Pond in Pelham, N.H. They currently have two daughters, Lauren, age 13, and Colleen, age 8, who also enjoy their summer vacations at Little Island Pond.

Although now married, Ed's active submarine career was not over. He was subsequently assigned to the nuclear-powered USS Groton, a fast attack submarine carrying high-tech torpedoes and Tomahawk cruise missiles. The Groton's primary function was to shadow Russian subs while undetected. Ed remembers great ports of call all over the Mediterranean, but one incident in Turkey he will never forget.

The Groton was tied up at the dock when a sudden and violent storm erupted. The waves were crashing over the hull and water was washing into the forward hatch. Most of the crew was out on liberty, but Ed and the others on board knew they had to immediately take the ship into deeper water to keep it from being damaged. With only a third of the crew, they quickly backed away from the pier without even removing the mooring lines. They now had ropes dangling in the water, a skeleton crew and an air purifying system that was down for repairs. Until the storm passed, the Groton spent the night circling in the harbor, in reverse to prevent the ropes from entanglement in the propeller, and on the surface for fresh air. It was not pleasant.

After six months on board the Groton, Ed was promoted to Chief Petty Officer. A year and a half later, Ed was once again transferred to shore duty. This time he became an instructor and curriculum developer at the Navy's Submarine School in Groton.

It was here that he had his back operated on because of an old injury he had received on the Turtle. He had two discs removed and a spinal fusion. Several years later, when it was time for Ed to go back on board a submarine, the medical doctors told him his sailing days were over. It was now 1998 and Ed had 18 years of service in the Navy. He could have stayed in for his 20 years with shore duty, but Ed felt that it was time to give some other deserving Navy officers an opportunity and decided on early retirement.

After leaving the service, Ed had to have another back operation. Finally, after a long recovery, Ed was feeling better and felt he could return to work. In 2000 he became the Veterans Agent for North Andover and Boxford. Chief Petty Officer Ed Mitchell, thank you for your service and the many years of sacrifices you made to keep our country out of harm's way.

Bill Callahan
WWII

By: Tom Duggan, Jr. - January, 2006

NORTH ANDOVER, MA - Lawrence native Bill Callahan served his country in two wars, World War II and the Korean War. After completing his military service, he has also spent decades volunteering in the community and working to help others.

When Bill Callahan graduated from Lawrence High School in 1945, the 17-year-old knew that he needed to learn a trade to get a job.

America was in the heat of World War II and, coming from a military family (his dad was a Navy man), Bill decided to enlist in the Navy and learn electronics. His father even took him to the recruiter to sign him up.

Bill quite vividly remembers his first day of boot camp. He went by train from Boston to a Navy facility at Sampson, New York. "It was April 12, 1945, the day President Roosevelt died," Callahan recalled.

"We threw together our uniforms and stood in the rain in commemoration of Roosevelt's dying day," Callahan added.

While at boot camp, Callahan says he always had trouble learning how to march. "I have short legs and could never keep in step," he recalls. Every time the drill instructor caught him out-of-step, he had to "watch a 'foolish' clothesline" from midnight to 4 a.m. the following night. This, unfortunately, happened more often than Callahan would have liked.

Boot camp lasted 10 weeks and Bill was then assigned to a small aircraft carrier, the USS Puget Sound. The ship carried 800 men and 30 planes. The Puget Sound was stationed in the South Pacific during the war.

Bill Callahan enlisted as a seaman, which involved scraping paint, followed by painting, and a few days later scraping off the paint again. He also swabbed the deck. Later, he was fortunate enough to become the chaplain's yeoman aboard ship.

"We had one priest and he was the chaplain for all of the services. I was the one assigned to assist him," says Callahan.

Bill served in World War II until the war ended. After returning to the states, he says he wanted to learn more about electronics and decided to sign up for a U.S. Naval Reserve program.

Bill remembers that there was a reserve center near the Lawrence Veterans Memorial Stadium. Bill signed on and eventually achieved a rating for electronic technician third class.

When the Korean War broke out, Bill learned that the United States Navy needed electronic technicians, and again Bill answered the call to serve and went off to war.

This time, Bill Callahan was assigned to the USS Block Island II, an escort carrier stationed off the coast of Korea providing the technical assistance that the Navy needed. While in Philadelphia waiting for the refurbishing of the Block Island II for the war, Bill and his wife had their only daughter, Betty. "It was hard, of course, having the baby at home for two years while I was at sea," he said. Bill says that the Navy was very good to him and his family, providing diapers and other items for Betty while he was at sea.

Bill Callahan's daughter Betty now works at the North Andover Senior Center where he is able to see her several times a week.

Bill says that one of his most memorable moments was outside the U.S. Navy Hospital where Betty was born. "They were filming the movie 'The Greatest Show on Earth' and I got to meet the great Jimmy Stewart."

While at sea, Bill's shipmates had a contest to select the "Most Typical American Girl." The winner was a young lady from Pennsylvania. When the Block Island II arrived in San Diego after the war, they paid for her transportation and flight to San Diego. Unfortunately, when she came off the plane, all of the men were disappointed because she was pregnant.

However, there was a big USO event at the time featuring the Andrew Sisters and Bill was called on stage to sing with them.

Bill served two years in the Korean War until it ended.

For his service in both wars, Bill Callahan received the World War II Victory Medal and the Pacific Theater Medal, and the Korean Medal for the Korean War.

After completing his service, Bill worked for 22 years at Honeywell in the Woodmill Building in Lawrence. Bill lived in Lawrence until five year ago, when he moved to North Andover.

After serving his country in two wars, Bill Callahan's interest in public service continued. Bill was instrumental in helping the Bread & Roses festival establish itself in Lawrence and he has always been eager to volunteer in the community.

Bill is currently a member of the American Legion Post 219, is an active volunteer with the North Andover Senior Center and helps out at the Sutton Hill Nursing Home, working with veterans and running the men's club.

He still volunteers at Bread & Roses. He also sings in a group called Vocal Airs, in North Andover.

A while back he was fortunate enough to represent the United States with the Garrett players in Finland.

The Valley Patriot would like to thank Bill Callahan for his military service to our country and all of his many years of public service to the community. We are proud to honor Bill Callahan as our Patriot of the Month..

John Doherty

By: Dr. Charles Ormsby - December, 2005

ANDOVER, MA – John Doherty had a lot of family history to uphold. His family had lived in Andover for over 150 years and the Doherty Elementary School is named after his uncle, Bill Doherty, after he served 39 years on the Andover School Committee. John's service to his town and country, which is still continuing, has upheld these traditions in a way that would make any family proud.

John has lived in Andover for all of his 64 years. All, that is, except for a couple of years in Southeast Asia in the late 1960s ... but more on that in a moment. He attended elementary and Junior High in the Andover public schools and then transferred to Phillips Academy. After graduating from Phillips, John attended Harvard where he studied Latin and Greek, and joined the ROTC. He would normally have begun his two-year service commitment immediately after he graduated cum laude in 1963, but the Army granted him a one-year extension to attend the University of

Pittsburgh. In 1964, after completing the requirements for his master's degree, John began active duty as an Army second lieutenant.

Upon commissioning, John headed straight for nine weeks of infantry training at Ft. Benning, Ga. Although the Vietnam War was in its early stages, the infantry-training program was still focused on thermonuclear or limited war scenarios with the Soviet Union. Halfway through training, the focus shifted to jungle warfare. Nobody had to ask why. John remembers this training to prepare young officers to be platoon leaders as being very intense, seven days and nights per week, and very hands-on. John loved it!

U.S. Army Intelligence School at Ft. Holabird, Md. was next. The technology was cutting edge and involved extracting intelligence data from overhead photography taken over denied areas such as Cuba, Germany, Hungary and Vietnam.

doherty5During this period, John was itching to go to Vietnam and see action. His country was at war and, therefore, that was where he should be. The Army saw things differently. They saw John's language major from Harvard and his maximum score on the Army Language Aptitude Test and sent him to Verona, Italy. John repeatedly requested re-assignment to Vietnam and even offered to switch with other soldiers being shipped to Nam, but the Army always refused. In May of 1966, after 11 months in Italy, John got his wish and was assigned to the 55th Military Intelligence Detachment at Nha Trang, Vietnam.

At Nha Trang, a beautiful port on the coast of Vietnam just north of Cam Ranh, John was assigned prisoner interrogation duty but he continued his quest to be assigned to a combat unit. Eventually, he was told to "find a home." So he did.

John picked the 2nd Battalion of the 7th Cavalry (2/7th Cav) – famous because it was originally General Custer's unit. John felt at home in the 2/7th Cav. He was assigned to provide specialized intelligence for II Corps – one of Vietnam's four military regions.

Soon after being placed with the 2/7th Cav, Gen. Westmoreland assigned John's unit to a province that was nearly overrun with Viet Cong. The province had a very weak Army of the Republic of Vietnam (ARVN) presence and Westmoreland wanted it cleaned up. The 2/7th Cav was heavily armed and was just the unit to do it. John was assigned to plan raids and ambushes against the Viet Cong. Having previously faced the weaker

ARVN forces, Charlie was unprepared for the highly professional, cutting-edge 2/7th Cav forces that came at them with "an attitude." The local Viet Cong were destroyed.

doherty4John had access to high-level intelligence, radio intercepts and information from local agents. One of John's responsibilities was to determine the enemy's "order of battle" – i.e., the specific units deployed by the enemy and their past history, so that they could be effectively engaged. John interrogated numerous prisoners who felt fortunate to be captured by American forces and not by the South Vietnamese, since ARVN soldiers were known for their brutality.

John, promoted to captain at this point, recalled his use of a "lie detector" machine during interrogations. The unit had two large colored lights on top, one red and one green. The unit had a switch under the table to control the lights. The machine didn't reveal anything about the truth of a prisoner's answers, but it had a powerful psychological effect. As John sat behind the desk with his pistol on top, his bayonet stuck in the desktop, and a mean-looking ARVN soldier/interpreter by his side, he would ask questions and control the lights. He would turn on the green light when routine questions were asked and when the prisoner was likely telling the truth. When John asked a more sensitive question or suspected a prisoner might be lying, he would flip on the red light and the ARVN soldier, seeing the red light, would jump out of his chair and run towards the prisoner with a half-crazed look on his face. To the prisoner, it was all very believable … heck, if the Americans could invent a way to see in the dark — night vision devices — they could probably invent a truth detector.

During this period, John took possession of a very valuable prisoner/defector. He had come into camp sick with malaria and dysentery and with one of the surrender leaflets that were scattered by US/ARVN troops.

doherty2He was faced with either dying or defecting and decided on the latter. This was not your usual prisoner! He was French/Vietnamese, 6 feet

1inch (most Vietnamese were 5 feet tall) and was very well educated ... at the Sorbonne! He had graduated from the Soviet Airborne School at Ryazan and had a great deal of high-level intelligence to offer. When word got to Gen. Westmoreland in Saigon, John was ordered to "protect him with your life" and a helicopter was soon dispatched to bring the prisoner to Saigon.

When John's first tour of duty in Vietnam was over, he decided he really liked what he was doing and wanted a second tour. After completing a 30-day leave of absence — granted to all soldiers who signed up for a second tour – John reported back to Saigon expecting to be reassigned to the 2/7th Cav. However, that was not what the Army had in mind. Instead he was sent to the Ancient Imperial City of Hue in I Corps – the military region closest to North Vietnam. At first, John was very disappointed. While he initially didn't want to change units, he came to like his new assignment. He was now working with the ARVN 1st Infantry Division – the best unit in the South Vietnamese Army.

John now interrogated prisoners from the North Vietnamese Army – NVA – and, using intelligence gained from them and other sources, became the I Corps target coordinator. In this role, he planned radar-based air strikes, naval gunfire, and even B-52 strikes – including a series of secret B-52 missions known as "Arc Light."

doherty3John's second tour took a different twist when an Australian warrant officer attached to the 1st ARVN Reconnaissance Unit was wounded and John was assigned to take his place. Finally, John was in the field with ARVN forces ... a group of about 100 soldiers ... conducting very quiet, sneak-and-peek operations in one of the more dangerous places in Vietnam.

During this period John was living off C-rations and rice, sleeping in hammocks to avoid rats and snakes, and spending his days walking through rice paddies. John's ARVN liaison was 1st Lt. Tan, a 31-year old Vietnamese who had been fighting the communists since he was 15-years old. Sixteen years of wartime experience develops good instincts. John noted that Lt. Tan often picked trails that avoided potential ambushes and/or minefields.

On one occasion John had to overrule Lt. Tan and, sure enough, they entered a mined area. John stepped on something odd but it didn't explode

... at least not until John had moved away. John pointed at the questionable object to warn others, but it was too late. A South Vietnamese soldier lost his foot when the mine exploded. John believes it was only the heavy mud surrounding the mine that kept it from "springing" apart and exploding when he took his foot off it.

John had a lot of respect for the enemy. Their soldiers were very resourceful and changed tactics quickly when needed. They were tough and fatalistic. NVA soldiers routinely had tattoos that said, "Born in the North – Died in the South." They were dedicated and ready to die. Many ARVN soldiers were equally brave. Some would dress up as NVA soldiers and infiltrate enemy positions to gain needed intelligence.

In December 1967 the previously wounded Australian returned and John was re-assigned to his former duties in Hue. He might have thought this would be less dangerous, but he would have been wrong.

On January 31, 1968 at 2:40 a.m., John was sleeping in his compound in Hue. He was just south of the "Perfume" river that divided Hue. Suddenly, all hell broke loose. Mortars, 122 mm rockets, and RPGs were exploding all around his compound. Hue was ground zero for the largest North

Vietnamese attack of the war – the Tet Offensive.

John's first reaction was, "What the <expletive deleted>?" He could see the explosions and RPG trails. He pulled his boots on and grabbed his AK-47. The building was being plastered with enemy fire. He could see the green tracers from enemy rounds being fired in his direction. He and fellow soldiers returned fire, shooting at shadows and muzzle flashes throughout the night. A mortar struck near John's position and he was wounded in the right leg.

Specialist 1st Class Frank Doezema probably saved John's life. Doezema was manning a machine gun and faced the first massive assault of NVA troops. He gunned down three NVA soldiers attempting to set demolition charges. When he was finally hit by an RPG, he still continued to fire at attacking units. Regrettably, the RPG had blown off Doezema's leg and he died before he could be given the needed medical care. He was later awarded the Army's Distinguished Service Cross.

The day before the attack, John noted that he had traveled through Hue in the open on a routine assignment. At the time, NVA forces were already in Hue in force, but were still awaiting the order to attack. John, almost certainly, passed right through NVA positions and was an easy target but they held their fire.

The battle of Hue raged on for a month. During the first week of the battle, John went on numerous missions within the city to attack enemy positions and to free trapped friendly forces. On one occasion, John's patrol rescued two senior ARVN officers who were surrounded by NVA forces.

On February 7th, 1968, John went on an impromptu patrol near the local soccer stadium. As he and others were slowly moving from tree to tree, Gunnery Sergeant George P. Kendall, Jr. stepped in front of John and took an entire burst from a Soviet RPD machine gun – a burst that was probably meant for John. In the ensuing battle, an RPG struck near John and shrapnel hit John in his right knee. He was eventually able to hobble back to his compound a quarter mile away, at which point he was dressed down for engaging in "unauthorized combat."

After having his wound tended, John returned to the scene of the battle to retrieve Kendall's body and do a little payback. He returned with an M42 Duster – a tank chassis armed with several 20 mm cannons. After obliterating the enemy machinegun position and retrieving Kendall's body, his unit was on its way back to the compound when John was hit by friendly fire. One of the men in John's unit was not a trained infantry soldier, since even cooks and bottle washers were in the fight at this point. When he was told to point his 40 mm grenade launcher away from his fellow soldiers and toward the enemy, he mistakenly fired it into the ground. After the grenade bounced off the ground and a nearby wall, it exploded and wounded John in the same knee that just took shrapnel.

Unfortunately, the new wound required some real surgery and there was no more morphine. All that was available was Darvon, but the surgery to extract metal from John's knee went ahead anyway.

John wasn't evacuated from Hue until February 14th. It wasn't a routine evacuation. John was loaded into a Huey helicopter with a pilot and a door-gunner. After takeoff, they flew 10 feet above the river at 85 knots and then right over thousands of NVA troops. The NVA were everywhere! John had 5 magazines of ammo and, despite being wounded, fired out the door continuously during his evacuation. The helicopter was hit numerous times, including rounds through the door and into the bulkhead that John was propped up against. Only 5 rounds were left when John ceased firing.

John made it to Saigon, but the city was also under attack during the Tet Offensive and John's combat wasn't over yet. A few days later, word was received that another attack was imminent. Sure enough, at midnight the attack came. A mortar round landed across the room — about 20 feet from John — and he again received shrapnel wounds, this time to his back, face, and head. His helmet was also dented and he couldn't hear anything or focus his eyes.

On the 14th of February 1968, two weeks after the Tet Offensive had begun, and 7 days after John had been scheduled to complete his tour and become a civilian, he was finally evacuated from Vietnam. This time he was glad to leave, but he refused to hand over his rifle until he was safely on the waiting Continental Airways 707. John didn't feel entirely safe until he was out over the Pacific, and for good reason; mortar explosions were still erupting on the airfield as they started their takeoff roll.

John officially left the Army on February 20th, 1968. After returning to Andover, John worked for Raytheon for a short period and then attended Boston College Law School. After graduation, John was a prosecutor for 14 years – the last 4½ at the federal level. He married his wife Denise in 1984 and has a 16-year-old daughter, Margaret. John switched to a private law practice in Andover in 1984 and continued his legal career until 1998 at which time he took his current position as the town's Veterans Service Officer.

John Doherty, thank you for your service.

Capt. Doherty has been awarded the Bronze Star, three Purple Hearts, the Vietnamese Medal of Honor, two Vietnamese Crosses of Gallantry, and two Vietnamese Wound Medals (earned while he was an advisor to ARVN Forces).

Frank Shimko, E-4 Communications Specialist

By: Dr. Charles Ormsby - October, 2005

METHUEN, MA - Frank Shimko, E-4 Communications Specialist Frank Shimko didn't think his future lay in Nebraska, so at 19 he enlisted in the Army. It was the summer of 1965. Not long afterwards, he found himself on the other side of the world and in harm's way.

Frank was born in Cheyenne, Wyoming in 1946. His dad was a career Army Master Sergeant who served his country for 32 years. Although his dad had numerous duty stations, Frank did most of his growing up in Edgar, Nebraska. In fact, he was able to stay in the same school in Edgar for 12 years. Edgar was a quiet town of approximately 650 residents ... very quiet and very flat ... much too quiet and too flat for Frank.

Frank graduated from high school in 1965 and, shortly thereafter, decided he had to get out. The Army seemed like the ideal solution. Oddly, Vietnam didn't worry Frank that much ... either that, or Nebraska worried him more!

Frank's first stop was Ft. Leonard Woods in Missouri for basic training. Advanced Infantry Training at Ft. Gordon, Georgia was next and where

Frank became a Communications Specialist as part of the Signal Corps. Graduation in March 1966 was rewarded with orders for Vietnam. Frank was not overly concerned when he received his deployment assignment; Vietnam was just too foreign to his hometown experiences while growing up.

His tour of duty started with a 24-hour flight, by way of Hawaii, to Tan Son Nhut Airbase outside Saigon. A C-130 flight brought Frank to Qui Nhon where trucks were arranged for the trip to An Khe Airbase in the Central Highlands. At An Khe, Frank and the 509th Signal Battalion was attached to the 1st Air Cavalry Division. (Note: It was the 1st Air Cavalry stationed at An Khe that launched the first major helicopter assault in modern warfare against the North Vietnamese Army in 1965 - as depicted in the Mel Gibson movie, "We Were Soldiers.")

Also based at the An Khe Airbase were Montanyard Tribesmen and Republic of Korea (ROK) troops allied with the American effort.

As is common for troops that are forward deployed, living conditions were less than luxurious. Frank's picture of his "home" while at An Khe was accompanied by the following captions: "Wall-to-wall dirt" and "Plenty of wild pets." The pets Frank was referring to were mice, rats and snakes — not pets you would normally want around the house!

As a Communications Center Specialist, Frank was often called upon to travel by helicopter to "HongKong Hill," a small Army hilltop communications center for the Central Highlands area. As this was a remote outpost and enemy troops were often operating in the surrounding jungle areas — both above ground and in a maze of tunnels built to resist the French occupation in the 1950s — Frank routinely served guard duty that exposed him and his fellow soldiers to enemy activity. On more than one occasion, Frank and others on guard duty saw what appeared to be enemy movement and they responded with either rifle fire or by throwing hand grenades.

The An Khe Airbase, on the other hand, was a very large and highly protected area because it was the main American air base in the Central Highlands region. It was surrounded by a 100-yard wide, clear-cut perimeter and was well guarded. While this was very effective in keeping out enemy troops, it did not prevent mortar attacks that could be very lethal.

The best defense against enemy mortars was a lot of sandbags to dive behind when necessary — and liberal use of 105 mm Howitzers to discourage the enemy from firing mortars in the first place. Frank's other caption with the pictures of his tent that he called "home" for a year was the following: "My alarm clock was constantly going off – Oh, no … that was the 105 Howitzers!" Sleep deprivation is a common recollection of combat soldiers and Frank's experience with the incredibly loud 105s is no exception.

As protected as An Khe was, Frank did venture out several times alone to visit nearby Vietnamese villages. Looking back, Frank says he knows that was probably not a very smart thing to do. He says he certainly wouldn't make that choice again under those circumstances. Nevertheless, he did get to see several small villages and had the opportunity to hand out candy and gum to the Vietnamese kids. He even joined in some jump-roping games and enjoyed the local food without any ill effects.

Looking back on his year in Vietnam, Frank recognizes that the experience took him from boyhood to manhood. The hardships associated with collapsing tents, foot-deep mud, monsoon rains, bugs, rats, and snakes were made all the more difficult because of incoming mortars, out-going Howitzer fire, ever-present danger, lost companions, and sleep deprivation. In March 1967, Frank Simko, once just a Nebraska boy, came home a man with a lot of memories – good and bad – to last a lifetime.

Coming home from Vietnam!

While Frank was in Vietnam, he wasn't aware of the split in public opinion back in the states regarding the war effort. He spoke to students in Edgar after he returned and received a warm reception. While Frank did not evidence any strong emotions on the subject, it is clear that he is still disturbed to this day by the more extreme anti-American protests that raged while Americans like him risked their lives for freedom in Vietnam.

Frank says that he has never really spoken in detail about his Vietnam experience prior to this interview, even to fellow veterans. He just keeps it to himself.

He still reacts instinctively when he hears sirens or helicopters – these are responses he will probably never shake. He thinks that some of the memories of that era may be suppressed and has occasionally considered hypnosis as a possible way to bring them back. But he is not sure he wants to remember and concludes that it is probably better to let the memories slip away.

When Frank returned to the States, he briefly served at the Army Officer War College in Carlisle, Pa. and then was transferred to a Civil Defense site in Maynard, Mass. It was during this period that he met Elli, currently his wife of 36 years. Frank and Elli lived in Lawrence for 14 years and raised two children while Frank worked for Gibson Motors. Methuen has been their home for the last 22 years where Frank now works for the city. Frank has been the Commander of the Methuen VFW for the last 5 years and Elli has been Women's Auxiliary President for the same period.

Frank Shimko, thank you for your service to our country.

Frank left the Army in 1969 as an E-4. He received the Good Conduct Medal, the National Defense Service Medal, the Vietnam Service Medal with one bronze service star, the Republic of Vietnam Campaign Ribbon w/device, the Republic of Vietnam Gallantry Cross w/Palm Unit Citation, and the Marksman Badge with rifle bar.

Frank Shimko (left) at Ft. Gordon awaiting deployment to Vietnam, late 1966

Pfc. Alexander "Alex" Milne

By: Dr. Charles Ormsby - September, 2005

NORTH ANDOVER, MA - Alexander Milne rarely speaks of his wartime experiences, even with fellow veterans. Such conversations were uncommon even with his brother, Donald, who served on the Battle-ship Texas at Normandy, Iwo Jima and Okinawa, and who passed away two years ago. Alex found it difficult to explain the reluctance veterans have when it comes to recalling their experiences in the war. Maybe it is modesty. Maybe it's the painful memories of the suffering and of the loss of their fallen comrades. In any case, it is just difficult.

Alex, currently a resident of Andover, was born in Fall River, Massachusetts in 1925 and graduated from North Andover's Johnson High School in 1943, just shy of his 18th birthday. In December 1941, when Alex was a junior and only 16 years old, Brockleman's Market on the corner of Essex and Lawrence Streets burned down. The next morning Alex and his boyhood friend, Bill McEvoy (a current and well-known resident of North Andover), walked to the scene of the fire to see what remained. On their way home, a car pulled up and the driver shouted out, "The Japanese have bombed Pearl Harbor!"

Shortly after Pearl Harbor, Donald, who was a year older than Alex, enlisted in the Navy and began his WW II service. After graduation in 1943, Alex turned 18 and registered for the draft. He was notified in September to report to the Army, which immediately sent him to basic training at Camp Perry, Ohio. After basic training and several months at the Rossford and Camp Flora Ordinance Depots, he was shipped to Texas for training in preparation for infantry replacement deployment.

Alex was lucky when it came to berth assignments for the "cruise" to Liverpool, England. He left from the Port Authority docks in New York on an upper-deck berth on the cruise ship Louis Pasteur, a ship that had been designed to be a high-speed civilian ocean liner. The war changed that and, on the ship's maiden voyage, it was used to save France's gold reserves – all 213 tons – by transporting them to Canada.

After arrival and for the next week or so, no two nights were spent in the same place. From the Louis Pasteur, Alex went by train to spend a night on a floating dock in South Hampton harbor. Then several smaller ships transported Alex and his fellow soldiers to the port of La Havre, France to spend a night in a "tent City" on a hill outside the port. The next morning they were loaded in "40 or 8" boxcars – a WW I term for boxcars that could accommodate forty men or eight horses – and they were on their way to Belgium. The trip to Belgium was less than first class – let's just say there were no "facilities", dining or otherwise, in the boxcar.

Belgium was the gathering point for replacement troops for Allied forces fighting the Germans. Alex spent one night in a huge mill building in Belgium with approximately 1000 other soldiers awaiting orders. He didn't have to wait long. The next morning Alex and two others were assigned to the 1st Army Group, 69th Infantry Division, 271st Infantry Regiment, Company C.

Once assigned to the 271st, Alex proceeded immediately to the Battle of the Hurtgen Forest, one of the bloodiest and most costly battles fought in U.S. history. Conservative estimates list U.S. casualties at over 24,000 killed with 9,000 more lost to trench foot, disease and combat exhaustion.

Alex joined the battle of Hurtgen Forest after the Allies were in the process of slowly pushing the Germans out. Alex remembers the Hurtgen Forest as a dark and frigid place with nothing but dirt logging roads and constant shelling by the Germans using 88mm artillery. Shells would hit the tops of trees and then ricochet, explode and rain shrapnel down on the American positions. "They knew where we were" Alex said, "and the German 88s were the most perfect weapons of WW II. They could be used for anti-air operations, artillery, or leveled and used like massive rifles."

Stephen E. Ambrose, in his book Citizen Soldier, described the battle as being "fought under conditions as bad as American soldiers ever had to face, even including the Wilderness and the Meuse-Argonne. Sgt. George Morgan of the 4th Division described it: 'The forest was a helluva eerie place to fight. You can't get protection. You can't see. You can't get fields of fire. Artillery slashes the trees like a scythe. Everything is tangled. You can scarcely walk. Everybody is cold and wet, and the mixture of cold rain and sleet keeps falling.' Troops more than a few feet apart couldn't see each other. There were no clearings, only narrow firebreaks and trails. Maps were almost useless. When the Germans, secure in their bunkers, saw the GIs coming forward, they called down pre-sighted artillery fire, using shells with fuses designed to explode on contact with the treetops. When men dove to the ground for cover, as they had been trained to do and as instinct dictated, they exposed themselves to a rain of hot metal and wood splinters."

Alex described the living conditions during this period: they were worse than deplorable. It was one of the coldest German winters on record. Troops slept on the ground amidst 4 or 5 inches of snow. They had no tents or sleeping bags … only their ponchos to wrap around themselves. Men woke up so cold they couldn't move. Those who were up had to lift their comrades and get them standing by a tree to slowly gain the ability to move. No smoke meant no fires and no hot coffee or hot meals … just cold C-rations. Even with these memories, Alex thinks the weeks preceding his arrival were even worse and the troops suffering even more intense.

While occasionally a "lunch truck" would happen by, cold C-rations were the norm during meal breaks. The frontline troops didn't even carry mess kits — one badly packed mess kit could rattle and threaten the security of an entire squad or company.

Alex Milne was awarded the Combat Infantry Badge, the Bronze Star, the Purple Heart, the European Theater of Operations Medal with Two Stars, the Vic-tory Medal, the American Defense Medal, the Good Conduct Ribbon, and the Sharp-shooters Award.

The reader may not fully appreciate the incredible casualties taken by U.S. Forces in the Hurtgen Forest ... especially during the battle's early stages. As noted above, Alex was one of the "replacement infantry." There were many such replacements. Why? Here is a very short excerpt from the history of 271st commenting on the casualty rates during the period just before Alex's arrival at the front:

"Replacements flowed in to compensate for the losses but the Hurtgen's voracious appetite for casualties was greater than the army's ability to provide new troops." Lieutenant Wilson recorded his company's losses at 167 percent for enlisted men.

"We had started with a full company of about 162 men and had lost about 287." Sgt. Mack Morris was there with the 4th and reported: "Hurtgen had its fire-breaks, only wide enough to allow two jeeps to pass, and they were mined and interdicted by machine-gun fire. There was a mine every eight paces for three miles. Hurtgen's roads were blocked. The Germans cut roadblocks from trees. They cut them down so they interlocked as they fell. Then they mined and booby-trapped them. Finally they registered their artillery on them, and the mortars, and at the sound of men clearing them, they opened fire."

When Alex's unit finally exited the forest, it was a godsend. Finally: rolling hills, flatlands, and fields.

Here Alex had the luxury of spending one night in a farmhouse. You can detect the relief in his voice as he describes the immense pleasure of spending one night indoors ... even if it was with twenty other soldiers in cramped quarters and on the floor. Alex remembers the pleasure of washing his hands in the sink, "It wasn't a bath but it still felt awfully good!"

Most of the action during this period was not close combat. The threats were from constant shelling by artillery, and numerous mines and booby-traps set by withdrawing German troops. The Germans would set their mines and booby-traps and register their artillery – as described above – and then stand off 5 to 10 miles and shell the American troops as they moved into the new areas. When artillery shells were incoming, which happened ten or twelve times a day, troops would dive for cover before moving out again.

Crossing the Rhine River was a major milestone for U.S. troops. Alex crossed the Rhine at a town called Neider-Breisig - not far from the famous Remagen Bridge where the first Allied crossing took place. Alex and his regiment spent several days helping the Corps of Engineers as they built a pontoon bridge. Alex remembers loosening his jacket filled with numerous heavy objects before crossing over ... he didn't need to be weighted down if the bridge collapsed or the truck went over the edge. The other major milestone for Alex at Neider-Breisig was taking a shower ... his first shower since leaving New York 6 weeks earlier!

On April 15, 1945, Alex had a very close call. Just before nightfall his squad was ordered to cross an open field. Suddenly, "the sky lit up like Fenway Park." Artillery shells timed to explode a hundred or so feet above the ground started going off everywhere. The entire squad turned and raced for cover. Alex jokes that he thinks he passed everyone as he ran from the field. But this was just a preview of coming events.

The next day, Alex was riding on a tank when artillery shells started to rain down on his convoy. Everyone jumped into the nearest gully. Initially, Alex was in the ditch with a medic but the medic soon left to attend a wounded soldier. Shortly thereafter a shell landed about 12 feet from Alex and about 5 feet above him. Shrapnel tore into his neck, shoulder, left leg, and back... one piece lodged in his lung. The concussion from the shell was so intense that Alex only re-members bits and pieces of what happened next. He vaguely remembers that the medic returned to help stabilize him - probably leaving Alex earlier saved the medic's life, since the medic had been positioned even closer to the point of impact than was Alex. Soon, Alex was placed on the hood of a jeep and rushed to a field hospital.

Alex spent fourteen months in hospitals before he was well enough to be released. He had to constantly fight infections while recovering from major operations. At one point, about the time his family was first able to visit him, Alex's weight had dropped to 99 pounds. Twenty-year-old Pfc. Alex Milne was finally released and discharged on June 28, 1946. He still carries shrapnel from that artillery shell in his neck.

Alex worked for the Davis & Furber Textile Company in North Andover for ten years, then with the Andover branch of McCartney's Clothing store for another 27 years. He lived in North Andover until 1953 when he moved to Andover. Alex and his wife Mary have four sons: Alex, Robert, David, and Gary who all still live in Massachusetts.

Alex Milne, thank you for your service and the sacrifices you made for our freedoms.

The Boddy Brothers
Charles and Edward

June, 2005

LAWRENCE, MA - They were literally the lifeblood of the American troops fighting against the Nazis and Japanese during World War II. The mariners of the Merchant Marine may have been civilians, but their task of supplying food, arms, medicine, and supplies was critical to the war effort.

Often facing Japanese subs or German U-boats, these brave men gave life to the battlefield for American soldiers and kept them one step ahead of the enemy. When they finally returned home, however, their status as civilians prevented them from receiving many of the benefits that the government rightfully gave to our military veterans.

Charles and Edward Boddy were young and energetic when World War II broke out. They were also patriots. Growing up in Lawrence, they were part of a group of friends called " Tally Ho," because they hung out at a lounge called The Tally Ho. All their friends were between 21 and 30 years old. Before the war they went to the beach, played hockey at Hills Pond and visited Hofreau's to see the latest bands play.

But on Sunday, December 7, 1941, their lives would change forever. That was the day when the Japanese launched a sneak attack on Pearl Harbor, and the "Tally Ho" friends were deeply moved by this treacherous act and all the terrible events going on in the world. They talked about what Pearl Harbor meant to them and felt they had to contribute to the national defense. By the end of December 1941, Charles Boddy and 25 young men from their group joined the war effort.

Charles Boddy says he saw an ad in the local paper which said "Maritime needs sailors, $75.00/month." On December 27, 1941, he signed up to join the Merchant Marine. He said he wanted to wait until after Christmas so that he could spend what might be the last Christmas holiday with his family.

A week later, on January 3, 1942, Charles was off to Hoffman Island in New York Harbor for three months of basic training. Then, on April 13, 1942, he was assigned to serve on a United States Navy Transport named the USS Siboney. On its first trip, the ship carried 2,200 GI's to Belfast, Ireland where troops and supplies were desperately needed. The mariners then sailed to Scotland, transferring more supplies before returning home to New York.

Charles completed nine other trips during the war, watching fellow mariners lose their lives trying to keep troops stocked with food, ammunition and supplies. For six months, in the harsh and inhuman winter conditions along the Arctic Circle, he carried troops to Labrador, Greenland and Finland. He participated in convoys bringing shells and explosives to our Russian allies at Odessa so that the eastern front could be defended against Hitler's invading forces. At that time, supplies could not be funneled through Nazi controlled Western Europe and the transports had to travel behind enemy lines and risk submarine attack to supply Russian forces.

He made two trips aboard the SS Seatrain Texas to North Africa where he delivered locomotives, railroad cars and over 180 tanks to our Allies fighting the forces of Rommel, better known as "The Desert Fox." Historians attribute the delivery of these Sherman tanks as a decisive factor in the Allied victory at El Alamein.

Charles said his most memorable and dangerous trip was carrying 4,200 tons of one-hundred pound bombs to our allies in England. The bombs eventually made their way to Germany via air force bombing missions over Berlin. "The ship had six hatches and every one of them was filled with bombs. It was very dangerous," Charles said. "We were on a ship filled with bombs! One mistake, one problem and we all would have blown into the sky"!

Charles recalled another harrowing situation: "For about eight weeks we were exposed to the enemy's buzz bombs when our ship, the USS James Gunn, was involved in a collision in Belgium. We were forced to discharge the cargo and repair the ship right there."

By 1943, Charles had accumulated enough sea time to attend officer's training school at Fort Trumbel in New London, Connecticut. He graduated in November and shortly thereafter signed on to the USS Alabama out of Boston. Charles sailed until December of 1944 when he went to Maritime School in Boston for his Second Officer's License. His last trip with the Merchant Marine was on July 28, 1945. "One of my proudest and most patriotic feelings was looking over a convoy of 100 ships and thinking of the contributions we were making towards winning the war," he stated.

In September of 1942, at the age of 20, Charles' younger brother Edward "Ward" Boddy also enlisted in the Merchant Marine. Prior to joining up, he had worked as a welder in the Bath Shipyard and then built invasion barges at the Boston Navy Ship Yard.

Ward was subsequently sent to Sheepshead Bay in New York for his basic training. He never could have dreamed of the dangers he would face on the open seas. He trained for three months before going to work for the Standard Oil Company on a gasoline barge. The barge was towed by a tugboat and supplied oil, gasoline and other fuels to U.S. ships. "The fuel we were carrying was highly flammable... there was no smoking at all on the ship ... one spark and we would all be dead," he said.

While overseas, Ward's father had a heart attack and stroke, which allowed Ward to return home where he was able to sign on to a barge with Standard Oil in Boston so he could care for the family.

When things settled down, Ward left for New York where he worked for Alcoa Aluminum, hauling food, flour, mail and cars to Trinidad – still dangerous waters for the Merchant Marine.

His next adventure was an invasion run aboard a U.S. Army transport bringing troops to Liverpool. There, they picked up more troops and brought them to Normandy for the now famous "D-Day" invasion. On the way, the Merchant Marine lost one of their ships, the Susan B. Anthony, when she hit a floating mine and sunk. Fortunately, the troops and crew were rescued with no loss of life.

Ward was also stationed in Belfast Harbor for a month, but says his most memorable moment was aboard the SS Lewis Luckenbach. "I loved to play the piano and I was pretty good at it," he now says, humbly. "The Luckenbach had been converted into a hospital ship [the Louis A. Milne] and transported wounded soldiers back to the states from different battlefields. On the day the hospital ship was christened, Kate Smith came to sing 'God Bless America.' It was such a thrill because it was one of the first times she had ever sung it for the troops," he said.

Ward's piano playing onboard the Lutinback was a great morale booster for the wounded soldiers, proving that whether delivering supplies, fighting on the battlefield or providing comfort to wounded soldiers, every contribution made by Americans during the war effort played an important part of the ultimate victory over the Japanese and Nazis.

For his service in the Merchant Marine, Charles Boddy received several medals, including the Russian Medal for transporting munitions and supplies across the Arctic Circle and behind enemy lines to Russian ports. His brother Ward received three North Atlantic Combat medals and several citations.

After the war ended, Ward joined another brother, Raymond, in the furniture business at Boddy Furniture in downtown Methuen. Raymond had also subsequently joined the Merchant Marine. A fourth brother, Leonard, served in the army. "Leonard went in as an enlisted man and came out as a captain," Charles said.

Charles' daughter, Ann Haggerty (a former Valley Patriot of the month), is presently in the army reserves and served in Operation Iraqi Freedom. She is an assistant principal in the Lawrence public schools. Charles' son, Charles Boddy, Jr., is the City Solicitor for Lawrence.

Charles (Sr.) and Ward Boddy are now actively trying to get a bill passed in Congress, H.R. 23. While other World War II veterans received the GI Bill, home loans, health care benefits and other rewards for their wartime service, the heroes of the Merchant Marine were denied these benefits. H.R. 23 is called "The Belated Thank You to the Merchant Mariners of World War II Act of 2005".

It provides $1,000 per month to WWII mariners or their widows in lieu of benefits not received after World War II. Charles and Ward hope that our government will recognize the contribution of fellow mariners with the passage of this bill.

The Valley Patriot wants to honor and thank all the Boddy brothers for their patriotism and service to our country at one of the most dangerous times in our nation's history. We also urge our readers to contact their congressman and urge support of H.R. 23. For additional information, visit the Merchant Marine web site at www.usmm.org.

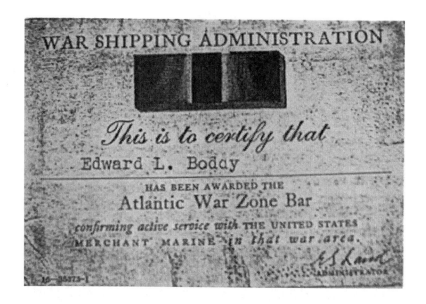

Corporal
Theodore (Ted) R. Eaton

By: Dr. Charles Ormsby - March, 2005

NORTH ANDOVER, MA -The Eaton family has a proud history of serving in the U.S. Armed Forces. When Ted Eaton was in his early teens, he had three brothers who signed up for duty in WW II (John and Lindy in the Army, and Frank in the Navy). In the summer of 1948 the world was generally at peace and Ted, now 17 years old, thought the Army might be a good place to gain some needed skills.

After enlisting, Ted requested training in radio repair. The Army, however, less interested in civilian skills than building a fighting force, sent Ted to Fort Meade, Md. to learn how to drive tanks. Eventually, Ted did get some radio-related training. His next stop was Ft. Monmouth, N.J. where he was trained as a radio operator. Graduating at the top of his class, Corporal Eaton was assigned to the 3rd Armored Cavalry Regiment Light.

If it hadn't been for President Truman's Secretary of State, Dean Acheson, Ted may have had a quiet enlistment and then been returned to civilian life. But Acheson, probably hoping to appease Stalin and the Chinese communists, decided to announce to the world that Korea and Taiwan were outside the American Far Eastern security cordon. He might as well have invited the communists to dinner.

On June 25th (Korean time), 1950, the North Korean communists invaded South Korea without warning. Just a few days later, Corporal Eaton, who was on weekend clerk duty at the time, got the order, "Contact your Company and tell them to get in here immediately … they're shipping out to Korea on Tuesday." That's how fast it happened.

Ted did not leave for Korea immediately with the rest of his Company. In fact, because Ted had a triplet brother assigned to Europe, he had his choice of orders: Korea or Europe. What would you do? Ted reflected on his family's record of military service and gave the only answer he could, "Send me where Uncle Sam needs me the most." With the South Korean Army trapped and being decimated on the north side of the Han River and the North Korean Army streaming south winning victories against U.S. Forces, the answer was obvious. Ted was going to Korea. Before shipping out Ted was assigned to the 20th Signal Corps based out of Ft. Bragg, N.C.

By the end of July 1950, the North Korean Army had captured nearly the entire Korean peninsula. The US Army finally established the Pusan Perimeter in early August after General Walker had issued his "Stand or Die" order. Fierce fighting around Pusan in August and early September led to MacArthur's brilliant (but risky) flanking invasion at Inchon on September 15th.

Corporal Eaton, having arrived just before the Inchon landings, remembers the mad dash to transport supplies by rail and truck to the infantry. While Ted had not been trained as a truck driver, that is what Uncle Sam needed. Ted soon found himself behind the wheel in a truck convoy in close proximity to the fighting northeast of Seoul. You may feel some comfort when surrounded by fellow soldiers in a convoy, but that secure feeling vanished one day when Ted found himself separated from the trucks he was following. All of a sudden, with no trucks in front of him, Ted became the lead driver without much of an idea where he and those following him were going. Luck (or intuition) prevailed and Ted found the intended destination that day, but he knew he never wanted to lose sight of the trucks ahead of him ever again.

Shortly thereafter, Ted was assigned Temporary Duty (TDY) to the 2nd Infantry Division, 8th Army as a radio operator (finally something he was trained for!). U.S. forces were rapidly pushing northward and on October 19th the North Korean capital of Pyongyang was captured. Ted remembers reaching the Yalu River (the North Korean – Chinese border) in late November. Everyone was excited and talking about being home for Christmas. The Chinese had different plans.

In late November the Chinese attacked in force along the Yalu. Ted remembers being ordered on November 27th to "shoot anyone coming over that hill" because they would be Chinese. Within days the 8th Army was in full retreat and Ted's Division was surrounded by Chinese troops (plus some Russian advisors). If the Division didn't fight its way out, Ted would be killed or captured.

As the battle raged, Ted was in a "deuce and a half" (2 ½ ton) truck. Under the plywood canopy in back, Ted had his radio equipment set up and was handling classified/coded message traffic to and from his unit. Suddenly, radio silence was ordered (probably to avoid giving away their position) and Ted was told to get down. He couldn't have transmitted much longer anyway because, as he lay on the bench in front of his radios, the truck was ripped with machine-gun fire. Both the driver and the right seat passenger were wounded and the streak of bullets raked across the radio stack just above his head. The driver yelled, "Eaton, GET OUT!" but Ted had one more job to do. He had to set the fire grenade that was designed to destroy everything in the truck (especially the secret codes) that might have value to the enemy. As Ted rolled off the back of the truck, he was grateful to see a jeep had just pulled up. At this point, Ted effectively became a member of the infantry.

Ted remembers how difficult it was to distinguish friendly troops from the enemy and his concern that he never shoot at friendly forces. At one point he encountered an enemy soldier crawling on the ground with his head up and screaming. Before firing, Ted noticed that the soldier had no legs ... they had just been blown off. Knowing he no longer constituted a combat risk, Ted left him alone and he was later helped by U.S. medics.

The 2nd Division finally broke through enemy lines on Ted's 20th birthday, November 30, 1950. When he told a fellow soldier "this was one heck of a way to spend his birthday," the soldier reached into a hiding space and pulled out a fifth of Canadian Club. Ted had never tasted whiskey and remembers that it "burned like hell going down!" Finally, Ted got a ride back to Seoul and his few days as an infantry soldier (albeit, unofficially) were over.

After arriving in Seoul, Ted's unit was renamed the 8075th Army Service Unit and assigned TDY to the 51st Fighter Wing, 5th Air Force which was relocating to Kyushu Island, Japan. Ted served the 51st as a radio teletype operator coordinating air strikes originating from U.S. airbases in Japan. Ted was in Japan from Christmas 1950 to April 1951. In April, Ted returned to Korea and assigned TDY to the 11th ROK (Republic of Korea) Division in Intelligence.

During most of 1951, the Korean conflict saw vicious fighting around the 38th parallel during seemingly endless UN resolutions and ceasefire attempts. With a truce imminent (finally agreed to in November of 1951), Ted was sent stateside. Ted was finally discharged in May of 1952.

Ted often speaks to schools about his experience in Korea. He tells them that there is no glory in war ... it is torture. While he skips over the more gruesome aspects of warfare, he also tells them that war is hardest on the children. Adults can find some way to fend for themselves, Ted says, but children are often seen just huddling together or picking through garbage to survive. He remembers children whose only English was, "GI, have candy bar?" While U.S. troops couldn't help them all, a few were "employed" as houseboys (see earlier photo) to provide them the necessities of life.

Theodore Eaton, thank you for answering Uncle Sam's call to duty.

Corporal Eaton was awarded the Korean Service Medal with Four Battle Stars, the United Nations Service Medal, the American Defense Medal, and the Good Conduct Medal. He has been active in the VFW for over 50 years and served as the Massachusetts State Commander from 1986 to 1987.

Note: All photos from the Korean War period in this article were taken by Corporal Eaton and taken from his personal collection.

Sylvio "Sy" Uliano

By: Tom Duggan, Jr. - February, 2005

METHUEN, MA - Cpl. Uliano can still hear General George C. Patton telling the troops not to worry about going into combat. Patton told them, "First, the enemy fires and you duck. Then, you fire and the enemy ducks." This quote seemed humorous when Sy Uliano relayed the story, but I'm sure it was less humorous at the time. Other Patton quotes, while pretty much right on the mark, were more chilling. For example, Patton also told them, "The reason we're here is to kill German soldiers. The sooner we kill them

all, the sooner we can go home." And, go home is just what Cpl. Uliano and his fellow soldiers wanted to do. To do that, Sy and the 3rd Army followed Patton's strategy, "Attack! Attack! Attack!"

Sy Uliano's military career started out quite modestly before the war. He signed up for the National Guard in 1940 so he could earn $1 for each Sunday drill session. You had to be 18 to join the Guard, but 17-year-old Uliano wasn't fazed; he just lowered his birth year by one on the signup form.

With war clouds looming, Sy was called up for one year of training as a forward artillery observer and was now assigned to the Yankee Division (102nd Artillery Battalion, 104th Combat Team).

Sy arrived in France shortly after the D-Day invasion and was quickly put to work helping supply Patton's 3rd Army, which was doing its best to outrun its supply lines. Initially, Sy drove trucks as part of the "Red Ball Express" but his career as a truck driver was short lived. The Army had a more exciting assignment in mind. It was time to join Patton's 3rd Army as a Forward Artillery Observer … the job Sy was originally trained for.

Sy remembers the day he first saw General Patton … it was the day Patton spoke the words previously quoted. These words struck home. While Artillery units were typically located several miles behind the front lines, as a forward observer, Sy would only be 25-50 yards from the infantry engaged in eyeball-to-eyeball combat. Recalling his first day of combat, Sy chuckled as he relayed his initial exposure to incoming mortar rounds. When Sy first heard the shells and the accompanying explosions, he dove into a nearby foxhole … right on top of a high-ranking American officer! After dressing down the new arrival, the officer told Sy, "What are you doing? Those are our shells!"

After daily exposure to mortar and artillery barrages, Sy soon was able to tell friendly shells from German artillery. But even experienced soldiers aren't immune from feeling fear. Sy told of the many times he tried to crawl into his helmet when under fire. Going home was a thought that he must have often savored.

Shortly after Sy's unit joined the 3rd Army, all hell broke loose. In late December 1944, the Germans launched one of the largest attacks of the war. The two-month-long Battle of the Bulge was under way.

When the attack began, the Germans took 68 very surprised American troops captive. The Germans promptly marched them into a clearing at Malmédy and machine-gunned them (this event was prominently depicted in the movie "Battle of the Bulge", which Sy noted was generally a pretty accurate portrayal of the battle).

Sy had the unpleasant experience of being in the unit that first discovered the murdered American prisoners. The bodies were immediately inspected to see if any soldiers were still alive. Sy was surprised to discover one of the two American soldiers who miraculously survived the ordeal.

While German prisoners were generally treated well by American soldiers, Sy related that, after particularly gruesome displays of German cruelty were un-covered (such as at Malmédy), it was not uncommon for angry American infantry to dispatch German captives. The practice never lasted long because higher-ups desperately wanted enemy soldiers brought in alive to secure much-needed intelligence.

Patton, of course, was known for his aggressive military campaigns. Sy recalled that if Patton saw a unit stalled by the side of a road, he would tell them they had three minutes to get moving or they would be busted in rank.

Once, when Sy's unit was waiting to cross a bridge over the Rhine that was under attack by the German Luftwaffe, his Captain told Patton they were waiting until nightfall or until the attack ceased. Patton responded, "This is what I think of the Germans." He walked over to the bridge and, fully exposed (in more ways than one), urinated in the river. He then ordered them to cross without delay.

By the time it was Sy's turn to cross the bridge it was dark, but the German attack continued. When Sy was half way across the bridge, the convoy stalled. Sy prepared to jump in the river if an attack came, but was told he would never be rescued in the dark. Luckily, the traffic jam broke and he made it across safely.

Once, when entering an enemy-occupied town, the word came that Sy and his unit were surrounded and they were ordered to turn around and fight their way out. Gunners were told to fire at anything that moved in any of the buildings. Sy stopped in the middle of this story to note that he prayed to the Lord five or six times every day that he would survive. Pointing skyward, Sy said, "Someone up there was listening."

Seven months of combat were concluded with the surrender of Germany in 1945. By the time the war in Europe was over, Sy had toured France, Belgium (including a stop in Bastogne), Luxembourg, Germany, Austria, and Czechoslovakia. He earned numerous medals including the Bronze Star, the American Defense Service Medal and the European African Middle Eastern Theatre Campaign Ribbon. Sy remained in Europe for two months following the war to help with post-war reconstruction and finally returned to the U.S. in August of 1945.

Sy lives in Methuen with his WWII sweetheart, Dora, whom he married in 1947. Sy remains active as a youth baseball coach in Lawrence, a passion he has pursued for 36 years. Near his home in Methuen is the Sy Uliano baseball field that was dedicated to him in 1994.

Sy, thank you for your service in defense of our country and for your continuing contributions to the Merrimack Valley.

Bronze Star Dates. 8 Nov. through 12 Dec. 1944 Place: East of Nancy, France Partial Citation: "During the offensive operations against the enemy … Corporal Uliano, Artillery Liaison Noncom-missioned Officer, performed his duties in an outstanding manner, despite adverse climactic conditions and difficult terrain often times under enemy fire… His performance contributed materially to the successful execution by his Battalion of its fire missions. His courage, initiative, and unusual devotion to duty reflect the highest credit upon Corporal Uliano and the armed forces of the United States." – Award of Bronze Star, HQTS 26th Infantry Division, February 1945.

Cpl. Sy Uliano's Medals earned while Serving in Europe during World War II

Jack Fitzpatrick

By: Tom Duggan, Jr. - October, 2004

METHUEN, MA - Methuen Resident Jack Fitzpatrick served in the U.S. Army after graduating from Merrimack College and Suffolk University. Upon Returning home, he became a community activist. Jack was recently appointed to the Airport Commission following in the footsteps of his father, who was also an Airport commissioner.

Jack also serves on the Board of Directors of the Sargeant Club, is a member of the Holy Family Men's Guild, The Sons of Italy, and the Knight of Columbus. He also works in Mayor Michael Sullivan's office.

His son-in-law is a Lt. Col. Marine, presently stationed in Iraq.

For serving his country and continuing to serve our community, The Valley Patriot is honored to name Jack Fitzpatrick of Methuen, our Valley Patriot of the Month. We thank him for his years of service to the country and community. He has made our community a better place to live.

Corporal Larry DeBenedictis U.S. ARMY, KOREA

By: Beth D'Amato - January, 2017

BILLERICA, MA. - When I met Larry DeBenedictis, he had just returned home from a wake for an old friend. That friend was U.S. Army LT. Colonel John W. Watson Jr. He passed away unexpectedly at the age of ninety. LT. Colonel Watson was a fellow Korean War Veteran and had spent 3 ½ years as a POW. Larry reminisced about their friendship and wondered out loud how his good friend had done so well in life after all he witnessed during the war.

Larry's modesty about his own military service is something I've encountered quite a bit lately. While interviewing veterans, they are always more concerned about their fellow soldiers than themselves. As a matter of fact, the very first thing Larry said to me was, "Beth, I just want to clarify that I'm no hero." I looked at him almost defiantly and said, "I'm sorry sir, but I strongly disagree. Whether you saw combat or not is irrelevant. You unselfishly served OUR country and therefore, you are a hero."

Lawrence Robert DeBenedictis was born in Medford, MA on June 4, 1929, and was one of twelve children. His father a Master plumber had hoped Larry would join him in running the family plumbing business.

After high school, Larry attended Franklin Tech in Boston and took courses in plumbing, heating and air conditioning. He received a master plumber's license at the age of twenty one making him one of the youngest licensed plumbers at that time. With his skills, Larry had an interest in joining the Navy but was drafted into the Army before he had a chance to enlist.

He was drafted on August 17, 1951, at the age of twenty two and became a Corporal in the Army.

Larry was sent to Korea to help the South Koreans fight against the Communist army of North Korea. While serving, Larry showed leadership skills and was put in charge of a squadron. He would have anywhere from eight to ten men under him. Their assigned combat area was vastly out in the open. Because of this, they did most of their patrol work during the night time hours so they could stay hidden from the enemy. The squad would venture out into "no man's land" far from their trenches and string coils of barbed wire in the hopes of slowing down the enemy. Larry was always careful not to go into territory that hadn't been cleared of land mines.

One night, Larry and another soldier stopped the barbed wire coils half way across the perimeter. A higher ranked officer told them it wasn't safe to stop there and to continue with the wire. Not able to ignore a direct order from a superior, Larry and the other soldier continued on. Suddenly, there was an explosion! Larry had stepped on a landmine.

He remembered waking up and looking down at his shredded clothes. One leg was severely injured while the remaining limb was a mere stump bleeding profusely.

The other soldier had been taken away to an aid station but Larry was left behind as they incorrectly assumed he was dead. Larry knew he needed to tie off his legs to stop the bleeding.

A couple of other soldiers at the scene helped fasten makeshift tourniquets. A medic finally arrived and shot Larry full of morphine. The medic marveled that he was still conscious and talking. Larry told the medic that if he stopped talking he would surely die. After eventually reaching the aid station, Larry was heavily dosed with morphine and finally rendered unconscious.

The next time he woke up was in a hospital in Japan. However, before being shipped stateside, gangrene set into Larry's remaining leg and it had to be amputated. He finally arrived home in America in 1952 and was sent to Walter Reed Military Hospital in Maryland. By April of 1952, Larry was back home in Medford, MA.

While Larry was in the service overseas, he was receiving letters from a young woman. Her name was Carol and she was a friend of one of Larry's sisters. Carol waited anxiously for Larry to return home and when he did, the courtship began. In November of 1953, Larry and Carol married and moved to the town of Billerica, MA. They had two sons.

Being fully disabled, the army retired Larry and he was given a stipend but it wasn't enough to live on. Larry then went to VA Tech College (some of the tuition was paid by the government) and he got a job as a building inspector for the town of Billerica.

Like all amputees in the early days, Larry was fitted with wooden legs. He was able to use crutches to do his job as a building inspector. As the years went by he would be fitted with more modern prosthetics, the most recent one being computerized.

Presently, Larry is as independent as he can be. He drives a specially equipped van (paid for by the Veterans organization). He does errands and enjoys food shopping. He clips coupons and buys food to bring to the Billerica Food Pantry. Larry spends around $300 on each monthly visit to the pantry.

Larry is still active in his military organizations: the DAV Disabled American Vets, Korean War Vets Association both the Greater Lowell and Boston chapters. He attends veteran functions, parades and of course the funerals of his fellow veterans. He also spends a great deal of time at the Bedford VA Hospital where he visits the veterans and other soldiers.

As we were wrapping up the interview, Larry's wife Carol showed me the medals he had received. In a small, delicate box was the Army CIB (Combat Infantry Badge), the Bronze Star – V for Valor, a Purple Heart, Good Conduct Medal and two Battle Stars for service in Korea.

These medals reveal only a fraction of the story concerning the bravery of Corporal Lawrence Robert DeBenedictis. This is the same gentleman who at the beginning of our visit tried to tell me he wasn't a hero. We beg to differ! It was an honor to meet him and a privilege that he allowed me tell his story. Thank you for your service, sir!!

John MacDonald
U.S. Air Force Desert Storm

By: Tom Duggan, Jr. - October, 2016 - October, 2016

Lowell Mayor Rodney Elliott gives John MacDonald a "Valley Patriot Hero Veteran Award" at the 2015 Valley Patriot BASH.

LOWELL, MA - This month, The Valley Patriot honors and recognizes Lowell resident John MacDonald not just for his service to the country as a military veteran, but also because of his tremendous work helping our veterans here at home.

John MacDonald enlisted in the United States Air Force in 1989 and was initially stationed at Davis-Monthan Air Force Base in Tucson, Arizona.

A year later he would find himself deployed to Saudi Arabia during Operation Desert Shield.

MacDonald was stationed at King Khalid military city about 20 miles from Kuwait/Saudi border, and just a few miles from the famous highway to hell. There, he was part of a firefighting unit tasked with saving and retrieving crashed American and allied pilots as they lifted off and landed from the base.

Within the first month or two of arriving in the Middle East, MacDonald's unit was awarded the best fire department in Air Force.

"We were the most forward operating location in Saudi Arabia. It was a place where international allied troops were constantly flying in and out," MacDonald told The Valley Patriot.

All the Iraqi and foreign prisoners of war were brought to the base and held until a final determination can be made.

MacDonald says that F16's come through on a regular basis, and eventually his unit was turned into a MASH (Mobile Army Surgical Hospital).

When MacDonald came back from the Middle East he brought back with him, a good conduct medal, national defense ribbon, Kuwaiti defense ribbon, outstanding service with valor, and the short tour ribbon.

MacDonald says that Iraqi SCUD missiles were fired at his base all the time and recounted how he was eating "chow" one afternoon when he saw a PATRIOT missile take out one of the Iraqi SCUDS headed for his location.

"It's funny, when we came back from the Middle East, the first people to greet us at the airport were the Vietnam Vets. It was amazing that these guys, men who were spit on and called baby killers, and never got the welcome home they deserved, they were the ones standing there for the next generation of soldiers coming home from battle." MacDonald said.

It was then, that he says, he realized more needed to be done here at home for our veterans, in particular the Vietnam vets.

Last month MacDonald, one of the original board members of Veterans Assisting Veterans, organized an official "Welcome Home" concert for Vietnam Veterans at the Lowell Memorial Auditorium where they raised thousands of dollars for local veterans' causes.

VETERANS ASSISTING VETERANS

The VAV is a group of veterans that volunteer their time to assist their fellow vets. MacDonald said he got involved because our veterans today are "not being treated much better by our government than the Vietnam vets were when they came home."

"I was sick of reading so many stories of how the government was screwing over our vets at the VA. They still aren't getting the help they need. I saw so many guys coming back, in rough shape. Many of us were involved in other veteran organizations that just didn't suit us. There were too many things going on, and not a lot of actually helping our vets. Our mission at VAV is to raise money and help as many local vets as we can . What's made us successful is that 100% of what we raise goes directly to local veterans."

MacDonald says that VAV is more effective because there's very little paperwork and they are able to react to things right away. "We vet out individuals who need the help. We determine if they are worthy of us spending money, and once we do, we go out and service their needs."

Two months ago Veterans Assisting Veterans, in cooperation with New England Veteran's Liberty House, found out that a WWII veteran in Lawrence was about to lose his home because he couldn't pay his mortgage.

MacDonald, along with JT Torres and other veteran volunteers went to his house, cleaned it, and then gave him a check for the balance of his mortgage.

MacDonald is also a big supporter of police and spoke at pro police rallies sponsored by The Valley Patriot in 2015 and 2016. At the recent Welcome Home Vietnam Vets benefit concert he gave an award to the Lowell police for their bravery in keeping the citizens of Lowell safe.

With all that going on, MacDonald and his group, Veterans Assisting Veterans has been able to place POW/MIA Chairs at Cawley Stadium in Lowell, the Veteran's Memorial Stadium in Lawrence, and many others, so those who did not come back will never be forgotten.

Each Year, VAV sponsors a black tie Gala in Burlington to raise money for their programs, and honor the medical corps units of each branch of government.

For these reason and so many more, The Valley Patriot honors and recognizes Lowell resident and hero veteran John MacDonald as our Valley Patriot of the Month.

Veterans Helping Veterans Hold Service for Military Men Killed by Muslim Terrorist in Tennessee

APRIL, 2106 - LOWELL, MASSACHUSETTS - More than 65 people showed up last month at the Lowell VFW as 'Veterans Assisting Veterans' held a memorial service for the four Marines and one Navy man who were killed last week by a Muslim terrorist in Tennessee at a recruiting center. Air Force veteran and WCAP radio host, John Macdonald, organized the event after Massachusetts Secretary of Veterans Services, Francisco Urena, asked Macdonald if his organization could hold a service in Lowell for the slain troops. MacDonald read the names of each serviceman killed in the terrorist attack as veterans, their families and members of the community held candles in silence. Lowell City Councilor Bud Caulfield then lead the crowd in singing the national anthem. Killed were: U.S. Navy Petty Officer 2nd Class Randall Smith, Lance Cpl. Squire "Skip" Wells, Gunnery Sgt. Thomas J. Sullivan, Staff Sgt. David Wyatt, Sgt. Carson Holmquist.

WWII, U.S. Army PFC Louis Panebianco Receives High School Diploma September, 2016

By: Maria Fiato - The Lawrence School Department gave an honorary high school diploma last month to US. Army, PFC. Louis Panebianco, who served in the 36th Infantry, Charlie Battery, 155th Field Artillery during WWII. Panebianco, who now lives in Salem, NH, served in many theaters of combat, including; Germany, Algeria, Naples, French Morocco, Arno, Rome, Rhineland, and Foggia. During the depression Panebianco had to leave school to go to work and provide for his family. He would later be drafted for the war, where he served with such distinction that he earned the: Purple Heart, Good Conduct Medal, Victory Medal, European-African Campaign Medal, and the nation of France even honored him with the highest medal of Honor, the Legion of Honour Medal.

WWII Vet William Bellmore Turns 101

August, 2016 - Mr. William Bellmore of 10 Monterey Dr., Methuen, celebrated his 101st birthday last month. He was honored for his service in WWII as a Chief Machinist Mate (1943-1944) by Methuen Mayor Steve Zanni and Veteran's Services Director Hargraves as well as his family and veteran friends. Bellmore was a Chief Machinist Mate, served as a Construction Battalion USNTC (United States Naval Training Center), NLFED (Naval Landing Fleet Equipment Depot) Albany California, US Naval Hospital, Oakland California, US Naval Hospital, Bainbridge, Maryland. His job was to maintain and repair all the Navy fleet troop landing craft. He also maintained all equipment at two hospitals. He was then honorably discharged with a perfect 4.0 final average.

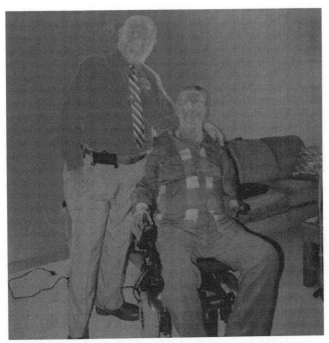

Sgt. Richard Lussier
U.S. Army, 78th Infantry Division

By: Tom Duggan, Jr. - May, 2016

NORTH ANDOVER, MA - Last month The Valley Patriot went along with Gerard Maguire, the Veteran's Services Coordinator for the towns of North Andover and Boxford as he delivered a custom fitted, electric wheelchair for a WWII hero veteran who lost his arm in battle and now is unable to walk.

Richard Lussier fought against the major offensive push by the German military near the end of World War II. Serving with headquarters, 78th Infantry Division, at only nineteen years old, Lussier would display an act of bravery so great that it earned him the Silver Star. The battle raged from December of 1944 through January of 1945, a period of about sixty days. It was a decisive battle turning the tides of victory in the direction of the Allied Armed Forces against the German military.

Sergeant Lussier, now ninety-one years old, recalls the day he entered an old farmhouse. Once inside, he cleared the first floor. But, startled by a noise that came from the direction of the cellar, Sergeant Lussier descended the stairs where he had discovered that there were 27 German soldiers hiding from the advancing American army.

Sergeant Lussier, tired, afraid, and armed with his M-1 Garand, raised his weapon toward the enemy. The German soldiers, as it turns out, were also tired and afraid. Thinking this was the end, Sergeant Lussier prepared to fight to the end when, amazingly, the German soldiers just laid their weapons on the ground and put their hands in the air!

Sergeant Lussier, still alone, then marched the Nazi soldiers out to where his unit was just arriving.

The battle continued to rage and the 78th Infantry Division would advance to Berlin. The following day, after making the capture of the 27 German soldiers, the 78th ID was engaged in a fierce gun battle where Lussier was shot in the left arm.

"Just before we were to go into Berlin, I saw the rifle scope of a sniper. We were the support troops for the Battle of the Bulge," Lussier told The Valley Patriot.

"I saw him laying down and he had a beat on me with the telescope of his rifle and he was aiming right at me while I was walking down the trail. I said to myself, 'I think he's going to shoot at me, I better shoot first.'"

"I had my rifle in my right hand. I fired a shot towards him, but he fired at me too at about the same time. His bullet hit my rifle, went up the rifle and hit me in the shoulder. I was left handed and I would have shot from the left if I had thought about it, but it was such a quick thing there was no time to think."

"I think you can understand that when you are in the military you do what you are told. So, I had to fire my rifle from the right as I was trained, even though I was left-handed. They didn't care if I was left-handed or what. I probably would have had a better shot if I had fired from my left."

"I remember when the bullet hit me, I hit the ground. Those medics were right there for me and I said to them 'get that guy'. But, they weren't there to go after him; they were there to help me. The medic picked me up, hauled me up the hill behind the lines and saved my life."

Lussier's wound was so severe that his arm would have to be amputated. While Lussier lay in a hospital bed for over a year recovering from the surgery, Berlin fell to the Allied Armed Forces, specifically as the Soviet armies advanced leaving a peaceful entry for the other three allies to advance on Berlin.

During his tenure in the United States Army, Sergeant Richard Lussier was awarded The Silver Star, The Bronze Star, The Purple Heart for wounds sustained in a firefight and the Berlin Occupation Medal!

His son, Raymond was in Special Forces in Vietnam, something that he says makes him "very, very, proud."

Sergeant Lussier, has served and remains a proud soldier! Thank you Sgt. Richard Lussier for your service and your sacrifice. We are honored to name you as this month's Valley Patriot of the Month.

EDITORS NOTE: Richard passed away just a few short weeks after he was honored in the pages of The Valley Patriot.

Harold Paragamian WWII

September, 2015

NORTH ANDOVER, MA - Merrimack College awarded a Bachelor of Arts degree to Methuen resident Harold Paragamian on June 2nd.

Mr. Paragamian, 90, took occasional classes at Merrimack between 1969 and 1998, earning an Associate's degree along the way. A recent audit of his courses determined he is eligible for a Bachelor of Arts in Liberal Arts, which will be dated 1998.

He told an interviewer in 2010, "You're never too old to learn."

An Army veteran of World War II, Mr. Paragamian earned four campaign stars during 14 months of fighting, from Normandy to the Rhineland, with the 113th Cavalry Reconnaissance Squadron. He retired in 1995 after 40 years working at Fort Devens in Ayer.

Merrimack College was founded in 1947 by the Order of St. Augustine at the behest of then-Archbishop Richard Cushing, who was responding to the concerns of a Merrimack Valley manpower commission that returning World War II servicemen needed to be educated for the civilian workforce.

Mr. Paragamian has been active in the local Armenian-American community and a regular attendee of St. Gregory Armenian Apostolic Church.

The diploma was presented by Merrimack College President, Christopher E. Hopey in a ceremony in Our Mother of Good Counsel Chapel. Many of

Mr. Paragamian's friends and family attended and joined a reception after the ceremony.

Paragamian was featured in the Armenian Mirror Spectator back in 2010 where he talked about his service in WWII.

"You wondered if you would ever come out of it alive," he said. "There were some bitter days. Not only was it devastating to see your own men killed, it was also painful to see Germans die. The human element is very close to me."

His military service spanned four decades as a Civil Service employee working in the Army Post Exchange at Fort Devens, Ayer, whether it was as a forklift operator or sales advocate, before retiring in 1995.

"Through the grace of God, I have much to be thankful for," he adds. "I count my blessings each and every day. World War II veterans are dying every day. Hopefully, I can still make a small difference."

Bruce Arnold Salvucci

By: Tom Duggan, Jr. - April, 2015

LAWRENCE, MA - The Valley Patriot newspaper gave away one Hero Veteran Award at their annual BASH on Friday to WCCM radio legend, Bruce Arnold Salvucci. The award was presented by Massachusetts Secretary of Veterans Services, Francisco Urena, who himself is a 2014 winner of The Valley Patriot Hero

Veteran Award. Urena presented the award to Bruce's wife and children at The Valley Patriot's 11th Anniversary BASH on March 20, 2015.

Radio Legend Bruce Arnold Salvucci may be most widely known for his decades on WCCM radio for shows like Purely Personal, The Hot Line Program, and as sidekick to our good friend Ronnie Ford who passed away two years ago. But what most people may not know is that Bruce Arnold was also a veteran.

By his own admission, Bruce Arnold has only once ever talked publicly about his experiences as a human guinea pig while serving in the army as part of Operation Hardtack, Joint Task Force Seven…the atomic bomb testing site. That one time in his entire life that he talked about his harrowing ordeal was on the Paying Attention radio program in the year 2000 with Tom Duggan, Jr. who somehow...the way only Tommy can do...got him to open up live on the air.

Tom has said many times since then, that it was one of the most riveting stories he has ever heard, on or off the radio.

Bruce Arnold enlisted in the Army in October of 1956...and graduated as a Broadcast Specialist. He was assigned to Ft. Bragg, North Carolina for duty with the Post Public Information Office for the 18th Airborne Corps and the 82nd Airborne Division with the Fort Bragg Radio and Television Dept.

From August of 1957 to August of 1958, he was stationed on Eniwetok Atoll in the Marshall Islands, still with Armed Forces Radio at Station WXLE. As Program Director, he was also stationed at the Army Pictorial Center in Long Island, NY producing and directing army training films, narrating and some acting. Bruce Arnold was discharged on October 10, 1959. PFC, SP5

Bruce Arnold is not only loved for his many years on radio helping people and sharing his gifts on the air, but for his amazing sacrifices as a member of the United States Army. His love for the army was so strong that he only once in his life talked publicly about his ordeal, because he once explained, he didn't want what happened to taint the honor of the men and women of the US Army.

Merchant Marine
Jake Collins

By: Tim Imholt - September, 2014

I had the pleasure recently of sitting down and talking with Jake Collins, this month's Patriot of the Month. Mr. Collins served in the Navy during World War II as a Gunner's Mate aboard the USS AOG-17 named the USS Mettawee.

The Mettawee was a gasoline tanker that was used to deliver precious aviation gasoline to places like Guadalcanal, Bougainville, the Solomon Islands, and Funafuti. Mr. Collins explained to me that this was a tanker originally designed for civilian use, but due to the massive need of men and equipment at the start of the war it was quickly converted for use by the US Navy. It had a cargo capacity for fuel of 750,000 gallons and had six gun emplacements to protect herself. Mr. Collins' job was to man the three inch 50 dual-purpose gun mount on the fantail of the vessel.

Think about this for just a minute, Gunner's Mate Collins and 61 other men were riding around in the Pacific to some islands that were not known to be calm places, like Guadalcanal, in what can only be described as a floating bomb. The fuel they carried was for aircraft and as a result this was a ship that the Japanese had an intense interest in taking out of the logistics chain.

The now 92-year old Mr. Collins and I discussed this at length. We are both veterans of the Armed Forces (although I was Army, and much more recently). There is an aspect of the combat soldier's life that not a lot of people who haven't been in the military just never think about (not that there is anything wrong with that). Logistics, and supply are keys to successful combat operations.

Why you ask?

It is very simple. Think about the job of this ship. It was to deliver airplane fuel to these islands that were constant hot spots for fighting the Japanese. If this precious fuel does not arrive to those islands, those airplanes do not take off. If those fighter aircraft don't take off that means that the Japanese could bomb the Marines on those islands without mercy, and they would have.

As a result the Japanese with their submarine community or fighter/bomber aircraft would want to destroy if they could. Destroying this ship would not only take out 750,000 gallons of airplane fuel but also degrade the US military's ability to resupply the aircraft in the region. That made this vessel and her crew a highly strategic target for the Imperial Navy.

That made Mr. Collins' job all the more important. His job was to man the guns on the rear of the ship and ensure that no enemy fighter/bomber aircraft, or ships come up and do harm to this vessel and her crew. Mr. Collins himself was at his gun one day during the war when a Japanese Zero came straight at his ship flying very low to the water, making it a tricky shot to get off. The Zero was thankfully destroyed a few hundred yards from the AOG-17, allowing her and her crew to make delivery of their precious cargo.

I asked Mr. Collins if there were any events that stuck out in his mind after all these years. He did, after all, spend several years of his life on this ship. He said, and I agree, there could be a book written about it, but I thought I would highlight just a few.

When part of the way to a destination island to pick up more fuel the steering on the ship failed. They had no repair or replacement parts to fix it at sea. What the crew had to do was to use the communication system on the ship from the bridge to where the rudder could be reached to have the Captain send down orders on which way to turn. The men would then go and manually turn the rudder according to the Captain's instructions.

Sounds easy right?

Sure…on a rowboat. This ship when full with fuel had a displacement of 2,270tons. These men had to literally throw their backs into moving a rudder against the water and the momentum of the ship to turn it as needed. The men would work four hours shifts in teams of six to accomplish this task. According to Mr. Collins recollection every time he pulled that duty he would instantly go back to his bunk and pass out exhausted, covered in sweat.

On another trip Mr. Collins had a story that in the Army we would have called a SNAFU (it is an acronym well worth Googling if you don't know what it is.) When they filled up with crew supplies on a trip to one of the islands one of the water tanks that the crew would use for drinking water was half filled with gasoline, then someone at the filling port realized the mistake and started loading water…without removing the gasoline or cleaning the tanks. That means that a good half of the fresh water supply for the journey was gone. The men got creative on the deck on rainy days to save water using the natural shower to bath, clean clothes, and other parts of life that one would use fresh water for. Now that is American ingenuity at work!

Mr. Collins did say he was glad he wasn't the first one to try to drink that water, as the person that did turned green before spitting it out.

He had many more stories about his time on this vessel ranging from when a Japanese bomber passed directly overhead to a trip to Lai Tai Harbor to refuel some airplanes that were aiding the Australian military while they were engaged with the Japanese.

All of those stories and instances are well worth a column of their own. But I would feel as though I missed something if I didn't say that Mr. Collins had a girlfriend he corresponded with the entire time he was gone. She was a radio instructor in the Army. They were eventually married and remained so for over sixty years. They had a very interesting hobby they shared.

They would deer hunt together. That isn't something too many married couples do any longer. I asked him when he stopped deer hunting (remember he is 92 years old).

His answer is all you ever need to hear to know what kind of a man this is. He is someone who will never quit, no matter what. He told me 4 years ago. When he was 88 years old. I was astonished I said really? What finally made you quit? His answer shocked me even more. He said, "Too many of my friends have died and I can't eat the whole deer myself."

In other words he would, and by the look of him could, still go out today and enjoy that hobby.

I think people like Jake defined what made the United States during and after the war. He is the type of person we need more of, and someone I strive to be much more like. I want to thank Mr. Collins for taking the time, and I wish him many more years to come. I fully expect to hear from him for years to come.

Tim Imholt

Tim is the author of several historic fiction novels including a series about a Marine in the Pacific during WW2 called China Bones available on Amazon.com.

Jason Kooken
National Guard
Amesbury Police Officer

Jason Kooken at the National Law Enforcement Officers Memorial in Washington, D.C. touching the name of slain Lawrence Police Officer, Thomas Duggan, Sr.

By: Tom Duggan, Jr. - April, 2014

Last month The Valley Patriot awarded Amesbury Police Officer Jason Kooken with The Valley Patriot, Officer Tom Duggan Sr. Law Enforcement Award. Officer Duggan's granddaughter did the presentation to Officer Kooken.

Every year, Jason Kooken bicycle rides his way down to Washington, DC to the National Law Enforcement Memorial to raise money for children of police officers who have been killed in the line of duty.

Jason's work ethic and morals show that my grandfather, Officer Thomas J. Duggan, Sr, still lives in him every day. In 2010, when my father, Tom

426

Duggan, Jr. read the names of Massachusetts police officers who were killed in the line of duty at the Police Memorial in front of President Obama's Cabinet and 25,000 law enforcement officers from all over the country ... Officer Jason Kooken was there and wearing a bracelet bearing the name of Lawrence Police Officer Tom Duggan, Sr. on his wrist because he had just biked from New England to Washington DC in my grandfather's name as he had done previous years.

When the ceremony was over, Jason and my dad met by chance at the memorial wall where my grandfather's name is etched in stone forever.

As Officer Kooken was touching the name of Tom Duggan Sr., on Panel 36W of the National Police Memorial he and my dad stood side by side in awe not having ever met.

As they both stood there silently remembering the tragedy that lead to the murder of Officer Duggan, Jason Kooken recognized my dad and introduced himself.

When my father admitted he was in fact the son of Officer Duggan, Kooken took the bracelet bearing Officer Duggan's name off his wrist and handed it to him right at the memorial wall in front of my grandfather's name.

My dad cries every time he tells this story and that's why he was unable to tell this story here tonight.

As time went by, our family came to learn that Jason Kooken also organizes fundraisers for children whose parents were killed in the line of duty.

He runs events for widows and disabled officers through Law Enforcement United, and then puts on a uniform and goes back to work protecting the public as an Amesbury Police Office Officer.

If anyone deserves an award named the Tom Duggan, Sr., Law Enforcement Award, it should go to the man who, not having met anyone in our family, not having ever met Tom Duggan, Sr., yet honors him every year with his rides to Washington, DC in his name. Jason Kookan is the true definition of a hero police officer, a hero military man; and Amesbury Police Chief Ouellet ... we want YOU to know that the Amesbury Police Department is very lucky to have him on the force.

Ed "Hoppy" Curran

By: Tom Duggan, Jr. - September, 2004

METHUEN, MA - Ed "Hoppy" Curran is a Vietnam Veteran who served with the 4th Division and the 243rd Field Service Co. in the Pleiku Province from 1967 to 1968.

He worked for the Lawrence D.P.W. as a Park Foreman for 27 years and was appointed Director of Veteran Services for the City of Methuen in October 1998. Hoppy is a Methuen resident who donates a great deal of his time to raising money for various charities and veteran's causes. He is a TRUE Valley Patriot!

For putting his life on the line for his country and continuing to serve our community long after coming home, The Valley Patriot is proud to name Ed "Hoppy" Curran of Methuen as our Valley Patriot of the Month. We thank him for his years of service to his country

Sergeant First Class Christine LeCain

By: Tom Duggan, Jr. - June, 2004

LAWRENCE, MA - Sergeant First Class Christine LeCain grew up on Mount Vernon Street in Lawrence and is the daughter of John and Theresa Gilhooly. She is also the granddaughter of Ann Ciccone, all of South Lawrence.

Christine has been a Mental Health Counselor for the United States Army for

15 years. She went to grammar school at Saint Patrick's School and graduated from Saint Mary's High School. She holds a Bachelor's Degree in both Psychology and Sociology and is completing a graduate degree in Educational Psychology.

Christine received THE BRONZE STAR for exceptionally meritorious achievement while assigned with the 21st Combat Support Hospital in support of Operation Iraqi Freedom. Her superb dedication to duty during combat operations assured mission accomplishment and reflects great credit upon her, her command and the United States Army.

She is serving her second tour in Iraq as the Detachment Sergeant for the 98th Medical Detachment for Combat Stress Control. Her first year was spent in Mosul, Iraq. The day before she was supposed to return the United

States, she and her soldiers were sent back to Iraq, this time to Najaf. Rather than spending their time at the mobile hospital set up in the region to which they are assigned, Sgt. LeCain and the soldiers under her command go right to the fighting men and women in the field to give mental counseling. This initial counseling is intended to reduce the incidents of Post-Traumatic Stress Disorder among combat soldiers. For her dedication and service to her country and community, we proudly select Christine LeCain as our Valley Patriot of the Month and thank her for making our country and our lives better.

Haggerty, Leonor & Lopez

By: Tom Duggan, Jr. - May, 2004

LAWRENCE, MA - Marjorie Haggerty was called to active military duty on February 7, 2003 to serve our country and defend it against terrorism. She safely returned home on

October 8, 2003. Sgt. Haggerty joined the Lawrence Public Schools, October 15, 1973 as a teacher. In August of 1994 she became an Assistant Principal and is currently at the Oliver School where she supervises and directs personnel assigned to the building. She also assists in the supervision, evaluation and improvement of the instructional program and process.

Bienvendio Leonor was born on October 5, 1979 and raised in South Lawrence.

Bienvenido attended the Kane Grammar School and Greater Lawrence Technical School where he played on the varsity football team. In July of 1998 he went to basic training in Fort Jackson, South Carolina, graduated in September and went on to Advanced Individual Training at Fort Gordon, Georgia. Bienvendio became a City of Lawrence employee in July 2001 as a hydrant and valve technician and was later deployed to Camp Arifjan, Kuwait with the Bravo Company of 368th . In Kuwait, he was in charge of setting up all of the communications for the company consisting of over 150 soldiers and vehicles and worked security duty for part of the perimeter inside of the camp which supported over 4,000 soldiers.

Angel Lopez was born on July 20, 1979 in Pontiac Michigan and moved to Lawrence in 1982. He lived on Prospect Hill, attended the Leonard School and went on to Greater Lawrence Technical School where he was involved in the Peer Leadership Program and was a member of the National Honor Society. In

2000, while Angel was attending Northern Essex Community College on a Presidential Scholarship, he enrolled in the U.S. Army Reserves. He began working for the City of Lawrence, Water Department in October of 2000. In January of 2001 he left for boot camp at Fort Jackson, South Carolina and went on to Advanced Individual Training in Automated Logistics where he graduated with distinction. In February of 2003 after being promoted to Sergeant, he was assigned to active duty with the HSC 368th Engineer Battalion and deployed to Camp Arifjan, Kuwait where he administered security, repaired vehicles, and built roads, camps and housing for soldiers in Iraq.

For their service to their country and community, The Valley Patriot honors Marjorie Haggerty, Angel Lopez and Bienvendio Leonor as our Valley Patriots of the Month. They have made our country safer and our community a better place to live!

Ray "Butch" Buchonis

By: Tom Duggan, Jr. - April, 2004

LAWRENCE, MA - These three Lawrence men captured the Japanese flag in the Philippines in 1943. They are James E. Hanlon (deceased), fireman first class, formerly of 15 Nesmith Street, Gerard J. Lehoux (deceased), fireman first class, formerly of 319 1/2 Lowell Street and current resident (also pictured on right) Ray (Butch) Buchonis, seaman first class, formerly of 163 Union Street.

The men's ship convoyed reinforcements to Leyte, in the Philippines and helped clear the sea lanes for advancing ships.

The Lawrence, Massachusetts Coast Guardsmen returned to the United States after serving ten months aboard a Coast Guard-manned frigate which rescued seven Army scouts trapped behind Japanese lines in the Philippines. Since that time, Ray (Butch) Buchonis has been an active member of the community and a tireless advocate for the restoration of The Lawrence WWII Veteran's Memorial Stadium. For his continued service to his country and community we select Ray (Butch) Buchonis as our Valley Patriot of the Month and thank him for making our country and our lives better.

Tech. Sgt. Donald G. Boulette

By: Kate Cotnoir - May, 2010

LOWELL, MA - Technical Sergeant Boulette was born in Lowell, Massachusetts. He was raised in the town of Billerica, Massachusetts, where he attended Billerica Memorial High School, graduating in 1995. Boulette entered the Marine Corps on 12 June 1995.

He went to Recruit Training at Parris Island, South Carolina and was assigned to Fox Company, 2nd Recruit Training Battalion. During his training he distinguished himself as Series High Shooter, achieving the second highest rifle score out of a company of 593 recruits.

Upon completion of recruit training, Boulette completed Marine Combat Training at Camp Geiger North Carolina, and was then assigned to attend the Marine Corps Small Arms Repair Course, held at United State Army Ordnance Center and School, Aberdeen Proving Grounds, Aberdeen, Maryland. Boulette finished first in his class and was meritoriously promoted to the rank of Lance Corporal in January 1996.

Boulette reported for duty with Ordnance Maintenance Contact Team –1, Lawrence, Massachusetts in January 1996 where he served as a small arms repairman. He was promoted to Corporal in October 1996.

In July 1997, Boulette was selected to be a member of Marine Security Detachment, USS Constitution, during OPSAIL 200 and the events commemorating the ship's 200th birthday. During this time he was involved in the day to day security functions required to protect this national treasure, and was aboard the ship when it sailed under its own power for the first time in 116 years.

In January 1998 Boulette was promoted to the rank of Sergeant. In March of that year he trained with the Norwegian military and other members of NATO, above the Arctic Circle at Camp Osmarka, Norway, in support of Operation Strong Resolve '98.

In July 1999 Boulette completed the Sergeant's Course held at Camp Crowder, Missouri. Also during this time he began serving as a Squad Leader, and later Platoon Sergeant for second platoon of Ordnance Contact Team −1. He also performed duties as the Armory NCOIC, and Unit Training NCO.

In May 2000 Boulette received a Bachelor of Arts Degree (Cum Laude), in Communications, from Framingham State College, in Framingham, Massachusetts. Boulette was also the founder and team Captain of the Framingham State College Men's Lacrosse Club Team.

Boulette completed the Small Arms Repair Refresher Course held at Aberdeen Proving Grounds, Aberdeen Maryland in October 2000 finishing second in his class.

In June 2002 Boulette was hired by the Billerica (MA) Police Department. He attended the 8th Massachusetts Police Officers Course, held at Massachusetts National Guard Base, Camp Curtis Guild, Reading, Massachusetts. He served as Platoon Leader throughout the duration of the 22-week course, supervising 35 other student police officers. He now serves as a Patrolman for the Billerica Police Department and is the Master-at-Arms of the department Honor Guard. He has been credited with three separate lifesaving actions.

In June 2003 Boulette was promoted Staff Sergeant (E-6). The following month he completed the Staff NCO Academy held at Camp Crowder, Missouri where he was named to the Commanding General's Honor Roll for completing the course with a 95.55% cumulative average.

In October of 2003 Boulette participated in his first marathon, completing the 28th Marine Corps Marathon in Washington D.C. In

December 2003, he completed his postgraduate studies. In February 2004 Staff Sergeant Boulette received a Master of Science Degree In Criminal Justice Administration from Western New England College, Springfield, Massachusetts.

On January 5, 2004, SSgt Boulette was called to active duty in support of Operation Iraqi Freedom – II. He was assigned to I Marine Expeditionary Force, 1st Force Service Support Group, Combat Service Support Battalion – 1, Combat Service Support Company – 121. After completing pre-deployment training in Camp Pendleton, CA, Boulette deployed to the Iraqi theater of operations in Feb 04 and served at Camp Fallujah until Oct 04. While at Camp Fallujah Boulette served as the Senior Small Arms Repairman for the Infantry Weapon Repair Shop, he was the Platoon Sergeant and Training NCO for Ordnance Platoon, he also served as the SNCOIC of the company area guard.

In October of 2005 Boulette attended Primary Marksmanship Instructor School held at Weapons Training Battalion Quantico, VA. He finished in the top 10 students academically, and was also the Rifle High Shooter for the course. He was awarded MOS 8530, Marksmanship Coach and MOS 8531 Primary Marksmanship Instructor/Combat Marksmanship Trainer. Following the completion of his training, Boulette became the lead marksmanship instructor for the 4th Maintenance Battalion.

In Feb - March 2006 Boulette completed the Army's Combat Lifesaver class held at Devens Reserve Forces Training Area. During this time Boulette also received certification from the Massachusetts State Police, as a Basic Firearms Safety Instructor.

In May 2006 Boulette served as Primary Marksmanship Instructor and Range SNOIC during OCT-1's annual rifle and pistol qualifications. Under his tutelage, the unit achieved 100% qualification. In August of 2006 Boulette traveled to Omaha, Nebraska to serve as PMI/CMT for Engineer Maintenance Company's annual rifle qualification. In just five days, despite inadequate range operations equipment, and severe weather conditions Eng Maint Co achieved a 99% percent qualification rate out of 202 shooters. For his efforts Boulette received a Certificate of Commendation.

Boulette last served as the SNOIC of the Infantry Weapon Repair Section of Ordnance Contact Team One, Devens, MA and was the unit's Primary

Marksmanship Instructor. He has voluntarily participated in 89 military funerals honors details in his career. He was Honorably Discharged from the United States Marine Corps on 5 Oct 2006.

In February 2009 Boulette enlisted in the United States Air Force Reserve as a Technical Sergeant with the 439th Security Forces Squadron, Westover ARB, Chicopee, MA.

Boulette completed the Security Forces Apprentice Course in Dec 2009. He was the class Honor Graduate and received school's highest achievement award, the Sgt. Louis H. Fischer Award. This award is given to students who complete the course with a 97% or higher average and who fire expert with both the M9 pistol and the M4 Carbine. Of the over 5000 students who complete the Security Forces Apprentice course annually, less than 1% receive the Fischer Award.

Boulette now serves as a Fire Team Leader and Designated Marksman for Squad 3 of the 439th Security Forces Squadron.

Technical Sergeant Boulette's personal awards include the Navy and Marine Corps Commendation Medal, and the Navy and Marine Corps Achievement Medal. He has also been awarded the Military Outstanding Volunteer Service Medal for prolonged volunteer work in his community. His hobbies include reading, competitive pistol and rifle shooting, lacrosse, and Brazilian Jiu Jitsu.

Dominic Scarpignato

By: Gary Mannion, Jr. - April, 2010

LAWRENCE, MA - In August of 1942, Dominic Scarpignato did what most boys his age were doing; he enlisted in the Navy. Almost a year after Pearl Harbor, boys like Dominic flocked to serve their country without a second thought. At 19 years of age, Dominic left his job at the American Wood Company in Lawrence, MA, along with his mother, his four sisters and his beloved Mary and joined the other young men ready to lay their lives on the line for the love of their country. He left the only place he had ever known to attend the Navy's boot camp in Newport RI and then to join the crew of the destroyer, the USS Conway, to which he was commissioned in October of 1942. After the boat left the port in Boston, it headed to Norfolk, Virginia to join its task force. On December 5th they received their orders to head to the Pacific Islands to face whatever lay ahead.

They headed toward the Panama Canal, though the sailors all knew that they were not allowed to pass through. They waited till the cover of darkness and then made their way across the canal. A month later, they were in the Pacific. On the way, the ship was instructed to take part in gunnery practice. Dominic was assigned to man a 40mm gun and set to his task. It was a 1,150 pound gun that shot 120 - 160 rounds per minute. It was the most efficient close-in air defense weapon on any warship during WWII and manning it was no mean task. Dominic set to his task with determination. While it was a routine task, there really is nothing routine about dealing with such a deadly piece of equipment and, at one point during the practice, a shell from the gun, exploded violently and Dominic was hit. A piece of shrapnel from the exploding shell pierced young Dominic's chest. Fortunately no one else was injured. Dominic was given medical care aboard the ship and recovered from his wound by the time they reached the Pacific Islands on January 5th, 1943. They stayed in New Caledonia for about a month and then were ordered to sail with their task force to act as a cover group in case the US met any enemy fire during their withdrawal from Guadalcanal.

On January 29th they were given orders to intercept a Japanese fleet By nightfall of that evening they were under attack from Japanese planes. One of the ships that the Conway was sailing with, the USS Chicago, was hit by two torpedoes and was paralyzed. The next day the Conway and the USS Lavallette were in charge of towing the Chicago back to port. They set about following their new orders. At about 4 p.m. that afternoon they received alarming information; the Japanese had sent twin engine bombers after the three ships. Almost instantly, chaos broke out aboard the ship. A few minutes later they were under attack by a second enemy torpedo air attack. The Chicago was hit five more times and, ultimately, sunk. Dominic, along with the other gunners on the Conway, continued to fire at the planes above and, with the help of the Army Air Corp, they were successful in shooting down almost all of the eleven twin engine bombers that had attacked the three ships.

Soon after the battle, the Conway was ordered to make its way through the islands. They had a short stop on an island called Tuilagi. Scarpignato recalls the event saying "a torpedo boat pulled up aside our ship and a crowd gathered around. I couldn't really see him, but a tall lanky guy came aboard. He said he was from Boston and, since our ship was commissioned there, he headed up to the captain's quarters to see if he knew anyone. Later we found out that the guy's name was Lieutenant Kennedy. We had no idea at that point that we were standing inches from a future president."

On August 15th 1943, Dominic encountered one of the toughest experiences in the war that he ever had to face. The Conway was ordered to Vella LaVella in the Solomon Islands. Early that morning the crew of the Conway found itself, once again, under air attack. Over and over again throughout the day they were subjected to intervals of relentless fire. Despite these waves of bombardment, the Conway came out unscathed. Despite repeated vicious onslaughts from the enemy, the Conway sailed under a lucky star, always managing to emerge unharmed.

In late August of 1944, Dominic and the USS Conway made their way back to the United States after 21 months of continuous service outside of the U.S. The men of the Conway were given a 30 day leave. Dominic didn't have to think twice about what to do with his time; he made his way back to Lawrence, Massachusetts. He recalled taking his first walk down Broadway: "I had just gotten here and was walking down Broadway and someone spotted me and called my mother. Before I knew what was happening, she was chasing me down Broadway". Not only was that reunion with his mother one that remains close to his heart but reuniting with the love of his life, Mary Marchese, also of Lawrence, was one that he has and always will treasure. Not more than a few weeks later he proposed to Mary and married her at Holy Rosary Church in Lawrence on his 30 day leave. They then set off for a honeymoon in New York city. That honeymoon was cut short when the Navy had need of Dominic Scarpignato. He was to report back to his ship in San Francisco; just one more in a long line of sacrifices he made with neither complaint nor reserve.

After Dominic returned from his 30 day leave, the crew set out for the Pacific again. He finished his deployment on the Conway during the next two years serving in Korea and in China. In 1945 he served a short stint in Washington D.C. at a naval school. In1946 Dominic was honorably discharged from the navy and returned to Lawrence, to his wife, Mary, and to his family. In all, the USS Conway was responsible for sinking 2 cruisers, and 1 merchant ship. They were credited with shooting down 9 planes, and participating in 33 island invasions. After 4 years of service Dominic had also been awarded a total of 10 battle stars. Despite over 40 confrontations in the Pacific, the Conway had never been hit. After returning home, Dominic returned to the Lawrence Wood Mill and later worked at the Lawrence Packaging company. He and Mary had one son.

Dominic is a special kind of person, one of that "greatest generation". In keeping with that fact, Dominic, in 1963, seventeen years after he left the Navy, joined the Navy Reserves. He continued to serve his country as a reservist from 1963 to 1979. He served in Newport RI and on a few different ships including the USS Galveston, the USS Valley Forge, and the USS Ranger. Even today, Dominic still continues to serve his community. As a volunteer in the city of Lawrence, Dominic serves as a greeter and many other different roles at the Mary Immaculate housing center. This past year he was awarded by the city with a certificate for his 20 years of voluntary service. Dominic may not see his contribution as heroic, but we do. Dominic gave his life for his country numerous times without a second thought. Because of men like Dominic, we have the freedom to honor his achievements as a patriot today!

The Moran Brothers

By: Gary Mannion. Jr. - March, 2010

LAWRENCE, MA - Webster's dictionary defines a patriot as one who loves his or her country and supports its authority and interests. The Moran family was such a family; one of the many families, over the years, that has shown its support for its country. Born and raised on Willow St. in Lawrence, Massachusetts, the Moran boys learned very early what it meant to serve your community.

Their father, John A. Moran, was a firefighter for Lawrence for over 41 years and retired as a lieutenant. The family was made up of 5 boys: John, Freddy, Joe, Howie, and Moe, and one girl named Grace. All five of the boys served their country in the armed services. At one point, in 1944, four of the five boys were serving at the same time. John was the eldest. His brothers always referred to him as the luckiest of them. John was drafted in 1944 and only served until the birth of his third child, about 6 months later. During his short stint in the Navy, he served on the aircraft carrier, the USS Lexington as a second-class seaman. Returning home to his wife and three children, he went to work at Davis and Furber of North Andover.

The next three brothers were the middle brothers and together saw the most action in the war. Joe was the first one to enter the war. He entered in 1942, at only 17 years of age. He was assigned to the U.S.S. Elmore as a 3rd class radio man. The Elmore was an attack transport which transported close to 1500 troops at a time. He later also served on the U.S.S. Turner and U.S.S. Fisk, both of which were destroyers. Joe served in many places during the war, among them the Marshall Islands, Guam, the Philippines and Okinawa. Joe served until 1945 and was honorably discharged, returning back to work at the Arlington Mills.

Joe was joined by his brother, Freddy, in 1943. Freddy was the only of the four brothers who fought in the Air Corps during WWII, rather than the Navy like his brothers. Freddy was a corporal in the US Army Air Corps. Freddy spent most of his 3 years in Guam and the pacific theater as a radioman, with the 10th air force dealing mostly with P38's. He was honorably discharged in 1945. In 1950, as the Korean War started, Joe was called back into the service and gave 3 more years to his country and was again honorably discharged in 1953. Joe was also the recipient of the Bronze Star, and several battle stars.

In 1944, Howie joined the others in service to his country. Howie left boot camp and headed out to Treasure Island, located in San Francisco, California. As fate would have it, this was at the very same time that his brother, John, was being discharged and was on his way home. John also happened to be passing through San Francisco. Neither of the two brothers knew that the other one was going to be there. It was just by luck that they both happened to be out one night and bumped into each other. It came as a shock to both of them that they were clear across the country and happened to see each other.

Howie continued on to serve most of his time in Okinawa, Japan. He was a 3rd class store keeper and was in charge of about 33 men. He also served on the U.S.S. Ajax, a small repair ship that held close to 200 men. In 1948,

Howie was hospitalized at the San Diego Naval Hospital and was discharged from there soon after. After coming home he went back to work with his brother, Joe, at the Arlington Mills and eventually went to work with the Lawrence Rubber Company, and then for the city of Lawrence in the Parks Department for 33 years.

The 5th and youngest brother, Moe, served in the US Army from 1958-1962. He was a private 1st class and spent most of his time serving in Germany. He was involved with a lot of rebuilding to the country after the devastation that followed WWII. He was the only brother not to be serving during a time of war and was discharged right before Vietnam really got off the ground. Moe, however, continued to serve his community when he left the military; he followed in his father's footsteps and became a firefighter in Lawrence.

A patriot is someone who loves and supports his or her country. Most of us, when we think of it at all, do think of ourselves as patriots but that feeling, for many of us, is never put to the test. To profess love for one's county is easy; to prove it, as the Moran brothers did, is a terrifying and life-threatening proposition. Many of us take an interest in the goings on in our community and country. Some of us go so far as to get involved in politics or community groups of some sort. But how many of us have the courage to express our feelings for our country as the Moran brothers did? How many make that ultimate commitment of risking their lives for it? In the years that so many young people are free to go off to college, enjoy the birth of adulthood, friends, family and freedom, the Moran brothers lived without any of that in order to ensure that we, and millions like us, would be free to enjoy our lives as we have. How sad and cruel that, for so many of us who have enjoyed the fruits of their sacrifice, we have done so without a thought for the men who risked, and even gave their lives that we might know such pleasure.

It was an early Monday morning and Joe and Howie, the last living Moran brothers, were sitting in the kitchen of Joe's house. Over coffee, they told tales of their time in the service, some they shared willingly and others more reluctantly with a request that they not be shared. They talked about engaging in battle on the shores of Okinawa, and the pain of watching fellow soldiers lose their lives in that same battle, of watching a kamikaze headed straight for another American ship and feeling helpless as they watched and prayed for the brave souls aboard the ship. Most of us will never fully understand the horror of such scenes.

Talking to the last two living Moran brothers, Joe and Howie, what is most striking is their humility. They were both reluctant to speak much about their experiences. They expected no gratitude or recognition for all they had gone through. They spoke, instead, of the men, some they had known and many, many that they had not, who had made the last and greatest sacrifice in those times, never coming back to live normal, quiet lives as the Moran brothers had. Rather than accepting any acknowledgement, they insisted that much of the time, it was simply about being at the right place at the right time. For the Morans, it had been a simple equation; their country needed them and they had answered the call. There was never any question of doing otherwise. Rather than seeking any honor for this, they feel that they have already been honored simply by being able to have shown the measure of their devotion to the country they love.

It is exactly this that makes these men real patriots. Between the five of them, the Morans have seen more of war than most families. Yet they did so quietly and without a second thought. And, rather than seeing anything special in what they did, they insist instead, on giving others credit for their brave and, in many cases, heroic actions. The Moran brothers are true patriots. John, Freddy, Joe, Howie, and Moe were willing to give their youth and risk their safety to serve their country honorably and, in the end, they were fortunate enough to have made it home. They consider themselves the lucky ones. Those who know them consider them true patriots.

FROM THE PUBLISHER

Growing up in Lawrence, Massachusetts I spent a great deal of time listening to my grandfather, Everett Martell, recounting details of his time in WWII as a cook on the U.S.S. Admiral Hughes transport ship and the liberated POW's from the island of Corregidor in the Philippines

In my younger years, these stories would make me daydream and wonder why I had to hear about the liberation of Corregidor the 200th time. When I grew older, however, these stories began to have real meaning. As I read more about the march on Corregidor and the torture the American soldiers endured at the hands of the Japanese, I began to understand and appreciate my grandfather's stories and his service.

I wish I could remember all of Pepere's stories, the many vivid details he described about the battles and the men he and his shipmates transported to and from the war. Moreover, I wish I had written them down in some detail now that he has passed. My aunt and uncle, Frank and Dorothy Incropera (my father's sister and her husband) raised me to attend all the various veterans' events in the community. Whether it was Veteran's Day, Memorial Day, or a park being named for a local veteran who lost his life, my aunt and uncle raised me to want to attend such events for all those who could not attend because they gave their lives for their country.

My father, Thomas Sr., rarely talked about his time in the Navy, but having a father who was a Vietnam Era veteran, combined with all the other pro-veteran forces in my life, led me to feel a profound sense of pride for our servicemen and women.

Thank you to my family, our writers over the last 13 years, our editors, delivery drivers, advertisers, and supporters. Thank you to my business partners Ralph Wilbur and Dr. Charles Ormsby. But, the biggest thank you is to all those who served our country!

~ Tom Duggan, Jr., Publisher – The Valley Patriot

INDEX

Made in the USA
Middletown, DE
03 February 2017